Between Crown and Community

Between Crown and Community

Politics and Civic Culture in Sixteenth-Century Poitiers

HILARY J. BERNSTEIN

Cornell University Press
ITHACA AND LONDON

First published 2004 by Cornell University Press

Printed in the United States of America

Library of Congress Cataloging-in-Publication Data

Bernstein, Hilary, 1966–
   Between crown and community : politics and civic culture in sixteenth-century Poitiers / Hilary J. Bernstein.
      p. cm.
   Includes bibliographical references and index.
   ISBN 0-8014-4234-6 (cloth : alk. paper)
   1. Poitiers (France)—History—16th century.   2. Poitiers (France)—Politics and government—16th century.
3. France—History—Wars of the Huguenots, 1562–1598.
I. Title.
   DC801.P77B47 2004

                                        2004001135

Cornell University Press strives to use environmentally responsible suppliers and materials to the fullest extent possible in the publishing of its books. Such materials include vegetable-based, low-VOC inks and acid-free papers that are recycled, totally chlorine-free, or partly composed of nonwood fibers. For further information, visit our website at www.cornellpress.cornell.edu.

Cloth printing   10 9 8 7 6 5 4 3 2 1

For my parents

Contents

Figures and Tables

Acknowledgments

This work on the political culture of Poitiers has grown from my initial fascination with the ways defined groups of people relate to each other. Individual opinions and group representations interact to create points of view independent of both. It is now my pleasure to acknowledge all of the help, advice, and support that I received during the long process of researching and writing this book. It would not be what it is without the discussions, suggestions, camaraderie, moral support, and monetary resources I have been fortunate to experience along the way.

This work could never have been completed without the generous monetary contributions of several granting agencies and universities. A Mellon Dissertation Fellowship and a Bourse Châteaubriand from the Ministère des Affaires Étrangères, France, funded research at the earliest stage. The History Department of the University of Pennsylvania, a Career Development Grant from the University of California at Santa Barbara, and a Travel and Research Grant from the Interdisciplinary Humanities Center of UC Santa Barbara enabled me to return to the archives for further research and afforded me the time and resources for revision. My thanks also go to UC Santa Barbara for according me a leave and to Jack Talbott and Pat Cohen, successive chairs of the History Department, for permitting some creative course scheduling to help me finish revising. I also owe a debt of gratitude to the librarians and archivists who facilitated my research. I wish to thank the staffs of the rare books departments of the Firestone Library at Princeton University and of the Van Pelt Library at the University of Pennsylvania and the Département des manuscrits occidentaux of the Bibliothèque Nationale de France. In Poitiers, I spent long hours at the Médiathèque municipale (formerly the Bibliothèque municipale) and the Archives départementales de la Vienne, and I thank the staffs of both institutions fondly for their help and patience with a persistent reader over the years.

Many people, in several academic communities, have provided the invaluable help and friendship I needed to bring this work to fruition. At Princeton University, the Dissertation Writers' Group offered useful, friendly criticism. I would also like to thank Alastair Bellany, Luis Corteguera, Cynthia Cupples, Vince DiGirolamo, Kristin Gager, Brad Gregory, Kate Jansen, April Shelford, Moshe Sluhovsky, Leslie Tuttle, and Ben Weiss for their reading of my work, helpful suggestions, and friendship. In Poitiers, my warmest thanks go to Nicole and Pierre Pellegrin, Alain Gabet and Sandrine Painsard, Sébastien Jahan, Emmanuel Dion, and Francis Metais for their interest in my work and willingness to share theirs, long-standing friendships, and enduring hospitality. I owe them more than I can express. Alain Gabet's help was also instrumental in obtaining one of the illustrations for this book; I thank him for this instance of his characteristic generosity. In Paris, Paul Cohen, Hugues Daussy, Emmanuel and Anne Dion, Gabrielle Houbre, and Chuck Walton made my time there a pleasure. I also owe a great debt of gratitude to Robert Descimon, who welcomed me to his seminar in 1992–94 and has continued to offer invaluable perspectives and advice; his work has inspired my own.

Back in the United States, numerous colleagues and friends have offered important suggestions, references, and insights. My thanks go to Megan Armstrong, Sara Beam, Michael Breen, Barbara Diefendorf, Claire Dolan, Jim Farr, Annette Finley-Croswhite, Lloyd Moote, Mark Potter, and Kevin Robbins, whose comments and conversation have helped me to push my conclusions further. Phil Benedict and Mack Holt read the earliest version of this work in its entirety and made excellent suggestions for revision. I have greatly enjoyed my discussions with Chris Stocker on French urban governance and thank him for permission to cite several of his unpublished papers. I am also particularly grateful to Jim Collins and Mack Holt for organizing a workshop for younger historians of early modern France, in which, together with fellow participants Megan Armstrong, Michael Breen, Greg Brown, and Sarah Chapman, they provided crucial advice and encouragement for this work. I have benefited extraordinarily from their suggestions and the exhilaration of discussing our projects for two intensive days in July 2001. In Santa Barbara, my colleagues have provided a supportive environment in which to complete this work. My general appreciation goes to all of them, but I would particularly like to thank Adrienne Edgar, Sears McGee, Erika Rappaport, and Marianne Robins of Westmont College for reading chapters, discussing ideas, and offering moral support.

I owe an immense debt to my teachers, for the help and training they have unstintingly provided over the years. Tony Grafton supervised my first work on urban historiography and municipal settings and, thanks to his vast knowledge of European culture, has provided important insights and encouragement to place my work within a larger European context. Bill Jordan not only read the earliest version of the work with careful attention and offered important criticisms but has also consistently provided encouragement and the kind of practical advice that has enabled me to complete and publish this book. Finally, the debt I owe to Natalie Davis, my graduate advisor, is more than I can express. Her approach has guided and inspired me at every stage; it was she who first impressed on me the necessity to balance guiding ideologies with historical voices of dissent, a concern to which I have tried to pay attention throughout this work. Her unfailing enthusiasm and confidence spurred me on as I began this project, and her continuing support has meant much as I revised the work. To her, and to everyone else who has helped to form my appreciation of the past, I express my sincere gratitude.

Just as I owe much to others for their help and advice while I conceptualized, researched, and wrote this book, I have accumulated important debts during the publication process. I would particularly like to thank my editor John Ackerman, director of Cornell University Press, for his support of my work and for an editorial style that happily combines humor with a calming influence. I am also grateful to Louise E. Robbins, production editor, for her help and careful attention during production. Additionally, I wish to thank the editors of *French Historical Studies* for permission to use material from my article "The Benefit of the Ballot? Elections and Influence in Sixteenth-Century Poitiers" in chapters 1, 4, and 10 of this work. My thanks also go to the Office de Tourisme of Poitiers, the Musées de Poitiers, and the A.D.A.G.P. (Société des auteurs dans les arts graphiques et plastiques) for permission to reproduce several illustrations.

Academic communities are important, but I have saved my most fundamental debts for last. Without the affection and patience of friends and the unstinting love and understanding of my family, I could never have completed this work. My gratitude therefore goes to Julie Breeze, Madeline Brown, Sarah Gille, Alexandra Moellmann, and Jie Zhao for always being ready to listen, and my deepest thanks go to my parents, Howard Bernstein and Joan Bernstein; my husband, Xiao-bin Ji; my sisters, Christina Bernstein and Debbie Dowell; and my grandmother, Pearl Katz. Each has contributed so much through love and support, but I dedicate this work to those who first gave me the confidence to pursue my interests—my parents.

Abbreviations

ACP	Archives communales de Poitiers
ADV	Archives départementales de la Vienne
AHP	Archives Historiques du Poitou
AN	Archives nationales, Paris
Annales: E.S.C.	*Annales: économie, sociétés, civilization*
BNF	Bibliothèque nationale de France
Brilhac	Belisaire Ledain, ed., *Journaux de Jean de Brilhac conseiller en la sénéchaussée de Poitou de 1545 à 1564 et de René de Brilhac conseiller au présidial de Poitiers de 1573 à 1622,* AHP 15:1–48. Poitiers: Imprimerie Oudin, 1885.
BSAO	*Bulletin de la Société des Antiquaires de l'Ouest*
Isambert	[François André] Isambert et al., eds. *Recueil général des anciennes lois françaises depuis l'an 420 jusqu'à la révolution de 1789.* 29 vols. Paris: Belin-Le-Prieur, 1822–33.
Le Riche	A. D. de la Fontenelle de Vaudoré, ed., *Journal de Guillaume et de Michel Le Riche, avocats du roi à Saint-Maixent (de 1534 à 1586).* Geneva: Slatkine Reprints, 1971.
MMP	Médiathèque municipale de Poitiers
MS	Manuscript
MS Clair.	Collection Clairambault, BNF
MS Fr	Manuscrit français
MSAO	*Mémoires de la Société des Antiquaires de l'Ouest*
Ordonnances	*Ordonnances des rois de France de la troisième race, recueillies par ordre chronologique.* 21 vols. Paris: Imprimerie Royale (Impériale, Nationale), 1723–1899.
Reg.	Register

SAHP   Société des Archives Historiques du Poitou
SAO   Société des Antiquaires de l'Ouest

The new year began on 25 March in Poitou in the sixteenth century. All dates in the text have been converted to the new style, unless otherwise indicated.

Between Crown and Community

Introduction

When Jacques de Hillerin, student of law and theology, arrived in Poitiers early in 1589, he spent the first few days viewing the city. Having first visited the cathedral St. Pierre, which he proclaimed "la première," he walked back uphill to Notre-Dame-la-Grande, a collegial church conveniently located in a public square. He then took advantage of the church's proximity to the royal judicial *palais* to enter this imposing building, where the main hall was twice the size of the one at Angers, testifying to the importance of Poitiers's presidial court. In the days following, Hillerin turned his steps toward the collegial and abbey church of St. Hilaire-le-Grand, probably crossing its large bourg by the rue de la Tranchée. After mounting the church's bell tower to view the whole city, but only briefly because of the tower's perilous condition,[1] the eager student descended and completed his tour along the ramparts to the southeast of the town, passing the small parish church of St. Grégoire and the fortified Tison tower, and arriving finally at the collegial church of Ste. Radegonde.[2] Hillerin, like all visitors to Poitiers, was particularly impressed by the city's size. Describing it as approaching Paris in its dimensions, although far less populated, he echoed in more complimentary terms Emperor Charles V's 1539 assessment of the city as "un grand village."[3] Yet, if Poitiers was so large that it required several days to see it

---

[1] The bell tower was in fact to fall less than a year later, on 22 January 1590. ADV G534, 66v.

[2] Jacques de Hillerin, *Le Chariot chrestien a quatre roues, menant a salut, dans le souvenir de la mort, du iugement, de l'enfer, & du paradis* ... (Paris, n.d.), 21. See also [Charles-Auguste] Auber, "Jacques de Hillerin, Poitevin et conseiller au parlement de Paris: biographie des XVIe et XVIIe siècles," *BSAO,* 1st ser., 6 (1850–52): 53–102.

[3] Hillerin, *Chariot chrestien,* 21. Charles V's words are reported in Gaston Dez, *Histoire de Poitiers* (Poitiers, 1969), 139.

properly, Hillerin did not make his tour in the most economic fashion. Rather, he visited the city's sights in order of their importance, making the cathedral, located on the extreme eastern side of town, down a steep incline, his first stop, but getting around to see Ste. Radegonde, a stone's throw from the cathedral, only several days later.

When Hillerin took up his lodgings in Poitiers and joined the many students frequenting the four faculties of the university, the city was an important regional capital. Historic center of the county of Poitou, in the sixteenth century it boasted many of the institutions and attributes that made cities important destinations for travelers and bustling communities for inhabitants. With its important royal courts, university, prolific printing shops, wealthy religious institutions, cathedral, numerous parishes, markets, impressive domestic architecture, extensive fortifications, and château, Poitiers guided the surrounding region in legal, religious, cultural, and military matters and provided a vital center for exchange of ideas, information, and goods.

Indeed, Justus Zinzerling, writing for Germans making a tour of western Europe in 1612, liked Poitiers so much that he counseled his compatriots to stay there for the whole second winter of a five-year peregrination. In describing the sights to be seen in this first city of Poitou, Zinzerling echoed Hillerin's movements: one was first to visit the cathedral, with its remains of the beard of St. Peter, then go to Notre-Dame-la-Grande, and finally to see the foul-smelling stone that consumed corpses,[4] the sepulcher of Geoffroy the Great Tooth, and the cradle of St. Hilaire, all preserved in the church of St. Hilaire-le-Grand. Once the intrepid German tourist had witnessed these sacred wonders, he could turn his attention to the other attractions of the town: the partially dismantled château, the palais, the university, and the cabinet of curiosities of Monsieur Constant, apothecary.[5]

Just as Hillerin and Zinzerling planned to pass a considerable moment in Poitiers for their edification and entertainment, I propose that we take the time to inquire into the many facets of the city's public culture and political life. Cities in sixteenth-century France formed worlds unto themselves. Surrounded by high, fortified walls, they were divided physically and emotionally from the surrounding countryside. Governed by urban councils whose character and organization had evolved over time, they also stood apart legally and culturally because of their special privileges, political customs, and historical traditions. Their particular environments inspired and informed the imaginations, identities, and loyalties of their inhabitants. This is why Renaissance historians such as Poitiers's Jean Bouchet constructed

---

[4] The stone was generally known as "la pierre qui pue." See Lecointre-Dupont, "Notice sur le monument nommé La Pierre Qui Pue," *MSAO*, 1st ser., 9 (1843): 65–76.

[5] Jodocus Sincerus [Justus Zinzerling], *Voyage dans la vieille France, avec une excursion en Angleterre, en Belgique, en Hollande, en Suisse et en Savoie*, trans. Thalès Bernard from the 1616 Latin edition of the *Itinerarium Galliae* (Paris and Lyon, 1859), 148–52.

elaborate mythical origins for their citizens (Poitevins, Bouchet argued, were descendants of the red-haired Scythians, who could trace their ancestry to Hercules and a half-serpentine mother),[6] and why Charles de Bourgueville, *lieutenant général* of the royal *bailliage* court at Caen, dedicated his old age to recording the history of his city and province, lovingly describing how he and his fellow citizens could stroll along the ramparts, watch boats arrive from the *hôtel de ville* (city hall), and appreciate the chestnut arcades of the older houses on the Île Saint-Jean.[7]

In addition to their local importance, sixteenth-century cities also constituted an essential element of the greater political body of the French kingdom. When Catherine de' Medici and her advisers planned Charles IX's grand tour to introduce him to his kingdom in 1566, they thought almost entirely in terms of the cities to be visited, and the king's entourage in fact stayed in cities for slightly more than three-quarters of the nights of his voyage.[8] As the prime centers for royal justice, financial administration, defense, and commerce, cities merited the attention of the French crown, even if royal policies concerning cities were not always consistent. The politically savvy Catherine de' Medici, like her one-time son-in-law Henri IV, recognized the importance of cultivating clients among the notable inhabitants and merchants of the principal cities of the kingdom, so that "never will a city have any other will but [the king's] and never will [he] have any difficulty in making [himself] obeyed."[9] For the royal vision of order, plenty, and security, the fate of mid-sized cities and regional centers such as Poitiers was therefore essential, even if their ties to the monarchy were not quite as symbolically intimate as in Paris, as profitable as in Lyon, or as visible as in parlement cities such as Rouen and Toulouse.[10] The assorted judicial officials, financial officers, lawyers, bourgeois, and merchants who gathered weekly in Poitiers's

[6] Jean Bouchet, *Les Annales d'Aquitaine. Faicts et gestes en sommaire des roys de France et d'Angleterre, pays de Naples & de Milan* ... (Poitiers, 1644), 4–8. The half-serpent, half-woman mate of Hercules recalls Mélusine, fabled founder of the house and fortress of Lusignan. On the subject of Poitiers's origins, see Georges Thouvenin, "La fondation de Poitiers selon les humanistes de la Renaissance: à propos d'une ode de Scévole de Sainte-Marthe," *BSAO*, 3d ser., 7 (1927): 734–63.

[7] Charles de Bourgueville, *Les recherches et antiquitez de la province de Neustrie, à présent duché de Normandie, comme des villes remarquables d'icelle, mais plus specialement de la ville et université de Caen* (Caen, 1833), preface: 7; bk. 2:9–18.

[8] Jean Boutier, Alain Dewerpe, and Daniel Nordman, *Un tour de France royal: le voyage de Charles IX (1564–1566)* (Paris, 1984), 31, 132.

[9] Quoted in Boutier et al., *Tour de France royal*, 252. For Henry IV, see S. Annette Finley-Croswhite, *Henry IV and the Towns: The Pursuit of Legitimacy in French Urban Society, 1589–1610* (Cambridge, U.K., 1999).

[10] Robert Descimon, "Le corps de ville et le système cérémoniel parisien au début de l'âge moderne," in *Statuts individuels, statuts corporatifs et statuts judiciaires dans les villes européennes (moyen âge et temps modernes)*, ed. Marc Boone and Maarten Prak (Leuven-Apeldoorn, 1996), 73–128; Richard Gascon, *Grand commerce et vie urbaine au XVIe siècle: Lyon et ses marchands (environs de 1520–environs de 1580)* (Paris, 1971); Philip Benedict, *Rouen during the Wars of Religion* (Cambridge, U.K., 1981); Robert A. Schneider, *Public Life in Toulouse, 1463–1789: From Municipal Republic to Cosmopolitan City* (Ithaca, 1989).

hôtel de ville to administer to public affairs certainly saw themselves as exercising an authority that devolved to them from the crown, even as their positions obligated them to provide for what they believed was the "public good" of their own community. If we are to understand the wider political culture of early modern France, therefore, we must delve into the processes of governance and the political assumptions that prevailed within these urban centers.

The role of urban institutions in shaping European political culture has long inspired implicitly ideological debates. For the Belgian historian Henri Pirenne, medieval cities became the enclaves of personal and economic liberties that have since guaranteed our civil society,[11] and for many historians of the medieval communal movement, these sworn associations of mutual aid among urban inhabitants seemed to presage important ideals of community responsibility and political participation that underlie the democratic tradition.[12] Yet these same urban institutions could also be co-opted to create the worst iniquities: namely, political oligarchy, commercial protectionism, and social exclusion.[13] French cities in the sixteenth century were neither the exemplars of modern democratic practices nor the rigid domains of hierarchical privilege, however; rather, the cities were a creative mixture of seemingly contradictory traditions. They constituted unique political environments, in which corporate bodies claimed to act for the good of the whole and citizens interacted to form political views that balanced the more absolutist pretensions of the monarchy.

In recent years, the cities of early modern France have generated extensive interest. Scholars such as Guy Saupin and Barbara Diefendorf have analyzed municipal institutions in great depth and have uncovered the family connections and alliances of those who served in city government.[14] Historians interested in the social practices and cultural assumptions of city dwellers—whether artisans in Dijon, notaries in Aix-en-Provence, bourgeois in Bordeaux, or notables in Agen—have worked to reconstruct the family ties and characteristic attitudes of different sectors of urban populations and have analyzed the role that civic institutions played in their lives.[15] The con-

---

[11] Henri Pirenne, *Medieval Cities: Their Origins and the Revival of Trade,* trans. Frank D. Halsey (Princeton, 1952). Lucien Febvre also adopts this view for the sixteenth century in his *Life in Renaissance France,* trans. Marian Rothstein (Cambridge, Mass., 1977), 91–121.

[12] Susan Reynolds, *An Introduction to the History of English Medieval Towns* (Oxford, 1977); Albert Vermeesch, *Essai sur les origines et la signification de la commune dans le nord de la France (XIe et XIIe siècles)* (Heule, 1966).

[13] Michel Mollat and Philip Wolff, *Ongles Bleus, Jacques et Ciompi: les révolutionaires populaires en Europe aux XIVe et XVe siècles* ([Paris], 1970); Fritz Rörig, *The Medieval Town* (Berkeley, 1967).

[14] Guy Saupin, *Nantes au XVIIe siècle: vie politique et société urbaine* (Rennes, 1996); Barbara B. Diefendorf, *Paris City Councillors in the Sixteenth Century: The Politics of Patrimony* (Princeton, 1983).

[15] James R. Farr, *Hands of Honor: Artisans and Their World in Dijon, 1550–1650* (Ithaca, 1988); Claire Dolan, *Le notaire, la famille et la ville (Aix-en-Provence à la fin du XVIe siècle)* (Toulouse, 1998); Christine Adams, *A Taste for Comfort and Status: A Bourgeois Family in*

cern to understand the spread of the Reformed faith in French cities led Natalie Davis to inquire into the working life and ways of thinking of women and men in Lyon and prompted Davis and Philip Benedict to explain the composition of Reformed communities in the urban context.[16] The importance of the Wars of Religion for sixteenth-century society and politics has prompted numerous historians to examine the critical moments of the spread of Reformed belief, the outbreak of the wars, and the hostilities of the Catholic League in cities throughout France.[17] The religious wars, their work shows, are particularly important for understanding French cities in the sixteenth century, not only because the wars brought about intense hostilities and threats to public order that challenged social and political alliances and patterns of governance, but also because they gave cities a clear stake in broad religious issues and political policies affecting the entire kingdom.

This book combines many of these approaches to shift the focus squarely onto the nature of civic political culture in the sixteenth century. In his quest to explain the radical characteristics of the Catholic League in Paris, Robert Descimon began to ask how urban institutions reflected assumptions about civic governance, how the composition of city councils influenced the wider Parisian population, and what impact more localized institutions, such as the militia, had in the lives of average citizens.[18] I take a similar approach to understanding Poitiers's urban environment. This work unites a focus on municipal institutions with the ways that urban officials conceived of their governing role; examines the elaborate processes through which officials arrived at workable decisions at the same time that it studies the ceremonial means through which an urban identity was constructed and maintained; and specifically asks to what extent the urban population accepted civic traditions and municipal authority. How did contemporaries justify the au-

---

Eighteenth-Century France (University Park, Pa., 2000); Gregory Hanlon, *L'univers des gens de bien: culture et comportements des élites urbaines en Agenais-Condomois au XVIIe siècle* (Talence, 1989); Julie Hardwick, *The Practice of Patriarchy: Gender and the Politics of Household Authority in Early Modern France* (University Park, Pa., 1998); Jonathan Dewald, *The Formation of a Provincial Nobility: The Magistrates of the Parlement of Rouen, 1499–1610* (Princeton, 1980); Michael P. Breen, "Legal Culture, Municipal Politics and Royal Absolutism in Seventeenth-Century France: The *Avocats* of Dijon (1595–1715)," (Ph.D. diss., Brown University, 2000).

[16] Natalie Zemon Davis, *Society and Culture in Early Modern France* (Stanford, 1975); Benedict, *Rouen.*

[17] Michel Cassan, *Le temps des guerres de religion: le cas du Limousin (vers 1530–vers 1630)* ([Paris], 1996); Wolfgang Kaiser, *Marseille au temps des troubles, 1559–1596: morphologie sociale et luttes de factions,* trans. Florence Chaix (Paris, 1992); Kevin C. Robbins, *City on the Ocean Sea: La Rochelle, 1530–1650; Urban Society, Religion, and Politics on the French Atlantic Frontier* (Leiden, 1997); Penny Roberts, *A City in Conflict: Troyes during the French Wars of Religion* (Manchester, U.K., 1996); Stéphane Gal, *Grenoble au temps de la Ligue: étude politique, sociale et religieuse d'une cité en crise (vers 1562–vers 1598)* (Grenoble, 2000).

[18] "La Ligue à Paris (1585–1594): une révision," *Annales: E.S.C.* 37 (1982): 72–111; "Le corps de ville et les élections échevinales à Paris aux XVIe et XVIIe siècles: codification coutumière et pratiques sociales," *Histoire, économie et société* 13 (1994): 507–30; "Milice bourgeoise et identité citadine à Paris au temps de la Ligue," *Annales: E.S.C.* 48, no. 4 (1993): 885–906.

thority of the governors over the governed? How did institutional patterns and assumptions about the proper conduct of decision making influence the conclusions reached? In a world of strict social distinctions, were there possibilities for the disenfranchised to influence civic policies and to play a role in political life? In a century of intense religious hostilities, how did religious choices influence patterns of political authority? Not only do Poitiers's experiences offer an instructive contrast with Parisian ones but, by focusing on the "long sixteenth century," this book reveals greater continuities between the concerns of the religious wars and the comparatively neglected periods preceding them than have previous urban studies. This work further departs from other urban studies in characterizing the political attitudes shaping interactions between cites such as Poitiers and the French crown and the consequent role that cities were thought to play within the kingdom. Although many historians have represented the sixteenth century in general, and the period of the religious wars in particular, as the last gasp of civic independence from the growing power of the French monarchy, I show that both urban officials and the kings of France understood that civic authority was dependent on royal support and that they valued cooperation over autonomy to maintain the status and usefulness of urban communities.

Poitiers provides an excellent place to watch the sixteenth-century political process at work. Located south of the Loire River, it was outside the orbit of cities subject to close royal supervision. Yet, as capital of a province permanently attached to the French crown, it did not insist on the independence that still inspired the outlying provinces in the sixteenth century. The citizens of Poitiers could point with pride to a tradition of city government that dated back to the communal movement of the high Middle Ages. At the same time, though, the city's general importance as an administrative and judicial center meant that royal officials also found their home in Poitiers. Growing in numbers all over France in the sixteenth century, they came to dominate Poitiers's civic administration. Finally, Poitiers's religious experiences placed it at the heart of the intense debates of the second half of the sixteenth century. An important center of Reformed belief by 1560, the city became a bastion of ultra-Catholic sentiment by the fifth religious war (1574–76), and of pro-League politics after the death of Henri III (1589). Since these religious changes and loyalties had an important effect on the city's political institutions and traditions of self-representation, its religious experiences provide a further important element in understanding the political culture of the sixteenth century.

Poitiers in the Sixteenth Century

Poitiers was a large city by sixteenth-century standards. Its walls, built in the twelfth century, encompassed an area second in size only to Paris, even if a good portion of the space was sparsely inhabited and given over to gardens and vineyards. Yet the city still boasted a substantial number of inhabitants, enjoying a population that may have approached twenty thousand by the end of the century.[19] Such a large conglomeration of people automatically made Poitiers an important regional market, but the city was not known for its industrial productivity. In the late medieval period, the armaments of Poitiers had been highly regarded,[20] but in the sixteenth century, the city produced little for an international market. If an important merchant such as Lorin Richier was training a German apprentice in the early part of the century, later notary contracts would mention destinations and commercial contacts no farther than Lyon via Clermont.[21] Poitiers was at a great commercial disadvantage compared with nearby cities such as La Rochelle and Niort; whereas the former boasted an important port on the Atlantic and the latter sat on the Sèvre River, Poitiers was inaccessible by water. Merchants and artisans certainly constituted an important part of Poitiers's lesser notability and served the city and surrounding region with goods, but the commercial aspect of the city was never predominant in its reputation or importance.

Since the fifteenth century, Poitiers had been an important center of law and learning. Within the jurisdiction of the Parlement of Paris, Poitiers still boasted one of the largest and busiest royal *sénéchaussée* courts in France and after 1552 possessed one of the "great" presidial courts. Because Paris was inaccessible for many litigants, numerous suits were settled definitively in Poitiers. The court's jurisdiction included an unusually large geographical area, and its highest officials enjoyed the special privilege of wearing red robes on ceremonial occasions, an honor usually reserved for parlementary judges.[22] Judges, lawyers, and legal personnel not only crowded the streets of Poitiers, but also dominated many of its political institutions. Legal officials exerted an overwhelming presence in the hôtel de ville, and they played their part in the city's poor-relief administration, vestries, and confraternities. The sénéchaussée and presidial courts were far from the only legal bodies in Poitiers, however. The mayor of Poitiers also administered justice, as

[19] There is no accurate way to assess Poitiers's population, since no complete tax rolls have survived. Extrapolating from a militia assignment of 1512, we may estimate a population of approximately fifteen thousand for the early sixteenth century. Gérard Jarousseau, analyzing the incomplete tax roll of 1552, arrives at a figure of roughly twenty thousand for the mid-sixteenth century. Gérard Jarousseau, "Un rôle d'imposition de Poitiers en 1552: étude des structures sociales et économiques de la ville," *Actes du 87e Congrès des Sociétés Savantes, Poitiers 1962, Bulletin philologique* (1962): 481–92; ACP Reg. 11, 161–66, 169–72 (6 and 29 Apr. 1512). See also Robert Favreau, *La ville de Poitiers à la fin du moyen âge: une capitale régionale*, 2 vols. (Poitiers, 1978), 572–75.

[20] Dez, *Histoire de Poitiers*, 45.

[21] ACP Casier 44, 1523–63 (Inquiry dated 3 June 1527); ADV E⁴24.19, Act dated 6 July 1588.

[22] Favreau, *Ville de Poitiers*, 276–80, 393–400; Ch. de Gennes, "Notice sur le présidial de Poitiers," *MSAO*, 1st ser., 26 (1860–61): 359–528, esp. 365–67, 417–20. Jean de Brilhac, *lieutenant criminel* of Poitiers, mentions wearing red robes at the entry of Elisabeth on her way to marry Philip II of Spain in November 1559. See Brilhac, 5–6.

FIGURE I.1. Poitiers during the siege of 1569. This general view of Poitiers from the east, painted by François Nautré in 1619, shows the city under siege by Coligny's forces. Photo Musées de Poitiers, Ch. Vignaud. Reprinted with permission.

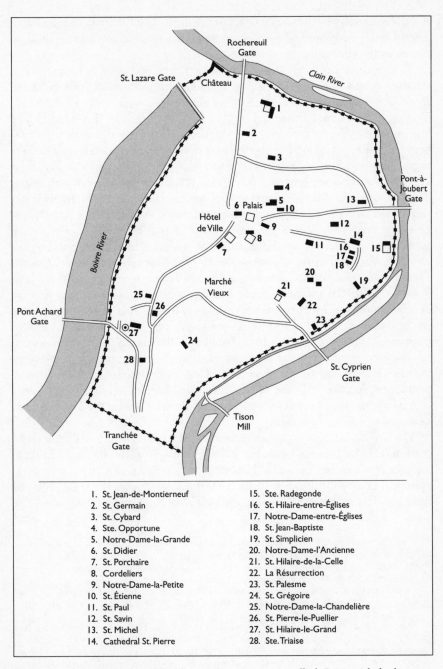

Rochereuil
Gate

Clain River

St. Lazare Gate

Château

Pont-à-
Joubert
Gate

6 Palais

Hôtel
de Ville

Boivre River

Marché
Vieux

Pont Achard
Gate

St. Cyprien
Gate

Tison
Mill

Tranchée
Gate

1. St. Jean-de-Montierneuf	15. Ste. Radegonde
2. St. Germain	16. St. Hilaire-entre-Églises
3. St. Cybard	17. Notre-Dame-entre-Églises
4. Ste. Opportune	18. St. Jean-Baptiste
5. Notre-Dame-la-Grande	19. St. Simplicien
6. St. Didier	20. Notre-Dame-l'Ancienne
7. St. Porchaire	21. St. Hilaire-de-la-Celle
8. Cordeliers	22. La Résurrection
9. Notre-Dame-la-Petite	23. St. Palesme
10. St. Étienne	24. St. Grégoire
11. St. Paul	25. Notre-Dame-la-Chandelière
12. St. Savin	26. St. Pierre-le-Puellier
13. St. Michel	27. St. Hilaire-le-Grand
14. Cathedral St. Pierre	28. Ste. Triaise

FIGURE I.2. Map of Poitiers. Adapted from Robert Favreau, *La ville de Poitiers à la fin du moyen âge* (Poitiers, 1978), 643.

did the *conservateur* of the privileges of the university, the body of merchants after 1566,[23] and several religious bodies that had kept their seigneurial rights within the walls.

The university only reinforced the legal flavor of Poitiers's civic culture. Chartered by Charles VII in 1431, it taught students in all four faculties. Pride of place, however, went to its faculty of law, which many people, including Hillerin, ranked second only to Paris, Bourges, or Toulouse.[24] The students were divided into four nations, but in the sixteenth century, the Bretons had the reputation of being the most serious, since the Parlement de Bretagne admitted Poitiers graduates by preference.[25] The academic and legal communities also supported a developed market in books and pamphlets. The Marnefs and Bouchets were among several families of printers who put out works of high quality, and others routinely published the latest pamphlets and news they could get from Paris.[26] Enguilbert II de Marnef set up shop in the palais itself, and gloried in the numbers of lawyers and literary men who stopped in for conversation and intellectual exchange.[27] Indeed, Poitiers also enjoyed its share of cultural life. Early in the century, Jean Bouchet, historian and poet, could frequent a group of like-minded literary connoisseurs, and by the 1570s well-known figures met at the proto-salon of the dames des Roches to talk on polite subjects and to try their hand at impromptu verses.[28] In the 1580s, Guillaume Bouchet published his *Serées,* in which he regaled readers with essays in the form of witty conversations that he claimed had occurred around Poitiers's supper tables over the preceding few decades.[29] In the sixteenth century, Poitiers was far more than a stop along the way between Bordeaux and Paris; it was a center of Renaissance culture in its own right.

The city was also an important religious center. The bishop of Poitiers held considerable lands and wealth, but luckily for the hôtel de ville, most of these were located outside the walls. In contrast to many French cities, therefore, episcopal and civic administrations were not at odds, and the bishop played little political role in Poitiers until the period of the Catholic League.[30] The

[23] See the royal edict of May 1566 creating a merchant jurisdiction in Poitiers. A copy exists in MMP Dom Fonteneau, 23:173–83.

[24] Hillerin, *Chariot chrestien,* 22–23.

[25] Hillerin, *Chariot chrestien,* 23–24.

[26] On printing in Poitiers in the sixteenth century, see A[uguste] de la Bouralière, "L'imprimerie & la librairie à Poitiers pendant le XVIe siècle," *MSAO,* 2d ser., 23 (1899): 1–392.

[27] La Bouralière, "Imprimerie," 76, 119.

[28] Jennifer Britnell, *Jean Bouchet* (Edinburgh, 1986), 7–10; Henri Ouvré, *Notice sur Jean Bouchet: poète et historien poitevin du XVIe siècle* (Poitiers, 1858), 26–29; Auguste Hamon, *Un grand rhétoriqueur poitevin: Jean Bouchet 1476–1557?* (Paris, 1901), 71–106; Jules-Levieil de la Marsonnière, "Le salon de Mesdames Desroches aux Grands Jours," *MSAO,* 1st ser., 8 (1842): 37–58.

[29] *Les serées de Guillaume Bouchet, sieur de Brocourt* (Paris, 1873). This work was first published in 1584.

[30] Favreau, *Ville de Poitiers,* 233.

municipal government, along with Poitiers's other institutions, was careful to carry out the bishops' entries in their customary form, but other religious bodies proved far more threatening to the urban administration.[31] Most cities in early modern France hosted a large number of religious establishments, and Poitiers was no exception.[32] Five collegial churches were located in all corners of the city, and one, St. Hilaire-le-Grand, still held seigneurial rights over a bourg that was nevertheless within the walls. Two male abbeys, two female convents, four mendicant establishments, and a variety of chapels and charitable hospitals also sat within the walls or very near them. With twenty-seven parishes in the sixteenth century, Poitiers was filled not only with churches, but also the *curés* (vicars), *vicaires* (curates), priors, and chaplains who staffed them. With so many altars, the city could not lack for saintly advocates on its behalf, but three patrons stood out above the rest: the Virgin, St. Hilaire (fourth-century bishop of Poitiers), and Ste. Radegonde (queen of France and founder of the abbey of Ste. Croix) each accorded special protection.[33]

Poitiers's history had marked it as an administrative and religious hub. When the Romans conquered Gaul, the city became an important Roman administrative center, and by the high Middle Ages, it was the undisputed capital of the counts of Poitou-dukes of Aquitaine, who held there a large and magnificent court.[34] When its twelfth-century countess Eleanor married Henry II of England, Poitiers passed into the set of territories administered by the Plantagenets. Yet it would not remain under English influence for long. Philip Augustus seized the city in 1204, and Poitou and its capital became a part of France.[35] It is likely that Eleanor of Aquitaine was the first to grant Poitiers a commune, but Philip confirmed the privilege and organized the communal government according to the *Établissements de Rouen* (Statutes of Rouen).[36] After being handed to the English for a short period during the Hundred Years' War, Poitiers had the opportunity to show its undivided loyalty to the kings of France by welcoming the dauphin Charles in 1418, after he had been forced to flee Paris.[37] Many of the privileges that the city would boast in the sixteenth century date from this period, and it was at this time that the city developed a relationship of special loyalty to

[31] For instructions for and accounts of bishops' entries in Poitiers, see ACP Casier 43, Reg. 18, N°1, 4v–5r (1555); Brilhac, 8–9 (1564); ADV J110 (seventeenth-century ceremonial).

[32] See, for example, Claire Dolan, *Entre tours et clochers: les gens d'église à Aix-en-Provence au XVIe siècle* (Sherbrooke and Aix-en-Provence, 1981).

[33] See chapter 7.

[34] Favreau, *Ville de Poitiers*, 22–23, 105–6, 112–13.

[35] On the dynastic concerns of the Plantagenets and Philip Augustus's seizure of Poitou, see W. L. Warren, *King John* (London, 1961).

[36] A. Giry, *Les établissements de Rouen: études sur l'histoire des institutions municipales de Rouen, Falaise, Pont-Audemar, Verneuil, La Rochelle, Saintes, Oléron, Bayonne, Tours, Niort, Cognac, S-Jean-d'Angély, Angoulême, Poitiers, etc.*, 2 vols. (Paris, 1883), 1:352–59.

[37] Favreau, *Ville de Poitiers*, 262.

the French crown. In the sixteenth century, Poitiers's notables would frequently make reference to the city's past service and affection in attempting to obtain further privileges.

The religious divisions and civil wars of the sixteenth century had a profound impact on the Poitevin capital.[38] An important Protestant community had developed by the mid-1550s, and this group managed to obtain control of the city in 1562. Even more traumatic than this incident, however, was the sack of the city by royal troops when they arrived to liberate it from Huguenot control. In 1569, Poitiers again fell into active fighting when the admiral Coligny laid it siege, and the young Henri de Guise arrived to help put up a strong defense. During the fifth religious war, the city contributed provisions to the royal camp at Lusignan and was under constant fear of attack because of the machinations of Jean de la Haye, lieutenant général of the sénéchausée and slippery commander of the *politique* faction in Poitou. The alarms of the fifth religious war helped to build ultra-Catholic allegiances in Poitiers and, following a lengthy struggle, the city adhered to the Sacred Union after the assassination of Henri III in 1589. For the next five years, it would operate as an important League center, countering Protestant La Rochelle to the west and royalist Tours to the northeast. Henri IV graciously accepted its rendition in the summer of 1594, but Poitiers's municipal governors soon found that the terms of their relationship with the king no longer rested on the same rhetorical history of loyalty and service of which they had made such good use under the Valois.

Political Culture in Poitiers

Three guiding ideas or arguments shape my analysis of Poitiers's political life. First, I argue that municipal government provided a unique sphere of activity, in which a system of assumptions and carefully articulated rules guided the behavior of the participants. Many of these procedures owed much to general sixteenth-century group dynamics and were typical of the numerous corporate bodies that played an important role in the early modern French state. Town councillors, for example, were just as concerned with issues of precedence in seating and speaking as any judge, cathedral canon, or nobleman. Other procedures, however, arose from the administration's particular claim not only to assert a corporate privilege but also to embody the communal origins of civic government. Therefore, while Poitiers's governors claimed to hold seigneurial authority over the inhabitants, they also clung to a notion of equality of service to the public good. In theory, such different models of authority and responsibility might have created irrecon-

---

[38] A more detailed description of Poitiers's experience during the Wars of Religion may be found in the Introduction to Part II.

cilable tensions. All participants desired unanimity but were forced to accept the disagreement that resorting to majority decision entailed. In practice, though, the very process of arriving at workable decisions mediated between these two opposing models. To achieve consensus, participants had to appeal to a range of interests, often presented as competing expressions of civic values.

Any work that concentrates on politics in the urban sphere requires an approach to the characteristics constituting political culture and process. Should we look only at the actions of political bodies and not at what was said, as Mark Konnert chose to do for the *corps de ville* (municipal governing body) of Châlons-sur-Marne; or should we theorize along with Quentin Skinner that political statements and the context in which they were uttered interacted in a dynamic way to produce coherent ideologies?[39] Should we privilege expressions of intention and assume that ideas have emotive force, or should we emphasize the concerns of family and alliance that may have influenced individuals to act in a certain way? This question is fundamental to long-standing debates about the nature of urban society, in which German Reformation historians have contrasted values of symbolic unity with the practical pressures exerted by elites to account for religious change,[40] and in which French historians have variously focused on ideologies or social factors to explain allegiances during the Catholic League era.[41] In this work, I have engaged to take seriously both the language of politics and the part that underlying motivations had to play in formulating behavior.[42] The words that people uttered and the ways that these words were written down were not obfuscations of real motivations and concerns, but were themselves an integral part of the political process. They therefore not only constitute the way in which politics was actually carried out but also reflect how individuals imagined and understood the process in which they were participating. Rhetoric, in both of its senses, was therefore essential to political life,

[39] Mark W. Konnert, *Civic Agendas and Religious Passion: Châlons-sur-Marne during the French Wars of Religion, 1560–1594* (Kirksville, Mo., 1997), 21; James Tully, ed., *Meaning and Context: Quentin Skinner and His Critics* (Princeton, 1988).

[40] See, in particular, Bernd Moeller, *Imperial Cities and the Reformation: Three Essays*, ed. and trans. H. C. Erik Midelfort and Mark U. Edwards Jr. (Durham, N.C., 1982); Thomas A. Brady Jr., *Ruling Class, Regime and Reformation at Strasbourg, 1520–1555* (Leiden, 1978).

[41] While Frederic Baumgartner focuses on political and religious ideologies, Wolfgang Kaiser and Annette Finley-Croswhite trace familial and political alliances among members of the competing camps. Both approaches tell us something important about the movement of the Catholic League but assume different motivating factors for individuals' choices in the sixteenth century. See Frederic J. Baumgartner, *Radical Reactionaries: The Political Thought of the French Catholic League* (Geneva, 1975); Kaiser, *Marseille;* Finley-Croswhite, *Henry IV and the Towns.*

[42] The kinds of records that have survived for Poitiers, however, have partially determined the relative weight of these approaches. Although Poitiers's town council records for the sixteenth century are extensive (although not complete) and of high quality, often recording individual opinions as well as final rulings, the city's tax records, notarial documents, and baptismal records have not fared as well. Therefore, no full reconstitution of family ties or social interests would be possible, had I set out to do so.

just as ceremony has been shown to be not just incidental to, but constitutive of, particular understandings of society and polity.[43] Linguistic conventions helped to define the possible in civic endeavors. These conventions provided an acceptable means for raising difficult matters at the same time that they set limitations on how these matters could be discussed and influenced how individuals defined their responsibilities in regard to them.

It was also important that representations of politics were not unique to a few governing bodies but were generally understandable to the rest of the urban population. Over time, the municipal government developed a history of its own privileges and of the city, which justified its authority and defined its relationship with the crown. But this history would have been of limited use had it not formed a well-known part of the general understanding of civic identity. By recounting an important miracle story and celebrating it publicly each year, the entire community reinforced its understanding of Poitiers's past and enlisted this past to define the city's relationship to the French monarchy and its religious destiny. Reacting against the view of a profound gulf between elite and popular cultures in early modern Europe, historians have recently sought to integrate these urban populations into the "public sphere," as theorized by Jürgen Habermas for the late eighteenth century in France but extended far earlier than Habermas intended. In this view, instead of standing dumbfounded at the sight of elaborate Latin inscriptions and humanistic motifs celebrating the king's official presence in their city, urban populations rather debated public matters thanks to an ever-growing number of pamphlets commenting, usually negatively, on royal and local affairs. The experiences of Poitiers in the early seventeenth century have specifically served to uphold this argument for the translation of a more modern public opinion back to a civic world divided over religious controversy.[44] In suggesting that both elites and common people in Poitiers shared a fund of local traditions that defined the city's identity, I am ascribing to neither of these views. Rather, I am maintaining that although different kinds of associational bodies in Poitiers had different methods of proceeding, different attitudes toward their membership, and different conceptions of their past, there was still a shared approach to, and language of, politics that could be inter-

[43] For example: Edward Muir, *Civic Ritual in Renaissance Venice* (Princeton, 1981); Barbara A. Hanawalt and Kathryn L. Reyerson, eds., *City and Spectacle in Medieval Europe* (Minneapolis, 1994); Peter Arnade, *Realms of Ritual: Burgundian Ceremony and Civic Life in Late Medieval Ghent* (Ithaca, 1996).

[44] Jürgen Habermas, *The Structural Transformation of the Public Sphere: An Inquiry into a Category of Bourgeois Society,* trans. Thomas Burger and Frederick Lawrence (Cambridge, Mass., 1989); Jeffrey K. Sawyer, *Printed Poison: Pamphlet Propaganda, Faction Politics, and the Public Sphere in Early Seventeenth-Century France* (Berkeley, 1989). For examples of popular incomprehension of public symbols, see Lawrence M. Bryant, *The King and the City in the Parisian Royal Entry Ceremony: Politics, Ritual, and Art in the Renaissance* (Geneva, 1986); Philippe Guignet, *Le pouvoir dans la ville au XVIIIe siècle: pratiques politiques, notabilité et étique sociale de part et d'autre de la frontière franco-belge* (Paris, 1990), 82; and Boutier, Dewerpe, and Nordman, *Tour de France royal,* 334–35.

preted in the city at large. Communication of political concepts was possible because governors and governed fundamentally agreed about what constituted a well-ordered society and shared assumptions about how history could serve as a language to express current goals.

Second, therefore, this work examines the relationship between municipal institutional culture and the wider civic polity. Although the city government claimed to govern in the interests of all, it nevertheless had to confront a range of judicial, financial, and clerical bodies that exerted their own corporate privileges within the same urban environment. Exclusive membership rules, as well, did not preclude occasions for wider consultation with Poitiers's inhabitants, both in their imagined role as the estates constituting the city and through their participation in organizations for poor relief and the militia. Although membership in the corps de ville was an honor far beyond the hopes of most of Poitiers's inhabitants, they could still exercise some control over public affairs through participation in their parish vestries, confraternities, and guild organizations. Despite these possibilities for interaction, however, municipal policies that were deemed to ignore the public interest could draw intense popular opposition, and the corps de ville was forced to recognize that it could not carry out its directives without a strong measure of implicit popular consent. Such was the case when a group of city councillors found their project to provide navigable river access to Poitiers impossible to execute. Intense debate over the proper responsibilities of municipal government and competing notions of the "public" sphere over which it should preside prevented the completion of this seemingly advantageous project. Reactions to Henri II's October 1547 edict prohibiting royal officials and men of the law from serving on city councils throughout France also reveal the fund of resentment that could build against municipal policies thought to benefit narrow interests at the expense of the wider community. Still, as this incident shows, Poitiers's inhabitants accepted the premises of municipal government more than they disputed them. When a body of merchants took advantage of the royal edict to demand that they be elected to office in the hôtel de ville, they were more concerned to gain positions for themselves and their families than to question its authority. William Beik has shown how fragile was the authority of municipal officials who could not retain the tacit support of a large portion of the urban populace and how urban populations attempted to visit retribution on officials whom they deemed radically to have violated understandings of a just political order.[45] Poitiers's experiences show us that tensions over political and economic issues could exist even when no violence occurred but that, despite these problems, there was normally a strong measure of agreement over the nature of civic political authority. This agreement allowed cities like Poitiers

[45] William Beik, *Urban Protest in Seventeenth-Century France: The Culture of Retribution* (Cambridge, U.K., 1997).

to endure the hostilities of the religious wars without fundamental changes in their internal political hierarchies or in their external place in the kingdom.

Urban political life in France existed only in constant reference to royal authority, and Poitiers's relationship with the French monarchy therefore forms my third area of analysis. In the past, scholars have pointed to the sixteenth century as the turning point in the story of the growth of French absolutism, when the towns finally lost their late-medieval independence to growing state control. Thus, Bernard Chevalier has argued that the period from 1450 to 1550 constituted the high point of cordial relations between French cities and the crown, when "Renaissance monarchs" from Louis XI to François I granted their "good cities" virtual internal autonomy in exchange for an assured defense.[46] Such positive relations are said to have deteriorated during the religious wars of the second half of the sixteenth century, however, so that many historians view urban willingness to adhere to the Catholic League and to oppose Henri IV as a last attempt to retain such urban autonomy in the face of a developing monarchal state.[47] Undergirding this view is the assumption that as royal authority grew, urban autonomy decreased, and as royal institutions developed in administrative culture and personnel, municipal traditions necessarily declined. Yet Poitiers's experiences show that royal authority and civic traditions were not antagonistic and that local elites did not view their relationship with the French crown in these terms. Basing their city's identity on a tradition of special loyalty to the kings of France, forged during the worst years of the Hundred Years' War and maintained throughout the sixteenth century, city officials sought above all to maintain a stance of cooperation with, and not opposition to, the crown. Their attitude reflects what William Beik has found for French politics and society in general: the state should not be conceived as an organism separate from society and expanding at its expense; rather, the state itself constituted a process of interaction between the interests of monarchs, local elites, and lesser subjects.[48] Therefore, although historians who tie a decay of municipal rights and customs to the coattails of developing royal institutions assert that French cities joined the Catholic League in a last attempt to reassert their quickly dwindling independence, Poitiers's example contradicts this conclusion. Although the capital of Poitou was an ardent League city and held out against Henri IV until very late (July 1594), urban

---

[46] Bernard Chevalier, "L'état et les bonnes villes en France au temps de leur accord parfait (1450–1550)," in *La ville, la bourgeoisie et la genèse de l'état moderne (XIIe–XVIIIe siècles)*, ed. Neithard Bulst and J.-Ph. Genet (Paris, 1988), 71–85.

[47] Bernard Chevalier, *Les bonnes villes de France du XIVe au XVIe siècle* (Paris, 1982); Robert Descimon, "Ligue à Paris" and *Qui étaient les Seize? étude sociale de deux cent vingt-cinq cadres laïcs de la Ligue radicale parisienne (1585–1594)* (Paris, 1983); Baumgartner, *Radical Reactionaries*.

[48] William Beik, *Absolutism and Society in Seventeenth-Century France: State Power and Provincial Aristocracy in Languedoc* (Cambridge, U.K., 1985).

elites were so far from looking for autonomy that they clamored for a League prince to enter the walls and to guide them through turbulent conditions. The religious wars brought many changes to the balance of power within Poitiers's governing institutions, but they did not bring out any republican intentions. Throughout the League period, Poitiers continued to look to a central power. The religion of the sovereign, and not his authority over them, was the key issue that motivated Poitevins to launch into prolonged civil war. This enduring view of the connection between the city and central authority further allowed Poitiers to recognize Henri IV as king of France without having to revise fundamental political assumptions. Yet the new Bourbon king, once he felt secure of his kingdom, soon displayed his preference for a more active and personal style of royal supervision that altered the ways in which king and city made reference to their past relationship.

PART I

I   Corps *and Community*

Privilege and Political Authority

"Gentlemen," intoned Maurice Roatin as he stepped down from the mayoral chair on 14 July 1595,

> there is great debate between those who take it upon themselves to discuss the
> excellence and provision of governments. Some give the prerogative and pride
> of place to monarchy, or government by a single individual; others prefer aris-
> tocracy, or government by a small number; still others prefer democracy, or pop-
> ular government, to any other kind of state. Yet everyone agrees that states that
> are conducted and supported by the wisdom and authority of a single kind of
> government cannot last long, assigning to this simple [unmixed] method of gov-
> ernment the cause behind and reason for the sudden subversions that occur in
> them. . . . Moreover, although the states that historians point out to us as long-
> lived as well as those that flourish today take their names from the form of gov-
> ernment that is foremost and dominates in them . . . , it is abundantly clear that
> if we consider them up close, we will then see and judge that the solidity of their
> foundations rests on the fortunate association of the three types of government.

Nowhere, Roatin continued, did this mixture of government operate to better effect than in the Roman republic, in which the monarchy of the consuls,
the aristocracy of the Senate, and the democracy of the people had ensured
its success for over one thousand years. Poitiers, moreover, was especially in-
debted to the wisdom of its founders. Having obtained the right of community from the king, they had modeled every aspect of their city government
on the Roman example:

> I am able to say that this *Maison Commune* is truly a model and abbreviated
> image of the inimitable grandeur of the Roman state, in that we may see the

authority of the Consulate in the person of the mayor; that of the Senate corresponds to the peers and *échevins* [aldermen]; and just as the most important affairs in Rome were discussed in the presence and put to the vote of the people, in the same way the most important matters that come up for deliberation in this college cannot and must not be decided except by the advice of the Mois et Cent [broad council].

Yet although Poitiers benefited from every Roman practice to ensure good order and justice in the city, the founders did make one improvement. Whereas in Rome administrative responsibilities were divided between numerous public officials, in Poitiers the mayor held responsibility for all aspects of urban administration. Preceded by sergeants wherever he went, the mayor consulted with Poitiers's deliberative bodies and executed their decisions, heard civil and criminal suits in first instance, assured the food supply and visited the markets, enforced religious order, and maintained the guard and safety of the city. The burden was heavy, but the reward in public service was great.[1]

Roatin's speech is curious on several fronts. At the end of the sixteenth century, it was not unusual for city officials to remind their colleagues of the nature and responsibilities of their offices. In this, they were adapting the practices of the French parlements and lesser courts to the municipal realm.[2] Neither was it unusual for political theorists to discuss contemporary institutions in light of Aristotelian political categories, or to look to ancient Rome as a source of legitimacy. It was inaccurate, to be sure, to claim that a Polybian view of mixed government was universally accepted in France as the ideal model of the polity. Not only had Jean Bodin refuted the very possibility of a mixed constitution in his influential *Six livres de la République*, but in Roatin's own audience sat Adam Blacvod (Blackwood), one of the sixteenth-century's foremost exponents of royal absolutism.[3] Yet what was most curious about Roatin's speech was the way in which he sought to apply the idea of mixed government to Poitiers. He did not, as we might expect, equate city government with an aristocratic or democratic element of the greater French monarchy but identified all three kinds of authority within one urban sphere existing under the grant of the French kings. Although he explicitly compared Poitiers's administration with the Roman republic, it was not clear whether the enhanced powers of the mayor made the French

---

[1] ACP Reg. 54, 211–18; quotations, 211–12, 213.

[2] For changing styles of eloquence in these discourses, see Marc Fumaroli, *L'âge de l'éloquence: rhétorique et 'res literaria' de la Renaissance au seuil de l'époque classique* (Geneva, 1980).

[3] Jean Bodin, *Les six livres de la République*, 6 vols. (Paris, 1986), 2:7–30. On Adam Blacvod's absolutism, see chapter 8. On theories of mixed government and their use in the Renaissance and early modern period, see J. G. A. Pocock, *The Machiavellian Moment: Florentine Political Thought and the Atlantic Republican Tradition* (Princeton, 1975), esp. 77–80 and chaps. 7–9.

provincial capital a better example of monarchy, aristocracy, or popular rule. Further, although in the Roman example popular participation assured the democratic element of government, Roatin's exposition grounded all three types of political authority within the urban administration. Just as Contarini did in describing the constitution of Venice in the early sixteenth century, Roatin limited Poitiers's political community to those who held civic office and precluded "the people" from any public role.[4]

Like most city governments all over France, Poitiers's corps de ville was highly exclusive and oligarchical. In cities such as Paris, Nantes, Marseille, Limoges, La Rochelle, and Dijon, limited numbers of professional and family groups dominated city offices, and in Poitiers, self-co-optive elections and lifelong office accentuated this tendency.[5] Elite families felt a sense of pride and proprietary interest in government. This was why Jean Le Roy, échevin of Poitiers, beguiled the hours elaborately illustrating an armillary of all the mayors of the city, and why Jean Darnal ensured that lists of Bordeaux's *jurats* accompanied every year of his updated history of the capital of Guyenne.[6] In this system, there was little room for regular popular input in town government. Few cities continued to hold general assemblies, and places like Dijon, where poor winegrowers showed up every year to voice their votes in municipal elections, were rare.[7] Given these realities, Mayor Roatin's evocation of a Polybian mixed constitution was *not* a very convincing way to describe urban government. Ideas of divided jurisdictions, with their implications for popular participation, actually ran counter to the single corporate status of Poitiers's corps de ville and contradicted municipal officials' preferred view of their own authority.

It is important to understand how elites and general inhabitants understood political authority in the urban arena of the sixteenth century. How members of Poitiers's corps de ville accounted for their own stewardship of the civic realm and how they imagined their relationship with the inhabitants both informed and grew out of daily decisions they made about government. The more an urban administration laid emphasis on its own prerogatives and privileges, the greater would be its claims unilaterally to define civic order and obstinately to fight any challenges to its decisions. Conversely, the greater

---

[4] Gasper Contareno [Contarini], *The Commonwealth and Gouernment of Venice* (1599; reprint, Amsterdam and New York, 1969).

[5] Diefendorf, *Paris City Councillors;* Robert Descimon, "L'échevinage parisien sous Henri IV (1594–1609): autonomie urbaine, conflits politiques et exclusives sociales," in *La ville,* ed. Bulst and Genet, 113–50; Saupin, *Nantes au XVIIe siècle;* Kaiser, *Marseille;* Annette Finley-Croswhite, "Absolutism and Municipal Autonomy: Henry IV and the 1602 Pancarte Revolt in Limoges," in *Society and Institutions in Early Modern France,* ed. Mack P. Holt (Athens, Ga., 1991), 80–97; Robbins, *City on the Ocean Sea,* 93–106, 253–73; Mack P. Holt, "Popular Political Culture and Mayoral Elections in Sixteenth-Century Dijon," in *Society and Institutions,* 98–116; and Breen, "Legal Culture," chaps. 2–3.

[6] MMP MS 574, 2r; Jean Darnal, *Supplement des chroniques de la noble ville & cité de Bourdeaus* (Bordeaux, 1620), 10v, 31v et seq.

[7] Holt, "Popular Political Culture," 105–11.

its tendency to see its role as representative, in one of the many senses available in the sixteenth century, the more it might acknowledge and include other groups as part of an active political community. Poitiers's city government advanced as a fundamental tenet its undivided control over urban institutions. Basing its view on a theory of dominion in which the mayor and échevins held in fief from the king the military and civil jurisdiction over the city, the corps de ville saw its governing powers as the result of a set of royal privileges granted to it as a corporate body. Having received its mandate from a source superior and exterior to the urban sphere, the municipal government looked upon itself as the sole legitimate arbitrator of order within the city and tied the obedience and respect it demanded to the honor of the entire community. The virtue of positing such a system of authority was that to challenge any aspect of it was also to doubt the king himself. And although the hôtel de ville or the city at large could resist individual royal demands, no one ever represented royal prerogative as anything less than absolute until the period of the Catholic League.

At the same time, contemporary assumptions about the ends of government, ideas of representation, and a history of communal values all dictated that the corps de ville recognize a political role for the inhabitants. Just as sixteenth-century theories of absolute authority of the French monarch did not preclude discussion of the mutual responsibilities and relationship between king and people, members of Poitiers's city administration saw their connection with the population at large as far more complex than between governors and governed.[8] Although town council members would have rejected the notion that they were delegates or representatives of the people in the modern sense, their claims to act for the common good established an important link with the rest of the urban community.

Political relationships in sixteenth-century cities continued to draw on understandings of the polity and representation that had grown out of the medieval traditions of church government, conciliar writings, communal foundations, and corporation theory. Just as the Catholic Church could be perceived as the mystic body of Christ, gathered or expressed in a council authorized to make decisions for the whole, city councils could be seen as the embodiment or epitome of the greater civic community and thus able to act for the good of all.[9] In Paris, as Robert Descimon explains, a complex

[8] Claude de Seyssel, *The Monarchy of France,* ed. Donald R. Kelley and trans. J. H. Hexter (New Haven, 1981); Quentin Skinner, *The Foundations of Modern Political Thought,* 2 vols. (Cambridge, U.K., 1978), 2:189–348; Nannerl O. Keohane, *Philosophy and the State in France: The Renaissance to the Enlightenment* (Princeton, 1980), chap. 1; William Church, *Constitutional Thought in Sixteenth-Century France: A Study in the Evolution of Ideas* (Cambridge, Mass., 1941); and J. Russell Major, "The French Renaissance Monarch as Seen through the Estates-General," *Renaissance Quarterly* 9 (1962): 113–25.

[9] Ernst H. Kantorowicz, *The King's Two Bodies: A Study in Medieval Political Theology* (Princeton, 1957); Pierre Michaud-Quantin, *Universitas: expressions du mouvement communautaire dans le moyen-âge latin* (Paris, 1970); Georges de Lagarde, "Les théories représenta-

network of ceremonial occasions helped to express the idea that the disparate elements of the city were organically and mystically united in one civic community, with the *bureau de ville* at its pinnacle.[10] Poitiers's communal tradition supported this sense of connection and accountability. The hôtel de ville chose to downplay the city's early communal history, but the origins of its political organization in the values of the sworn association and mutual aid could not be denied. Neither, ultimately, could the right of the inhabitants to be consulted on matters of special interest to themselves. According to corporation theory, as it had developed through canon and civil law, the governors of a corporate group, or fictive person, oversaw and tended to it as a guardian would a ward. Communes, with their rights to sue and to be sued, were of course prime examples of such collective personalities. Yet the famous dictum of *Quod omnes tangit ab omnibus tractari et approbari debet* (what touches all must be decided by all) also dictated that persons had to be consulted on matters affecting them as individuals.[11] In fact, it was precisely when the hôtel de ville recognized that a decision would directly affect a sector of the urban community that it formally invited its input. This resort to outside opinion did not follow any rigid principles; indeed, it was in the interest of the corps de ville to leave delineations of the political community and their respective rights suitably vague. Yet this practical admission of other groups into the decision-making process reflected a very important reality of municipal government. Despite references to exclusive privileges, urban officials had to recognize that for decisions to be effective, they had to have a measure of popular support. Whether this consent was obtained through a formal process of consultation with the various corps and estates that were thought to compose the city or through an informal process of sounding out one's neighbors, its absence endangered the legitimacy of municipal policy.

Implicit in the hôtel de ville's insistence on its rights to determine order within the city, then, was its tacit admission that cooperation was necessary to ensure proper regulation. The claim of members not only to consider the

---

tives du XIVe–XVe siècle et l'Église," in *Xe congrès international des sciences historiques, Rome, 1955* (Louvain and Paris, 1958), 66–67; Achille Darquennes, "Représentation et bien commun," in *IXe congrès international des sciences historiques, Paris 1950* (Louvain, 1952), 35–51, esp. 39–40.

[10] This sense of Parisian identity did not compete with the city's relationship with the kings of France, but rather was dependent on its dual role as royal capital and civic community, mediated through its relationship with God. Descimon, "Le corps de ville et le système cérémoniel."

[11] Yves M.-J. Congar, "Quod Omnes Tangit, Ab Omnibus Tractari et Approbari Debet," *Revue historique de droit français et étranger,* 4th ser., 35 (1958): 210–59, esp. 214; Lagarde, "Théories représentatives," 73; Antonio Marongiu, "Q.o.t., Principe fondamental de la Démocratie et du Consentement, au XIVe siècle," *Album Helen Maud Cam: Studies presented to the International Commission for the History of Representative and Parliamentary Institutions,* XXIV (Louvain and Paris, 1961), 104. Bodin (*République,* 3:188) confirms that this rule still informed theories of corporate association in the sixteenth century.

particular good of their corps but also to act for the common good of the populace opened the back door to consent and accountability even as the front was staunchly secured by corporate privilege. In her analysis of the political rhetoric of the consulate of Aix-en-Provence, Claire Dolan found that the *consuls* resorted to references to the common good only when laying their case before the king but fell back on an argument for order when dealing with the urban community. From these findings, Dolan concluded that ideas of the common good did not truly motivate consular decisions but provided a convenient defense against attempted royal incursions.[12] Such a view certainly does not hold for Poitiers. Here, prescriptions for order did not contradict, and in fact depended on, values of harmony and consensus that made the city a moral whole rather than a disparate assortment of competing interests.

Although the relationship between civil authority and civic unity often remained implicit in municipal decision making, periodic substantial revisions and promulgations of *police* ordinances provided an opportunity for the corps de ville to remind the population of the theoretical basis of its administration. Nowhere are the emotive attributes of the police of Poitiers elaborated more explicitly than in an introduction to the ordinances of 1567. Having overseen their revision, their acceptance by the Parlement of Paris, and their subsequent publication, Mayor Maixent Poitevin composed an introduction to the regulations designed to explain their virtue to the population at large.[13] "Just as we see that in a private house," began the mayor, resorting to the classic comparison of civil and family government,

> the father of the family (people of Poitiers) teaches and remonstrates with his children and domestics what their duties are and how to carry them out, in order to maintain the order and government of his house in a good state and honorably to increase the welfare which is in his hands; in the same way, the laws and ordinances in a town and city teach the citizens how they should live with each other. They show them what is just and reasonable and invite them all to uphold the public good and general tranquility through honorable reasons and means, while keeping them from vice through punishments and fines in line with what the case requires.[14]

[12] Claire Dolan, "Des images en action: cité, pouvoir municipal et crises pendant les guerres de religion à Aix-en-Provence," in *Les productions symboliques du pouvoir XVIe–XXe siècle,* ed. Laurier Turgeon (Québec, 1990), 65–86.

[13] ACP Casier 10, D53. Although no copies of the ordinances' first impression have survived, an item in Poitevin's mayoral account for 1566–69 indicates both that they were printed in Poitiers and that they did not sell as well as expected. See ACP Casier 37, K21. The ordinances, however, were to appear in subsequent compilations of Poitiers's police statutes. The widow of Jean Blanchet, for example, published not only the actual ordinances, but also all of Poitevin's supporting materials in *Reglement et ordonnances pollitiques, faictes par les maire pairs, conseillers, escheuins & bourgeois de la ville de Poictiers, . . . pour le repos public & reglement du fait de la police en ladicte ville* (Poitiers, [1606]).

[14] ACP Casier 10, D53, "Oraison au peuple de poict[iers]," 1r.

Such laws, continued Poitevin, are necessary, because we cannot always be sure that people will consistently follow the path of virtue.

> For the law is nothing other than a guide for good living, and as such the governing principle of cities, which pertains equally to everyone, according to which each person must range himself and conform his values and habits of living. Otherwise, he will find himself as one lost, and the cause of misfortunes, disagreements, and dissensions within the commonweal. . . . Therefore, the towns and cities without laws and good ordinances have no life worthy of human beings; neither do they have any feeling or acquaintance with reason and honor; nor especially any form of public order. This is due to the fact that their members, who are the citizens, no longer get along with each other and no longer feel within themselves the virtue of the law, which flowing and seeping in through the minds of men, makes them, all in one agreement, undertake and do useful and profitable things for the whole body of the public. As a result, when the law is scorned and ignored, the city, which is called thus due to the unity and concord of the citizens, must rather be identified as a den and assemblage of beasts of different kinds, which attack each other and fight among themselves up until the point that they have torn each other to pieces and miserably devoured each other. But in the opposite case, when each person restrains himself and obeys the order and ways for living that the laws and statutes of the region prescribe, we would see everyone assured of a good peace and tranquility and richly endowed with all kinds of goods.[15]

For Poitevin, then, the law was the soul or lifeblood of the city, which, in ordering the actions of the inhabitants, combined them in a union of common purpose.[16] As a result, the city as an entity could be understood on both a material and a figurative level, being at the same time the body of inhabitants and the principle of harmonious association uniting them. Further, since the law was the activating principle that assured a humane order to an otherwise disparate assemblage of social groups, the municipal government was to be found at the heart of the civic body. Through its activities in both making and executing the laws, the council was to play an important, even determining, role in defining the specific qualities of the union of the inhabitants. Yet this authority came at a price. If police statutes were seen to go beyond concerns for practicality and fairness to inspire and to mediate civic unity, then councillors had to be sure they could bear this moral weight. Although Poitevin placed the onus on Poitiers's inhabitants to regulate their actions according to the laws passed down to them, the corps de ville possessed

---

[15] ACP Casier 10, D53, "Oraison au peuple de poict[iers]," 1v–2r.

[16] Poitevin is here echoing a general tendency of constitutional theorists of the second half of the sixteenth century to see the law as "the constitutive structure of the polity," or the crucial element binding society together. Keohane, *Philosophy and the State,* 43.

an even greater responsibility to assure that its decisions were conduits for harmonious action and the common good.

Municipal Privilege

At the heart of the hôtel de ville's perception of itself as a specially privileged body responsible for the government of Poitiers was its relationship with the kings of France. Every 14 July, the mayor and twenty-four échevins swore an oath between the hands of the king or his representative, most often the lieutenant général of the sénéchaussée. When Henri III visited Poitiers in 1577, the councillors proudly swore to the chancellor in the presence of the king that they would "be good and loyal subjects, obedient to the king; guard his city and prevent it from being captured through plots [*monopoles*] or otherwise; and immediately reveal them and alert his Majesty to them."[17] The licentious behavior of the royal court during its stay in Poitiers shocked some of the inhabitants,[18] but Henri III no doubt made up for this trouble when he affirmed the council's assurances:

> They have offered us . . . the homage, oath of fidelity and duty by which the said twenty-five échevins of the said town are obliged to us through their offices, in accordance with the ancient institution and creation of their college, for the guard and government of the said [town] thus committed to them.[19]

City council and king therefore concurred that the authority of the hôtel de ville derived from an oath of fealty investing it with the military guard and rights of justice and police over the city. As Yves Barel has pointed out for the medieval period, the fact that a seigneur considered a town as a vassal did not necessarily mean that the corps de ville acted as a collective seigneur or that the population considered it that way.[20] Yet for Poitiers's municipal government, one aspect of seigneurial control was crucial to its self-definition. Because it saw its authority to administer the city as deriving "downward" through a direct relationship with the king, it could respond to calls for public accountability or participation on its own terms.

Swearing an oath of fealty for the guard of the city was far from unique to Poitiers's corps de ville. All town governments probably performed this action,[21] and city councils as exalted as Paris's bureau de ville anxiously

---

[17] ACP Reg. 42, 656.

[18] Le Riche, 287–89.

[19] ACP Reg. 42, 677.

[20] Yves Barel, *La ville médiévale: système social, système urbain* (Grenoble, 1977), 10.

[21] Article 27 of the Edict of Crémieu (1536) specifies: "Ordonnons aussi, qu'és eslections qui seront faites de Maires, Escheuins, Consuls & autres ayans administration des affaires communs, nosdits Baillifs, Seneschaux, & autres nos Iuges ressortissans en nosdites Cours sans

sought to swear their oaths in the king's presence.[22] Many city officials probably did not equate their oath with seigneurial dominion, but Poitiers was at
least not alone in this view. The city council of Périgueux conducted its deliberations under the aegis of *les citoyens seigneurs,* and Niort's municipal
officials claimed to exercise military guard and civil and criminal legal jurisdiction from the king "by right of barony, by fealty and liege homage, with
the duty of one glove or five sous tournois for all obligation, payable at each
change of seigneur."[23] Poitiers's municipal government also placed special
emphasis on a tradition of the city's unswerving loyalty to the French crown
that it had worked hard to construct.[24] When Charles VII granted letters
patent permanently attaching Poitou to the royal domain and extinguishing
the historical position of its counts, the corps de ville of the county's capital
city began to see itself as fulfilling that role.[25] As a result, the city council
took pride in seeing the mayor not only as the king's captain in Poitiers but
also as the first baron of Poitou.

The unusually exclusive composition and practices of Poitiers's hôtel de
ville enhanced its ability to interpret its authority over the inhabitants as one
of command. Although opinions differ concerning when the town was first
organized as a commune, it clearly held this status by 1204, when Philip Augustus confirmed this right by charter.[26] The king also sent the city a copy
of the popular *Établissements de Rouen* (Statutes of Rouen), in adopting
which Poitiers joined the group of towns characterized by a government of
one hundred peers, with councils of twelve *jurés,* twelve échevins, and a
mayor.[27] By the sixteenth century, this organization had changed somewhat.
The corps de ville was composed of a council of twenty-five notables, including the échevins and the mayor, and a body of seventy-five bourgeois
that joined the smaller council to consult on important affairs, including fi-

---

moyen, president & concluent respectiuement, *reçoiuent le serment,* & procedent à l'institution
selon les Statuts & Ordonnances des villes . . ." (emphasis mine), in Pierre Neron and Estienne
Girard, *Les edicts et ordonnances des Tres-Chrestiens Roys, François I. Henry II. François II.
Charles IX. Henry III. Henry IV. Lovys XIII. et Lovys XIV. Sur le faict de la Iustice & abreuiation des Procez* (Paris, 1666), 5.

[22] Robert Descimon, "Les scrutateurs des élections échevinales à Paris (mi-XVIe/mi-XVIIe
siècle): des médiateurs de fidélité," in *Paris et ses compagnes sous l'Ancien Régime: mélanges
offerts à Jean Jacquart,* ed. Michel Balard, Jean-Claude Hervé, and Nicole Lemaître (Paris,
1994), 198.

[23] Augustin Thierry, *Essai sur l'histoire de la formation et des progrès du Tiers État suivi de
fragments du Recueil des monuments inédits de cette histoire,* 2d ed. (Paris, [1853]), 302, 325.

[24] See chapter 7.

[25] Edict of Charles VII, dated Aug. 1436 from Tours. For a printed version, see *Ordonnances,*
15:677–79.

[26] For discussions of the origins of Poitiers's communal status, see: Favreau, *Ville de Poitiers,*
51–53, 69–78; Giry, *Établissements de Rouen;* and Prosper Boissonade's introduction to *Recueil de documents concernant la commune et la ville de Poitiers,* ed. E. Audouin, 2 vols., AHP
44, 46 (Poitiers, 1923, 1928), 44:xiii–lxxxviii; 46:vii–lxxxiii.

[27] Giry, *Établissements de Rouen,* 1:7, 358–60. Copies of the *Établissements* may be found
in ACP Casier 1, A2, and MMP MS 51, 27v–32r.

nances and elections, in an assembly known as the Mois et Cent (because it was composed of one hundred members and was supposed to meet once a month). The former distinction between échevins and jurés had all but disappeared, except that échevins who had formerly served a term as mayor were granted precedence over those who had not. This one-hundred-member body had also become entirely self-perpetuating. Although privileges that Philip Augustus accorded in 1222 specified that the citizens of Poitiers were to elect the mayor, councillors, and échevins, by the sixteenth century any notion that the inhabitants were to participate in the selection of the members of the corps de ville was long a thing of the past.[28] Unlike in many other French cities, there was no oath of bourgeoisie in Poitiers, so the inhabitants would have been hard-pressed to identify who the "citizens" might be. Members of the corps de ville alone therefore voted replacements for vacancies among the seventy-five bourgeois and twenty-five échevins, and once a man acquired his position, he held it until either resignation or death. Only the office of mayor changed annually. There were also no stipulations to ensure representativity among those who held office. Beyond the requirements, occasionally set aside, that members have reached the age of majority (twenty-five years) and be permanent residents of the city, there were no statutory limitations on who could serve. The fact that échevins were elected from the body of seventy-five bourgeois, frequently while serving a term as mayor, made the organization even more exclusive.[29]

Circumstances in Poitiers thus lent credence to the hôtel de ville's view of its own authority. Merchant Michel Bibard, for one, was certainly inclined to accept it. During an assembly called to prevent a possible uprising in Poitiers over the *gabelle* (salt tax) in 1548, he suggested that the city should alert the king of its fears, since "the mayor and échevins hold [the city] from him by fealty and homage."[30] At the same assembly, though, René de Champalays, canon of St. Hilaire-le-Grand, proposed that they meet the emergency by electing a captain and a special council of twelve to deliberate in secret, following the example of the Republic of Venice.[31] Such a suggestion hardly credited the claims of the mayor and échevins to hold the guard of the town in military fief from the king. Objections also came from presidial court judges in the heat of antagonism caused by the Catholic League. Hurling insults at former mayor Maixent Poitevin for his presumption in interfering

[28] "Cives Pictavenses singulis annis eligere majorem et duodecim scabinos et duodecim juratos." Audouin, ed., *Recueil de documents,* 44:74. Audouin speculates, however, that the phrase "cives pictavenses" could have referred to the one hundred peers rather than to a general assembly (74 n. 1).

[29] I analyze Poitiers's electoral practices in "The Benefit of the Ballot? Elections and Influence in Sixteenth-Century Poitiers," *French Historical Studies* 24, no. 4 (2001): 621–52.

[30] ACP Reg. 30, 21 (14 Aug. 1548).

[31] ACP Reg. 30, 18. Henry Heller also recounts some of the opinions expressed in this assembly in his *The Conquest of Poverty: The Calvinist Revolt in Sixteenth Century France* (Leiden, 1986), 188–89.

with their guard of the gates in 1588, several legal officials declared that the guard did not belong to all of the échevins, but only to those who were also judges of the presidial court. They therefore implied that military authority accrued to them as royal judicial officials rather than as city councillors, a view that Poitevin, a lawyer, denounced as insulting to him personally and injurious to the interests of the king and to the échevins, who had all sworn an oath of fidelity to the crown.[32] Evidence thus indicates that the municipal government's view of its authority was generally known throughout Poitiers. At the same time, competing versions of political relationships were likely to surface when extraordinary conditions drew other groups to help make decisions affecting the entire city.

If the municipal government placed strong emphasis on its privileges, it had extensive privileges on which to draw. Poitiers, like many other French cities, was responsible for its own defense. Like Nantes, it could require that the parishes belonging to the *châtellenie* send men to perform the *guet*, a service that in the sixteenth century was frequently converted to a work detail.[33] Louis XI considerably increased the city's privileges in the military sphere by exempting first the échevins, then the whole *Cent*, and finally the inhabitants from the *ban et arrière-ban* (a feudal military obligation) in 1463, 1467, and 1472, respectively, each time on the charge of defending the city.[34] That Poitiers was never the preferred residence of the region's royal governor also enhanced the mayor's military role. In the first half of the sixteenth century, Jean de Daillon, comte du Lude, lieutenant général to the governor of Guyenne, spent much of his time in Bordeaux.[35] After his son, Guy, was invested with the governorship of Poitou in 1562, he still had to rush from Niort to Poitiers in 1569 when Condé's forces threatened to attack.[36] For a short period, from late 1573 to 1577, the mayor and échevins even had the charge of defending the royal château, a situation they quickly but ineffectively tried to claim as standing since time immemorial.[37] It was not until

---

[32] ACP Reg. 47, 466 (25 May 1588).

[33] ACP Casier 42, Reg. 11, 27r–34r (1453–1454); 37v–46v (1487–1488); Reg. 47, 196 (1 Nov. 1587). For Nantes, see the parish accounts of Saint-Martin de Chantenay, in S. de la Nicollière-Teijeiro, ed., "Comptes de la fabrique de Saint-Martin de Chantenay, 1481–1506," *Revue de Bretagne, de Vendée et d'Anjou* 37 (1875): 174–85. Chantenay spent a considerable sum in 1494 to equip a soldier to complete the parish's military service.

[34] ACP Casier 2, A26 (1463), A27 (1467) and A28 (1472). See also Giry, *Établissements de Rouen*, 1:371; Favreau, *Ville de Poitiers*, 323–24.

[35] *Lettres adressées à Jean et Guy de Daillon, comtes du Lude, gouverneurs du Poitou*, ed. Bélisaire Ledain, 2 vols., AHP 13–14 (Poitiers, 1882–83), 13:xiv.

[36] Robert Harding explains that the governor of Poitou was subordinate to the governor of Guyenne until July 1560, when Poitou was established as a separate government. Guy de Daillon held the position of lieutenant général to Antoine de Bourbon, governor of Poitou, from August 1560 to November 1562, when Lude became governor in his own right. *Anatomy of a Power Elite: The Provincial Governors of Early Modern France* (New Haven, 1978), 43. On the events of 1569, see H[enri] Beauchet-Filleau, ed., *Le siége de Poitiers par Liberge suivi de la bataille de Montcontour et du siége de Saint-Jean-d'Angély* (Poitiers, 1846), 16–17.

[37] BNF MS Fr 15559, 17r; Brilhac, 23.

Jean Jay, sieur de Boisseguin, was appointed lieutenant général for the king in Poitiers in 1574 and captain of the château in 1577 that the city council had to deal with a regular, external military authority.[38]

The hôtel de ville also possessed substantial rights of justice and police. Although its legal jurisdiction was limited by comparison with other towns in the thirteenth century,[39] a 1369 grant from Prince Edward of England (the Black Prince) considerably enhanced its judicial rights by granting the mayor jurisdiction over almost all criminal and civil cases.[40] Its police jurisdiction gave the urban administration the right to pass general ordinances, and unlike in many other cities, members of the corps de ville took on the burden of enforcement themselves. Although Paris appointed individuals as subsidiary police officials (and eventually sold these offices to those willing to pay), Poitiers's city government held a *Mois* annually to apportion out duties of visitation to members of its own corps.[41] The hôtel de ville also exercised considerable control over artisanal production. Although Poitiers was a *ville juré*, where artisans formed corporate groups that appointed their own officers to enforce statutes that members had sworn to uphold, the urban government retained important powers over them. No craft could be sworn in Poitiers without municipal ratification, and new masters were required to pay an entrance fee to the mayor.[42] The candle makers found to their dismay that the city council could also dissolve disobedient guilds, just as the woodworkers discovered that it would create a new master over their objections.[43] Many of these cases found their way to the mayoral court. Expediting all varieties of civil and criminal cases and possessing (or so it claimed) exclusive jurisdiction over police matters, it heard in first instance all suits involving commercial and guild disputes, assault, assignment of guardians, and drawing up of inventories.[44] Once a consular (merchants')

[38] ACP Reg. 41, 127–29 (17 June 1574); Reg. 42, 683–85 (14 Oct. 1577).

[39] Giry, *Établisssments de Rouen*, 1:366–67.

[40] He reserved to himself the crimes of lèse-majesté and counterfeiting and the act of execution. See *Ordonnances*, 15:675–76; Audouin, ed., *Recueil de documents*, 46:242–43.

[41] Robert Descimon, "La vénalité des offices politiques de la ville de Paris (1500–1681)," *Bulletin de la S.H.M.C.* (1994), nos. 3–4: 17–18, 21, 24–26.

[42] For a good discussion of the difference between sworn and unsworn crafts, see François Olivier-Martin, *L'organisation corporative de la France d'ancien régime* (Paris, 1938), 90–105. Olivier-Martin points out that in Poitiers the crafts were governed in a manner intermediate between the practice of the sworn and open *métier* (199–200). On guild organization in general, see Émile Coornaert, *Les corporations en France avant 1789*, 2d ed. (Paris, 1968); and for Poitou, Prosper Boissonnade, *Essai sur l'organisation du travail en Poitou depuis le XIe siècle jusqu'à la Révolution*, 2 vols. (Poitiers, 1898–99). The account for 1586–89, for example, contains the names, trades, and entrance fees for all new masters named during this period. ACP Casier 37, K28.

[43] ACP Reg. 46, 107–10 (20 Oct. 1586); 276 (13 Apr. 1587).

[44] The only records to survive from the court in the sixteenth century are gathered in ACP Casier 44, 1523–63; 1560–86; 1583; and 1506–7. Only Casier 44, 1523–63, and part of 1560–86, contain actual sentences of the mayoral court. The other documentation is composed of extracts made for a legal suit of 1583. Because this suit pertained to criminal jurisdiction, the majority of sentences preserved concern assault, guardians, and inventories.

court was set up in Poitiers in 1566, though, many small commercial disputes probably eluded the mayoral jurisdiction.[45]

Other privileges enhanced the prestige of city council members and increased their ability to oversee important urban affairs. Poitiers was the first city to obtain the privilege of *noblesse de cloche* when Charles V conferred hereditary noble status on the mayor, échevins, and councillors in 1372 in gratitude for their active role in returning the city to French rule.[46] When Charles VII, showing similar appreciation for Poitiers's loyalty in a later phase of the Hundred Years' War, founded a university in the regional capital, he also granted the hôtel de ville supervisory powers over it, including the duty to ratify the doctors regent.[47] In 1552, the corps de ville was so dissatisfied with the medical doctors available in the city that it overrode the judgment of the medical faculty and appointed its own candidate.[48] The one area of urban administration that always posed a serious challenge, however, concerned fiscal matters. All inhabitants of Poitiers were exempt from the *taille,* a direct royal tax, but almost all were subject to the usual range of indirect impositions. The corps de ville could not impose or collect any of these taxes without a specific royal commission, and it was required to renew its major source of revenue, the *dixième,* or indirect tax on wine sold at retail, every six years.[49] Such limitations meant that the city council was frequently strapped for funds. In 1577, the deputies in charge of organizing the royal entry for Henri III refused to act until René Arnoul, a rich bourgeois, agreed to lend them three thousand livres tournois to complete their preparations.[50]

When compared with other city governments in France, then, Poitiers possessed relatively strong political privileges, but weak economic ones. When François I decided to reward the cities of Cognac and Angoulême, the first for being his place of birth and the second for its loyalty to his house, he granted to the former exemption from the taille, rights of middle and low justice, and a sénéchaussée court, and to the latter a university.[51] These were thus desirable privileges at the beginning of the sixteenth century, and Poi-

[45] See Pierre Rambaud, "La jurisdiction consulaire de Poitiers (1566–1791)," parts 1 and 2, *BSAO,* 3d ser., 6 (1924): 643–72; 7 (1925): 210–31. No documentation survives from this court in the sixteenth century.

[46] Letters patent dated Dec. 1372. ACP Casier 1, A19, or, for a printed version, *Ordonnances,* 5:563–64.

[47] *Ordonnances,* 13:179–81. See also ACP Reg. 30, 193 (4 Mar. 1549) confirming this arrangement.

[48] ACP Reg. 32, 144–47 (21 Nov. 1552).

[49] Kings granted Poitiers the right to collect the dixième for variable periods of time, but six years was the most common period in the sixteenth century. See, for example, ACP Casier 20, G49 (1540), G50 (1546), G51 (1552), G52 (1562), and G53 (1575).

[50] ACP Reg. 42, 626–27 (18 May 1577); 629–34 (27 May 1577); Casier 37, K24 (final account for the entry).

[51] Cognac: letters patent dated Feb. 1515. *Ordonnances des rois de France: règne de François Ier,* 9 vols. (Paris, 1902–92), 1:128–32; confirmation of François II, dated Nov. 1559 from Blois. Marie-Thérèse de Martel, ed., *Catalogue des actes de François II,* 2 vols. (Paris, 1991), 1:254. Angoulême: edict dated 27 Dec. 1516 from Amboise. Isambert, 12:100–102.

tiers held them all. Poitiers also matched all of the political privileges of well-endowed La Rochelle, so that if Louis XI gratified Bourges by granting it the same municipal liberties and jurisdiction as the Atlantic port, Nantes selected Poitiers for its model over Angers.[52] It would be a mistake for us to take some of these highly sought-after privileges, such as criminal jurisdiction and rights of police, for granted: Paris's bureau de ville lacked the one, and Lyon's city council coveted the other.[53] Neither did Poitiers, like Rouen, Aix, Rennes, or Toulouse, have to tolerate the heavy thumb of a resident parlement.[54] Poitiers had the advantage of an important sénéchaussée and a first order presidial court,[55] but unlike Toulouse, it did not have a sovereign court that saw fit to appoint the *capitouls* (city councillors) unilaterally ten times between 1500 and 1562.[56] In fact, unlike most cities, Poitiers could proceed with its elections without interference, at least in theory. In contrast to La Rochelle, the hôtel de ville did not send its three mayoral candidates to the king's lieutenant for his final selection, and unlike Bourges and other cities affected by François I's 1536 Edict of Crémieu, the lieutenant général did not preside in electoral assemblies.[57]

Yet Poitiers's economic privileges appear quite insubstantial when compared with those of other important cities in the kingdom. La Rochelle had access to twenty-five percent of all rights arising from the sale of wine from Saintonge, the Île de Ré, and other surrounding islands, significant customs duties on all merchandise and wine leaving the port, and various other han-

---

[52] For a listing of La Rochelle's most important privileges, see François II's confirmation, dated December 1559 from Blois. *Catalogue des actes de François II*, 1:312. On Bourges: Jean Chenu, *Recveil des antiqvites et privileges de la ville de Bovrges, et de plvsievrs autres villes capitales du royaume* (Paris, 1621), 26–33, esp. 30. Nantes: AC Reg. 40, 193–96 (18 Apr. 1572).

[53] In Paris, the royal *prévôté* court, meeting in the *châtellet*, held criminal jurisdiction. Jean-Pierre Babelon, *Paris au XVIe siècle* (Paris, 1986), 264. In Lyon, Charles IX's edict of 1572 creating police tribunals actually increased the police responsibilities of the hôtel de ville, which explains why he had to issue special letters patent ordering the *sénéchal* and presidial court to carry them out. Guillaume Barbier, *Recveil des privileges, avthoritez, povvoirs, franchises, & exemptions des preuost des marchands, escheuins, & habitans de la ville de Lyon* (Lyon, 1649), 168–78.

[54] See Benedict, *Rouen*, 33–34; Sharon Kettering, *Judicial Politics and Urban Revolt in Seventeenth-Century France: The Parlement of Aix, 1629–1659* (Princeton, 1978), 47; Henri Carré, *Le Parlement de Bretagne après la Ligue (1589–1610)* (Paris, 1888), 504–15; Thierry Mailles, "Les relations politiques entre le Parlement de Toulouse et les Capitouls, de 1540 environ à 1572," in *Les parlements de province: pouvoirs, justice et société du XVe au XVIIIe siècle*, ed. Jacques Poumarède and Jack Thomas (Toulouse, 1996), 509–21; G[ermain] de La Faille, *Annales de la ville de Toulouse depuis la reunion de la comté de Toulouse à la couronne*, 2 vols. (Toulouse, 1687–1701), 2:22, 53–54, 75–76, 93.

[55] When it was created in 1552, Poitiers's presidial court was larger than most others, with twelve *conseillers* and a *greffier d'appaux*, and at two thousand livres received a greater sum in *gages* than any other presidial. Edict dated Mar. 1552 from Reims. Neron and Girard, *Edicts et ordonnances*, 191, 197–98.

[56] La Faille reports this as happening in 1513, 1517, 1519, 1524, 1528, 1549, 1550, 1557, and 1561–62 (*Annales*, 1:323; 2:8, 16, 65, 152–53, 188, 228, 250).

[57] Robbins, *City on the Ocean Sea*, 31; Chenu, *Recveil des antiqvites*, 141–42. On the Edict of Crémieu of 1536, see Neron and Girard, *Edicts et ordonnances*, 5.

dling fees.[58] Lyon could impose an indirect tax on merchandise sold outside its celebrated fairs of up to 1,000 livres per year without any special letters or royal permission. It also had perpetual right to raise the dixième.[59] Both Orléans and Tours received substantial royal help to stimulate trade.[60] Poitiers's weak economic privileges reflected its relative lack of commercial vitality in the sixteenth century.

Still, even if Poitiers's trade was not booming, its stance of special loyalty to the French crown paid off. Over the course of the sixteenth century, the city was able to keep many of its privileges in the face of royal legislation that tended to scale back urban liberties. The hôtel de ville was thus able to gain a derogation from Henri II's 1547 edict limiting the kinds of men who could be elected to municipal office,[61] and the city council eventually pulled off the coup of retaining its civil jurisdiction, despite the well-known provision of the 1566 Ordinance of Moulins depriving all city governments of this liberty.[62] Neither was the corps de ville forced to undergo any changes in organization at the behest of the crown. As Annette Finley-Croswhite has argued, the crown's tendency to reduce the numbers of councillors and échevins in cities throughout France did not necessarily reflect any royal desires to limit municipal liberties. Indeed, Henri IV represented his reduction of Lyon's twelve échevins to four plus a *prévôt des marchands* as a mark of his singular affection for the city.[63] Yet places such as Bordeaux and La Rochelle undeniably owed reductions and reorganizations of their administrations to perceived disloyalty. When Bordeaux supported the gabelle uprisings in 1548, the capital of Guyenne saw the twelve jurats and mayor who had been elected an-

---

[58] *Catalogue des actes de François II*, 1:312; Robbins, *City on the Ocean Sea*, 41–42, 68; David Parker, *La Rochelle and the French Monarchy: Conflict and Order in Seventeenth-Century France* (London, 1980), 65–67.

[59] Edict of Charles VIII, dated Dec. 1495 from Lyon. Barbier, *Recveil des privileges*, 10–11.

[60] Orléans: edict of François II, dated 28 Nov. 1560 from Orléans, concerning maintenance of roadways entering the city, *Catalogue des actes de François II*, 1:231. Tours: letters of François I, dated May 1517 from Paris, granting Tourangeaux exemption from taxes on all cloth and woolen manufactures, *Ordonnances de François Ier*, 2:69–72; edict of François I, dated June 1542 from Éclaron, concerning the silk industry, *Catalogue des actes de François Ier*, 10 vols. (Paris, 1887–1908), 4:339; edict of François II, dated 16 Jan. 1560 from Blois, concerning expanding the walls to accommodate cloth workers, *Catalogue des actes de François II*, 1:93. For royal support of Tours's silk industry, see also L. A. Bosseboeuf, "La fabrique des soieries de Tours," *Mémoires de la société archéologique de Touraine* 41 (1900): 204–35; Bernard Chevalier, *Tours, ville royale (1356–1520): origine et développement d'une capitale à la fin du Moyen Âge* (Louvain and Paris, [1975]), 351–53.

[61] See chapter 6.

[62] Ordinance dated Feb. 1566 from Moulins, Article 71. Isambert, 14(1):208. The city council obtained the derogation from Moulins when Henri III reconfirmed Prince Edward's 1369 charter granting Poitiers civil and criminal jurisdiction. Although Giry remarks that the derogation was only implicit, an addition to the 1506 inventory of Poitiers's titles indicates that the text of the confirmation included the king's explicit consent to the derogation. See Giry, *Établissements de Rouen*, 1:380 n. 2; ACP Casier 43, Reg. 15 (Henri III's confirmation, dated May 1575 from Paris); and Casier 42, Reg. 13, 40 (inventory of 1506, no. Acvi).

[63] Finley-Croswhite, *Henry IV and the Towns*, 86–87; edict of Henri IV, dated Dec. 1595 from Chauny, Barbier, *Recveil des privileges*, 49–53.

nually since 1378 reduced to six jurats elected every two years.[64] Faced with
dire (but inaccurate) warnings about La Rochelle's loyalty in 1535, François
I reduced its one-hundred-member corps de ville to twenty and appointed
Charles Chabot de Jarnac, the noble who had raised the alarm, as perpetual
mayor.[65] Poitiers, by contrast, kept its twenty-five-member council and one-
hundred-member corps de ville intact. When Henri IV ordered a reduction in
the numbers of bourgeois in 1609, his goal was merely to return a corps
swollen by the effects of the Catholic League back to its customary size.[66] In
1576, Poitiers's mayor and échevins even managed to acquire the additional
boon of having all of their civil and criminal suits tried before the court of the
conservateur of the privileges of the university in first instance.[67]

Over time, more aspects of urban life became subject to municipal supervision. When war threatened in 1512, the lack of a permanent militia meant
that companies had to be hastily formed.[68] Yet once the governor instituted
six militia companies, each commanded by a captain with his lieutenants and
ensigns, in preparation for the siege of 1569, the militia became a permanent
fixture in the city's defense. Unusually, two of the six captains were always
clerics: a canon of St. Hilaire-le-Grand and the cathedral St. Pierre were each
to serve.[69] As in many other French cities, Poitiers's elites also faced the explosion of urban poverty with increasingly institutional approaches.[70] Backed
by general royal edicts and favorable rulings in the Grands Jours (judicial
sessions) of Poitiers, city and royal officials began to supervise the many *aumôneries,* or charitable houses, that had fallen into neglect—sometimes despite the ardent opposition of their administrators.[71] Further, in 1532, not
long after Paris began its poor-relief regime, the corps de ville and clergy
gathered to agree on a system of regular collections in the parishes and dis-

---

[64] Gabriel de Lurbe, *Chroniqve bovrdeloise composee cy devant en latin* (Bordeaux, 1619),
29v, 41v–43r.
[65] Robbins, *City on the Ocean Sea,* 78–81. The original structure of La Rochelle's government was restored in 1548 (92).
[66] *Arrêt* dated 9 Apr. 1609, ACP Reg. 64, 146–51. This incident is discussed in more depth
in chapter 10.
[67] Letters patent of Henri III, dated May 1576. ACP Casier 3, A43. This was an advantage
because these suits went immediately to the Parlement of Paris on appeal.
[68] ACP Reg. 11, 161–66 (6 Apr. 1512); 169–72 (29 Apr. 1512).
[69] ACP Reg. 64, 175–79; *Siége de Poitiers,* 22.
[70] The literature on poor relief in sixteenth-century France is extensive, but for important
studies on Lyon and Toulouse, see Natalie Z. Davis, "Poor Relief, Humanism, and Heresy," in
Society and Culture, 17–64; Barbara Beckerman Davis, "Poverty and Poor Relief in Sixteenth-
Century Toulouse," *Historical Reflections* 17 (1991): 267–96.
[71] Royal edicts on lay supervision of aumôneries and *hôpitaux:* edict dated 19 Dec. 1543
from Fontainebleau, Isambert, 12:841–43; edict dated 15 Jan. 1546 from Saint-Germain-en-
Laye, Isambert, 12:897–900; edict dated 12 Feb. 1554 from Paris, Isambert, 13:355–58. Decisions of the Grands Jours of Poitiers: arrêt of 27 Oct. 1531, described in ADV G1100
(inventory for litigation concerning the aumônerie of Notre-Dame); copy of an arrêt of 19 Dec.
1579 in ACP Casier 11, D58. Litigation against Guillaume Bienvenu and his son Jean Bienvenu,
aumôniers of Notre-Dame: ADV G1100; G1286, 42r; ACP Casier 54, 1556–57; Casier 54,
1565–66, 28r–v.

tributions to the needy.[72] A decade later, the hôtel de ville and delegates from the clergy set up a weekly Sunday meeting (appropriately named the *dominicale*) to make decisions on poor relief, undertook citywide solicitations for weekly contributions, and established means for assessing the needs of the poor and distributing aid.[73] This system would require periodic revitalization, and Poitiers may have kept its eye on beacons such as Lyon and Paris for guidance,[74] but the hôtel de ville so continued to dominate the city's regime for poor relief that the bishop would attempt to seize direction of its meetings during the Catholic League period.[75]

It was no wonder, then, that Maurice Roatin trumpeted the powers of the mayor or that Maixent Poitevin waxed lyrical over the unifying qualities of the law. Thanks to its privileges and participation in sixteenth-century institutional trends, Poitiers's hôtel de ville kept an eye on all areas of urban governance and laid its hand on most. Civic order, city councillors believed, arose from their corps' undisturbed enjoyment of a series of special rights. This being the case, the prestige of the corps de ville and the honor of its individual members nourished their city's health and its reputation throughout the kingdom. Historians have often marveled that urban elites would sacrifice hours in tedious debate, market supervision, and accounting—and would pay for the privilege. We speculate that the rewards in enhanced authority, honor displayed through processions and special robes, and a chance at nobility must have been worth it. But this is to leave out a crucial element. Because the authority of the city government was so closely tied to its ability and responsibility to assure the common good, municipal officials could seek individual honors at the same time that they exulted in an ethic of public service. Privilege and service were thus not antithetical, but reinforcing, goals.

Honors and Obligations of Office

As a corporate body asserting authority over public life, the hôtel de ville placed great emphasis on maintaining the prestige and defending the privi-

---

[72] ACP Reg. 19, 117–29 (25–29 Jan. 1532); 153–60 (18 Mar. 1532). Paris is described as beginning poor relief in 1530 in Ern[est] Coyecque, ed., "L'assistance publique à Paris au milieu du XVIe siècle," *Bulletin de la Société de l'Histoire de Paris et de l'Île de France* 15 (1888), 106.

[73] ACP Reg. 26, 115–17 (6 Dec. 1544); Casier 53, 1544, 2v–3r and passim (inauguration of the dominicale and subsequent deliberations); Casier 49, 1544–45 (rolls of contributions).

[74] On 1 December 1555, the dominicale decided to print Poitiers's ordinances on the poor "semblable a celle des ordan[ances] des pauvres de La ville de lyon." ACP Casier 53, 1555–56, 10r. In 1557, a new organization for poor relief, involving an intendant in each parish, was proposed in the Mois, and it was in place by 1561. Reg. 35, 20–28 (10 Aug. 1557); Casier 53, 1555–56, 138r. The similarities between this organization and that described for Paris in print sometime between 1555 and 1557 suggest that the Parisian model influenced the provincial city. See Coyecque, "Assistance publique."

[75] ACP Reg. 51, 152–53 (9 Mar. 1592); 155–58 (16 Mar. 1592).

leges that would assure its superior place within the city and Poitiers's status within the kingdom. Members thus portrayed agreement and unity within the administration as crucial to ensure its authority over the inhabitants and the surrounding region. In reaction to a series of challenges to municipal election procedure in 1549, François Doyneau, senior échevin, chastised the company for its division and discord and insisted that "good peace and concord" among the members of the corps de ville had always acted to maintain its authority.[76] Members also set great store in upholding their own dignity, equating the honor showed them as public officials with the authority of the city government. When the échevin Hilaire Macé was insulted during his exercise of a commission concerning the city's artillery in 1512, the culprit was imprisoned for his "great insult and rebellion" against the municipal government. Only after his father had appeared to plead his case, and after the young offender had retracted his statements and asked Macé's pardon, "crying, on his knees, bare-headed, and hands joined" in supplication and humility, did the council consent to remit his fault and set him free.[77]

If even a youth's disrespect could threaten municipal authority, the city government battled outside attempts to belittle its prized privileges all the more fiercely. During the Estates General of 1588 the city council found its cherished right of nobility under attack. When Poitiers's delegates for the nobility arrived at Blois, they found that the assembly for the second estate had already recognized a rival delegate from Poitou, elected by a group of rural *gentilshommes* who sneered at the échevins' nobility.[78] When the dispute went before the royal privy council for resolution, the council's brief passionately sought to counter assertions that the échevins lacked the estate to appoint noble deputies for their county.[79] The council later asked the comte de Brissac if it would make sense for the current échevins to be denied noble status when so many noble Poitevin families owed their origins to the hôtel de ville. "Not that we wish to say that our house is the mother of all [noble descendants] of Poitou, but of a good number," the councillors explained in a letter soliciting his help.[80] The death of the mayor shortly afterward gave the corps de ville the chance to affirm his nobility and status of first baron of Poitou. The body therefore lay in state surrounded by the spurs, gloves, and *heaulme* (helmet with visor) that announced his nobility, and when the mayor's remains were escorted to his parish church, these objects were carried reverently before him. Six seigneurs, representing the other barons of Poitou, accompanied the body. In short, the mayor was buried "en chevalier" as échevin René de Brilhac commented in his journal.[81] Noble status

76 ACP Reg. 30, 222 (16 Apr. 1549).
77 ACP Reg. 11, 228–29 (14 June 1512).
78 ACP Reg. 48, 130–35 (24 Oct. 1588).
79 ACP Reg. 48, 150–60 (7 Nov. 1588).
80 ACP Reg. 48, 203–8; quotation, 207.
81 ACP Reg. 48, 259–76 (19 Jan. 1589); Brilhac, 22.

was thus a crucial component of municipal privilege, enhancing not only the honor of individual members but also the status of the corps de ville among the bigwigs of the region.

That leaguers and royalists would risk a citywide ceremony of mourning and come together to honor their deceased mayor in January 1589 indicates how crucial the échevins' privilege of nobility was to Poitiers's municipal elite. Noble status was not only the sign of, and justification for, the respect and deference city officials expected from the inhabitants; it was also the goal of many urban dwellers hoping to achieve a social boost beyond the urban sphere. François Barrault, *enquêteur* in the sénéchaussée, may have been seeking this coveted, if not altogether secure, nobility when he spent months in Paris on town business in the hope of being elected échevin. Yet noble status was not the only practical enticement for civic office. When Jacques Herbert sought election to the corps de ville, his family's tradition of membership formed the chief argument for his qualification.[82] But since his family already enjoyed nobility thanks to municipal service, this could not have been Herbert's chief motivation. He and others like him may have been drawn by the power to rule on important issues. This was certainly the presumption of a deputy from Agen who complained that if Henri IV instituted *élus* (royal financial officials) in Agenais, there would no longer be any good reason to be a consul. "Adieu liberties! privileges!" he warned his colleagues. "*Consular* offices will not [*sic*] longer have their luster or power; . . . If we do not take care, we shall be *consuls* only to have the streets cleaned."[83]

For Poitiers's corps de ville, the authority of the group went hand in hand with its prestige, just as members' status reflected their impact on many areas of urban life. The quest for honors and advancement induced many people to seek municipal office, but the concrete functions of city government also demanded that members acknowledge, if not embrace, their responsibilities for the public welfare. Thus, Jacques Regnault, mayor of Poitiers in 1537, reminded the company that both honor and service to the public were to motivate each member of the city government. He proclaimed that he

> took it to be a beautiful and glorious thing to be a good bourgeois or a good échevin who feels an affection and will toward the commonwealth, of which the histories are infinite . . . and even he who is a member of this current body must proclaim and consider himself fortunate, not in order to describe himself as receiving the attendant honors without acting for the guard and defense of the town, but extremely fortunate to say that he is of the present body in order to guide and administer the government of the said noble town of Poitiers.[84]

[82] ACP Reg. 25, 147–51 (30 Jan. 1543).
[83] Quoted in J. Russel Major, *From Renaissance Monarchy to Absolute Monarchy: French Kings, Nobles, and Estates* (Baltimore, 1994), 139.
[84] ACP Reg. 20, 255–56 (29 June 1537).

His words were echoed at the end of the century by Mayor Maurice Roatin:

> I would point out that just as a shadow follows the body, difficulty and labors accompany honor; that you have been called to this body and have been honored with your places in it not only to enjoy its attributed privileges and rights but in order to be more solicitous toward the public and in order to show a more precise diligence in the conservation of this town than the other inhabitants.[85]

Active service to the public, of course, was a value honored more in the breach than in the observance. Active members such as Maixent Poitevin protested that a crowd of people were seeking office without any intention of rendering service, and Jean Estivalles pointed to an obvious problem when he complained about low attendance except at elections.[86] These complaints were real, since average attendance at municipal assemblies over the course of the century hovered around one-third.[87] Given these notable lapses, could city officials really have kept public service strictly before their eyes, or did they simply seek the advantages of their extremely distinguished positions? To find out, consider the examples of Maixent Poitevin and Jean de Brilhac, two former mayors whose exemplary service to the hôtel de ville Jacques Foucquet particularly singled out for praise (although not by name) in his mayoral harangue in 1583.[88]

Maixent Poitevin was in a position to benefit from his membership in the corps de ville. Arriving in Poitiers as a young man, he used an inheritance pooled among his siblings to marry the daughter of Jean Durand, bourgeois and established lawyer in the sénéchaussée.[89] Having risen to mayoral office for the period of 1564–66, Poitevin may have taken advantage of this prestigious position to arrange an advantageous marriage for his own son in 1566.[90] Nobility, however, was Poitevin's chief reward for public office. In his remarkable final testament, in which he explained why he was disinheriting his son, Jean Poitevin, canon of Ste. Radegonde, he denounced his offspring's claims that he was not an *écuyer*, or noble, and insisted that his own father had already held that estate.[91] The ex-mayor further concentrated on materially enhancing his seigneury, La Bidollière, and attempted to pass it on to his heirs as noble property that could not be divided or sold.[92] Yet these

---

[85] ACP Reg. 54, 10 (1 July 1594).

[86] ACP Reg. 43, 117 (31 Mar. 1581); Reg. 34, 143–69 (30 Dec. 1556).

[87] For details on attendance rates, see Hilary Bernstein, "Politics and Civic Culture in Sixteenth-Century Poitiers," (Ph.D. diss, Princeton University, 1996), 187–97.

[88] ACP Reg. 44, 287 (1 July 1583).

[89] ADV G⁹ 114, testament of Maixent Poitevin, dated 24 June 1594, 12–13. For information on Jean Durand, Poitevin's father-in-law, see ADV G⁹ 85, testament of Jean Durand, dated 8 Aug. 1532.

[90] ADV G⁹ 114, testament, 19.

[91] ADV G⁹ 114, testament, 1, 15.

[92] ADV G⁹ 114, testament, 5–8.

attempts to "arrive" were clearly inadequate for this provincial *avocat* (barrister), since he asked for letters confirming his nobility from the city council in 1574.[93] These letters may have provided just the proof he needed in his legal suits. In all of his self-justifications, however, Poitevin did not mention his extensive public service. True, in describing the long history of honors accruing to his ancestors, he divided his family into those who had held important ecclesiastical offices in Poitiers and Rome and those who had left their mark on nearby Saint-Maixent through their notable civic administration.[94] But if Poitevin did not evoke his consistent attendance at council meetings, his active part in defending Poitiers from Protestant soldiers in the siege of 1569, his leading role in municipal deliberations throughout the religious wars of the 1570s and 1580s, and his devotion to enforcing police ordinances and overseeing repairs of the fortifications, he did not spend any less time accomplishing these charges. Poitevin gained important benefits from being an échevin, not the least of which was a firmer claim to noble status, and he was able to fulfill what he must have seen as a familial tradition of involvement in public affairs. But he also took time out from his frequent lawsuits against his rebellious son to spend considerable energy performing the time-consuming and no doubt annoying tasks that fell on Poitiers's city officials. The personal benefits of municipal office did not overshadow Poitevin's real dedication to urban government.

Jean de Brilhac, *conseiller* (judge) in the sénéchaussée and *lieutenant criminel* (chief judge of criminal cases) from 1559, was less assiduous in his municipal duties than Poitevin. He was, however, a good man in a crisis, going on deputations to important nobles in 1548 and 1557, and standing up against occupying forces in 1562.[95] Brilhac's personal papers, however, indicate that Poitiers's city government was among the last things on his mind. In his journals of petty accounts and memoranda, he almost never mentioned municipal business, and as he began to record important events in Poitiers more frequently after becoming lieutenant criminel, he took the point of view of the judicial official rather than the échevin.[96] In recounting the entry into Poitiers of Elisabeth de Valois on her way to Spain to marry Philip II, Brilhac noted approvingly that the judicial officials were privileged to walk "separately and ahead" of the corps de ville; during the episcopal entry of 26 August 1564, "la justice" were honored to march near the bishop.[97] Brilhac clearly identified his own importance with his judicial, and not his municipal, status on ceremonial occasions.

[93] ACP Reg. 42, 101–103 (15 Nov. 1574).

[94] ADV G⁹ 114, testament, 9–11.

[95] ACP Reg. 30, 81–84 (29 Aug. 1548); Brilhac, 3–4; Alfred Barbier, "Chroniques de Poitiers aux XVe et XVIe siècles: deuxième partie: première guerre civile à Poitiers (1562)," *MSAO*, 2d ser., 14 (1891): 182–84.

[96] ADV SAHP 102 (Papier journal de Jean de Brilhac, 1539–65) and 51 (Papier journal de Jean de Brilhac, 1535–43). Extracts of these journals are published in Brilhac, 1–9.

[97] Brilhac, 5–6, 8–9.

Meanwhile, the Brilhacs were doing their best to enhance their social position. Jean's eldest son, François, married into a local robe family, through which he could boast brothers-in-law who exercised the offices of *maître ordinaire* in the Chambre des Comptes of Paris and conseiller in the Parlement de Bretagne.[98] An inventory of Jean de Brilhac's property two years before he died also indicates that he had extensive holdings in the barony of Ruffec with an important *maison forte* at La Riche.[99] Given that the Brilhacs were on their way to becoming *bourgeois gentilshommes*,[100] it may seem surprising that two of Jean's sons followed him as échevins of Poitiers. If one's goal was to elevate one's family into the world of the sovereign courts and robe nobility, a continued tie with city government and its lesser avenue to noble estate was ill-advised. Yet just as François followed his father as lieutenant criminel (this may have been a disappointment, given his marriage), he and his brother, René, became members of Poitiers's *échevinage*. What beside a sincere obligation to one's city could prompt the Brilhacs, and other more successful upwardly mobile elites, to take on the limitations, as well as the benefits, of municipal office?[101] In Poitiers, the hôtel de ville exerted enough authority within the city to make membership attractive, just as judicial and financial elites retained a strong commitment to guiding public policy through civic institutions.

[98] ADV SAHP 20, contract of marriage, dated 14 June 1565, and contract dated 15 June 1566.

[99] ADV SAHP 49, Papier des debtes et affaires pour monsieur de la Riche, 1586. See especially the *rentes* that Brilhac owed on his seigneury of La Riche.

[100] The reference is to George Huppert, *Les bourgeois gentilshommes: An Essay on the Definition of Elites in Renaissance France* (Chicago, 1977).

[101] For a similar sense of civic service expressed by a much more successful royal official, see Vincent Gallais, "Entre apprentissage et ambition: la culture politique d'un procureur du roi au présidial de Nantes, Jean Blanchard de Lessongère (1602–1612)," in *Les officiers "moyens" à l'époque moderne: pouvoir, culture, identité,* ed. Michel Cassan (Limoges, [1998]), 367–86.

2   *Public Politics and the Need for Consent*

The view from the hôtel de ville missed important aspects of the city's political terrain. When people thought of Poitiers in the sixteenth century, they rarely considered its municipal government. Instead, the city derived its reputation and vitality from its university faculties, substantial legal business generated in the sénéchaussée and presidial courts, and the powerful religious presence of its bishop, collegial church chapters, mendicant orders, and monastic institutions. Each of these bodies possessed its own agenda and exerted influence over its surroundings. As much recent work on parochial and neighborhood associations has shown, too, inhabitants did not depend solely on city government to provide a channel for political activity. Merchants, artisans, and legal personnel who had virtually no chance to obtain exclusive municipal offices could nevertheless express some measure of control over their lives through parish government and confraternity membership. Between the reigns of François I and Henri IV, these outlets for popular participation became more integrated into municipal structures, as Poitiers followed the general trend to institutionalize urban poor relief, the militia, and market control. Although these changes certainly decreased the public spaces in which Poitiers's inhabitants could make independent decisions, they also in effect increased the numbers of people who participated in citywide political structures. Urban society was hierarchical and authoritarian, to be sure, but just as kings could not rule effectively without the support of elites and subject bodies, neither could an exclusive political corps enforce order without the tacit acceptance of the greater urban community.

The Need for Consent

The model of municipal seigneury over the inhabitants of Poitiers proved inadequate in many respects. Just as municipal officials' desires for honors and influence did not crowd out their ideals of public service, the hôtel de ville's view of its powers over the urban population did not preclude assumptions that the inhabitants could occasionally play an active role in government. Although the idea of seigneurial dominion implied that the corps de ville obtained its authority uniquely from the crown, municipal pretensions to reconcile individual interests for the common good suggested that consultation was occasionally appropriate and that the urban administration was in some sense accountable for its decisions. Indeed, most people who explicitly theorized the relationship between city governments and urban populations in France through the reign of Henri IV maintained that municipal officials played a mediating role between the king and the people. Claude de Rubys, *procureur* (solicitor) of the city of Lyon in the mid-sixteenth century, for one, took this position. In his work dedicated to describing the privileges and functioning of the Lyon urban administration, he identified city government as one of the "democratic" elements of the French state and explained that the *consuls échevins* of Lyon, like their Roman and Spartan forebears, acted as the mediators between the people and the crown. It was their job to inform themselves of the people's grievances, to represent their interests to higher authorities, and thus to preserve their liberty.[1] In Paris, the bureau de ville was also seen as an intermediary body between the king and the Parisian population, but this time its influence extended in both directions. Rather than simply championing the people's needs to the king as in Lyon, it was also described as a repository of royal authority in governing the inhabitants.[2] Such ideas also informed Charles Loyseau's description of the nature of municipal officials in his *Cinq livres du droit des offices* (1609). As administrative officers sworn in by royal officials and often confirmed by the king, mayors, échevins, and consuls played a role in preserving an order that emanated from the crown; as watchdogs over their city's privileges and serving at the pleasure of the voters, though, they also implicitly retained a responsibility to the electorate. For Loyseau, these two aspects of municipal office were not inherently contradictory, since he insisted that it was often useful for royal officials to take their turn to serve as city councillors.[3]

Such views of city government as mediating between the concerns of the crown and the people worked well in communities where the inhabitants

---

[1] Claude de Rubys, *Les privileges, franchises et immunitez octroyees par les roys treschrestiens, aux consuls, eschevins, manans & habitans de la ville de Lyon, & à leur posterité* (Lyon, 1574), 44.

[2] Descimon, "Le corps de ville et le système cérémoniel," 77.

[3] Charles Loyseau, *Oevvres . . . , diuisees en deux tomes . . .* (Geneva, 1636), 816–17, 820–21, 823–26, 829.

played some role in electing their urban officials. In Poitiers, however, where popular input in elections was entirely lacking, it was more difficult to imagine the corps de ville as direct representatives of the inhabitants, even if in the sixteenth century, deputies of the people could still act in a particularly paternalistic style.[4] Yet even in Poitiers, the hôtel de ville had to recognize that it could not always dictate for the inhabitants and that, despite its pretensions to rule on all matters of police and urban administration, one corps could not determine the process of government. Other groups had to be consulted and provided the opportunity to participate in deliberations, either because a decision affecting their interests was required or because of the council's determination that the situation called for special levels of cooperation and public support. In these occasional extensions of the active body of municipal participants, the corps de ville left the question of its relationship to the inhabitants and the definition of the constituent parts of the civic community suitably vague. Indeed, doing so was in its interests, since a lack of specific rules for consultation assured it the greatest latitude of political action and prevented other interest groups within the city from claiming a right to participate.

The realities of urban administration dictated that the corps de ville include other groups in its decision-making process. When important matters arose, therefore, the mayor summoned them to lend their points of view or their consent to the deliberations of the Mois. Those who joined municipal assemblies generally did so as deputies for the corporate groups composing the city: deputies of the bishop, church chapters, and non-mendicant orders appeared for the clergy, as did representatives of the university, sénéchaussée, *bureau des trésoriers généraux,* and *élection* on various occasions. Only notable inhabitants who did not belong to any of these corporate groups received personal invitations to attend when their input could provide valuable information about the mood of the city, as when armed opposition to the gabelle threatened in 1548. When the corps de ville sought the opinion or approval of the general body of inhabitants, it did so through the parochial divisions of the city. Inhabitants were expected to meet at parish assemblies called by their vestrymen after Sunday Mass, deliberate on the matter at hand, and then authorize the vestrymen to report their decision in the Mois.

The hôtel de ville's conception of the constituent parts of the urban community, however, was never consistently defined. In addition to the assumption that a shifting range of corporate groups composed the political community, the idea existed that the urban population, like that of the kingdom, was composed of an equally amorphous body of estates. If in 1558 échevin Antoine de la Duguie suggested that the clergy and the nobility be consulted concerning a new imposition that Henri II was assigning on the town so that all of the estates could act together,[5] identification of the estates

[4] Rubys, *Privileges,* 67–68, 83–93.
[5] ACP Reg. 35, 206–11 (9 Feb. 1558).

of Poitiers did not always follow such traditional lines. In 1531, for example, the Mois decided that new police ordinances promulgated by the Grands Jours of Poitiers that autumn were prejudicial to the members of the city, including the clergy, judicial officials, and merchants and common people, "who form the three estates."[6] The role that these urban estates played in political consultation was as inconsistent as their general conception. In 1536, the mayor summoned members of the clergy, the university, and the parishes to deliberate on letters addressed to the *manans et habitans* (inhabitants) and described all of these groups as forming a single body united in common feeling.[7] In 1557, however, the mayor responded to royal letters instructing the city to hold "a convocation and general assembly of all of the estates" to deliberate on an extraordinary subsidy by convening only clerical deputies. It was only after the clergy insisted that the king could not have meant to include them in the subsidy that the company decided to instruct the vestrymen to hold parish assemblies to deliberate on the letters and to begin the process of tax assessment.[8] Christopher Stocker has suggested that by the 1580s, Henri III and city officials concurred that right order could be best assured if police institutions incorporated representation from the estates composing the city, conceptualized not as aggregate groups but as the expression of a higher organizing principle. These assumptions would become even stronger during the Catholic League era.[9] Poitiers's experiences show that tendencies to conceive of the urban community as a moral whole encompassing the estates of the city long predated the last stages of the religious wars. But these experiences also indicate that such conceptions existed side by side with less organic definitions, identifying the city as the sum of corporate groups with their own interests to support.

Not only did the hôtel de ville show a convenient irregularity in its definition of the constituent parts of the civic community and under what circumstances they should be asked to participate in decision making, but its pronouncements concerning the relationship between the urban administration and the body of the inhabitants were equally inconsistent. In spite of municipal pretensions to seigneurial command, most sixteenth-century theories of urban government assumed that city officials and the people, however selected or constituted, formed one united corps. This assumption was present in notions of the city as a religious whole as well as a body composed of head and members, and in Poitiers it received historical support from the city's status as a commune. Even the municipal officials' habit of summoning corporate groups when their interests were at stake implicitly confirmed

---

[6] ACP Reg. 19, 76–83 (8 Nov. 1531); quotation, 80.

[7] ACP Reg. 20, 43–55 (21 Aug. 1536).

[8] ACP Reg. 35, 69–77 (11 Sept. 1557); quotation, 73.

[9] Christopher Stocker, "Urban Police and Confessional Politics in Sixteenth Century Orléans" (paper presented at the Western Society for French History annual meeting, Santa Barbara, Nov. 1990), 10–11.

this view. According to the political assumptions expressed in the formula of *Quod omnes tangit,* matters concerning the general interests of the group could be decided by a limited number acting in its name, whereas decisions affecting members' particular interests required their consent. The key requirement in the application of this principle, then, was that the group in question constitute a corporate whole with a legal personality, which in this case would include both the municipal administration and the entire urban population. Poitiers's corps de ville, to be sure, never explicitly maintained that it was operating under these guidelines. Yet it summoned the hotel owners and bread sellers in 1511 to tell them that both the public good and their individual interests required stricter attention to weights and measures;[10] it instructed the vestrymen to hold parish assemblies to obtain the inhabitants' consent for weekly contributions to the poor or to support the cleanup of garbage;[11] and it invited deputies of the clergy to commit funds for the *communauté des pauvres* or to contribute its part to financing royal troops.[12] On these occasions, it acknowledged that when public policies would have a direct impact on private interests and property rights, the affected groups should be given an opportunity to deliberate, and it consequently implied that when these interests were not in question, municipal officials could decide for the whole.

Despite the advantages of conceiving of the city as a single political body, the hôtel de ville could also view the general population of Poitiers as constituting a separate juridical entity. The body of inhabitants could receive official correspondence requiring it to act explicitly, as when in 1513 and 1538 royal letters addressed to the manans et habitans of Poitiers prompted the municipality to summon the vestrymen to obtain their parishioners' opinions.[13] It could also be held legally accountable, as when in 1559, the Mois ruled that it could not be held liable for arrears in royal tax payments since the commission to collect the tax had been addressed directly to the inhabitants.[14] Grants of privileges confirmed this sense that the inhabitants of a city formed a separate group from their governing body. François II, for example, confirmed the privileges granted to the clergy, bourgeois, and inhabitants of Tours without mention of its city government in 1559, and Guillaume Barbier, in an introduction to his compendium of the privileges of Lyon, specified which belonged to the prévôt des marchands et échevins of the city and which to the population at large.[15] Poitiers's hôtel de ville occasionally acted as if considerations involving the city's privileges required

[10] ACP Reg. 11, 32–33 (17 Sept. 1511).
[11] ACP Reg. 19, 173–76 (27 May 1532); Reg. 20, 373–76 (30 Oct. 1537).
[12] ACP Reg. 19, 124–29 (29 Jan. 1532); Reg. 32, 1–3 (26 July 1551); Reg. 42, 36–40 (9 Aug. 1574).
[13] ACP Reg. 11, 485–95 (9–10 June 1513); Reg. 20, 514–21 (18 May 1538).
[14] ACP Reg. 36, 194–202 (24 June 1559).
[15] *Catalogue des actes de François II*, 1:51; Barbier, *Recveil des privileges*, iii–xxviii.

the inhabitants' special consent. In 1541, lieutenant général François Doyneau proposed that since Poitiers needed to take special steps to have important privileges reconfirmed, the parishes should be assembled to express their wishes on the subject.[16] Similarly, when the other towns of Poitou questioned Poitiers's right to apportion the burden of royal subsidies for the entire county in 1558, the council ruled that the parishes should appoint deputies to express their opinions and to delegate authority to act to the corps de ville.[17] Such procedures implied that the inhabitants possessed a separate voice from the municipal government on issues concerning the city's general liberties. Yet the hôtel de ville abandoned such distinctions and denied the inhabitants a separate corporate status when these distinctions did not work in its favor. When a group of merchants in Poitiers brought suit against the municipal government under the auspices of the manans et habitans of the city, for example, urban officials argued that this characterization had no meaning, since every member of the corps de ville was also an inhabitant, and it was impossible for a person to sue himself.[18]

Even in a city such as Poitiers, then, with a corps de ville recruited internally and jealous of its privileges, limited opportunities for groups of inhabitants to have an impact on municipal policies did exist. Such consultation arose from general political assumptions concerning the rights and personality of corporate bodies and the hazy notion that the inhabitants' interest in the city's liberties and prestige prescribed that their ratification of municipal activities at least be secured. The realities of government also played a large part in prompting officials to invite other groups to join the decision-making process. Enforcement of urban policies could prove extremely difficult if they met with significant public opposition, so that when other groups had palpable interests at stake, it made practical sense to hear their views and to gain their cooperation from the beginning. Yet the interests of the hôtel de ville also dictated that the conditions for consultation remain imprecise and that, under the guise of its authority over the police and military defense of the city, it alone should determine when other groups be invited to participate in political deliberations. By and large, the bodies over which municipal officials claimed authority showed themselves willing to act within these parameters. Many municipal policies met with active resistance, but the various groups making up the urban community recognized the corps de ville's ability to summon interested parties and to serve as arbiter of the civic welfare.

Interactions with Municipal Government

Despite tendencies to disobey municipal policies when it suited them and to challenge the privileges of the hôtel de ville when they clashed with their

---

[16] ACP Reg. 23, 250 [Apr. 1541].
[17] ACP Reg. 36, 25–28 (14 and 21 Nov. 1558).
[18] ACP Reg. 29, 179–89 (20 July 1548). See chapter 6.

own, Poitiers's inhabitants and corporate groups were still willing to recognize the municipal government's authority to set policies for the well-being of the city and to cooperate when they were summoned to take part in deliberations. Parishioners, it is true, frequently reacted to the administration's call to assess wealth and to nominate deputies to assign tax liabilities with extreme reluctance, occasionally rejecting their vestrymen's call to assemble, questioning the Mois's decision to meet the city's debts through taxation, or trying to prevent the selection of deputies through a stubborn refusal to register a choice.[19] Parishioners could also thwart the corps de ville's intentions, as when several parishes refused to authorize a municipal deputy to act on their behalf in a dispute over the city's financial privileges.[20] Yet the parishioners of Ste. Radegonde also asked the council to intervene when their vestrymen appeared to have connived at inaccuracies in the tax rolls, and the residents of the rue des Basses Treilles complained to échevin Jean Palustre about a neighbor who was flouting recent plague ordinances by accepting victims of the illness into her hovel. Thanks to the tip, the council could punish the woman for her offenses and send the sick to the plague hospital.[21]

The guilds, too, could stubbornly resist municipal police ordinances. The butchers, for example, had to be summoned repeatedly to explain why they were not keeping their counters stocked with meat as their statutes required.[22] In 1549, as the mayor was examining the main meat market to make sure there were adequate provisions, he was insulted by one of the butchers and found that others were illegally acting as farmers of taxes on skins and leather.[23] Despite frequent instances of resistance, however, artisans sought the hôtel de ville's permission to become sworn crafts and to operate under its watchful eye. The linen weavers (1537), the shoemakers (1557), the carpenters (1567 and 1572), the roofers (1572), the dyers (1572), and the dressmakers (1574) all petitioned to become sworn crafts, and the candle makers, after being disbanded for monopolistic practices in 1587, humbly requested to be reinstated six months later and promised to meet their obligations toward the city's artillery in exchange.[24] The guilds also turned to the authority of the city council and mayor's court to resolve their differences. In 1538, the woodworkers appeared in council to complain that their journeymen were holding separate assemblies. One week later, the jour-

<hr/>

[19] See chapters 5 and 6 for examples of each.

[20] ACP Reg. 23, 263–68 (26 Apr. 1541).

[21] ACP Reg. 42, 963–65 (3 Nov. 1578); Reg. 47, 119–21 (14 Sept. 1587).

[22] For example, ACP Reg. 11, 13–18 (18 Aug. 1511); Reg. 19, 171–72 (13 May 1532); Reg. 19, 223–28 (9 Jan. 1533); Reg. 22, 302–3 (19 Apr. 1540); Reg. 31, 238–40 (1 June 1551); Reg. 42, 712–22 (13–17 Mar. 1578).

[23] ACP Reg. 30, 168–71 (4 Feb. 1549).

[24] Linen weavers: ACP Reg. 20, 325–27 (27 Aug. 1537); shoemakers: ACP Reg. 34, 171–75 (7 Jan. 1557); carpenters: ACP Casier 10, D55; Reg. 40, 134–38 (3 Mar. 1572); roofers: ACP Reg. 40, 139–45 (10 Mar. 1572); dyers: ACP Reg. 41, 42–43 (22 Dec. 1572); dressmakers: ACP Reg. 42, 54–59 (13 Sept. 1574); candle makers: ACP Reg. 46, 180–87 (3 Jan. 1587); 357–60 (22 June 1587).

neymen equally appealed to the échevins to uphold their cause, but the council ruled in favor of the masters.[25] In 1586, the painters sued one of their craft for making dishware without a hammer.[26] In 1603, two visitors of the tailors of clothing complained in the mayoral court that when they had attempted to stop two journeymen from working independently in the home of one of Poitiers's notables, they had been insulted, imprisoned, and even beaten before they were able to escape.[27]

To obtain what they wanted, the craftsmen needed to frame their desires in ways that would meet with municipal approval, but not all guildsmen showed equal sophistication in their dealings with the hôtel de ville. The hotel owners, tavern keepers, and bread resellers learned only through experience how to represent their interests in a political language that the council would accept. Summoned to discuss new police regulations in 1511, the group first simply failed to appear and then annoyed the council with what it considered a useless response. "And because the abovementioned [hotel owners, tavern keepers, and bread resellers] were unable to give any response or declare any valid propositions for the police of bread," the secretary recorded, the council passed its police measures as originally drafted, but not before issuing "many remonstrances on the great welfare of the police and commonwealth" of the city.[28] Shortly afterward, however, the bread providers had developed a workable approach to dealing with the council. When they were formally informed of the proposed police statutes, one of their number speaking for the whole reported that they had held deliberations and that the greater and wiser part of their body desired to be governed by the statutes of Paris.[29] Using the terms of corporate decision making thus assured craftsmen a hearing, but it could not always guarantee that they would achieve their aim. Although the linen weavers commissioned Jean Baron, a bourgeois and well-known lawyer in Poitiers, to present statutes by which they wished to be governed, the Mois denied their request, for many reasons that it characterized as "good and valid" but did not specify.[30] To secure their interests, guildsmen also needed confidence and group solidarity to stand up to the hôtel de ville, and the butchers had an ample supply of both. When the council threatened that it would dissolve their guild if they did not obey police measures, the butchers responded by calling the échevins' bluff and resigning their craft in a body. The council quickly ruled that the butchers' four sworn officials would meet with the mayor to work out a compromise.[31]

Poitiers' prestigious religious bodies and royal institutions also gener-

[25] ACP Reg. 20, 443–45 (11 Feb. 1538); 453–56 (18 Feb. 1538).
[26] ACP Reg. 46, 138–46 (17 Nov. 1586).
[27] ACP Casier 45, 1601–15, articles for an inquiry dated 24 July 1603.
[28] ACP Reg. 11, 32–33 (17 Sept. 1511); 39–42 (13 Oct. 1511); 45–46 (17 Oct.); 47–50 (20 Oct.); quotation, 48–49.
[29] ACP Reg. 11, 53–54 (29 Oct. 1511).
[30] ACP Reg. 20, 325–27 (27 Aug. 1537); 340 (14 Sept. 1537).
[31] ACP Reg. 42, 712–22 (13 and 17 Mar. 1578).

ally recognized the municipal government's authority to oversee affairs of general interest and to judge when it was appropriate to convene different groups to discuss matters important to the city. As powerful corporate groups with their own histories, privileges, and influence over the city's neighborhoods, they certainly did not approve of all of the corps de ville's claims about its own privileges and administrative rights. The élus of the élection of Poitiers attempted to claim jurisdiction over the collection and payment of all indirect taxes, including both the dixième that the hôtel de ville periodically renewed the privilege to collect and the royal subsidies that it assigned and collected in conjunction with parish deputies.[32] Ecclesiastical bodies retained extensive rights over portions of the city that conflicted with the municipal government's claims to exercise judicial and police jurisdiction. The abbots of Montierneuf and St. Hilaire-de-la-Celle each insisted that their traditional privileges gave them rights of high justice and fief over enclaves of inhabitants living near their monasteries, and the chapter of St. Hilaire-le-Grand proved an especially powerful opponent because of its rights of justice and police over the extensive bourg of St. Hilaire that covered the southern portion of Poitiers within the town walls.[33] Yet deputies of the clergy, royal courts, and financial institutions still availed themselves of the opportunities the hôtel de ville offered to participate in its deliberations, and they recognized municipal privileges when they did not conflict with their own. Although evidence indicates that the canons of St. Hilaire disputed their obligation to contribute to the guard of the city under the mayor's authority, the chapter still dispatched a canon to warn the council of its fears of a surprise attack in 1574 and cooperated in the resulting house-to-house search.[34] This level of cooperation was not a foregone conclusion for city governments. In Lyon, urban officials complained that notables and masters of the crafts refused to attend general assemblies when called on to do so, "out of a certain contempt and condemnation of them," and that they not only disobeyed the administration's ordinances regarding public health and the defense of the city, but also maintained that it had no right to issue them.[35] Poitiers's corps de ville certainly encountered powerful opposition to its policies, but it never faced the scorn for its public authority that plagued Lyon's city government. Poitiers's political privileges were older and more developed than those of Lyon, but the real difference may have rested in the social prestige of the

---

[32] ACP Casier 23, I23, XI, act dated 12 Feb. 1552.

[33] La Celle: ACP Reg. 19, 142–44 (26 Feb. 1532). Montierneuf: Reg. 23, 107–20 (22 Dec. 1540); Reg. 34, 341 (12 Apr. 1557); Reg. 46, 254–62 (6 Apr. 1587). St. Hilaire: ADV G639–642. On the history, organization, and privileges of St. Hilaire-le-Grand, consult [Alphonse Le Touzé] de Longuemar, *Essai historique sur l'église royale et collégiale de Saint-Hilaire-le-Grand de Poitiers* (Poitiers, 1857). I intend to study the relations between the clergy and municipal government of Poitiers in depth in a separate work.

[34] ADV G505, order of Artus de Cossé, dated 31 Jan. 1571, dispensing the chapter of St. Hilaire from doing the guard; ACP Reg. 42, 120–22 (15 Dec. 1574).

[35] Barbier, *Recveil des privileges,* 7, 260–64; quotation, 262.

échevins and bourgeois who claimed exclusive membership in Poitiers's municipal body.

Public Politics?

With a corps de ville practicing self-selection and lifelong tenure and with the opportunities to participate in civic deliberations determined by these same officials, the possibilities for inhabitants to affect their community through public action were limited. Still, the hôtel de ville did not have a monopoly on political activity, and associative bodies such as parish vestries, confraternities, and guilds provided many who could not expect access to municipal government the opportunity to exercise leadership roles, to consult with their neighbors, and to influence local decisions. Parish life and parochial institutions mattered to Poitiers's residents, and small notables found a sphere of action and influence there that testified to their prestige among their neighbors and their commitment to public life.[36] This is not to say, however, that parochial institutions fell below the sight lines of Poitiers's municipal elites. Members of the corps de ville certainly did not shirk or disdain local obligations, but neither did they orchestrate them entirely. In the parishes, efforts to distribute duties broadly meant that a variety of people at different social levels got their chance to act. Yet these concerns did not mean that styles of participation in parochial decision making differed radically from the habits of the hôtel de ville. Although associative bodies put the accent on commensality, their practices were still hierarchical, and important residents could still expect to exert undue influence over their decisions. Over the course of the sixteenth century, too, the sphere of parochial politics became more subject to municipal supervision. For some, this change may have meant a loss of self-determined public action; for others, it provided new ways to play some role in the broader structure of municipal government.

Poitiers's twenty-seven parishes constituted the basic unit of division among the city's inhabitants, as well as the primary forum in which residents could influence public affairs. The city's parish churches differed substantially in their prestige and ecclesiastic government: some, such as Notre-Dame-la-Grande and Ste. Radegonde, were administered by chapters of secular canons; others, such as St. Porchaire and St. Didier, housed a priory or important confraternity supporting numerous chaplains; still others, such as St. Michel, could barely support their curé. Most, however, possessed a lay-administered vestry, responsible for the upkeep of the church buildings

---

[36] Julie Hardwick also discusses the importance of these institutions to men of middling social standing in general, and to notaries in particular, as a way to participate in public life in her *Practice of Patriarchy*, 195–218.

and ornaments, the supervision of masses founded by parishioners, and especially, administration of property designed to support these functions. Inhabitants were able, indeed duty-bound, to influence the workings of their
parish church through their consent to property arrangements. When the
vestrymen of St. Germain wished to alienate a piece of land belonging to the
church in exchange for an annual rente, for example, they publicized their
intentions and came to an agreement with the highest bidder only with the
consent of a group of notable parishioners, who also signed the contract.[37]
When échevin René Berthelot proposed to make physical alterations to the
same church so that he could see the main altar from a new chapel he wished
to build in 1531, a group of twenty-five residents of the parish gathered
after parochial Mass on the convocation of the vicaire, as they were accustomed to do to treat the church's affairs, and unanimously agreed to Berthelot's request, in exchange for a bequest to the vestry.[38] The consent of the
parishioners was necessary even when the financial transaction involved
property belonging to the *cure*. When the curé of St. Porchaire determined
that one of the vineyards of his benefice was not producing a good income,
he presented his complaint before an assembly of parishioners, congregated
after Sunday Mass. After making a visit to the property and seeing its ruined
state, the parishioners authorized their parish priest to offer the vineyard at
rente to the highest bidder, and approved the resulting transaction after
parochial Mass on St. Porchaire's Day 1588.[39]

Many of Poitiers's inhabitants took the concerns of their parish extremely
seriously. Numerous testators left separate bequests to the vestry and the cure
of their church and recompensed their parish when they asked to be buried
elsewhere.[40] Michel Cartier founded a Mass to be said at the altar of St.
Michel in his parish church of Notre-Dame-la-Petite, "for the servitors of the
said parish, so that they will not have to go elsewhere and in order that they
be able to hear Mass from their curé or vicaire, with the prayers that he will
be required to make at the Mass," and bequeathed separate payments to the
parish priest, vestry, and bell ringer to underwrite his foundation.[41] Yves
Vernou, échevin and doctor regent of civil law, similarly explained that even
individuals with unmarried children ought to give a portion of their goods
to the church for the good of their souls and of their families, and bequeathed
an entire house to the parish priest of St. Étienne, "as much for his convenience as that of his parishioners, so that they may have easier access to their
curé." He supplemented this endowment with a generous gift to the vestry.[42]
Even when a chapter of canons administered the church's temporal affairs,

---

[37] ADV G⁹98, contract dated 12 Sept. 1549.
[38] ADV G⁹98, contracts dated 15 June 1531 and 14 Oct. 1532.
[39] ADV G⁹114, contract dated 31 May 1588.
[40] For example, ADV G⁹95, testament dated 28 Jan. 1495 (o.s.).
[41] ADV G⁹106, testament dated 28 Jan. 1522 (o.s.) and contract dated 7 Apr. 1526.
[42] ADV G⁹95, testament dated 31 Dec. 1541; quotation from a later copy of the original.

parishioners still sought to exert some influence over parochial concerns. The parishioners of Ste. Radegonde fought hard to retain rights that vestries normally possessed. When the canons insisted on appointing the bell ringer, the residents of the parish argued in court that because they had a separate parochial altar, they should naturally exercise functions normally associated with parish churches and that, despite what the canons claimed, the parish actually predated the chapter.[43] Decades later, when the canons requested that the parishioners of Ste. Radegonde maintain a lamp to be placed before the Corpus Christi, the parishioners agreed only on the stipulation that the canons refrain from saying masses that were distracting worshippers during the parochial service.[44] At Notre-Dame-la-Grande, although one of the canons always administered the vestry, the parishioners still selected lay deputies to represent the parish in municipal assemblies and negotiated with the chapter when it decided to melt down the small bell that signaled parish business.[45]

If parochial issues could involve numerous residents in public affairs, other residents took on the added burden of serving as vestrymen (generally called *fabriqueurs* in sixteenth-century Poitiers). Generally elected to office every two years, they were to collect the annual rentes due to the vestry, appoint and pay chaplains for saying special masses, hire craftsmen to do repairs or to add to the ornament of the church buildings, and work with legal counsel to pursue delinquents in court. When the parishioners of St. Porchaire met to draw up articles concerning vestry administration in 1633, they put special emphasis on the vestrymen's responsibilities to call parish assemblies regularly, to conclude all property transactions responsibly, to supervise parishioners' requests regarding burials, pews, and family chapels carefully, and to render account of their activities conscientiously.[46] Indeed, vestrymen were frequently required to keep detailed accounts of the parish's financial business and to pass on inventories of church valuables, religious services, and documentation to their successors.[47] They could also be required to maintain a box with which to collect the dead bodies of impoverished parishioners, to keep the grass mowed at the cemetery, and to make a collection at Mass every Sunday to meet parish expenses.[48] Their familiarity with parish affairs made the vestrymen natural figures to give account of their neighbors' property for tax assessments, to identify householders who could afford to contribute to poor relief, and to appoint individuals to collect the sums that residents were assigned.

[43] ADV G1346, legal decision dated 30 Dec. 1503.
[44] ADV G1589, 98v–99v (25 Feb. 1564); 101r–v (28 Feb. 1564).
[45] ADV G1286, account of the vestry of Notre-Dame-la-Grande, 1534–45, 36v. Parish bell: G1301, 154r (20 June 1577).
[46] ADV G⁹119, register of deliberations of the *fabrique* of St. Porchaire, 1630–80, 1r–5r.
[47] For examples, see ADV G⁹114, "Extraict des Rentes" (1536); G⁹85, "Registre des messes" (1560); and G⁹106, "Inventaire des tiltres" (1592–93).
[48] ADV G⁹114, "Papier du Revenu" (1592), 1r, 5r, 6r.

The vestrymen's authority, to be sure, did not extend to what was possible in England or in Italy. In communities such as Swallowfield, Mildenhall, and Southwark, church wardens presented parishioners to ecclesiastical courts for disrupting church services and behaving in ways that upstanding inhabitants deemed unacceptable, served as de facto overseers of the poor of the parish after the Poor Law of 1598, and kept remarkably detailed records of church attendance and charitable contributions.[49] In Bologna, not parish leaders but confraternity officials played a determinant role in the city's charitable organizations.[50] Still, Poitiers's vestrymen rated their obligations highly. Guillaume Bienassis, *fabriqueur* in 1540, took the interests of his parish of St. Paul to heart and refused to condone a questionable transaction accepted by the inhabitants.[51] An anonymous vestryman of St. Porchaire even envisioned the historical development and importance of his office. In 1559, he composed a small history of the church's vestry and the great works that had been accomplished since the early sixteenth century, implicitly contrasting the efforts to rebuild the church that previous vestrymen had been able to accomplish because of the financial generosity of the parishioners with his own difficulties in times of increasing religious tension and reduced charity.[52]

Parish life therefore provided numerous opportunities for individuals to have an impact on their local community, and many people availed themselves of this advantage. St. Porchaire's 1633 statutes governing vestry business assumed that different individuals would take up the posts of vestrymen every two years, and in general, residents tended to perform parish duties for limited periods of their lives.[53] Typical were men such as Fulgent Caillon, a master shoemaker living in the parish of Notre-Dame-la-Chandelière, who collected his neighbors' taxes in 1546 and served as vestryman in 1550;[54] Maître François Picherit, probably a procureur, who served as parish administrator (*intendant*) for the communauté des pauvres in St. Cybard in 1581 and 1589 and went from door to door to collect his neighbors' contributions;[55] and Louis Clabat, a merchant draper residing in the parish of

---

[49] Steve Hindle, "Hierarchy and Community in the Elizabethan Parish: The Swallowfield Articles of 1596," *The Historical Journal* 42, no. 3 (1999): 835–51; J. S. Craig, "Co-operation and Initiatives: Elizabethan Churchwardens and the Parish Accounts of Mildenhall," *Social History* 18, no. 3 (1993): 357–80; Jeremy Boulton, *Neighbourhood and Society: A London Suburb in the Seventeenth Century* (Cambridge, U.K., 1987).

[50] Nicholas Terpstra, "Apprenticeship in Social Welfare: From Confraternal Charity to Municipal Poor Relief in Early Modern Italy," *Sixteenth Century Journal* 25, no. 1 (1994): 101–20; idem, *Lay Confraternities and Civic Religion in Renaissance Bologna* (Cambridge, U.K., 1995), esp. chap. 5.

[51] ADV G⁹112, *procès-verbal* dated 15 Aug. 1540.

[52] ADV G⁹114, "Memoyre so [gap] A tous p[rese]ns et advenir," (1559–62).

[53] ADV G⁹119, register of deliberations of the fabrique of St. Porchaire, 1630–80. See especially the preamble to the election of 1633, 5r.

[54] ACP Casier 23, I23, 2r; Reg. 31, 140–43 (13 Apr. 1550).

[55] ACP Casier 54, 1581, 21r–22r; Casier 49, 1589, 18r–v.

Notre-Dame-la-Grande, who served as vestryman from 1540 to 1544 and collected taxes in 1547.[56] Occasionally, several members of the same family performed parish duties, either concurrently or over a period of time. Both Nicolas Clabat and Sire Rogier Clabat followed Louis Clabat's example of parish involvement, serving as administrator and collectors for Poitiers's poor regime over a period from 1565 to 1581.[57] Three generations of the Marnef family, master printers, were active in the affairs of their parish of Notre-Dame-la-Petite, attending parish meetings, serving as vestryman, and collecting contributions for the poor from 1508 to 1588.[58] Yet specific families, like individuals, did not generally monopolize parish offices or obligations. The numerous opportunities to serve meant that women could occasionally contribute to parish affairs, as when wives gathered linens for the aumônerie of Notre-Dame-la-Grande in 1568 and when Renée Legrier, wife of Girard Ernau, collected contributions for the communauté des pauvres in 1589.[59] The positive values attached to involvement allowed even Protestants, such as Tenneguy Percicault and Jean Boiceau, sieur de la Borderie, to act as vestrymen and to collect contributions for poor relief.[60] There were, to be sure, a few exceptions to these patterns. Maître Jacques Godard was elected vestryman of his parish of St. Étienne a year and a day after he took up residence there in 1539, and he continued to serve in this function until 1571.[61] No one could match Godard's three-decade record, but Maître Vincent Joubert served his parish of St. Hilaire-entre-Églises from 1538 to 1556, and François Boutyer, a baker, acted as a vestryman of St. Palesme from 1536 to 1550.[62] These "career vestrymen" formed the exception rather

[56] ACP Reg. 22, 279–82 (8 Mar. 1540); Reg. 23, 87–89 (25 Nov. 1540); 254–56 (20 Apr. 1541); Reg. 25, 125 (22 Dec. 1542); 174–80 (20–21 Mar. 1543); 406–7 (27 May 1544); Casier 23, I23, 2v.

[57] ACP Casier 54, 1564 (Jan. 1565); Casier 54, 1572–74, 22v; Casier 54, 1581, 13v.

[58] The founder of the family, Jean de Marnef, dit de Liège, attended a vestry meeting in 1508 (ADV G⁹106, contract dated 1 June 1508). His son, Enguilbert de Marnef, served as vestryman in 1559 (ACP Reg. 36, 76–88 [16 Jan. 1559]). Various members of the family took their turn as parish collector for the poor. See ACP Casier 54, 1558–59 (Notre-Dame-la-Petite); Casier 54, 1564 (June 1565); Casier 54, 1572–74, 11r–12r; Casier 49, 1589, 24r.

[59] ACP Casier 54, 1568, 1v–2r; Casier 49, 1589, 23v.

[60] Percicault: ACP Reg. 25, 397–99 (19 May 1544); Reg. 31, 140–43 (13 Apr. 1550). Boiceau: ACP Casier 54, 1558–59 (St. Hilaire-de-la-Celle).

[61] ACP Reg. 21, 217–19 (4 Jan. 1539); Reg. 22, 279–82 (8 Mar. 1540); Reg. 23, 87–89 (25 Nov. 1540); 254–56 (20 Apr. 1541); ADV G⁹95, contracts dated 26 and 27 Apr. 1542 and receipt dated 28 July 1552; Reg. 25, 33–36 (25 Aug. 1542); 125 (22 Dec. 1542); 174–80 (20–21 Mar. 1543); 406–7 (27 May 1544); Casier 53, 1544, 25v–26r (25 Nov. 1545); Reg. 27, 125–32 (3 May 1546); Reg. 28, 205–13 (26 May 1547); Reg. 29, 98–106 (5 Mar. 1548); Reg. 32, 179–80 (15 Feb. 1553); 282–89 (19 Aug. 1553); Casier 53, 1555–56, 2r–3v (Aug. 1555); 14v (2 Feb. 1556); Reg. 36, 76–88 (16 Jan. 1559); 160–66 (8 May 1559); ADV G⁹95, receipts dated 18 Feb. 1565, 29 Mar. 1570, and 16 Nov. 1571.

[62] Joubert: ACP Reg. 21, 107–13 (23 Nov. 1538); Reg. 25, 125 (22 Dec. 1542); 174–80 (20–21 Mar. 1543); 406–7 (27 May 1544); Reg. 26, 221–22 (4 May 1545); Reg. 27, 125–32 (3 May 1546); Casier 23, I23, account of Leon Guyvreau for 1546, 1v; Reg. 28, 205–13 (26 May 1547); Reg. 29, 98–106 (5 Mar. 1548); Reg. 31, 140–43 (13 Apr. 1550); 147–50 (20 Apr. 1550); Reg. 32, 179–80 (15 Feb. 1553); 282–89 (19 Aug. 1553); Casier 53, 1555–56, 2r–3v

than the norm, but their experiences show that parochial office provided real satisfaction and honors for men willing to take on the burdens of service to their local community.

In fifteenth-century Florence, Dale and F. W. Kent have shown, the men who made up the leadership of the *gonfaloni* (neighborhood associations) also tended to hold communal offices. Indeed, since the *gonfalonier* (captain of the association) composed the list of his neighbors eligible to hold city offices, only with a good reputation in his *gonfalone* could a Florentine accede to the honor of sitting on one of the city's many councils.[63] In sixteenth-century Rouen, men followed a *cursus honorum,* leading from the post of financial auditor to that of *quartenier,* finally to arrive at the coveted position of *conseiller-échevin.*[64] In Poitiers, however, undertaking parochial duties did not prepare residents to obtain a place in the corps de ville; the public realm of parish management and the privileged realm of municipal administration remained largely separate. This is not to say that Poitiers's bourgeois and échevins neglected their obligations to their neighbors. A significant number served as vestrymen and collected contributions for poor relief, but their election to the corps de ville tended not to follow, but to precede, their stint at parish service. Thus, Sire Guillaume Rogier, merchant furrier, was elected bourgeois in 1536 but served his parish of Notre-Dame-la-Grande in various capacities, including vestryman, from 1538 to 1556.[65] Jean Goislard performed his services to his parish after being elected bourgeois sometime between 1523 and 1531 and even took his turn as vestryman several years after serving as mayor in 1543.[66] If anything, being a member of the corps de ville helped to give local notables the clout and respect they needed to perform parochial duties successfully. Yet not all urban officials partook of parish affairs, and some of the most dedicated to municipal administration were relatively inactive on the parish level. Jean de Brilhac, for example, served as vestryman of St. Didier only a single time, as did Maixent Poitevin, a veritable workhorse for the hôtel de ville, in his parish of St. Cybard.[67]

The large numbers of people involved in overseeing parish affairs and the

---

(Aug. 1555); 14v (2 Feb. 1556). Boutyer: ACP Reg. 20, 43–55 (21 Aug. 1536); 501–5 (4 Apr. 1538); Reg. 21, 107–13 (23 Nov. 1538); Reg. 22, 279–82 (8 Mar. 1540); Reg. 25, 385–86 (5 May 1544); Reg. 30, 12–24 (14 Aug. 1548); Reg. 31, 140–43 (13 Apr. 1550); 147–50 (20 Apr. 1550).

[63] D. V. and F. W. Kent, *Neighbours and Neighbourhood in Renaissance Florence: The District of the Red Lion in the Fifteenth Century* (Locust Valley, N.Y., 1982), 17–18, 78.

[64] Benedict, *Rouen,* 36.

[65] ACP Reg. 20, 112–15 (4 Oct. 1536); 501–5 (4 Apr. 1538); Reg. 22, 279–82 (8 Mar. 1540); Reg. 29, 98–106 (5 Mar. 1548); Reg. 31, 147–50 (20 Apr. 1550); Casier 53, 1555–56, 14r (26 Jan. 1556).

[66] Since the registers of deliberation no longer survive for the period of 1523 to 1531, it is impossible to know when Goislard was elected bourgeois. He was elected mayor on 29 June 1543 (ACP Reg. 25, 243–47). For his parish involvement, see Reg. 20, 43–55 (21 Aug. 1536); 501–5 (4 Apr. 1538); Reg. 31, 140–43 (13 Apr. 1550); Casier 53, 1555–56, 14v (2 Feb. 1556).

[67] ACP Reg. 25, 385–86 (5 May 1544); ADV J1021, legal document dated 21 Dec. 1559.

lack of specific connection between this activity and municipal office meant that many men who did not have the notability or connections to enter the corps de ville could still act in a public capacity in their neighborhood. Granted, the possibilities for nonelites to participate varied with the social composition of their parishes.[68] In the wealthy parish of Ste. Opportune, where numerous legal officials and lawyers resided, men of the law dominated parish administration, and important échevins, such as Pierre Rat and Joachim Prevost, took their turns.[69] In the heavily mercantile parishes of Notre-Dame-la-Grande and Notre-Dame-la-Petite, Poitiers's most successful merchant-craftsmen tended to take on parish responsibilities, in the company of an array of smaller craftsmen, procureurs, and secular canons. A significant number of these merchants and procureurs, such as Louis Clabat, Guillaume Rogier, and Jean Bouchet, were successful enough to be elected bourgeois, but others, such as the Marnefs, Sire Jean Berier, tailor, and Jean Violette, goldsmith, were not.[70] Parishes with a more popular composition provided scope for local notables who were far below the level of the urban elite to play an active role in public life. In St. Hilaire-de-la-Celle, notaries André Chaigneau and Jean Chauveau were active, and in St. Germain and St. Jean-de-Montierneuf, artisinal parishes in the shadow of the abbey, merchant tanners such as Sire Jullien Barbillon, the younger, and important butchers such as Pierre and Hilairet Poupeau served along with procureurs, royal sergeants, and booksellers.[71] It is significant that "career vestrymen" such as Jacques Godard tended to reside in small, relatively poor parishes and never became members of the corps de ville.[72] Such men were big fish in small ponds; the lesser the sway of elite families in a parish, the greater the opportunities for smaller men to pull their weight in a public capacity.

Parish institutions and associational groups gave broader access for public involvement than the carefully monitored doors of the hôtel de ville, but, predictably for sixteenth-century society, a theoretical right of entrance did not give everyone an equal voice. Although all householders were summoned

[68] This situation contrasts with that of Nantes, where elites rarely took on vestry offices even in the most prestigious parishes. Hardwick, *Practice of Patriarchy,* 211–12.

[69] Rat: ACP Reg. 19, 258–64 (15 Apr. 1533); Reg. 20, 43–55 (21 Aug. 1536); ADV G⁹109, contract dated 4 Mar. 1541 (o.s.). Prevost: Reg. 21, 107–13 (23 Nov. 1538); Reg. 25, 385–86 (5 May 1544).

[70] Bouchet: ACP Reg. 15, 290–96 (27 Apr. 1517); ADV G⁹106, legal decision dated 8 Mar. 1506 (o.s.) and legal decision dated 19 Jan. 1542 (o.s.). Berier: ACP Casier 54, 1572–74, 111–12r; Casier 54, 1581, 14r–v; Casier 49, 1589, 24r; ADV G⁹106, legal decision dated 27 May 1585. Violette: Casier 54, 1558–59 (Notre-Dame-la-Petite).

[71] Chaigneau: ACP Reg. 21, 107–13 (23 Nov. 1538); Reg. 27, 125–32 (3 May 1546). Chauveau: Reg. 20, 501–5 (4 Apr. 1538); Reg. 32, 463–64 (29 June 1554). Barbillon: ADV G⁹98, contract dated 19 July 1585, legal decision dated 10 May 1588, and legal decision dated 1 Feb. 1588. Poupeau: ACP Reg. 22, 279–82 (8 Mar. 1540); Reg. 23, 87–89 (25 Nov. 1540); 254–56 (20 Apr. 1541); Casier 53, 1555–56, 2r–3v, 13r; Casier 54, 1564 (Jan. 1565).

[72] Jacques Godard may have been proposed as a candidate for bourgeois in 1532 but was not elected. See ACP Reg. 19, 183–89 (6 June 1532).

to attend the parish assemblies after Mass, in practice only limited numbers did so, and they were generally the most notable members of the parish. For the thirteen elections of new vestrymen of St. Porchaire that took place between 1633 and 1664, an average of just under twelve parishioners attended and signed the register.[73] Similarly, when the vestrymen of St. Germain disposed of a piece of parochial property, only eleven parishioners consented to the arrangements and signed the contract.[74] When the vestry of Notre-Dame-la-Petite was planning to build a new chapel in the church in 1508, a full thirty residents accorded Michel Mourault, lawyer in the sénéchaussée and "one of the principal parishioners of the parish," the right of sepulcher in it, but their names were carefully noted in descending order of notability, beginning with the local graduates in law and theology.[75] Yet these low numbers should not be taken entirely at face value. At a meeting of the parishioners of St. Michel in 1575 to witness the renting of a field, only twelve individuals, including the two vestrymen, were specifically named, but the official account of the proceedings indicated that others attended as well.[76] It is probable that humble parishioners were less likely to be mentioned in accounts of vestry business, especially when they were unable to sign their names to help validate property transactions.

Attendance at an assembly, of course, did not guarantee a person influence over the proceedings, and evidence is scarce to inform us how these meetings occurred. The few records of vestry elections that survive are far more concerned to detail the smooth transferal of accounts and inventories from one set of vestrymen to the next than to describe the elections themselves. No references or telltale complaints survive as at Angers or Paris, but neither do careful restrictions on who could be elected to office as Henri II imposed on the Parisian *quartier* assemblies in 1554.[77] Still, an account of the election of new vestrymen in St. Porchaire in 1593 suggests that the voting occurred aloud, since the candidates are described as having been nominated as well as elected, and that the election was concluded by majority decision.[78] Indeed, as the reference to a majority choice would indicate, parochial assemblies did far more than rubber-stamp previous decisions. The vestrymen of St. Michel called a meeting of the inhabitants in 1592 to de-

[73] ADV G⁹119, register of deliberations, 6r–29r.
[74] ADV G⁹98, contract dated 12 Sept. 1549.
[75] ADV G⁹106, contract dated 1 June 1508.
[76] ADV G⁹102, procès-verbal dated 20 Mar. 1575.
[77] Jacques Maillard, *Le pouvoir municipal à Angers de 1657 à 1789*, 2 vols. (Angers, 1984), 1:76–82; *Registres des délibérations du bureau de la ville de Paris*, 19 vols. (Paris, 1883–1958), 3:27–28; Descimon, "Le corps de ville et les élections échevinales," 510–11; and Robert Descimon and Jean Nagle, "Les quartiers de Paris du moyen âge au XVIIIe siècle: évolution d'un espace plurifonctionnel," *Annales: E.S.C.* 34, no. 5 (1979): 962–63. See also Bernstein, "Benefit of the Ballot?" 627, 630, 635–36.
[78] ". . . les parroissiens assemblez En Icelled. eglize . . . Ont procedde a la no[m]mina[ti]ons daultres procureurs & fabricqueurs Et [à] la pluralite des voix Ont este esleuz & nommez. . . ." ADV G⁹114, procès-verbal dated 6 June 1593.

cide how long a field should be rented out and, based on their opinion, offered the lease to the highest bidder for the specified term.[79] When the hôtel de ville instructed the vestrymen to hold meetings in their parishes to discuss funding carts to collect refuse throughout the city, the poor parishes of St. Simplicien and Ste. Triaise refused to contribute, and the vestrymen of St. Cybard, St. Pierre-le-Puellier, and St. Michel reported that not everyone in their parishes was favorable to the idea.[80] Further, parish business could lead to intense disagreement. In 1557, René Brochard, conservateur and vestryman of Ste. Opportune, and Joachim Prevost, seigneur des Chaulmes, inhabitant of the parish, protested the sale of a garden belonging to the cure that had occurred six months earlier, and accused the curé and the purchaser, François Bellucheau, conseiller in the presidial court and élu, of having acted secretly and against the interests of the parish.[81] Yet if parishioners could argue over property with vehemence and refuse to condone out-of-pocket contributions, parochial institutions reflected the same attention to social hierarchy as permeated other aspects of sixteenth-century urban life.

Despite ideas that parochial decisions should be made with the consent of the inhabitants and that responsibilities should circulate among a significant group of individuals, hierarchical principles played an important role in parish affairs. Elite parishioners, such as Michel Mourault of Notre-Dame-la-Petite and René Berthelot of St. Germain, could expect to have their wishes concerning private chapels and special burial rights respected, and François Bellucheau's dubious purchase of a garden belonging to the curé of Ste. Opportune was questioned only because other elite parishioners had it in their interest to do so. Further, many of the political styles of municipal government, including the practical influence of important members over the proceedings, exerted an influence on the parochial level. The articles that the parishioners of St. Porchaire passed in 1633 to regulate vestry matters noticeably relied on the example of the hôtel de ville. Just as Poitiers's mayor was required to survey the fortifications, the vestrymen were to complete a tour of the church buildings to assess needed repairs a week after their election, and like the mayor, they were supposed to convene the parish assembly once a month.[82] A meeting of the confraternity of Notre-Dame celebrated in the church of St. Didier also shows that considerations of symbolic brotherhood did not negate social hierarchies and that there was a significant overlap between members' influence within the confraternity and in the hôtel de ville.[83] Notable échevins, such as François Doyneau, lieutenant général, and

[79] ADV G⁹102, procès-verbal dated 19 Apr. 1592.
[80] ACP Reg. 23, 90–94 (29 Nov. 1540).
[81] ADV G⁹109, contract dated 8 July 1556 and draft of a legal decision dated c. 1557.
[82] ADV G⁹119, register of deliberations, 1v (articles 3–4).
[83] For these proceedings, see ADV E⁸4, deliberations dated 10 Oct. 1546. This confraternity was seemingly one of the most important in Poitiers, but the poor survival of these documents makes it difficult to be sure. For full references to the twelve confraternities (not including those

René d'Ausseurre, *lieutenant civil,* proposed the series of issues to be decided, advised the group on property matters and clerical vacancies, and saw their opinions and appointments passed unanimously. The language of these deliberations emphasized agreement and consent, but the proceedings were as structured as any of the corps de ville. It is unlikely, however, that all of Poitiers's confraternities and associational groups bowed to social superiors in such a structured way. With a membership that included the cream of Poitiers's elite, the confraternity of Notre-Dame acknowledged the respect owed to the city's most important judicial officials. The confraternity of Ste. Catherine, celebrated in the more popular parish of St. Germain, however, put much more emphasis on organizing festive events that would include a much greater part of the faithful.[84] As these examples show, parish organizations and religious groups offered Poitiers's inhabitants a range of experiences in which neither the rights of social influence nor assumptions concerning the values of broad participation entirely won out.

Over the course of the sixteenth century, the tendency of the hôtel de ville to create and to regularize public institutions such as the urban militia and the poor-relief regime increased municipal demands on parochial officials and the clergy. The increasingly regular subsidies that François I and Henri II required of the city increased the contact between the vestrymen and the corps de ville, since as deputies for their parishes, the vestrymen played a key role in judging parishioners' means and overseeing the appointment of deputies who would set rates of payment. At the same time, the deputies of Poitiers's communauté des pauvres relied on the vestrymen to perform essential services in identifying the needy, soliciting donations, and assuring that funds were collected. Thus, in 1532, 1545, and 1555, the deputies instructed the vestrymen to do the rounds of their parishes to obtain promises of weekly contributions and to draw up rolls of the needy, and in 1545 and 1556 the vestrymen were charged to appoint collectors and to constrain them to carry out their tasks.[85] Even after separate *superintendants* had been appointed to carry out these functions, the vestrymen were instructed to accompany them in a tour of their parishes.[86] Poor relief also drew the clergy

---

associated with specific crafts) I have found in sixteenth-century Poitiers, see my "Politics and Civic Culture," 211 n. 23. Compare this low number with the 80 confraternities in Rouen between 1435 and 1596, the 118 confraternities in Avignon over a similar period, and the 337 confraternities in Paris in 1621. Marc Venard, "Les confréries dans l'espace urbain: l'exemple de Rouen," *Annales de Bretagne et des pays de l'Ouest (Anjou, Maine, Touraine)* 90, no. 2 (1983): 321–32. For Poitiers's craft brotherhoods, see Pierre Rambaud, "Contribution à l'étude des confréries religieuses dans les maîtrises et corporations de Poitiers," *BSAO*, 3d ser., 1 (1909): 673–712.

[84] ADV E⁸11, "Cest La Myse," (1559–1571) and "1587. Recette des rents [sic]" (receipts and payments, 1586–91).

[85] ACP Reg. 19, 130–31 (5 Feb. 1532); Casier 53, 1544, 24r–v [no date]; 24v–25r (22 Nov. 1545); Casier 53, 1555–56, 2r–v (11 and 18 Aug. 1555); 23r (17 May 1556).

[86] ACP Casier 53, 1570–73 (21 Jan. 1571).

more firmly into the sphere of municipal government. Not only were the parish priests to recommend donations to their flocks, but Poitiers's church chapters, abbeys, and chapels were also to make regular contributions; in addition, the chapters were to select deputies to deliberate at the Sunday meetings.[87] Such changes allowed the corps de ville to increase its abilities to force members of the urban community to act according to its designs. Clerical institutions were now constrained to pay their contributions and to appoint deputies to attend the Sunday meetings, and after 1579, all collectors of donations were held legally responsible for the sums they were supposed to collect.[88] Yet this integration also gave more individuals the chance to participate in civic administration on a regular basis and to wield significant control over their neighbors. Although many clerics resisted expectations that they would play an active role in Poitiers's communauté des pauvres, Jean Gaillard, canon of Ste. Radegonde, nevertheless took a regular and active part in the bureau meetings that the corps de ville set up to deal with a plague epidemic in 1587.[89] As the religious wars politicized church attendance, as well, parish authorities such as the vestrymen and curés became central to determining religious loyalties, and thus their neighbors' rights to remain in their homes.[90]

Even in a city such as Poitiers, therefore, opportunities existed for residents who had little or no hope of ever holding municipal office to participate in public life. The corps de ville certainly placed great emphasis on the traditions and privileges that marked it as a separate corporate body and associated its judicial, military, and police functions with a seigneurial jurisdiction over the population. It also claimed sole responsibility to determine when the nature of public events required the input or consent of various groups within the city. This bid for authority was possible, in part, because Poitiers possessed few subsidiary bodies that linked local decision making with municipal government, especially before the religious wars necessitated the permanent institution of the militia. Such exclusive claims for authority, however, did not go undisputed. Inhabitants were able to participate in making decisions that affected public life on the level of their parochial assemblies, religious associations, and guild meetings, and these experiences provided a base to help them contest municipal policies

---

[87] See, for example, the arrangements for the communauté des pauvres instituted in 1544, in which the clergy named deputies, and a cleric was to guard one of the two keys to the grain supply. In 1545, the curés were enlisted to encourage their parishioners to contribute. ACP Casier 53, 1544, 2r-v (Dec. 1544); 7r-v (18 Jan. 1545). For clerical contributions, consult any of the accounts of the communauté des pauvres—for instance, ACP Casier 54, 1558–59, Ar-v.

[88] ACP Reg. 27, 29–30 (31 Aug. 1545); ADV G1589, 120v–122r (4 Aug. 1564); ACP Casier 11, D58, sentence of the Grands Jours of Poitiers, dated 19 Dec. 1579.

[89] ACP Reg. 47, 7–15 (20 July 1587); 31–32, 35–40 (25–26 July 1587).

[90] ACP Reg. 48, 3–8 (18 July 1588); 49–56 (8 Aug. 1588); Reg. 52, 133–35 (30 Dec. 1591).

that they considered unfair. The hôtel de ville developed a strong sense of corporate identity and elaborate procedures for decision making. But it could never govern without some attention to public opinion, as it found when cherished policies led to intense disputes in the decades preceding the religious wars.

3 "*Messieurs de la ville*"

Legal Men and Municipal Culture

In the decentralized city that was sixteenth-century Poitiers, the hôtel de ville and the royal palais stood in close proximity. Located within the contiguous, wealthy parishes of St. Porchaire and St. Didier, they were separated only by the principal butchery, the retail market, and sundry other marketing streets.[1] Although geographical proximity does not always entail institutional cooperation, in this case numerous individuals passed back and forth between the two buildings, alternating their roles in the royal judiciary with their responsibilities in urban administration. The situation benefited both institutions. With overlapping memberships, each organization could count on a certain measure of cooperation. Poitiers's municipal government may have owed much of its importance as an institution precisely to the fact that it included many of the city's most influential royal officials; judicial personnel, university doctors, and financial officers all sat among its ranks, lending their prestige and expertise to town government. Yet this marked official presence did not mean that the hôtel de ville lacked a corporate spirit and identity unique to itself. On the contrary, Poitiers's judges and lawyers were some of the most vocal advocates of a distinct municipal style that ignored the social and honorary distinctions that office generally conferred.

There were, of course, drawbacks to the situation. With many of the same people reaching decisions in the hôtel de ville and the judicial palais, the possibilities for the municipal government to act as an autonomous pole of political debate were much diminished. The heavy complement of royal officials also meant that other groups were poorly represented. Poitiers's wealthiest

---

[1] For the evolution and layout of Poitiers's markets, see Gérard Jarousseau, "Essai de topographie historique: le marché neuf de Poitiers créé à la fin du XIe siècle," *BSAO*, 5th ser., 4 (1990): 99–118.

FIGURE 3.1. Former hôtel de ville, before renovations. Reproduced from *Poitiers, "Ville de tous les âges," ses monuments, ses environs* (Poitiers, 1939). Reprinted with permission of the Office de Tourisme de Poitiers.

FIGURE 3.2. Poitiers's judicial palais and Tour Maubergeon. Reproduced from *Poitiers, "Ville de tous les âges," ses monuments, ses environs* (Poitiers, 1939). Reprinted with permission of the Office de Tourisme de Poitiers.

merchants and tradesmen complained of the difficulties they faced in gaining membership, and lesser notables were all but excluded. The overlap in membership therefore reinforced the authority of the institutions involved but decreased the extent to which the corps de ville could be said to reflect the city as a whole.

The extraordinary rise in the numbers of royal officials during the course of the sixteenth century is well known in the history of early modern France. Scholars describe a group with its own intellectual culture and rhetorical style, developing views on the family, and aspirations to nobility[2] that came not only to influence royal policy but also to determine it, not only to associate its interests with the state but also to claim small portions of it for its patrimony. In France's capital and important provincial cities, the story continues, this growth of an elite social group inevitably resulted in conflict.[3] If the battle for control of urban politics was waged within the hôtel de ville itself, the old merchant and *rentier* families found themselves hard-pressed to retain their dominance within civic institutions. Alternatively, opposing corporate bodies could vie for political ascendancy. Here, the municipal government saw its established jurisdictions limited and its traditional influence questioned at the hands of a parlement, lesser royal court, or seat of financial administration. The result was profoundly to alter the political character of the urban environment. With royal officials in control, the particularistic and participatory styles of government practiced everywhere in the late medieval period gave way to an administration assured by devotees of the state.

Bernard Chevalier has provided a particularly systematic expression of this model. He identifies the period of the mid-fourteenth through the mid-sixteenth centuries as one of extraordinary independence for France's *bonnes villes,* when cities acted as political partners with the crown in governing the realm. The new urban elite composed of merchants, lawyers, and officials cooperated during this time to impose their own interests and to further their families in the urban sphere. Although the number of lawyers and officials rose steadily from the mid-fifteenth century forward, it was only after 1550,

---

[2] Fumaroli, *Âge de l'éloquence;* Sarah Hanley, "Engendering the State: Family Formation and State Building," *French Historical Studies* 16, no. 1 (1989): 4–27; Arlette Jouanna, *L'idée de race en France au XVIe siècle et au début du XVIIe,* 2 vols. (Montpellier, 1981); Elery Shalk, *From Valor to Pedigree: Ideas of Nobility in France in the Sixteenth and Seventeenth Centuries* (Princeton, 1986); Huppert, *Bourgeois Gentilshommes.* Diefendorf discusses the marital strategies of Paris's city councillors in her *Paris City Councillors,* and Dewald explores this issue for the *parlementaires* of Rouen in *Formation of a Provincial Nobility.*

[3] Roland Mousnier, *La vénalité des offices sous Henri IV et Louis XIII,* 2d ed. (Paris, 1971). Although his focus is on a later period, see Michel Antoine's interesting distinction between the "judicial monarchy" that predominated until the demise of the Valois kings and the "administrative monarchy" that began under Henri II and his sons but came to fruition under Louis XIV. "La monarchie absolu," in *The French Revolution and the Creation of Modern Political Culture,* vol. 1, *The Political Culture of the Old Regime,* ed. Keith Michael Baker (Oxford, 1987), 3–24.

when the religious wars destroyed this late-medieval consensus, that royal officials began to disassociate themselves from the other groups, to develop their own culture, family strategies, and professional concerns.[4]

Poitiers's experience offers an instructive proviso to this neat sixteenth-century story. In some ways, the social and political trends in this provincial capital fit very well with the broader developments that historians have noted. In Poitiers, the rise in the influence and numbers of men of the law occurred early, but the general character of its elite corresponds well with Chevalier's social portrait. Yet in other ways, the city's experience points to the limitations of this model. In Poitiers, Chevalier's *trahison des bourgeois* never took place. Rather than retiring from municipal government to ensconce themselves solely in royal institutions, Poitiers's royal officials continued to play an active part in the hôtel de ville. Instead of imposing a different model of government based in a growing identification with the state, they actively maintained a civic rhetoric based in notions of independence and equality. Instead of attempting to limit the authority of the municipal government at every turn, they were happy to avail themselves of the benefits that membership conferred.

The willingness of Poitiers's officials to participate in municipal government points to the variability of French political realities and the elasticity of political definitions. Like Simona Cerutti's municipal councillors in Turin, Poitiers's legal officials were able to express ideas about civic government that were independent of the concerns of their judicial prerogatives.[5] Interpretation of the role of the state in urban government was not rigid, and officials adopted the view that coincided with their own interests in any given situation. Because they were assured significant influence within the hôtel de ville, there was no incentive systematically to challenge its authority. As William Beik has pointed out for the seventeenth century, the French kings ruled—even absolutely—through local elites, rather than against them.[6] In Poitiers in the sixteenth century, both the hôtel de ville and the palais provided useful channels through which political authority could flow.

Lawyers and Merchants in the *Cent*

The increase in the numbers of judicial personnel in Poitiers's town government occurred early. Although merchants and rentiers dominated the hôtel de ville at the end of the fourteenth century, the establishment of the university and the privileges granted to the sénéchaussée in the first half of the fifteenth century raised the numbers and improved the position of *gens de loi*

[4] Chevalier, *Bonnes villes*. See esp. chap. 6, "La trahison des bourgeois," 129–50.
[5] Simona Cerutti, *La ville et les métiers: naissance d'un langage corportif (Turin, 17e–18e siècle)* (Paris, 1990), esp. 111–19.
[6] Beik, *Absolutism and Society*.

Table 3.1.
Number of Cent with title of maître versus no legal title

	Échevins		Bourgeois		Total[a]	
Date	Maître	No legal title	Maître	No legal title	Maître	No legal title
17 Aug. 1531	24	1	59	13	83	14
22 July 1541	25	1	63	11	88	12
22 July 1547	25	1	65	9	90	10
6 July 1549	21	3	55	18	76	21
26 June 1551	22	4	53	22	75	26
1561–62	26	0	58	16	84	16
13 Sept. 1574	25	0	62	14	87	14
31 July 1582	25	1	66	8	91	9
28 July 1589	24	2	68	6	92	8
1592[b]	24	1	66	7	90	8

Source: ACP Registers 19, 23, 29, 30–31, 38, 42, 44, 49, 51, 53.
[a]Because of delays in elections, lists of members do not always contain one hundred individuals. The council may also contain more than twenty-five members if the mayor was not an échevin at the time of his election.
[b] This date shows full elections during the Catholic League period.

in Poitevin society. Indeed, Robert Favreau traces the steady increase of law graduates in the corps de ville from this time.[7] He finds that although only nine members of the Cent held the title of maître (meaning that they held a legal degree or exercised a profession associated with law) in 1412, their number had risen to eighty-eight by 1523.[8]

As table 3.1 shows, the percentage of members of the Cent who laid claim to a legal honorific remained relatively steady at 85 percent to 90 percent throughout the sixteenth century. The one reversal in the trend, visible in 1549–62, resulted from a royal edict in 1547 prohibiting election of gens de loi to municipal office.[9] Not only did the hôtel de ville elect a greater number of merchants in the five years after the edict, but five individuals who had previously been recorded as maître were now listed without this title. A consideration of the professions of the Cent reinforces this perspective. Individuals in the legal professions generally composed around two-thirds of the body, while financial officials varied between 5 percent to 15 percent of the group, and merchants and related professions ranged from 7 percent to 22 percent.[10]

---

[7] Favreau, *Ville de Poitiers,* 314–18, 490, 494–99, 510–12.
[8] Favreau, *Ville de Poitiers,* 494.
[9] See chapter 6 for this episode.
[10] I compiled these general figures by noting the professions of members of the corps de ville whenever they appeared in archival documents. I did not assume that an individual exercised the same profession throughout his life. Although the percentage of known professions is very low for the first half of the century, the fact that this information did not come from one type of document should help to make the professions that are known more representative. The one exception is again after 1547, when not only were more merchants elected, but the dispute also tended to make commercial professions more visible.

The sixteenth-century rise in the numbers of royal officials in Poitiers reinforced their numbers in city government, since new judicial officials often sought and were awarded places in the corps de ville. Occasional references document this growth: although the presidial court had twelve conseillers when it was created in 1552, that number had increased to twenty-two by 1562.[11] In an election of 1575, at least forty-three officials cast a vote, and Henri III created nine new offices in the 1580s.[12] Of a sample of thirty-five individuals who obtained judicial office during the sixteenth century, seven were elected to a place in the seventy-five or in the council within one year. Nine more were elected within five years, and a total of twenty-seven eventually combined their judicial duties with participation in municipal government.[13] As the financial administration developed and fiscal concerns became ever more important with rising taxes and the costs of religious war, moreover, financial officials were included in greater numbers within the corps de ville as well.

Poitiers's notable mercantile families inevitably suffered from this situation. Although merchants were elected to the town government in a slow but steady stream, it was only in the five years after the 1547 edict that they saw their influence significantly increase. Further, they were almost never elected to be échevins directly, and only four of their number were chosen for mayor in the sixteenth century. Within the group of merchants, moreover, the range of professions was very limited. Only the most wealthy dealers in cloth and silk, the elite of the apothecaries' guild, or the owners of Poitiers's best-known hotel establishments could hope to gain entrance to the corps de ville. Craftsmen were entirely excluded, with the possible exception of a surgeon. In fact, it is likely that some of the individuals exercising legal professions, such as a *greffier* (court clerk) and some of the less successful procureurs, were of lower social consequence than the few commercial men who sat in the Mois.

To be sure, Poitiers was not alone in the heavy legal composition of its town government, as gens de loi and royal officials came to sit on and to dominate town councils in many parts of France. In Paris, Dijon, and Montpellier, merchants saw themselves displaced by their fellow citizens in the legal professions.[14] In Limoges, 47 percent of the town councillors elected between 1602 and 1610 were royal officials.[15] Yet Poitiers experienced a

[11] Gennes, "Notice sur le présidial," 370–71.

[12] Brilhac, 11, 17, and 21.

[13] Since the records for Poitiers's sénéchaussée and presidial courts for the sixteenth century no longer exist, I have compiled this list of 35 officiers from mentions in Brilhac; Papier journal de Jean de Brilhac, ADV SAHP 102, 11–25v; and Extrait de la table des matières contenues dans le *Papier rouge* du greffe présidial de Poitiers (1559–1573), ADV SAO 245.

[14] Diefendorf, *Paris City Councillors;* Mack P. Holt, "Wine, Community and Reformation in Sixteenth-Century Burgundy," *Past and Present* 138 (1993): 66; and Frederick M. Irvine, "From Renaissance City to Ancien Régime Capital: Montpellier, c. 1500–c. 1600," in *Cities and Social Change in Early Modern France,* ed. Philip Benedict (London, 1989), 105–33.

[15] Finley-Croswhite, "Absolutism and Municipal Autonomy," 90.

Table 3.2.
Municipal officials with title of maître in Poitiers, Bourges, and Toulouse

Dates for Bourges and Toulouse (dates for Poitiers)	Mayor & échevins of Poitiers (%)	Mayor & prud'hommes of Bourges (%)	Capitouls of Toulouse (%)
1491–1500ᵃ	—	36	17
1501–10 (1503)	76	46	24
1511–20 (1513)	80	26	29
1521–30 (1523)	88	44	29
1531–40 (1533)	100	30	26
1541–50 (1543)	93	54/13ᵇ	34
1551–60 (1552)	85	2	34
1561–70 (1561–62)	100	13	33
1571–80 (1575)	96	4	33
1581–90 (1586)	92	26	33
1591–1600 (1595)	97	50	36

Source: Poitiers: membership lists in the town council registers; Favreau, *Ville de Poitiers,* 494 (1503–23); Bourges: "Liste des Maire et Eschevins," in *Privileges de la ville de Bovrges et confirmation d'iceux,* 3–62 (new pagination); Toulouse: La Faille, *Annales.*

ᵃThe date range for Bourges is 1492–1500 because of the reorganization of Bourges's municipal government.

ᵇThese percentages represent figures before and after Henri II's 1547 edict.

particularly acute rise in the numbers of judicial officials, legal practitioners, and law graduates who sat in the corps de ville. For example, although Bourges and Toulouse each possessed celebrated faculties of law, royal bailliage or sénéchaussée courts, and the latter city a parlement, the percentages of municipal officials with a legal background were noticeably lower (see table 3.2). In important commercial centers such as Marseille and Lyon, moreover, mercantile elites retained their predominant influence over municipal government.[16] Poitiers therefore constituted an extreme case of one model of civic government developing during the sixteenth century.

Legal Influence and Precedence in the Hôtel de Ville

The rise in the numbers of gens de loi and judges throughout France sparked debates over whether royal officials should participate in municipal administrative bodies, and if so, what place they should hold within them. With the edict of October 1547 the crown officially adopted the stance that no lawyers or judicial officials should sit on town governments, and this point of view even found fleeting expression in Poitiers. In an electoral contest of 1531, François Herbert the younger attempted to disqualify Jasmes de Lauzon as a candidate, on the grounds that since Lauzon was *avocat du roi*

---

[16] Kaiser, *Marseille;* Gascon, *Grand commerce,* 407–17.

(king's barrister) in Poitiers's sénéchaussée court, he could not concurrently hold the office of échevin.[17] The notion that royal and civic offices were incompatible, however, generally gave way to arguments that including royal officials and men of the law in city governments was a help rather than a hindrance to civic liberties and urban order. When an argument arose in Toulouse in 1536 over whether royal officials could be elected capitouls, opponents of the idea insisted that this act would go against the customs of the city, but supporters trumped them by arguing that admitting royal officials to the body would prove useful for Toulouse's city council.[18] For Claude de Rubys, men of letters were not just beneficial, but essential to Lyon's city government. Not only did men of the law possess knowledge that was critical for many aspects of urban administration, but their attention to learning also bred virtue and stamped out vice, making them ideal men to guide the city.[19] Charles Loyseau implicitly agreed with this assessment and based his approval of royal officials' participating in city government on the grounds that only they could prevent the disorder and disloyalty that many city councils had displayed during the Catholic League period.[20] By the early seventeenth century, in fact, the debate over the conflicts of interest that could arise if royal officials simultaneously acted in city administrations was largely over. When François Miron, lieutenant civil of the prévôté of Paris, was elected prévôt des marchands of Paris in 1604, an advisory pamphlet pointed out that no man had held these offices concurrently since 1544 but ascribed this fact to the heavy workload of both positions rather than to any inherent incompatibility.[21]

If royal officials were to act as members of city governments, however, their presence raised the thorny issue of what rules of precedence should operate within the body. Should men possessing a royal dignity precede their colleagues distinguished only through their role as city officials, or did their participation in a single corps make them equal within it? Men such as Loyseau and Rubys argued that royal officials and lawyers should have precedence. For Loyseau, any municipal councillor who held a royal office should always precede any councillor who did not, and Rubys argued that the noble qualities of men of letters fit them to precede actual nobles, royal officials who did not possess a legal grade, and all bourgeois and merchants, in that order.[22] Yet the question was not so easily resolved in practice, and in Poitiers it led to intense debates. Although members of Poitiers's corps de ville were frequently disposed to accord the royal officials within their midst

---

[17] ACP Reg. 19, 84–101 (15 Nov. 1531).
[18] La Faille, *Annales*, 2:101.
[19] Rubys, *Privileges*, 62–67.
[20] Loyseau, *Oevvres*, 829.
[21] A[lbert] Miron de l'Espinay, *François Miron et l'administration municipale de Paris sous Henri IV de 1604 à 1606* (Paris, 1885), 361–64.
[22] Loyseau, *Oevvres*, 827; Rubys, *Privileges*, 82–83.

special prerogatives and prestige, the members proved unwilling to sacrifice essential customs and procedures that set the municipal administration apart as a collegial governing body.

The influence of royal officials and men of the law in Poitiers went beyond their generally high numbers in the Cent. The city's most important judicial and financial officers also enjoyed an enormous amount of prestige and influence over the body. Many were chosen as échevins or mayor shortly after being elected bourgeois, unlike lesser legal practitioners and merchants, who generally acquired these positions only after long service in the seventy-five. The lieutenant général and the *président* of the presidial court were also accorded special honor.[23] Although seniority within the hôtel de ville was firmly determined by order of election, the rules were frequently bent for Poitiers's most important judicial officials. In 1512, lieutenant général Pierre Regnier was accorded the second seat to the right of the mayor, at the sufferance of Jean Favereau, himself *procureur du roi* (king's solicitor).[24] In 1579, when Mathurin Courtinier, *trésorier général* and bourgeois, was challenged for attempting to sit with the échevins, the financial official replied that he was asking no more than what had been accorded to René Brochard, lieutenant général.[25] A 1571 dispute between Jean de la Haye, lieutenant général, and Pierre Rat, président, reveals that according the président the second seat within the hôtel de ville had become routine. While la Haye protested that Rat, a bourgeois, should not be allowed to sit with the échevins, the président asserted his right to the place, following the tradition established during the tenure of François Aubert. Clearly siding with Rat, the secretary explained that "the said place after the mayor belongs to the said Rat because of the dignity of his office as head of justice in the region of Poitou. . . ."[26]

Not only could Poitiers's senior judicial officials expect municipal seating arrangements to reflect their special status, but these individuals often played an especially weighty part in the decision-making process too. Despite the seemingly automatic deference implied by honorary seating, office did not uniquely determine this role. Personality, ascendancy over the legal and factional battles of the palais, and no doubt interest in municipal affairs all influenced the degree of authority that the judicial head could exercise in the hôtel de ville. Although Pierre Regnier was rarely present at council deliberations in 1511–1513 and saw his election as mayor disputed in 1516,[27] his

---

[23] Before the founding of the presidial court in 1552, there was of course no président. Thereafter, the président took precedence over the lieutenant général. Because of the disputes arising from this situation, the offices were combined in 1586, when président Pierre Rat was also appointed lieutenant général. They were separated again in 1594, because of the double appointments resulting from League politics. On the history and composition of the courts, see Gennes, "Notice sur le présidial."

[24] ACP Reg. 11, 242–48 (22 June 1512).

[25] ACP Reg. 42, 980–86 (13 July 1579).

[26] ACP Reg. 40, 71–76 (31 Oct. 1571); quotation, 72.

[27] See ACP Reg. 15, 173–82 (27 June 1516), and Gérard Jarousseau, "L'élection du maire de Poitiers, Pierre Régnier, en 1516: observations sur les institutions communales de cette ville," *BSAO*, 4th ser., 14 (1978): 567–86.

successor François Doyneau may have been the most highly regarded member of the municipal government in the sixteenth century. In the early 1570s, likewise, Jean de la Haye could look back in frustration to the respect accorded to his predecessor François Aubert. Both Regnier and la Haye may have owed their comparative municipal insignificance to disputes originating with their judicial functions. Regnier had been involved in continuous litigation concerning exercise of his office,[28] and la Haye's complaints against Pierre Rat reveal dissatisfaction with the président's precedence over him. Doyneau, on the other hand, could boast ascendancy over court and échevinage alike. He had exerted such control over the cases and procedures of the sénéchaussée that the other judges had gone so far as to sue him in the royal Grand Conseil.[29] This conflict, however, did not deprive him of respect or render his judicial decisions any less definitive. In his work on the customary law of Poitou, for example, Guillaume Theveneau frequently referred to Doyneau's judgments to illustrate and even to prove his arguments.[30] Within the hôtel de ville, Doyneau's unusually developed ethic of civic responsibility often guided debate,[31] and his prestige allowed him a large influence in important matters such as the annual election of the mayor.[32] By the end of his life, respect for the judicial official ran so high that the municipal secretary even saw fit to record verbatim the patriarch's personal recipe against plague![33]

Cooperation and Tensions

Both the hôtel de ville and the royal palais benefited from such joint affiliation. A good proportion of municipal business involved legal activity, so that access to Poitiers's greatest legal experts proved a great advantage.[34] As relations improved with financial officials, the city also began to gain tempo-

---

[28] In the discussion preceding Regnier's election, Nicolas Claveurier protested that the Mois should not select an individual who had been convoked before the Parlement of Paris and declared abusive of his office. ACP Reg. 15, 180. See also Jarousseau, "Élection du maire," 576–77.

[29] Jean de Brilhac copied the whole of the request submitted to the Grand Conseil in 1529 into his *papier journal*. See ADV SAHP 102, 1r–25v.

[30] Nicolas Theveneau, *Annotations, ov paraphrase avx loix mvnicipalles, et covstvmes dv comte, et pays de Poictov* (Poitiers, 1561).

[31] For examples, see ACP Reg. 19, 209–11 (18 Sept. 1532); Reg. 20, 505–8 (5 Apr. 1538).

[32] For examples, see ACP Reg. 20, 757–64 (27 June 1539); Reg. 23, 323–29 (1 July 1541).

[33] ACP Reg. 32, 438–39 (30 Apr. 1554).

[34] Michael Breen makes the same observation for seventeenth-century Dijon, where avocats also played a significant role in the *mairie*. See his "Legal Cultue." By 1547, Poitiers's municipal government had begun to name certain members to act as special counselors in its lawsuits. These counselors were usually échevins and important members of the judicial establishment. For examples, see ACP Reg. 29, 1–15 (22 July 1547); Reg. 34, 1–4 (24 July 1556). In the 1580s, Georges Baron, Jean Boiceau, and Antoine Bouchet, Poitiers's most famous and well-respected attorneys, were members of the corps de ville and were named to oversee its legal activities. Reg. 46, 14–26 (25 July 1586).

rary access to royal funds. Inclusion of royal officials also assured the Mois of receiving the latest news from the king and royal administration. In its daily management, finally, the municipality did not have to prove the propriety of its expenditures to an outside authority, since its extraordinary accounts were reviewed by the lieutenant général.[35] The municipality could also involve royal officials directly in urban administrative concerns. Inhabitants who refused to pay their taxes found themselves called before the royal courts for their delinquency,[36] and the *gens du roi* played an important role in compelling the clergy to consent to changes in poor relief that the municipality inaugurated in the 1540s and 1550s.[37]

Yet the municipality benefited most in avoiding the challenge to its privileges that other urban administrations faced from competing bodies of royal officials. In Toulouse, the relationship between the parlement and the municipality was tense throughout the sixteenth and seventeenth centuries, and during the religious crisis of 1562 the judges actually removed all of the capitouls from office.[38] Hostilities and competition were also pronounced in Angers, and in Rouen the parlement simply dominated the process of urban administration.[39] Yet in Poitiers, although the two institutions did not always exist harmoniously, the présidial did not block the hôtel de ville's actions in retaining its privileges. In fact, royal officials cooperated to obtain derogations from the Ordinance of Moulins, and thus to preserve many of the municipal government's judicial rights that this royal edict initially curtailed.[40]

Royal institutions also gained in this symbiotic relationship. Enjoying an unusually large jurisdiction at the beginning of the sixteenth century, the sénéchaussée had consistently to combat attempts by the smaller towns in Poitou to obtain their own royal courts. In preserving the predominance of Poitiers over the surrounding region, the palais found a staunch ally in the

---

[35] For a straightforward statement that the lieutenant général had jurisdiction over the review of the municipality's extraordinary accounts, see ACP Reg. 20, 192–97 (26 Feb. 1537). Articles 94–95 of the Ordinance of 1560 (dated Jan. 1561 from Orléans) abolished the offices of *superintendant controlleur* of public funds in the cities, returned the supervision of these accounts to the mayors and échevins, and specified that the accounts should then be rendered to the *bailli*, sénéchal, or his lieutenant, as had been done in the past. See Isambert, 14:87.

[36] ACP Reg. 46, 146–48 (24 Nov. 1586).

[37] For example, see the legal proceedings against Guillaume Bienvenu, aumônier of the aumônerie of Notre-Dame, especially the "Salvations" of Bienvenu dated 1543 and the inventory of the procureur du roi dated shortly thereafter (ADV G1100). In 1545, the Mois decided to seek legal constraint against all inhabitants and clerical bodies that had not paid their contributions. ACP Reg. 27, 29–30 (31 Aug. 1545).

[38] M[ark] Greengrass, "The Anatomy of a Religious Riot in Toulouse in May 1562," *Journal of Ecclesiastical History* 34, no. 3 (1983): 369–70, 381–82; William Beik, "Magistrates and Popular Uprisings in France before the Fronde: The Case of Toulouse," *Journal of Modern History* 46 (1974): 585–608, esp. 587; and Schneider, *Public Life*, 68–69.

[39] Xavier Martin, "L'escamotage d'une réforme municipale: Angers, 1589," *Annales de Bretagne et des pays de l'Ouest* 91, no. 2 (1984): 116–17; Benedict, *Rouen*, 34–35.

[40] ACP Casier 42, Reg. 13, 40.

hôtel de ville. The municipality periodically joined the royal court in opposing attempts to limit the range of Poitiers's judicial dominion, and on one occasion at least the town council took the initiative against nearby Saint-Maixent.[41] When cities were being chosen as seats for the new presidial courts in 1552, moreover, the city government actively sought an installation in Poitiers.[42]

Despite general cooperation, frictions were bound to occur between two institutions that laid claim to maintaining order in the civic sphere. The municipality periodically protested that the presidial court was overstepping its bounds, both in the sentences it handed down and in the general edicts it passed on police matters.[43] When the hôtel de ville and the palais found their interests to diverge, moreover, the clash was most frequently with the lieutenant criminel over the boundaries of police jurisdiction. Around 1450, the municipality had submitted legal documents designed to prove that the mayor had the right to hear criminal cases in first instance and to punish criminals at the pillory.[44] In the sixteenth century, no lieutenant criminel seems to have disputed the municipality's right to hear criminal cases or to rule on police measures, but there was not a single criminal judge with whom the hôtel de ville did not find itself at variance over particular cases.[45] On the whole, however, the lieutenants criminels did not take full advantage of royal legislation designed to limit municipal arbitration of police and craft matters. Rather, both institutions concentrated on challenging the jurisdiction of seigneurial courts within Poitiers—particularly the less formally run courts of the chapter of St. Hilaire and the abbot of Montierneuf.[46]

Predictably, the tensions caused by the double authority of the hôtel de ville and the palais erupted in precedence disputes. Disagreement frequently involved the status of the mayor relative to the lieutenant général or other royal officials. Thus, in 1540, the council decided that the mayor would attend the funeral of the wife of the *sénéchal,* despite the difficulties over precedence that could arise.[47] Two decades later, Jean de Brilhac, lieutenant

[41] ACP Reg. 22, 302–3 (19 Apr. 1540). For other examples of decisions to help preserve Poitiers's legal jurisdiction, see Reg. 11, 473–80 (27 May 1513); Reg. 54, 130–33 (23 Jan. 1594).

[42] ACP Reg. 32, 64 (28 Feb. 1552); 68–69 (11 Mar. 1552).

[43] For examples of tensions, see ACP Reg. 31, 18–28 (22 Aug. 1549); Reg. 40, 223–27 (20 May 1572); Reg. 42, 302–6 (26 Aug. 1575); 435–37 (8 Mar. 1576).

[44] ACP Casier 9, D14.

[45] Amaury Pidoux and police jurisdiction: ACP Casier 9, D34; René Berthelot and jurisdiction over public entertainment: Reg. 32, 235–36 (3 July 1553); 311–13 (28 Aug. 1553); Jean de Brilhac and criminal jurisdiction: Casier 37, K21; François de Brilhac and religious prosecutions: Reg. 47, 312–14 (25 Jan. 1588); 323–31 (1 Feb. 1588); 331–40 (8 Feb. 1588); 366–70 (29 Feb. 1588).

[46] St. Hilaire: ADV G641, legal decision dated 16 Oct., 1525; G646, procès verbal dated 10–14 Sept. 1570; G642, extract of the registers of the Parlement of Paris dated 26 Jan. 1572 and royal letters of Henri III dated 29 Nov. 1577. Montierneuf: ACP Reg. 23, 107–20 (22 Dec. 1540); Reg. 46, 254–62 (6 Apr. 1587).

[47] ACP Reg. 23, 57–58 (23 Aug. 1540).

criminel, was prosecuting a precedence dispute that had arisen between himself and the mayor on the day of the coronation of François II.[48] Disputes also arose over the general relationship of the corps de ville to the royal administrative bodies. With such a high proportion of overlapping membership, the Mois was required to rule on whether its members would march with their professional corps (implying less honor for the municipality) or separately with the mayor (implying greater municipal prestige).[49] Revealingly, the hôtel de ville did not adopt the same approach at all times, but let the importance of the occasion dictate whether it insisted on marching separately from the royal officials or abreast of them. In 1577, the Mois made its assumptions explicit by concluding

> that for celebrated acts, such as entries of the king and queen, seigneurs, and ladies who come to the city, as well as for [processions to] greet and congratulate them, Monsieur the mayor and the corps de ville shall march separately without joining the judicial corps. And with regard to indifferent acts, such as funerary processions, Monsieur the mayor shall pray the judicial officials to march [separately]: that is, justice to the right and the échevins to the left.[50]

Thus, for all affairs of state, where the town would be representing itself to others, it was imperative for the municipality to maintain a separate presence and thus to preserve an independent identity. Where the audience was restricted to the urban milieu, however, the municipality could be less vigilant and recognize its effective partnership with the royal court.

Municipal Independence and Equality

With its composition heavily skewed toward royal officials, with many of its most important positions held by them, with the enormous influence that officials played in the decision-making process, and with the ceremonial deference accorded them, could the hôtel de ville maintain independence from the royal administration? The corps de ville certainly thought so. Whether merchants, lawyers, or royal officials, many échevins and bourgeois viewed the town government as an autonomous institution, with its own interests, traditions, and internal relations. Further, they saw this independence as resting specifically on the integrity of municipal tradition. Retaining privileges was important, to be sure, but so was preserving the

---

[48] ACP Reg. 37, 115–17 (1 Apr. 1560); 124–27 (6 May 1560); 128–29 (13 May 1560); 129–30 (27 May 1560); 132–37 (17 June 1560).
[49] For examples, see ACP Reg. 19, 11–20 (17 Aug. 1531); Reg. 47, 7–15 (20 July 1587); Reg. 53, 25–26 (4 Sept. 1592).
[50] ACP Reg. 42, 621 (3 May 1577).

practices of the hôtel de ville as defined by statute and customary procedure. The issue of precedence in municipal assemblies was so important precisely because it threatened to substitute external hierarchical considerations for established decision-making practices. Many members of the corps de ville invested these traditions with great meaning. For them, at least ideally, the municipality provided a space in which exterior social considerations did not hold, in which all members had an equal value dependent on their deliberations and expressed in their vote. Officials and subjects of a powerful monarch, they still could make reference to the notion of equitable sharing of responsibilities within a limited government of notables that formed the basis of contemporary republican ideology.

Disputes over precedence within the hôtel de ville provided an important forum in which to debate the relationship between municipal status and exterior authority. Over the years, the municipality had developed its own rules of precedence, based entirely on an individual's service within the town government. Former mayors presided over everyone else, followed by the échevins, and then, on a lower level, the bourgeois. Within each group, seating order was dependent on date of matriculation.[51] Yet exceptions were made to this order, and the rules of seniority were occasionally bent to acknowledge outside dignity. In the last quarter of the sixteenth century, in particular, the Mois found itself obliged continually to reexamine the sticky question of precedence in municipal assemblies. Two competing ideas were at stake: one assumed that exterior distinctions of honor and degree should permeate civic institutions; the other held that municipal integrity depended on its imperviousness to outside qualities. Yet the prerogatives of precedence went only so far. Even members who advocated conferring honorary places on important individuals held that exceptions in ceremonial order were to remain limited to seating. In the more crucial matter of the order of opinions, the rules of municipal seniority were to stand firm. Thus in 1575, responding to complaints over abuses in seating order, the council finally ruled that "as far as the seating order in this house is concerned, one will cede the honor to important personages of quality, but that when it comes to opining, each person will give his opinion according to the order of his reception and matriculation. . . ."[52] By 1582, the increase in the number of financial officials in the Cent had raised the problem of whether they were to be accorded the same honor that the judicial officials had traditionally enjoyed. After lengthy deliberation, in which members aired numerous competing opinions, the Mois finally concluded that both trésoriers and senior judicial officials who were échevins would be honored with special places, the financial officials to the right of the mayor and the judges to the left. Again, however, these exceptions were to be limited to seating, and

[51] See chapter 4 for further discussion.
[52] ACP Reg. 42, 329 (10 Oct. 1575).

each member was to give his opinion in the order prescribed by municipal custom.[53]

In each case, therefore, the Mois distinguished between two kinds of precedence—one negotiable, the other not. Whereas precedence in physical space could be manipulated to confer honor on specific members of the town government, the relational order defined by a theoretical space and determining the functioning of the institution could not. In this way, the hôtel de ville recognized two seemingly contradictory facts about its identity. Through alterations in ceremonial order, it accepted the dual nature of royal officials as honored servants of the king and as municipal officials and thus acknowledged the importance of including members of royal bodies within the municipality. In insisting on maintaining customary hierarchy in the process of government, on the other hand, it asserted the autonomy and integrity of municipal institutions. It created a realm in which administration could proceed according to the values and the dictates established uniquely through municipal statute and precedent.

Although some important financial and judicial officials insisted on having their office recognized within the hôtel de ville, not all their colleagues shared their point of view. In fact, royal officials were some of the most vocal advocates for retaining municipal procedures intact and thus for preserving the institution's integrity and unique political style. During the extended deliberations over precedence in 1582, the majority voted to accord judicial and financial officials a special place within the Mois, but others disagreed. Some, like Scévole (Gauthier) de Sainte-Marthe, trésorier général, held that no exceptions should be made, either in seating order or in the order of opining.[54] Louis de la Ruelle, doctor regent, was so adamant in this belief that he formally opposed the conclusions of the Mois.[55] Yet no one stated the case against recognizing outside dignities more forcefully than François Barrault, bourgeois and enquêteur. Proclaiming his zeal to preserve the privileges and liberties accorded to the hôtel de ville by the kings of France, Barrault argued that

> in order not to derogate from any point of the said rights and privileges, that in accordance with the statutes and ancient traditions, those who were received and matriculated first among the échevins and bourgeois, each according to the order in which he was received in his place, should preside, both in seating and in voting, indistinctly. And that in this regard, it is not fitting to comply with or conform to usual practices observed elsewhere to defer to preeminence

[53] Deliberations of 6 Aug. 1582, ACP Casier 4, B19. In fact, it seems that these stipulations were never carried out. During further discussions over precedence in 1595, René Boisson pointed out that the decision of 1582 had never been put into practice, because of the official opposition of a member of the Cent. ACP Reg. 54, 146 (25 Feb. 1595).

[54] ACP Casier 4, B19, 1v–2r.

[55] ACP Casier 4, B19, 2v.

of office, considering that this maison commune is a kind of popular order [*ordre popullaire*] [existing] under the grant and goodwill of kings, composed of two kinds only: that is, échevins and bourgeois.

This body of one hundred, continued Barrault, was charged to elect the mayor annually, and never in such elections was the quality of the candidate recognized or considered, the name and surname being all that was required on the ballot.[56]

Barrault, like Sainte-Marthe and La Ruelle but more explicitly, joined the issue of precedence to the municipality's institutional identity. Since the hôtel de ville owed its many rights and prerogatives to royal grant, any alteration in procedure would chip away at the basis for municipal authority. Yet if urban institutions were guaranteed by the king, they were also the product of ancient statute and common accord, which over the years had come to define civic procedure. The special bylaws of the municipality, stated Barrault and implied his colleagues, could not be sacrificed to the general social rules that obtained elsewhere without weakening the institution and damaging the ethic of communal government. This minor judicial official regarded the municipality as inspired by a different philosophy of membership and allegiance than royal institutions required. Within the Cent, professional dignities were irrelevant, and members participated in general decisions in an order strictly determined by experience and with an equality resting on each vote.

In the sixteenth-century setting, references to equality within such a hierarchical and exclusive body as the municipality were not contradictory. Discussing a very different type of civic regime, Francesco Guicciardini had explained that liberty, or the good of the state, was not dependent on universal political participation, but on the activity of men of ability. To ensure the common good, government necessarily had to be limited, but within the group of individuals fit to hold office, these responsibilities should be rotated frequently. In this way, everyone would enjoy the opportunity and the incentive to act to the best of his ability.[57] For Guicciardini, therefore, equality was distinct from democracy, and the situation in Poitiers accorded well with this view. In France as in Florence, the notion of equality was tied more to the possibility of exercising one's potential as defined by one's social status than to equal access to political authority. A government of notables with strict rules of access, the municipality could therefore adopt a special rhetoric of inclusiveness without worrying about its effect on the rest of urban society.[58]

[56] ACP Casier 4, B19, 3r–v.

[57] Francesco Guicciardini, *Dialogue on the Government of Florence*, trans. and ed. Alison Brown (Cambridge, U.K., 1994), esp. 17, 36–37, 100. See also Pocock, *Machiavellian Moment*, 219–71; Althanasios Moulakis, "Civic Humanism, Realist Constitutionalism, and Francesco Guicciardini's *Discorso di Logrogno*," in *Renaissance Civic Humanism: Reappraisals and Reflections*, ed. James Hankins (Cambridge, U.K., 2000), 200–222.

[58] Muir also discusses the possibilities for the coexistence of strict notions of hierarchy with an ethic of republicanism in the closed group of Venice's patricians in his *Civic Ritual*, 185–86.

Not only was equality possible, but it could even be identified as the essential principle of municipal government. "That which principally maintains and preserves towns, provinces, republics, kingdoms, even the whole human race in their being," explained outgoing Mayor Jacques Foucquet in 1583, "is equality."

> For whether peoples govern themselves through monarchy, aristocracy, or democracy, equality is always required. Although in a monarchy a single person commands, if the offices and functions are not distributed equally among subjects who are worthy and virtuous men, a remarkable disorder results.

The same was true in aristocratic and democratic governments.

> But when, on the contrary, these same charges and dignities are distributed equally among fellow citizens, men of property and honor, this practice sustains kingdoms, makes republics flourish, and preserves towns and cities in union and concord.[59]

Within the hôtel de ville, Foucquet continued, the annual election of the mayor assured this essential quality. Because no member of the corps de ville could expect to exercise this dignity for more than a year (or two), this sharing of office and open access to honor provided the same encouragement to virtue that fair weights and measures prompted in trade and equal division of property among heirs allowed within families.[60] If offices were perpetual, asked Foucquet, what hope would fellow citizens have of one day acceding to them? Greater than the pleasure of holding office indefinitely was the duty to pass it on to someone else, to render account of one's administration, and to become a private citizen once more.[61]

Foucquet was a conseiller in Poitiers's presidial court. His mayoral address, too, may have been influenced by the new style of parlementary harangues that had begun in Paris in the 1570s and may have spread to Poitiers during the session of the Grands Jours in 1579.[62] Yet despite his professional interests as an officer of the crown, Foucquet could still make reference to an ideal of civic corporatism, in which men of worth shared the task of governing on a rotating basis. Officials and men of law certainly wielded royal authority on the local level, but they were also important advocates of provincial concerns and civic ideals. Although historians may distinguish be-

---

[59] ACP Reg. 44, 283–84 (1 July 1583).

[60] This reference to equal inheritance was particularly significant in Poitiers, since Poitevin customary law called for equal division among all offspring of the deceased, without exception. See Jean Yver, "Les caractères originaux du groupe de coutumes de l'Ouest de la France," *Revue historique de droit français et étranger* ser. 4, no. 30 (1952): 18–79.

[61] ACP Reg. 44, 284–85.

[62] Fumaroli, *Âge de l'éloquence*, 469–71.

tween "the state" and "the city" and assume that supporters of the first could not also uphold the styles of the second, contemporaries did not draw such firm distinctions. Individuals such as Foucquet and Barrault could therefore echo some of the political outlook of an advocate of Florentine republican institutions. At the same time, though, their understanding of political structures could reflect the theories of monarchy, aristocracy, and democracy of France's best-known sixteenth-century political theorist, Jean Bodin.[63]

If royal servants and men of the law dominated Poitiers's town government throughout the sixteenth century, therefore, this situation did not erode notions of municipal independence and political integrity. By maintaining procedures that had been legislated or developed over time, members of the corps de ville sought to preserve a separate civic style that assured their own authority over the urban sphere. Whatever the realities of urban administration, they persisted in viewing decisions as reached through common agreement, through a process in which each individual invested his weightiest deliberation for the good of the whole. The municipal government was far from consistently functioning in this way, but the discrepancies between ideal representation and quotidian decision making cannot be explained by a sixteenth-century trahison des bourgeois.

[63] Foucquet's distinction between the type of state (monarchy, aristocracy, democracy) and the qualities requisite in each (equality, in particular) recalls Bodin's explanation that while states cannot be mixed in their nature, the means of government can vary. He writes: "Car il y a bien difference de l'estat, et du gouvernement: qui est une reigle de police qui n'a point esté touchee de personne: car l'estat peut estre en Monarchie, et neantmoins il sera gouverné populairement si le Prince fait part des estats, Magistrats, offices, et loyers egalement à tous sans avoir esgard à la noblesse, ni aux richesses, ni à la vertu." Monarchies could also be governed aristocratically. Bodin, *République*, 2:34.

4   *"Pour gouverner on Langage fardé"?*

Political Expression and the Decision-Making Process

Pierre Brunet, municipal secretary, began his register of deliberations in July 1542 with the following paen to piety and simplicity:

> Force or human prudence is worth little or nothing
> When artificial language is used in governing
>   [*pour gouverner on Langage fard(é)*].
> Asia, Greece, and valorous Rome,
> These empires no sooner adopted this way
> Than they fell. For, everything well considered,
> Far stronger is a powerful weakness,
> Speech short and true with sage simplicity,
> Which doubting itself, puts its faith in God.
> Such is the force, eloquence and wisdom
> Of the worthy men governing in this place.[1]

In avoiding the decadent language and moral decay of history's great but fallen empires, Brunet implied, Poitiers's corps de ville would ensure the successful administration of the city. Government did not depend on a fund of excessive or pretentious learning for its own sake but rested on the solid foundations of faith. Decision making was thus to be based in divine approbation, even inspiration. The municipal secretary's poetic invocation was itself a pretense. Politics and political language in Poitiers were anything but simple, and their complexities even ensured their success. The sometimes stylized representations of political argument, their recording in registers of deliberations, and the complicated processes of assignment of responsibility

---

[1] ACP Reg. 25, A (unnumbered first page).

reflected neither "decadence" nor dishonesty. They were rather the very means through which politics was conducted in the sixteenth-century urban world.

To explore the strategies and assumptions of decision making and the linguistic medium of the political process forms the goal of this chapter. The first section examines the town council registers as a source. In assessing what they say and do not say, it discusses the parameters of acceptable expression and argues that these limitations did not constitute impoverishment of language but formed the elaborated medium through which politics was conducted. In analyzing the registers' production, it presents recording as an integral part of the political process. The second section then turns to decision making. It examines the ways in which members expressed their opinions in council and the procedures for reaching decisions. It argues that although consensus was always desired, negotiation was continuous, and the process could break down at any time. Indeed, notions of majority decision and unanimity existed in constant tension, each providing a model for political decision, but each requiring a different conception of what this process was ultimately about. In order to grasp how the municipal government functioned as an institution, we must consider how members interacted, worked out solutions, implemented final decisions, and represented the process to themselves and others.[2]

Town Council Registers—the Medium

Brunet's decision to grace his register with an idealized representation of the character of political language testifies to the importance of the process of recording. And as the members of the municipality themselves did on occasion, we must turn to the registers of deliberations as a first step in understanding urban politics. Yet the registers speak a complicated language. Like any historical source, they were written for their own purposes and according to their own logic. They were not an "objective" account of what occurred either within the municipal government or within the town at large, but served as a record of the municipality's official point of view.[3] They are therefore just as much an argument as a report. Yet although one should never lose sight of the partial character or "bias" of the source, attempting

[2] My approach to political language has much in common with the interpretative methods set forth by Quentin Skinner and his commentators in Tully, ed., *Meaning and Context*. Skinner urges that one consider not only the argument of a text, but its ideological context as well as the impact it has in political terms, intended and unintended. Words, in this view, have a force through their very expression, both in terms of a contextually defined meaning and the speaker's intention to influence a situation.

[3] See the comments on this issue made by Jean-Pierre Andrault, "Une capitale de province à l'âge baroque: le corps de ville de Poitiers, 1594–1652," 3 vols. (Ph.D. diss., Université de Poitiers, 1988), 1:4.

to "look behind" what the registers are saying, to find out what was "really" happening, is inadequate. The recorded language of privilege and the minutiae of procedure were the terms in which municipal politics was conducted. The drawn-out processes of decision making were not so much evasion of responsibility as attempts at negotiation and creation of consensus. These attributes are therefore important in themselves as keys to the sixteenth-century political process. The registers certainly do not express all of the concerns and motivations behind municipal government, but they do provide us with a sense of what were the available and acceptable ways of presenting these concerns. The nature of the registers of deliberation and the process of recording hold important keys to the decision-making process, not only because the registers provide our only source for such considerations, but also because the act of recording was itself a part of that process.

The town council registers were subject to a range of interrelated definitions. First and foremost, they were records belonging to the hôtel de ville. Similar to the deliberations of church chapters, vestry groups, or confraternities that belonged to these institutions, but unlike notarial contracts and court records that belonged to the recorder, the registers were to be kept in the *trésor,* where they could be consulted as questions arose. Occasional attempts to collect all registers that had not been deposited in the town hall testify to the municipality's proprietorship over them.[4] At the same time, the registers were the product of the labors of the secretary, and during his term of office, this municipal official had sole responsibility for his own record. This unique responsibility often left the registers incomplete. Although the secretary was supposed to attend every meeting, he could not in practice be present at all of them, and often his absence meant that no record was taken of that day's proceedings.[5] At times, the secretary would delegate another individual to take the minutes in his absence, and this record would then be included within the register.[6]

The town council registers were not composed entirely in the heat of the moment but were the end product of a recording process. The secretary copied down the matters discussed and the decisions reached during the meetings of the town council and the Mois and later recopied these minutes into the final registers.[7] This process provided the opportunity for editing and embellishment, especially since the general practice seems to have been to save recopying until the end of the secretary's tenure, or at least until the

---

[4] ACP Reg. 35, 188, 196–206 (24 Jan. and 6 Feb. 1558).

[5] For example, a record exists for only seventeen of thirty-two known council meetings between 9 June 1578 and 23 February 1579. ACP Reg. 42, 808–10.

[6] ACP Reg. 36, 34–38.

[7] The registers of Michel Gillet, municipal secretary, make this process clear. Because he died before he could recopy several of them, his son was obliged to deliver to the municipality rough copies of the town council minutes, described as "grand quantite de papiers de plus[ieu]rs ann[ees] La plusp[ar]t diceulx sans ordre. . . ." ACP Reg. 35, 188. For an example of one of these uncopied registers, see Reg. 22.

end of the municipal year. In the register for 1589, for example, events occurring in September and October are noted integrally during the record for
August, revealing that this part of the register at least was not composed until several months later.[8] Certain registers cover relatively large periods of
time, and it is likely that they were copied all at once rather than gradually.[9]
The register for the 1594 municipal year even shows signs of having been recopied a decade later.[10]

The gap between the taking of the minutes and the final writing of the
register provided opportunities for alterations based on hindsight and revision, and the fortunate survival of both the collections of minutes and the
town council registers for 1538–39 and 1571–72 shows the changes that
could be made from one to the other. The identification of speakers has been
changed; topics of discussion are omitted or filled in; the explanatory text of
certain articles in the minutes appears in a fuller version in the register; whole
meetings disappear or are added; and it is common for opinions recorded in
the minutes not to appear in the register.[11] This reworking of the text shows
that the details of who said what and in what terms were important. It also
reveals that some of these decisions were not made in the heat of debate but
could be crafted later to reflect a successful point of view.

Once the register of deliberations was delivered to the hôtel de ville and
placed in the trésor with other municipal documents, it became a part of municipal law and precedent available as a reference for decision making. Faced
with a difficult decision, the members of the corps de ville often consulted
the town council registers to ascertain how similar situations had been handled. When the question of appointing a new mayor after the untimely death
of the incumbent came up in 1589, for example, the town council registers
were consulted to determine how the matter had been handled in the past.[12]
Similarly, on 12 December 1537, Mayor Antoine du Val presented a series
of extracts of police regulations concerning provisioning that he had made
from the town council registers, so that they could be written up, posted in
public, and submitted to Parlement for enhanced enforcement.[13] The registers of deliberations thus served as repositories not only for past decisions
but also for the body of municipal law.

The details of the recording process and the status of the town council

[8] ACP Reg. 49, 17–20 (18 Aug. 1589).
[9] ACP Reg. 32, for example, covers the period from 26 July 1551 until 24 February 1555,
and Reg. 42 spans from early May 1574 until 11 July 1580. The consistent handwriting of these
registers argues for their being copied at one time, rather than slowly over the years.
[10] Several times, in the articles at the beginning of the register and especially from 1 to 18
July 1594, the author mistakes the date and records "1604" instead of the proper year. See ACP
Reg. 54.
[11] These observations are based on a careful comparison of ACP Reg. 20 (recopied text) with
Reg. 21 (minutes) and of Reg. 39 (minutes) with Reg. 40 (recopied text).
[12] See Brilhac, 22, for this incident.
[13] ACP Reg. 20, 406–12.

registers as witnesses to past decisions played a part in encouraging the registers' most obvious characteristic: their representation of an official municipal policy and point of view. Their often detailed argumentation and frequent
silences therefore reveal much about the process and assumptions of government. First, the registers of deliberations served as an institutional, rather
than an urban, record. They thus generally detail only what transpired
within the hôtel de ville and make no attempt to provide an inclusive account
of events occurring in Poitiers. To be sure, the municipality had an important role to play in many of the crises of this century of imperial and civil
warfare and religious disturbance, but these events are reflected in the deliberations only to the extent that the corps de ville found it necessary to
reach a decision or to implement a policy relative to them. To take one example: in 1559 a significant religious riot broke out during the traditional
Easter Monday sermon at the Jacobins convent. What little we know of the
causes and form of the actual disturbance comes from other sources; the
town council registers mention only its repression.[14] Even situations that
must have had a distinct impact on urban decision making appear in the
town council registers only in a partial way. When Henri III visited Poitiers
in 1577, for example, the town council registers proudly record his entry and
the swearing of the mayoral oath directly in the hands of the king.[15] Otherwise, the registers only betray the presence of Henri III and his suite when
orders concerning the guard of the town were forthcoming. Not only do they
not mention the discussions that ultimately resulted in the Peace of Bergerac,
but they are also silent on Henri III's touching for the King's Evil at the cathedral St. Pierre at Assumption (15 August).[16] Similarly, the various sessions
of the Grands Jours of Poitiers—events important not only for their significant judicial decisions but also for the presence of the influential conseillers
and personnel of the Parlement of Paris in Poitiers—are mentioned in the
town council registers only to the extent that additional provisioning was required or that the municipality had submitted a legal suit for adjudication.[17]

If such silences are a product of the character of the town council registers as a municipal rather than an urban account, other choices concerning
what was recorded and what was omitted from the record are a result of the
hôtel de ville's desire to present a specific interpretation of events. The point
of view ultimately expressed, moreover, was not necessarily shared by every

[14] We owe an account of the riot to a letter written by François Aubert, lieutenant général,
to Henri II, dated 31 Mar. 1559. BNF MS Fr 15872, 69. The letter is also cited by Barbier,
"Chroniques de Poitiers," 3–5 n. 1. See ACP Reg. 36, 125–32 (28 Mar.–4 Apr. 1559) for the
response of the hôtel de ville.
[15] ACP Reg. 42, 647–51, 655–57.
[16] Brilhac, 13.
[17] See, for example, ACP Reg. 42, 840–42, 999–1012, for deliberations in preparation for
and during the Grands Jours of 1579, which met between 7 and 18 September. The only articles relevant to the Grands Jours during its time of actual seating concerned the care and feed-
ing of the judges' horses (11 and 14 Sept.).

member of the corps de ville, but in numerous cases indicated the victory of one representation of events over another. The secretary here played a key role in determining the manner in which events and arguments would be recorded. Partisan reporting is evident both in detailed representations of events and in significant silences. Unusually complete explanations for municipal decisions acted as a justification for them, designed to serve as a defense against possible challenge. When the town received royal letters requiring the loan of Poitiers's artillery in 1572, for example, Maixent Poitevin's opinion was recorded in full to justify a postponement of the decision. Poitevin's speech in the Mois lists all of the reasons that Charles IX could not possibly have intended to deprive the town of its principal means of defense, so that the loyalty of the hôtel de ville could not be called into question.[18] That Poitevin voiced the opinion was also important, since his activity in defending Poitiers from Protestant siege in 1569 had earned him the reputation of particular zeal in the defense of the town.

Although detailed accounts of events or the reasoning behind them served at times to protect the entire corps de ville from possible recriminations arising from their decisions, other narratives hint at factional pleading. The wealth of detail surrounding the attempts of Jean de la Haye, lieutenant général and leader of the *publicains* of Poitou during the fifth religious war (1574–76), to regain control of Poitiers provides one particularly telling example. Not only does the register of deliberations record Poitevin's identification of la Haye as a seditious individual, whose presence in the town would cause an uproar,[19] but the secretary also included numerous references to the lieutenant général's previous attempts to enter the city by stealth. In an article concerning payments for repairs to the Tison mill, the secretary recounted at length la Haye's use of it for the assault of the town. He also copied the whole of the clergy's procuration for an urban deputation to the king to present the case against la Haye, and he even composed a detailed description of a general procession that the hôtel de ville instituted to celebrate the failure of their opponent to gain entry within Poitiers's walls.[20] Such unusual expressions of animosity and lengthy descriptions point to the special concern of the municipal government to record its position against the lieutenant général. Yet the very intensity of the report suggests that the point of view to appear in the town council registers was not unanimous. Certainly, the municipal secretary sympathized with those within the corps de ville who had taken a position against this extremely powerful individual. But the very urgency expressed within the registers that la Haye not be allowed to reenter Poitiers testifies to the fact that he could still boast a group of supporters within the city. In this case, therefore, the registers of deliberations expressed

[18] ACP Reg. 40, 203.
[19] ACP Reg. 42, 73–74 (18 Oct. 1574).
[20] ACP Reg. 42, 61–62 (21 Sept. 1574); 183–84 (26 Apr. 1575); 199–204 (30 May 1575).

a viewpoint that was "partisan," not only because it involved special municipal pleading, but also because it was particular to a certain group within that body.

Although certain silences in the record hide internal division over specific issues, others are not so easy to explain. One of these is the overwhelming absence of any reference to Protestantism or to religious strife in the town council registers throughout the century, or at least until the period of the League. Unlike the registers of Dijon or Marseille, those of Poitiers discuss the presence of Huguenots and the execution of royal and municipal policies relative to them only cryptically.[21] Such a silence is difficult to interpret: the presence of both Catholics and Protestants within the hôtel de ville may account for the situation until the mid-1570s, but the dominance of staunch Catholics after this time makes unlikely any theories of calculated religious compromise. Indeed, the general policy of silence was at work as late as 1587, when an article concerning a tax to be levied on Protestants was subsequently altered to omit any overt religious considerations.[22] In this case, the Mois did not revise its decision relative to the Protestants but at some later date deemed making specific reference to them inappropriate. Such a consistent silence points to a general and conscious policy of averting any mention of religious difference. A full understanding of events therefore requires reintegration of religious factors back into the registers' account. At the same time, the reticence to record aspects of religious difference may provide an important tool for surveying contemporary conceptions of an acceptable language for politics.

Partial and partisan recording, therefore, does not mean that it was all just rhetoric. Indirect means of expression and the complications of a minutely orchestrated procedure were rather the medium in which and through which individuals conducted municipal politics. Legalism, attention to privilege, and a carefully regulated relationship between different institutions were all elements of a sixteenth-century style, which was not limited to the urban sphere. They were also elements in the processes of negotiation and consensus-building, and they were understood as such both by members of the municipality and by individuals who, because of their office, had busi-

[21] Holt notes that references to Protestants filled Dijon's town council registers throughout the 1550s and explains that the Dijon mairie had jurisdiction over religious matters because of its authority in civil, criminal, and police concerns. "Wine, Community and Reformation," 61, 65–66. The privileges of Poitiers's hôtel de ville were just as developed in this respect. For Marseille, see Kaiser, *Marseille*.

[22] The text is as follows, with words in italics representing crossed-out sections and underlined portions indicating their replacements: "[The mayor represented that the sieur de Boisseguin and the judicial officials] Avoient trouve bon qu'on *fist une tax Sur* mectast en amande ceulx qui *ont este* cy davent *de la pretendue Relligion pour navoyr encores este* navoient este en personne ou envoye aux gardes avecq Les catholicques [an oversight!] de lad ville nestant Raisonnable *Que Lesd pretendus* Quilz fussent a Leurs ayses en Leurs maisons Et que *Lesd catholicques* Les aultres employassent Leurs vies et biens et moyens pour Leur conservation. . . ." ACP Reg. 47, 126 (19 Sept. 1587).

ness with it. Just as the law had a rhetorical style developed from a combination of classical learning and court procedure,[23] municipal government had its own practices and modes of expression arising from a nexus of education and institutional structure.

Procedure and privilege allowed the hôtel de ville to navigate the difficult process of internal decision making and to negotiate the terms of its compliance with external demands. The relationship of counsel and confirmation between the twenty-five and the seventy-five permitted a multifarious approach. On the surface, neither body was willing to take the responsibility to reach a conclusion. On another level, though, the perpetual considering and reconsidering of the same issues allowed the formation of a consensus strong enough to ensure that the decision was actually carried out. The language in which the municipality chose to address royal officials also relied on the niceties of procedure to negotiate a compromise or to blunt the edge of confrontation. When the royal officials who had been commissioned to put order to the goldsmiths appeared in the Mois in 1556, for example, the corps de ville promised to lend the officials "every required favor, counsel, and support," but then went on to explain that the municipality's right of police gave the corps sole control over the sworn crafts, and that the present number of goldsmiths exactly fitted Poitiers's needs.[24] Outright expressions of disobedience were clearly impossible where the king's authority was concerned, but the hôtel de ville made its position clear nevertheless.

The events surrounding the Protestant takeover of the château in 1562 provide a particularly telling example of politics proceeding through legalism and of religious considerations receiving no overt expression. Faced with the necessity to protect royal tax receipts in May 1562 and worried about the Protestant sympathies of key financial officials in Poitiers, the municipality approached suspected Protestant François Pineau, *receveur général*, about the funds. The financial official reacted defensively, hoping that the council "did not wish to interfere with his office" (*entreprendere sur son estat*).[25] Only two days later, however, the receveur approached the lieutenant général, asking that he be allowed to guard the funds in the château. When the council was summoned to deliberate on the matter, it ruled that because the château was under the authority of the sénéchal, it could not possibly be turned over without his consent and suggested that Pineau apply to him or his deputy for permission to store the funds there. Since the lieutenant général by definition acted for the sénéchal and was an échevin, such advice

---

[23] See Ian Maclean, *Interpretation and Meaning in the Renaissance: The Case of Law* (Cambridge, U.K., 1992), and Fumaroli, *Âge de l'éloquence*.

[24] ACP Reg. 34, 27–37 (17 Sept. 1556); quotation, 30.

[25] The events described in this paragraph, occurring between 4 and 12 May 1562, are recorded in ACP Reg. 38, 139–84. For a published version, see Barbier, "Chroniques de Poitiers." The town council records for the period of 14 April to 16 June 1562 form *pièce justificative* no. 26, 161–218. For the quotation, see Barbier, 164.

could be interpreted as an outright refusal. Meanwhile, the receveur offered his own opposition to the hôtel de ville by demanding that the town pay its back taxes. When the council sent a delegation to the *général des finances,* the receveur's superior and fellow religious sympathizer, in order to explain that it was seeking remission for the sum, the général des finances informed the group that he had a matter to communicate and asked the mayor to convene the Mois. The mayor refused, holding that a Mois could not be assembled without the deliberation of the council and especially if the subject to be discussed was unknown. Over the next two days, the mayor would visit the général two more times and the council would assemble twice before a written order from the général finally forced the assembling of the Mois. When the général finally appeared in the hôtel de ville, it was to announce that he had installed the receveur in the château. He presented a written account of his actions to preserve the royal funds, protested any suspicions against his loyalty, and submitted a list of supplies to be delivered to Pineau. Because the général des finances and the receveur général were both Protestant sympathizers, the château was now in Protestant hands.

Throughout this complicated series of events, the hôtel de ville used legalism to approach a difficult situation. Although control of Poitiers's château was the matter at stake, the argument proceeded on the level of municipal jurisdiction and procedure. The cooperation of the mayor, the council, and the lieutenant général at first allowed the municipal administration to evade the financial officials' demands for the keys to the fortress, and once the receveur had actually ensconced himself there, debates over proper procedure in calling a Mois permitted the corps de ville to delay recognizing the fait accompli. These discussions may even have offered the possibility for compromise—ultimately not realized—between the municipality and the général des finances. The deliberations of the council and the discussions conducted outside of it did not occur on a plane hopelessly removed from the hard facts of religious divergence and military control. Instead, debate and action were intertwined at each step, even if the problem at hand was never overtly mentioned.

This discussion of important matters in a language seemingly unrelated to them was a general characteristic of sixteenth-century municipal politics. Concerns influencing decision making were various and could include ideological differences, the interests of family alliance, confessional considerations, professional rivalries, or personal animus. Certain of these aspects clearly factored into discussions carried on within the council and the Mois, as we may deduce from their very occasional mention in the town council registers. Arguments based on private interest, for example, appear extremely rarely in the record, but occasional denials of self-interested motivations show that such accusations did take place.[26] Complaints against

---

[26] For example, ACP Reg. 30, 161 (3 Jan. 1549).

personal animus do riddle the written statements that members of the corps de ville presented in opposition to specific municipal decisions, reflecting a vituperative climate of debate.[27] Yet when it came either to confronting a municipal official or to recording the matter in the town council registers, a translation or a flattening of language occurred. The potentially numerous means of expression were funneled, either consciously or not, into an acceptable form of reasoning or presentation, which became for all intents and purposes the political medium. The language of private interest may have been a standard element in municipal argumentation, but it was not generally appropriate to the town council registers.

If certain kinds of language and criteria for decisions were acceptable while others were not, the question then becomes, why? This is not to say that we should lose sight of the unstated or restated factors influencing decisions, only that the very language of legalism and the noted silences provide a means of access to the intellectual assumptions under which the municipality was operating. We have already noted that the town council registers studiously avoided any reference to the religious differences that influenced life in Poitiers from the 1530s until the end of the sixteenth century and beyond. Similarly, considerations of socio-professional background were rarely expressed in such terms. Viewed from this perspective, one of the most threatening aspects of the merchants' bid to obtain access to the hôtel de ville in the 1540s (an episode that is studied in detail in chapter 6) may have been the overt introduction of social considerations into electoral procedure. To decide why the municipality consistently rendered such elements of sixteenth-century life into other terms is therefore necessarily to explore contemporary assumptions concerning the purposes and means of government. Representations of the ideal functioning of municipal government and the roles of the members composing it influenced the choices of language in which that process was both carried out and expressed. In order, therefore, to enter the hazy world of urban political idea, we must now turn to a more detailed analysis of the decision-making process.

Giving an Opinion

Let us imagine a meeting of the town council or the Mois. We enter the échevinage from the rue de l'Aguilerie, the street leading from the Marché Vieux past the church of St. Porchaire to the intersection of the ways to the Cordeliers and to the judicial palais. The hôtel de ville has been located on this spot since 1260 and was rebuilt in 1439; the buildings of the university were

---

[27] See for example René Audebert's written request that his election to the seventy-five be confirmed, despite "certaine non Recepvable ne vallable oppo[siti]on faictes [par] maistres Guill[aum]e Rougier pierre et Jehan Ratz [blank] fume et Jehan charrier ses hayneulx et malveillants. . . ." ACP Reg. 25, 115 (28 Nov. 1542).

added between 1445 and 1466.[28] The central chamber of the échevinage is a large one located on the ground floor.[29] There is a special chair for the mayor, flanked on both right and left by the places of the échevins. Below these twenty-five seats are the places for the bourgeois.[30] In the middle is the *bureau,* the table on which all documentation under consideration is placed during meetings. It may be that the members crowd about two sides of the central table as at Lyon.[31] Perhaps the échevins and bourgeois face each other in a rectangular format similar to that in which the king, his highest officials, and the deputies were arranged during the Estates General at Orléans.[32] Each member of the corps de ville has his assigned place dictated by seniority. Although certain exceptions are made for the highest judicial officials and in certain periods for the trésoriers généraux, the general rule is that members sit in the order in which they are called in the roll.

Monsieur the mayor generally opens the meeting by presenting the matters for discussion. If the issues to be treated are complicated, he may have written out his presentation ahead of time, as Jean de Brilhac did for a Mois in September 1537.[33] But the mayor is not the only one to introduce matters for the consideration of those present. Échevins, or more rarely bourgeois, also bring up topics of concern, either through general interest, in their guise as municipal deputies, or because an inhabitant has asked them to raise the issue. Although councils are ideally supposed to be secret, inhabitants do not have to rely on the mediation of an échevin to have the municipality consider their concerns.[34] Groups of inhabitants in various corporate guises appear in council periodically, in order to ask that the municipality rule on

[28] Favreau, *Ville de Poitiers,* 69, 380–81; Philippe Rondeau, "L'ancien hôtel de ville de Poitiers," *MSAO,* 1st ser., 34 (1869): 132–36.

[29] Rondeau, "Ancien hôtel de ville," 139.

[30] The mayoral installation of 1587 mentions "La chaire majoralle" and the "haulx sieges" of the échevins. ACP Reg. 46, 402. That the bourgeois sat below the échevins is made clear by the description of the members of the corps de ville as "tant du hault q[ue] du bas." Reg. 23, 110 (22 Dec. 1540). The seating of the twenty-five to the right or left of the mayor is indicated by the description of Jean Claveurier in 1512 as "Installe a la dextre de mons[ieu]r Le maire" and of Jacques Regnault in 1537 as taking his place of échevin to the left. Reg. 11, 245 (22 June 1512); Reg. 20, 389 (12 Nov. 1537).

[31] See the extract of the *Livre du Grabellage de Lyon* showing a meeting of the *Consulat* in 1519, reproduced in André Latreille, ed., *Histoire de Lyon et du Lyonnais* (Toulouse, 1975), fig. 11.

[32] For a description of their seating, see *La description dv plant dv theatre faict à Orléans, pour l'assemblée des troiz estats, auec vn brief discours de la seance des tenans & representans lesdictz estatz* (Paris, 1560). The same description is included in Charlemagne Lalourcé, ed., *Recueil de pièces originales et authentiques, concernant la tenue des États-Généraux d'Orléans en 1560, sous Charles IX, de Blois en 1576, 1588 sous Henri III, de Paris en 1614, sous Louis XIII,* 9 vols. (Paris, 1789), 1:29–31.

[33] See ADV SAHP 51, Papier journal de Jean de Brilhac, 1535–1538, IIr–IVv (reverse pagination). The first article in particular is written out at length, complete with legal argumentation and citations.

[34] The emphasis on secrecy would become much stronger with the religious wars, but deliberations of 1533 already cite this principle to justify a decision concerning the functioning of the mayoral court. ACP Reg. 19, 277–85.

some issue concerning them. Royal officials with a direct commission from the king may also impart their concerns directly to an assembled gathering of the Mois. They then retire from the company so that the matter may be discussed.

Once the matters for discussion have been raised, the company gives its opinion on what needs to be done.[35] General discussion might sometimes occur beforehand.[36] The rules of municipal seniority generally determine the order of opining, and members tenaciously uphold their right to voice their opinions in their proper turns. This concern to speak within established order reflects more than a preoccupation with ceremonial precedence and honor, although these are certainly important matters. Rather, members of the municipality recognize that the order of giving opinions has important implications for the decision-making process.

Disputes over precedence within the corps de ville go far to illustrate the distinction between honorary and practical acknowledgments of hierarchy and seniority. They also reveal the importance assigned to the order of speech within the municipality as influencing the decisions that body ultimately reached. Although most members of the Cent were willing to grant important judicial and financial officials an honorary place close to the mayor irrespective of their order of induction, they also specified that such exceptions to the rules of municipal seniority did not extend to the opining process. It was one thing to acknowledge that the estates of some of the members conferred an authority and honor important to recognize even in the council chamber. It was another thing, though, to tamper with the functioning of municipal government, in which the order of speech played a crucial part.

The order in which the members of the corps de ville gave their opinions interacted with other concerns leading them to argue one point of view over another. The first individuals to give their opinions normally set the terms of the debate. Occasionally the senior échevin expressed his opinion on each matter under consideration, after which each member present contented himself with expressing agreement. Yet such endorsements were certainly not always the case. In giving his opinion—even an affirmative one—the

[35] Although the general format of the town council registers, in which matters are recorded one by one with the conclusions immediately following each article, might lead to the assumption that matters were raised one at a time, other factors indicate that all issues to be discussed were introduced at the same time. Secretaries such as Jean Bouchet often began their tenure in office by recording all articles of discussion and then listing all of the decisions together before adopting the more usual method of recording proposition and conclusion together. See ACP Reg. 19. When Jean Gaillaudon kept the minutes for Michel Gillet in the Mois of 12 Oct. 1540, he also listed every article to be discussed followed by a separate group of decisions. Reg. 23, 61–68. In the registers that record specific opinions, moreover, the members comment on every matter for discussion at the same time. See Regs. 20 and 32 for examples of registers in which opinions were frequently recorded.

[36] The reporting style of municipal secretary Pierre Clabat gives the impression that échevins raised matters concurrently with the mayor and that general discussion occurred before the opining process began. ACP Reg. 31 (1549–51).

person who had the floor was faced with several options. He could either agree with the person who had first expressed a particular opinion, citing him by name; he could concur with the individual who went immediately before him; he could restate the conclusions of others in his own words; he could add his approval to the most eloquent expression of a particular point of view; or he could announce that he agreed with the general consensus of the "*precedens.*" Each method of expressing his opinion had slightly different implications. Naming the individual with whom he agreed may have served to identify his preferred version of a general opinion, but it could also have been interpreted as a sign of deference or alliance. On the other hand, restating a general opinion in his own words may have had implications for his image of self-importance; alternatively, the echoing and reechoing of the same opinion may have reinforced the notion of unity among the members. Expressing agreement with the "precedens" may have had the same effect.

Over time, certain individuals stand out as having frequently obtained the agreement of the rest of the Cent. François Doyneau, lieutenant général and for a long period senior échevin, was certainly within this category, as were Jasmes de Lauzon, avocat du roi, Philippe Lucas, conseiller at the sénéchausée, and Pierre Rat, also conseiller. All four men could claim a deference and respect naturally due to their office. Doyneau and Rat were also from established Poitevin families that had played key roles in the intense factional disputes of the turn of the century, and they may have continued to represent the interests of opposing groups decades later. Yet their perspicacity and eloquence also prompted their colleagues to lend them special approval. De Lauzon had a propensity to express his views in highly theoretical terms that may have done much to elicit the approbation of his peers. Doyneau was generally acknowledged to be an effective and influential figure outside the community circumscribed by the town walls. When the council was attempting to assign deputies to go to court to plead for a reduction in royal taxes in 1548, for example, Guillaume Rogier expressed the opinion that if they could only persuade Doyneau to go, "he would do more in eight days than anyone else in a month."[37] Rat, likewise, had the reputation of informed and persuasive argument. Not only had he published a commentary on the customary law of Poitou,[38] but while in Poitiers Emperor Charles V had shown him favor by converting the Rat family arms from three rodents to a unicorn.[39] When it came to choosing a deputy to go to court to seek reduction of the royal subsidy in 1539, Jean Rogier therefore commented that "in his conscience, he knew no man who could do a better

---

[37] ACP Reg. 30, 134 (27 Nov. 1548).
[38] See his *Petri Rat Pictauiensis decurionis, in patrias Pictonum leges, quas vulgus consuetudines dicit, glossemata* (Poitiers, 1548).
[39] Dez, *Histoire de Poitiers*, 74 n. 143.

job than the mayor," and if Rat did not go, then they should send another member of the municipality who was an "homme de Replicque."[40]

Clearly, numerous reasons determined both a member's opinion on a given issue and how he chose to express it. The promptings of family alliance and professional allegiance were rife in this exclusive political body, but considerations of self-image, rhetorical style, and ideology also had their role. Yet in a system in which each person generally spoke only once in one round of opining, one thing was clear: if an individual did not have the opportunity to express his opinion early in the process, he had less hope of swaying the others to his point of view. Hence the importance of seniority. Seating order confirmed a hierarchy already established on the basis of royal office or municipal service; speaking order affected the ability of members directly to influence municipal policy and to heighten their prestige thereby.

Making a Decision

The opining process completed, a decision then had to be made. Having (officially) withheld his point of view during the discussion, the mayor now concluded based on the counsel he had just received. Yet just as numerous considerations had influenced individual opinion, the decision-making process was also a complicated one. In light of corporate procedure extending back to Roman law, municipal conclusions could rest on simple majority vote. Behind this practice lay the notion that a part of the group, and presumably the wisest part, could decide for the whole. Yet majority vote also necessarily involved difference of opinion, a reality of political life that the corps de ville was sometimes loath to recognize. Existing in opposition to such strictures were the traditions of unanimity and consensus, owing their intellectual origins to the communal movement and still very much alive, at least in the realm of ideology. No one would deny that the municipal government was a corporate body in the sixteenth century, but an underlying question was, should the emphasis be placed on its status as a corporation, or its existence as a unified organism? Individual conclusions, however arrived at, were also not necessarily conclusive. In fact, many decisions turned out to be unworkable and either had to be reconsidered or simply became dead letters. Decisions that had not been based on sound consensus were open to further negotiation, and the same processes that in other cases worked to arrive at acceptable conclusions were reenlisted to adapt policies so that they could be carried out. The process worked to collapse the dichotomy between majority vote and unanimous decision: major-

---

[40] ACP Reg. 22, 218 (16 Dec. 1539). An "homme de Replicque" was a man who tended to respond in a lively, humorous way.

ity decisions worked only if they were generally accepted, either by the whole of the corps de ville or by the leaders of its dominant groups.

The mayor frequently concluded according to majority opinion, even in cases in which significant disagreement occurred or in which, because of poor attendance, the "majority" constituted only a small portion of the Cent. In 1512, for example, the Mois concluded to uphold a decision of the échevins relative to the university, despite the active opposition of thirteen of forty-five bourgeois present.[41] In the sparsely attended Mois of 4 June 1549, the mayor concluded for the majority of four, when the three others suggested further study or insisted that there was an insufficient quorum to warrant deliberation.[42] The vote was even closer in a Mois of 1576, when the mayor broke a tie.[43] Even extremely large undertakings, involving considerable outlays in time and money and having profound implications for the duties of the municipality, could be pushed through by a majority in the face of significant opposition. The navigation project of 1537–42 discussed in chapter 5 is a prime example of an endeavor pursued in spite of significant dissent. Not all decisions, however, were reached in conformity with majority opinion. In 1549, for example, the mayor concluded that the mayoral election would be postponed for a week, even though only ten of twenty-four members counseled the delay.[44] Although the opinion of the majority normally determined the municipality's course of action, the mayor clearly could exercise some discretion in his conclusions. Indeed, nothing in his mayoral oath specifically obliged him to follow the counsel of the other members of the Cent.

Conclusions either in favor of majority opinion or in spite of it necessarily involved the recognition of dissent within the corps de ville. Despite desires for unity, members were forced to concede that disagreement and conflict were inevitable parts or consequences of the decision-making process. Indeed, the electoral process was nothing if not an institutionalization of the workings of disagreement. Elections were the only occasions when the municipality followed the rules of majority opinion to the letter and when the secretary would routinely (but not always) record the components of the vote in the register. The corps de ville adhered so tenaciously to the details of electoral procedure precisely because it assumed that expectations would be divided: the only way to channel discordant aspirations based on competing personal interests and to prevent overt expressions of conflict was to establish a set of rules that would define fairness.[45]

[41] ACP Reg. 11, 413–19 (25 Nov. 1512).

[42] ACP Reg. 30, 242–43.

[43] It is interesting that in this case the register specifically notes the division of opinion and the mayor's conclusion based on it: "Surquoy Apres q[ue] Led[i]t S[ieu]r maire a veu q[ue] le moys estoyt en pluralite de voix qui est q[ui]lz sont sept dun coste et vii de Lautre a conclud. . ." ACP Reg. 42, 438–44 (10 Mar. 1576); quotation 442–43.

[44] ACP Reg. 30, 247–51 (25 June 1549).

[45] See my "Benefit of the Ballot?" for a full discussion of this issue.

Disagreement among members could also entail the breakdown of the municipal decision-making process. Although the language of personal conflict was not usually an acceptable means of recording dispute, tensions still existed. Friction between members could result in the informal bypassing of municipal responsibility. In 1539, for example, tensions between Mayor Pierre Rat and Lieutenant General François Doyneau concerning the details of the entry of Emperor Charles V led the hôtel de ville to seek resolution of the problem through outside authority. In this case, the members of the municipal government resorted to the advice of the governor and the constable of France to resolve the difficulties created by the contrasting opinions of two powerful men.[46] Yet the prevalence of disagreement also required a means for individual members formally to record their opposition to specific measures and for the municipal administration to act in spite of such disapproval. When compromise was impossible, individuals could formally oppose a decision taken by the rest of the company, and they would be given an "act," or written acknowledgment, of their opposition. These actions, however, did not solve the problem but rather constituted an admission that it was irresolvable within the cadre of the hôtel de ville. By lodging opposition and obtaining a written recognition of it, disgruntled members were providing themselves with the necessary documentation to begin a legal suit against the corps de ville. These actions were thus the first step in a resort to a higher authority to adjudicate on a disagreement arising within the municipal context.[47] Any execution of an opposed decision was therefore provisional, to be carried out pending the judgment of a higher authority.

Such legal proceedings on the part of members of the corps de ville against the municipality were in fact relatively common. They were both the ultimate outcome of disagreements over policy and an extreme response to interpersonal conflicts played out within the realm of the hôtel de ville. The inventory of 1506, for example, contains a French translation of the final parlementary decision of a case that Nicolas and Jean Claveurier lodged against Pierre Prevost, Michel Mourault, and Jean Favereau. Disputed election procedure and the complaint that the defendants had caused the nineteen-year-old son of Favereau to be elected mayor formed the specific terms of the case, but the rivalry of the two groups extended far beyond municipal concerns to include the functioning of the sénéchaussée and even the prerogatives of the chapter of Notre-Dame-la-Grande.[48] Members of the corps

---

[46] See especially the deliberations of the Mois of 7 Dec. 1539. ACP Reg. 22, 198–203.

[47] Olivier-Martin remarks on the frequency with which corporate groups lodged oppositions against royal letters patent or judicial edicts, any body having the right to oppose a judicial decision to which it had not been a party. The act required that the court make a decision, either to overrule or to sustain the objection, but in either case to record it. *Organisation corporative,* 498–99.

[48] ACP Casier 42, Reg. 13, 28–30. Favreau provides a short analysis of the decision in *Ville de Poitiers,* 498–99, and discusses the early-sixteenth-century race for offices, 491–93. The legal proceedings over the judicial jurisdiction traditionally exercised by the chapter of Notre-

de ville also opposed general policy decisions and frequently contested the necessity to pay taxes.[49] They could also become embroiled over the execution of charges to which they had been deputed. François Roatin, for example, was engaged in endless legal proceedings against the hôtel de ville concerning his administration of a royal grant of 40,000 livres, designed to pay the debts of the town incurred during the siege of Poitiers in 1569.[50] Whether differences of opinion could be resolved by a reference to the "greater and wiser part" or whether they plagued municipal procedure through hostility, opposition, or legal resort, the corps de ville had to deal with them as an inevitable part of the governing process.

However prevalent disagreement, unanimity was always preferred. In times of difficulty, unanimity became essential, both as a standard to reassure members and as a means to protect the polity against threats to its integrity. Thus when danger threatened in the form of warfare or religious division, the corps de ville temporarily suspended its carefully worked out electoral procedures and directed its efforts toward electing a mayor, unanimously and aloud, who would inspire the confidence of the entire group. In 1512, for example, as fears of the translation of the Italian wars onto French soil loomed, Jean Favereau advised "that in the present Mois, nothing should be put to deliberation except only that each should ponder and deliberate according to his conscience to elect a mayor aloud and not by ballot, so that all could commonly recognize [*Affin que lon congnoisset notoirement*] the most useful and necessary individual for the good and profit of the town." The échevin went on to propose the election of Nicolas Claveurier, his former rival, who was unanimously elected.[51] Still, if unity could be employed as a special strategy, the concept retained an existence apart from any functional considerations. Unity was a good in itself; it was the ultimate end of the political process. And just as one strove to attain it within the larger community through police measures and the rule of law, many municipal decision-making procedures had as their avowed or implicit end the construction of unanimous opinion within that body. In an environment where dissension was so common, the creation of consensus could be a difficult business. And many of the painstaking strategies enlisted in the effort borrowed from the language of legalism and attention to minute procedural detail that was an essential characteristic of the municipal political process.

Distribution of responsibility formed a fundamental approach to municipal decision making. Especially if the matter involved examining documen-

---

Dame-la-Grande during the three days of Rogations dated from 1507 and opposed François Doyneau and Jean Claveurier, sénéchal of Notre-Dame, against Pierre Prevost, lieutenant général, and Jean Favereau, procureur du roi. See ADV G1097.

[49] See, for example, ACP Reg. 23, 155–61, 173–74 (10 Feb. 1541); Reg. 29, 153–55 (25 June 1548).

[50] See ACP Casier 22, H41; Reg. 46, 379–86 (6 July 1587).

[51] ACP Reg. 11, 253.

tation and rendering a legal judgment, its resolution was never dependent on the advice of one man. Although through much of the century the corps de ville assigned deputies responsibility to review its legal transactions and selected individuals to oversee especially complicated matters within its jurisdiction, the deputies' assessments met with routine review by other council members. Often, in reporting their opinion on a legal matter, échevins requested that others examine the case. Nicolas Le Roy's opinion that the suit pending against the abbey of Ste. Croix was doubtful of success but that others should study the documentation was typical.[52] So was the process through which the statutes of police drawn up by Maixent Poitevin were accepted. After the mayor had read the statutes in the Mois, that company ruled that the échevins should deliberate on them. The Monday Council did not then accept them but deputed two of their number to examine them closely. Only after their report, and a final reading of the articles in council one week later, did the statutes finally receive approval.[53]

If affairs that did not elicit noticeable disagreement could meet with multiple considerations and the inclusion of as many members as possible in the decision-making process, difference of opinion only accentuated this tendency. When the council could not agree over a matter proposed for discussion, the decision was often delayed. If the prospects for accord were particularly poor, the preferred approach was to ignore the issue until compromise seemed more attainable. Poitiers's governmental structure abetted such a procedure. A system based on life tenure in office and a two-part division in membership offered the potential for tensions and jealousies to develop,[54] but the interaction of two decision-making bodies could give to each a leeway that a unicameral system would lack. The relationship in which the council was generally to guide and to negotiate complicated matters and the Mois to make all important decisions allowed each group to resort to the other when it encountered difficulties in reaching a satisfactory conclusion. Matters in which decision was particularly difficult could be passed back and forth repeatedly between the two bodies, in the hope that either the more detailed analysis of the council or the more summary conclusions of the Mois would allow the consensus of opinion necessary for their resolution.

Agreement within the hôtel de ville, however, did not assure the execution of an administrative policy. The boundaries between municipal decision making and public acceptance of those conclusions were permeable. Members of the municipal government may have formed part of a special corpo-

---

[52] ACP Reg. 20, 132–35 (6 Nov. 1536).

[53] ACP Casier 10, D53.

[54] Although disputes often arose between individual members of the corps de ville, recorded occasions of friction between the town council and the Mois were rare. Jarousseau relates the most pronounced example of such tensions, occurring in 1515, in which a spokesman for the bourgeois accused the échevins of selfishness, of not informing the Mois of their decisions, and of engaging in activities that were not noble. "Élection du maire," 572–73.

rate group, but they also lived within the urban community and could both exert influence on, and be influenced by, public opinion. As a result, decisions that had prompted significant dissension within the corps de ville often met with resistance within the city at large. Inhabitants' resistance to paying their share of a subsidy to be used in affording Poitiers a navigable river, discussed in the next chapter, provides a particularly good example of this problem.

The political process, then, acted as a prism through which the opposed phenomena of disagreement and unity were refracted to form a viable approach to decision making and administration. Although majority vote and unanimity were both recognized means of determining group action, they were nevertheless based on very different assumptions. Decision making based on majority opinion derived its authority from Roman law, and civil lawyers could cite discrete portions of the *Digest* to support their general acceptance of this approach.[55] Unanimity, on the other hand, owed its intellectual origins to the Catholic Church, first as a necessary condition for decision making and later as an ideal for all group action.[56] The two approaches implied very different assumptions about individuals, their interactions, and the nature of the group. To rule that a conclusion be reached according to majority opinion implied an acceptance of disagreement; such an approach assumed that members were individuals with their own concerns and ways of approaching issues that could not be completely reconciled. This was not to say, however, that all possibilities for collective spirit or action were doomed to failure. Majority vote was, after all, the preferred method of proceeding in corporate groups, and if members expected to be able to voice dissenting opinions, they also consented that the determination of others guide the body when they found themselves in the minority. Majority decision making therefore had as profound resonances for theories of representation as it did for allowances for individual opinion.[57]

An emphasis on unanimity, on the other hand, went much further toward the definition of a collective spirit. The assumption that belonging to a group would lead its members to arrive at a consensual decision invested the collectivity with a moral force that went far beyond the notion of corporate per-

---

[55] Michaud-Quantin, *Universitas*, 273–74.

[56] Michaud-Quantin, *Universitas*, 276.

[57] Michaud-Quantin discusses this issue in terms of the seeming contradiction between majority decision making and the equally frequent maxim concerning representation within the collectivity of *Quod omnes tangit*. Although the two concepts were held to be contradictory until the beginning of the thirteenth century, by the end of the century canonists were holding that since the majority could legitimately act for the whole, a decision reached by over half, but not all, of the members of a collectivity still retained the status of having been approved by everyone (283–84). Brian Tierney similarly points out that by the thirteenth century, canon lawyers had reinterpreted the phrase to mean that what was required was the approval of a corporation as a whole, not that of each individual within the group. *Religion, Law, and the Growth of Constitutional Thought 1150–1650* (Cambridge, U.K., 1982), 24–25.

sonality. Although this point of view had been prevalent in the high Middle Ages to describe the associative spirit behind ecclesiastical collective groups, it was easily transferred as an ideal motivating secular collectivities. Communes may have been formed in various political circumstances with the general goal of establishing a customary law for their members,[58] but the swearing of an oath provided fertile soil for the ideal of unity to flourish.[59] Henceforth subject to the same law, or peace, and responsible for its enforcement, commune members could extend such ties into the realm of decision making and resort to the idea of unity to explain the relationship between them that was ideally to hold in that sphere. Elaborate theories of representation would not be necessary, since everyone would be in accord over the proper course of action.

Over time, the two different models of decision making, finding their sources in disparate traditions and embedded in varying understandings of collective identification, flowed into a single body of explanation of political life. The Catholic Church had early offered a bridge between the two ethics. In defining majority vote in terms of the *maior et sanior pars* instead of in simple numerical terms, it had introduced qualitative considerations into the procedure.[60] It had in effect provided an ideological space for complicated political concerns to play themselves out without the accusation of corruption or unacceptable dissent. The will of God could therefore be expressed in an opinion that was not unanimous.

Although the town council registers do occasionally make reference to decisions made by *la plus grande et saine partie,* the confluence of the ethics of majority and unanimous opinion generally proceeded otherwise: in the end

[58] Although the idea that communes were formed in eleventh- and twelfth-century Europe with the specific purpose of putting an end to arbitrary exactions and thus of defining the regulations and privileges under which their members were henceforward to live is common to all recent literature on the subject, Vermeesch, in his *Essai sur les origines,* is certainly the most adamant exponent of this point of view. Communes, for Vermeesch, were peace associations, where the notion of peace did not involve an idealized tranquility, but a code of rights and duties regulating the relationships between individuals and between the group and the seigneur. Michaud-Quantin supports this idea in making reference to the "liberties" sought by collective groups. See especially 268, where he explains that "Être libre, c'est pouvoir discuter les limites de sa soumission, posséder un *status* défini précisant les droits et devoirs." Jacques Le Goff follows Michaud-Quantin's presentation of the issue in the section "L'apogée de la France urbaine médiévale, 1150–1330," in Georges Duby, ed., *Histoire de la France urbaine,* 5 vols. (Paris, 1980–85), 2:264–75.

[59] Charles Petit-Dutaillis was the first exponent of the view that the mutual oath distinguished the commune from other organizations with equivalent privileges. Since his work, historians have all pointed to the importance of the mutual oath, without making it the sole determinant of commune status. Vermeesch considers the oath as an innovatory method of enforcement of the peace of the commune; Michaud-Quantin identifies it as a characteristic element of corporate bodies formed in the twelfth and thirteenth centuries and points to its special affective character as a horizontal rather than a vertical tie. Petit-Dutaillis, *Les communes françaises: caractères et évolution des origines au XVIIIe siècle* (Paris, 1947); Vermeesch, *Essai sur les origines,* 165–66; Michaud-Quantin, *Universitas,* part 2, chap. 3, esp. 238.

[60] Michaud-Quantin, *Universitas,* 276–81.

the political process itself provided the means to mix these two seemingly insoluble ideas.[61] Majority vote held sway only if supported by sufficient consensus—a consensus that may not have been based on numbers, but instead on the interactions of individuals or groups within the larger body. Unanimity, on the other hand, was not always a miracle of collective accord, but the result of a carefully orchestrated agreement worked out ahead of time by opposing groups. Sometimes such processes took place outside the hôtel de ville, and in these cases we can only surmise what the specific method must have been. At other times, however, the process of arriving at a generally acceptable conclusion occurred within the municipal administration itself. In practice, municipal decision making bridged the chasm between the two disparate ideals of majority consent and unanimous accord, while drawing on both conceptualizations to explain the activities of municipal government. If the municipal political dynamic seems so complex, its intricacies are in large part due to the necessity of working out in practice, through action and negotiation, differing conceptions of the relationships of members to each other and of individuals to the collectivity.

---

[61] This is not to say, of course, that divine intention was deemed irrelevant to the urban sphere. On the contrary, all decisions were held to proceed according to the will of God, whether the product of unanimity or patched-up dissent.

5 Navigating the Public Good

Civic Authority and the Clain River
Project in the Reign of François I

On 9 December 1539, Emperor Charles V made his official entry into Poitiers.[1] As a result of the discussions between François I and the emperor at Aigues-Mortes in July 1538 and the subsequent *entente* worked out by February 1539, the French king had granted his former enemy permission to cross his lands in a direct path between Spain and the Netherlands.[2] Poitiers was one of four cities given the honor and assigned the burden of providing the emperor with a full-scale welcome.[3] Charles V, having entered Poitiers by its southern Tranchée gate, proceeded through the bourg St. Hilaire, through the Marché Vieux, where the university had set up a theater celebrating the new harmony of the rival powers, past the parish church of Notre-Dame-la-Petite, where a fountain of concord welcomed him, and arrived at the cathedral St. Pierre. There he heard Mass and was then escorted to his lodgings.[4] The following day, after the mayor, accompanied by the échevins and bourgeois, had paid his respects and presented him with a gift, the emperor set out once more, but not before having expressed his pleasure with the town for its welcome.[5]

---

[1] For three separate accounts of the imperial entry, see MMP MS 51, 97v–102v, also transcribed in ACP Casier 42, Reg. 12, 526–40; ACP Reg. 22, 206–7 (9–10 Dec. 1539), with preparations discussed beginning on 10 Nov. 1539, 120–21; and *Triumphes dhonneur faitz par le commandement du roy a lempereur en la ville de Poictiers ou il passa venant Despaigne en france ce pour aller en flandres le neufuiesme iour de dece[m]bre lan mil ci[n]q ce[n]s xxxix* (Paris, 1539). See also Léo Desayre, "Charles-Quint en Poitou en 1539," *BSAO*, 2d ser., 6 (1894): 410–20.

[2] R. J. Knecht, *Renaissance Warrior and Patron: The Reign of Francis I* (Cambridge, U.K., 1994), 385–91.

[3] The other three towns were Bordeaux, Orléans, and Paris (Knecht, 391).

[4] ACP Casier 42, Reg. 12, 528–29, 531–32; Reg. 22, 206; *Triumphes dhonneur*, A4v–C3r.

[5] ACP Casier 42, Reg. 12, 532–33, 537–38; Reg. 22, 206–7; *Triumphes dhonneur*, C3r–C4r.

Everyone seemed to agree that the visit had gone extremely well. The town council had been doubly sure that all elements of the entry were honorably carried out, after it had received word of inadequacies at Bordeaux.[6] The emperor had received the mayor's greeting and the town's gift very favorably, and a laudatory account of the whole saw publication in Paris shortly afterward.[7] Poitiers had gone all out, ceremonially and financially. In light of the municipality's impeccable execution of royal orders, would it not be possible, the town council reasoned, to advance their obedience as an argument for the reduction of royal subsidies currently demanded of the city? In a Mois called to approve the expenditures of the entry, the participants overwhelmingly named Pierre Rat, mayor, to go to court to make the requisite arguments, and he departed soon thereafter.[8]

Rat did not in fact obtain remission of the royal subsidy. Instead, he returned to Poitiers with the king's permission to convert the 3,200 livres tournois still outstanding in royal taxes from support of royal troops to subvention of a project to make the Clain River navigable.[9] Although an important center of justice and learning, Poitiers had always been at a commercial disadvantage for lack of a navigable river. With royal prompting in 1538, therefore, the hôtel de ville had embarked on the ambitious project to make Poitiers accessible by water. Work had begun on the Clain River, but the necessary funding had proved wanting. Members of the corps de ville thus suggested that if the mayor could not obtain a simple remission of royal taxes, then he should request "that it would please the king to remit the monies with the requirement that the said sum be used to meet the needs of the navigation of the Clain River, begun according to his wishes and command. . . ."[10] In light of these instructions, Rat's trip was a success. Poitiers had shown its willingness to carry out royal directives in exemplary fashion, and in return the king had dedicated funds toward a public works project that would have enormous benefits for the city. Such, at any rate, was the story carefully recorded in the municipal register devoted to the privileges and prestigious exploits of the corps de ville. Should the message be unclear, Latin commonplaces glorifying actions taken for the public good moralized definitively on its meaning.[11]

---

[6] ACP Reg. 22, 171–72 (27 Nov. 1539).

[7] ACP Reg. 22, 207, records that the mayor gave the emperor the town's gift and made "une belle et ellegante oraison." The emperor "fut trescontant et Regracia mond. s[ieur] le mayre et Lad. ville" and offered the following reply: "Il men souviendra bien."

[8] ACP Reg. 22, 210–24, 233, 239. The specific goals of Rat's trip are not spelled out in the town council register but are stated in its description in ACP Casier 42, Reg. 12, 539. (This text is a seventeenth-century transcription of the original account, recorded in MMP MS 51, 97v–102v.)

[9] François I imposed this subsidy in Poitiers in April 1538 to support three hundred foot soldiers. It was an extraordinary tax, Poitiers being exempt from the taille. ACP Reg. 20, 499–501.

[10] ACP Casier 42, Reg. 12, 539.

[11] ACP Casier 42, Reg. 12, 540.

Despite this compelling narrative, the mayor's actions and the instructions on which they were based met with more hostility than approval in Poitiers. From its very inception, the project to make the Clain River navigable had aroused considerable opposition, both within the corps de ville and among groups of inhabitants with competing economic and proprietary interests. Several seasoned members of the corps de ville insisted that its exorbitant cost went beyond anything that the city could bear and frankly argued that the municipality lacked the authority and competence to undertake the work. The inhabitants of Poitiers's parishes were inclined to agree with them. For the previous several years, contentions over tax assessments had generated disaffection with municipal policies; with the subsidy now earmarked for the project, the potential for greater opposition to both emerged.

Competing economic concerns therefore ensured that the navigation project would meet with resistance, but the dispute was about much more than money. Rather, it grew out of two competing interpretations of the extent of authority and sphere of action that the corps de ville could assume in administering the interests of the city. The project's supporters saw its benefits as enhancing the "public good" of the urban community. On that criterion alone, they held that the hôtel de ville possessed the authority, and indeed the obligation, to carry out the project. Detractors did not dispute that access to river transport would bring benefits to the city, but they did have very different ideas about who should order, implement, and pay for the undertaking. In the sixteenth-century urban world, the public good was an ideal that everyone supported, but no one was inclined to explain. The debate over the navigation of the Clain River shows that in the first half of the sixteenth century, at least, members of the urban political community were struggling to define the concept. They did not dispute the importance of enhanced trade for the city, but they did disagree over who possessed the proper authority and competence to achieve this goal. The public good was thus understood not just as a result, but also as a process. This is why the arguments over the project took the form of whether the corps de ville was qualified to undertake such a difficult work and, especially, who should bear the financial burden. Conversely, those who objected to the project and the hôtel de ville's attempts to complete it expressed their resistance through refusals to pay their taxes. The repetitive debates of the city council, the continuous problems of tax resistance, and the repeated attempts of the municipal administration to enforce compliance are therefore our most important guides to understanding these opposing viewpoints and how a project supported by a significant portion of the urban elite was ultimately defeated. This is not only because these issues and the means to resolve them were integral to the urban political process as it functioned in the sixteenth century, but also because these questions of authority and public financial responsibility for the well-being of the city were precisely what was at stake in the affair.

As eager as some members of the corps de ville were to make the Clain River navigable, the project would never have gotten under way without strong support from the crown. Projects to make French rivers navigable certainly predated the sixteenth century,[12] but François I embraced them with particular enthusiasm. By issuing permissions for the work and letters condemning recalcitrants, the crown acted to assure that its general economic policies would be carried out at the local level and to combat competing proprietary interests. Armed with royal letters, the city government was able to claim that it was proceeding on direct orders from the king, and thereby to justify a decision taken with little input from the rest of the urban community. The "public good" that would result from the navigation project would certainly enhance Poitiers's commercial importance. But even more, it would increase the sphere in which the municipality could regulate public life and reinforce its ability to act almost unilaterally in any matter advantageous to itself. Crown and city government thus worked together to enhance the powers of each.

Bernard Chevalier has identified the period of 1450–1550 as the time of greatest cooperation between the crown and the cities, founded largely on a policy of royal laissez-faire.[13] The navigation project in Poitiers, however, shows a more active and dynamic relationship of mutual support, as crown and municipality worked toward a public good that would advance their interests in a similar way. Of course, to posit a mutually beneficial relationship between François I and an elite group of Poitiers's governors is hardly unusual. Since William Beik so cogently reminded us that early modern monarchy had to rest on some identity of interests between the king and elites who kept order in the provinces, views of a centralizing state at odds with local freedoms have ceded to examinations of the overlapping features of social interactions and political goals.[14] Yet if monarchy by definition depended on mutual support between crown and elites, the identity of those elites and the processes of interaction did change over time. In the reign of François I, the king placed confidence not only in individual urban dwellers to carry out royal policies, as the Bourbons would do, but also in the workings of those civic bodies that owed their extensive privileges to the crown, as later "absolutist" monarchs would not. Here lies a fundamental difference between François I and Henri IV, let alone Louis XIV. Yet the project also demonstrates that this model of public authority encountered significant resistance within the urban sphere. Faced with both external and internal dissent, the corps de ville was forced repeatedly to broach and to debate the subject, since tenacious disagreement prevented any conclusion from being decisive. Nei-

[12] Henri Sée, *Louis XI et les villes* (1891; reprint, Geneva, 1974), 321–22.
[13] Bernard Chevalier, "L'état et les bonnes villes"; *Bonnes villes;* "Pouvoir royal et pouvoir urbain à Tours pendant la guerre de Cent ans," parts 1 and 2, *Annales de Bretagne et des pays de l'Ouest* 81, no. 2 (1974): 365–92; 83, no. 4 (1974): 681–707; "The Policy of Louis XI towards the *Bonnes Villes:* The Case of Tours," in *The Recovery of France in the Fifteenth Century,* ed. P. S. Lewis (London, 1971), 265–93.
[14] Beik, *Absolutism and Society.*

ther appeals to royal authority nor pleas for the public good in the end sufficed to ensure general cooperation or to convince common opinion. In its attempts to make the Clain navigable, the hôtel de ville did manage to achieve much. But urban dissent in the end proved strong enough to prevent both king and city administration from bringing their plan to fruition.

The Royal Will

Poitiers's project to make the Clain River navigable fit within a long French tradition of attempts to improve commerce through enhanced river transport. Not until the reign of Louis XIV did Sébastien Le Prestre de Vauban elaborate a systematic plan to unite all of France through a network of canals and navigable rivers, and not until the eighteenth century were many of these projects completed.[15] Many of these undertakings, however, were adaptations of earlier plans and attempts, some of which dated back to the reign of François I, or earlier. Thus, the Canal de Languedoc, completed in 1681, was first conceived as a project to divert the Garonne River to Narbonne in 1539.[16] The Canal du Centre, joining the rivers Saône and Loire, was first proposed by François I in 1515.[17] The project to make the Eure River navigable from Nogent-le-Roi to Chartres, revived in the late-seventeenth century, had a venerable history extending back to 1440.[18] As this genealogy indicates, a large number of these earlier undertakings produced either inadequate or impermanent results. To achieve success, many had to await the direct involvement and more considerable resources of Louis XIV's administration.[19] The history of Poitiers's navigation project fits this pattern well. First undertaken in the fifteenth century, abandoned until the reign of François I, and then put aside until the end of the religious wars, it differs from like attempts only in that it was never successfully concluded.

The idea to make the Clain River navigable originated under the reign of Charles VII. On 13 January 1432, the king issued letters patent instructing that the Clain and Vienne Rivers were to be made navigable.[20] Although the

[15] Jean-Yves Chatel, *Les projets de transnavigation de Loire en Seine par les rivières d'Eure et du Loir et leur abandon: 150 ans d'utopie (1685–1840)* (Chartres, 1995), 19–20; Robert Bornecque, *La France de Vauban* (Paris, 1984), 17; Joseph-Michel Dutens, *Histoire de la navigation intérieure de la France, avec une exposition des canaux à entreprendre pour en compléter le système*, 2 vols. (Paris, 1829).

[16] Dutens, *Histoire de la navigation*, 1:111–13; [Joseph Jérôme Le Français] de la Lande, *Des canaux de navigation, et spécialement du canal de Languedoc* (Paris, 1778), 2–4, 14–21.

[17] Dutens, *Histoire de la navigation*, 1:208.

[18] Chatel, *Projets de transnavigation*, 5–6; Claudine Billot, "Chartres et la navigation sur l'Eure à la fin du moyen âge," *Annales de Bretagne et des pays de l'Ouest* 85, no. 2 (1978): 245–59.

[19] Beik, *Absolutism and Society*, 292–96.

[20] These letters patent from Poitiers no longer exist, but they are mentioned in ACP Casier 42, Reg. 13, inventory of 1506, 85.

orders seem to have been designed to validate efforts already begun on the Clain River, there is no evidence that any work was undertaken afterward.[21] In 1460–62, the subject was revived and substantial preparatory investigations undertaken, but again with no permanent result.[22] By 1477, legal disputes had broken out concerning fraud committed in the use of funds earmarked for the project,[23] and in 1478 Louis XI issued letters "mentioning that the king has accepted the offer made by the mayor, bourgeois, and échevins of the town of Poitiers of the sum of 4,500 livres tournois [in recompense] for the monies given for the parlement, navigation project, royal loans and other things [which have been] poorly used, and that he has acquitted and remitted all of the faults that each of them have allegedly committed, both in general and in their private persons, so that they can never be molested for them. . . ."[24] With this blanket pardon for malfeasance, the hôtel de ville dropped its fifteenth-century efforts to render the Clain River navigable.

When Poitiers's town council revived the idea in the 1530s, it could predict royal approval for the scheme. Although predecessors had certainly encouraged such projects, François I's interest in France's fluvial network was much keener. Could his early experience with the canals of Milan and the hydraulic projects of Leonardo da Vinci have piqued his enthusiasm?[25] If so, navigation projects also particularly advanced the king's economic policies and accorded well with the general patterns through which he interacted with the localities and promoted his own authority against competing seigneurial interests. Although the French court did not evolve any elaborate theories of political economy under François I, the king did have ideas about how to "make [his] subjects live in peace, repose, and tranquility, enrich them, and set them back on their feet [*remettre sus*]."[26] Considering gold and silver to be the life force of the body politic, the crown adopted measures designed to draw in precious metals from abroad, while stanching their outward flow. French products and industries were to be promoted and improved and foreign imports strictly regulated.[27] Royal memoires disparaged

---

[21] Rédet, in his collection of extracts from municipal accounts, presents evidence that original letters patent may have been issued in 1429 and that work had been undertaken by 1430 but was halted by November of that year. [Louis-François-Xavier] Rédet, "Extraits des Comptes de la Ville de Poitiers, aux XIVe et XVe siècles," *MSAO*, 1st ser., 7 (1840): 423–24. Jules-Levieil de la Marsonnière generally follows Rédet's account in his "La navigation du Clain," *BSAO*, 2d ser., 7 (1896): 238–39.

[22] Rédet, "Extraits des Comptes," 425–29; La Marsonnière, "Navigation du Clain," 239–40. See also the record of twenty-two receipts for the navigation project dating from 1462 in ACP Casier 42, Reg. 13, inventory of 1506, 96–98.

[23] See the royal commissions mentioned in ACP Casier 42, Reg. 13, inventory of 1506, 94.

[24] ACP Casier 42, Reg. 13, inventory of 1506, 105.

[25] V. P. Zubov, *Leonardo da Vinci*, trans. David H. Kraus (Cambridge, Mass., 1968), 15, 33, 39–40.

[26] Ordinance of 18 Feb. 1517 from Paris, *Ordonnances de François Ier*, 2:1.

[27] Georges-Pierre-Charles de Vaissière, ed., *Journal de Jean Barrillon, secrétaire du Chan-*

goods available only from abroad as superfluous luxuries, and accused those who engaged in foreign trade of "avarice and ambition . . . to enrich themselves by their inventions [and] impoverish everyone else."[28]

Projects designed to enhance the volume of internal trade and thus to foster local industry therefore met with royal encouragement. As early as 1518, François I had issued letters authorizing investigations to determine whether the Allier River could be made navigable from Issoire to Pont-du-Château, and in 1520 the prévôt des marchands and échevins of Paris received orders to render the nearby Serein, Vanne, Morin, and Ourcq Rivers navigable to ensure the proper provisioning of the capital.[29] Work had begun on the rivers Ourcq and Serein by 1529 and stretched into the 1530s.[30] Throughout his reign, François I authorized numerous projects, including work on the rivers Dore,[31] Sauldre (1518), Ille (1523),[32] Rhône (1523, 1528),[33] Orne (1531), Ouche (1531), Mayenne (1537), Eure (1538), Garonne (1539), and Vilaine (1539).[34] Obtaining these letters became so easy that in 1546, a Rouennais speculator managed to gain permission to make the Curre River navigable, despite its complete unsuitability for this purpose.[35]

Not only did the king grant permission in these cases, but he also upheld the developers' needs over existing proprietary rights. Although all navigable rivers belonged in the public domain by Roman law, no waterway was free of private concerns, such as mills and fisheries, that obstructed the flow of water.[36] Issuing royal letters condemning these properties subject to reimbursement, the king subjected individual interests to public wealth—a wealth that would eventually enrich royal coffers through indirect taxation. Thus, the letters that Poitiers obtained to force mill owners to make the necessary concessions to render the Clain River navigable resemble similar let-

cellier Duprat, 2 vols. (Paris, 1897–99), 1:274–302; Émile Coornaert, "La politique économique de la France au début du règne de François Ier," *Annales de l'Université de Paris* 8, no. 5 (1933): 414–27.

[28] Articles submitted to an assembly of deputies from the *bonnes villes* of France, 15 Mar. 1517, Vaissière, ed., *Journal de Jean Barrillon,* 1:282–83.

[29] *Catalogue des actes de François Ier,* 5:370; *Ordonnances de François Ier,* 2:610–12.

[30] *Catalogue des actes de François Ier,* 1:622 (Ourcq); 1:654 (Serein). It is possible to follow these projects through legal problems that the prévôt des marchands and échevins of Paris encountered by consulting the *Registres des délibérations du bureau de la ville de Paris,* 1:217 and 2:62–63, 66, 69–70, 73, 142, 201–4 (Ourcq) and 2:402 (Serein).

[31] Philippe Mantellier and Denis Jeanson, *Histoire de la Communauté des Marchands fréquentant la rivière de Loire et fleuves descendant en icelle,* 2 vols. (1864; reprint, Tours, 1987), 1:42.

[32] *Catalogue des actes de François Ier,* 5:413 (Sauldre); 8:600 (Ille).

[33] *Ordonnances de François Ier,* 3:260–62; *Catalogue des actes de François Ier,* 1:558.

[34] *Catalogue des actes de François Ier,* 6:261 (Orne); 2:12 (Ouche); 7:217 (Mayenne); 6:507 (Eure); 4:67–68 (Garonne); 4:36 (Vilaine).

[35] *Registres des délibérations du bureau de la ville de Paris,* 3:65–66, 69–70.

[36] Mantellier and Jeanson, *Histoire de la Communauté des Marchands,* 1:206–8. See also Paolo Squatriti, *Water and Society in Early Medieval Italy,* A.D. 400–1000 (Cambridge, U.K., 1998), esp. 6 n. 7.

ters issued to Paris and Chartres.[37] Royal edicts prohibiting all innovatory tolls on the rivers Loire and Rhône spoke to similar concerns.[38]

Despite the crown's interest in these projects, royal officials were rarely directly responsible for carrying them out. True, the judicial officials of Poitiers's sénéchaussée received the commissions to conduct the initial investigations and to pronounce on the navigational potential of the rivers in question.[39] The Parlement of Paris determined the costs of the Ourcq River project and entertained bids for undertaking the work.[40] The burden of the undertakings, though, rested with the communities along the banks. In like manner, the crown almost never provided direct funding for these projects. It did frequently authorize cities to keep indirect tax levies, as in Paris and Caen,[41] to gain relief from royal subventions, as in Poitiers and Tarascon,[42] or to raise special taxes on the surrounding countryside, as in the cases of Chartres, Rennes, and Poitiers.[43] Only in the case of Romorantin, however, does the king seem to have paid directly for navigational work on a river.[44] In these endeavors, therefore, François I adopted the patterns of support traditionally used to assure town fortifications rather than the direct involvement that refurbishing the royal châteaux or building the new defensive port at Le Havre entailed.[45] The navigation projects therefore fit the style of administration typical of Renaissance monarchy. The crown made it possible for local corporate groups to enforce policies and to engage in activities that benefited both simultaneously.

Work on the Clain

Executing royal orders, however, turned out to be a difficult and drawn-out affair. Although in Poitiers the hôtel de ville carried out substantial work between 1538 and 1542, these efforts most likely did not actually make the city

[37] Letters dated 23 Jan. 1540 from La Fère-sur-l'Oise, ACP Casier 10, D39; *Ordonnances de François Ier*, 2:61; *Catalogue des actes de François Ier*, 6:810.

[38] Letters dated 29 Mar. 1515 from Paris, *Catalogue des actes de François Ier*, 1:27; letters dated 9 July 1524 from Blois, ibid., 1:384.

[39] Investigation dated 14 Mar. 1538, ACP Casier 9, D35; opinion dated 7 Apr. 1538, ACP Casier 10, D36.

[40] *Registres des déliberations du bureau de la ville de Paris*, 2:69.

[41] *Catalogue des actes de François Ier*, 1:622; 6:261.

[42] Letters dated 6 Jan. 1540 from Paris, ACP Casier 10, D38; *Catalogue des actes de François Ier*, 1:558.

[43] *Catalogue des actes de François Ier*, 6:507; 4:50; letters dated 7 Apr. 1542 from Vauluysant, ACP Casier 10, D43.

[44] *Catalogue des actes de François Ier*, 5:413.

[45] On Le Havre, see André Corvisier, ed., *Histoire du Havre et de l'estuaire de la Seine* (Toulouse, 1987), esp. 45–51. The project cost the crown approximately 400,000 livres (48). For royal expenditure on châteaux, see Léon de Laborde, *Les comptes des bâtiments du roi*, 2 vols. (Paris, 1877–80). The *Catalogue des actes de François Ier* also lists numerous orders for payment both for the work at Le Havre and on various châteaux.

accessible to water transport.[46] The navigation project in Poitiers involved linking existing rivers to the network of waterways already supporting river traffic. Thus, the Clain River was to be navigable from Poitiers southward to Vivonne and northward to the Vienne River. The Vienne, too, needed work to make it navigable the short distance to Châtellerault, whence it was navigable until it met the Creuze River, which ultimately flowed into the Loire (see figure 5.1).[47] Once this work was completed, a boatman charged to evaluate the rivers estimated that the Clain could support boats carrying thirty to forty tons of merchandise in the winter and up to twenty tons in the summer.[48]

Having received royal permission to undertake the navigation project on 26 April 1538,[49] the hôtel de ville did not begin any of the actual work until the spring of 1539. It was not until March 1539 that former mayor Antoine du Val offered to pay for building the first lock and not until May 1539 that municipal deputies received full authority to act.[50] The work undertaken in this first summer involved improvements to the course of the Clain north of Poitiers.[51] Funding, however, was uncertain, and this probably limited the amount of work completed.[52]

When Rat returned from court with permission to divert the 3,200 livres tournois from payment of the royal subsidy to funding work on the Clain, the project's supporters had at last obtained a concrete source of funds. Although collection of these taxes proved extremely difficult, it did allow the hôtel de ville to supervise substantial work by the summer of 1540. By April, Jean Baptiste de Marine, an engineer from Florence, had been consulted, and his services were retained until the following October.[53] Under his supervision, a work plan for the Clain was drawn up sometime in 1540.[54] Deputies had been assigned to supervise the work in February, and a rotating system of responsibility existed by early June.[55] Purchase of the necessary materials began in earnest by the last few days of May 1540, and laborers were work-

[46] There are no mentions of the navigation project in the town council registers after 15 Nov. 1542. ACP Reg. 25, 82, 94. Although the records of the Mois of 26 Aug. 1552 declare that the Clain had been made navigable (Reg. 32, 125), Heller mentions requests for tax relief in 1553 claiming that the work on the Clain had never been finished. See *Conquest of Poverty*, 178.

[47] This work is spelled out in the investigation begun 14 March 1538; ACP Casier 9, D35.

[48] ACP Casier 9, D35, testimony of Étienne Mesme.

[49] Letters patent from La Coste Saint-André, ACP Casier 10, D37.

[50] ACP Reg. 20, 684–89 (10 Mar. 1539); 710–13 (19 May 1539).

[51] No evidence of the work survives in municipal records or accounts. The accounts of the canons of Notre-Dame-la-Grande, however, indicate that work was being done on their mills at La Jonchière in August 1539. ADV G1286, account of the fabrique of Notre-Dame-la-Grande, 1534–1545. A legal suit launched by miller Guillaume Parent against Antoine du Val in June 1539 also mentions damage done to his mill. ACP Reg. 20, 729–31 (2 June 1539).

[52] See ACP Reg. 22, 103–6 (18 July 1539), as well as 27–36, 73, and 77–78 (18 Aug. 1539), for discussions of funding possibilities.

[53] ACP Reg. 22, 304–5; Reg. 23, 61–68.

[54] Inquiry of 1596, *Affiches du Poitou*, 9 Aug. 1781, 125.

[55] ACP Reg. 22, 258–62 (12 Feb. 1540); 327–36 (2 June 1540), esp. conclusion, 336.

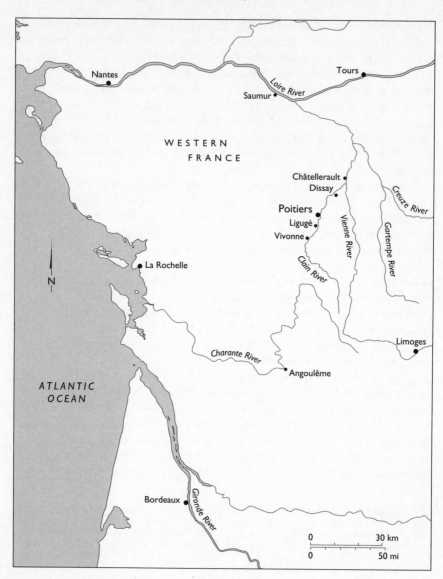

FIGURE 5.1. Planned network of navigable rivers, 1539–42.

ing by late June. By this time, each deputy was responsible for supervision and payment of workers for a week's time, a system that continued until late October.[56]

The Clain needed considerable changes to render it navigable. Although the work plan drawn up in 1540 no longer exists, specifications for the project when it was resumed in 1596 indicate the kinds and extent of alterations that were needed. Numerous mills, many of them owned by Poitiers's important religious establishments, obstructed its course, as did many small islands. The abbots of St. Hilaire-de-la-Celle and St. Cyprien and the abbesses of La Trinité and Ste. Croix each held rights to mills, fisheries, and other property along the river, and the cathedral chapter of St. Pierre, the chapter of Notre-Dame-la-Grande, the chaplains of Ste. Radegonde, and the chapter of St. Pierre-le-Puellier all owned interests in structures on the Clain.[57] Many of these structures required modifications to allow the passage of boats. In Poitiers, mills belonging to the Ste. Croix abbey and the group of mills called the *moulins de Chassaigne* had to be condemned. A small branch of the Clain had to be stopped up, an island that advanced too far into the river's course shortened, and various structures blocking traffic removed.[58] Of fifty-one mills mentioned in the 1596 work plan, twenty-six would require the addition of double gates or other work, and twenty-four were to be closed down entirely, because of diversion of the flow of water. Only one could remain as it was.

The hôtel de ville resumed its difficult and contested work on the Clain in the summers of 1541 and 1542. In 1541, it decided to solicit further advice from experienced workers from Angers and resolved that the bishop of Maillezais, who was also the prior of the abbey of Ligugé, should be forced to adhere to his agreement to pay for the gates to be installed there.[59] By the time that the corps de ville obtained royal letters authorizing it to levy seventeen thousand livres to continue work in 1542, only the stretch between Poitiers and Vivonne remained unfinished.[60] Further arguments with the prior of Ligugé indicate that this area needed further attention.[61] Yet when

[56] ACP Casier 36, K11.

[57] La Celle: *Affiches du Poitou*, 20 Sept. 1781, 147, and ADV 1H^{13}9 (mills near the faubourg Montbernage); St. Cyprien: *Affiches du Poitou*, 13 Sept. 1781, and ADV 1H^{1}7 (legal proceedings against La Trinité and the mills of Crainebot); La Trinité: ADV 1H^{1}7 (legal proceedings against St. Cyprien) and 2H^{2}29 (Tison mill and fisheries); Ste. Croix: ADV G1770 and 2H^{1}22 (Charruau mill), 2H^{1}13 (Bageon mill), 2H^{1}15 (mill of the Quatres Roues), 2H^{1}3 (Bageon mill and mills of the Quatres Roues and La Tour), and 2H^{1}23 (fisheries); Notre-Dame-la-Grande: ADV G1118 and G1226 (mills of La Jonchière in Dissay); Ste. Radegonde: ADV G1687; St. Pierre-le-Puellier: G1770 (Fief-le-Comte).

[58] Inquiry of 1596, *Affiches du Poitou*, 20 Sept. 1781, 151.

[59] ACP Reg. 23, 287–90 (16–18 May 1541).

[60] The letters patent of 7 April 1542 from Valuysant dedicate these funds to expenses to make the Clain completely navigable between Vivonne and Poitiers but do not mention any work to be done between Poitiers and Châtellerault. ACP Casier 10, D43.

[61] ACP Reg. 24, 193–202 (5 July 1542); 203–17 (11 July 1542); Reg. 25, 4–5 (31 July 1542); 18–21 (10 Aug. 1542).

the clergy refused any further contribution in the autumn of 1542, the hôtel de ville persevered no longer in its attempts.[62]

The Public Good

Why did the hôtel de ville launch into such a difficult, and in the end futile, undertaking? François I's love of navigation projects in general, and the potential navigability of the Clain in particular, certainly provided an impetus. When in 1542 deputies from the clergy accused the corps de ville of imposing the project on the city, échevin René d'Ausseurre could counter that it was "the king's own monument"(*du propre monument du Roy*), begun because "the will of the king was such that the river be navigable."[63] Yet in undertaking the work, the hôtel de ville was doing more than dutifully submitting to the royal will. The navigation project was likely to bring greater trade and prosperity to the city, and an active minority within the Cent was determined to reap these advantages. Self-appointed arbitrators of the civic realm, they felt a genuine duty to enhance the "public good." That the public good as they conceived it trespassed against numerous private interests did not lessen the imperative to achieve it. On the contrary, all enhancements to the public domain would likely augment municipal authority. The public good and the corporate interests of the hôtel de ville handily cohered.

We would look in vain for anything more than the most general justifications for undertaking the navigation project in the town council registers, and we must resort to the 1538 investigation and resulting opinion to ascertain the specific reasons evinced by its supporters. Deponents in the investigation particularly emphasized the commercial advantages to accrue to Poitiers, its surrounding region, and most generally to the whole of northern France, from the increased circulation of goods. River transport would enhance the wealth and population of Poitiers, provide more work for the poor, and prevent famines through increased access to grain supplies. Not only did Poitiers's status as a regional capital, university center, and home of prestigious religious institutions justify such efforts, but they would also benefit the cities on the Loire River and make the center of France more accessible from the Atlantic Ocean. The king, as well, would directly benefit through greater receipts from indirect taxes.[64]

The investigation therefore cited Poitiers's existing prestige and conversely its lack of mercantile importance as reasons to undertake the project. This

---

[62] ACP Casier 10, D44; ADV E⁴27.5. There is no indication in any of Poitiers's records that further work was executed on the Clain at this time.

[63] ACP Casier 10, D44, 5.

[64] Investigation, ACP Casier 9, D35, 3r–22r.

concern for the city's commercial health was not misplaced. The corps de ville frequently decried the number of idle poor within the walls and forcibly sought to stimulate Poitiers's meager cloth industry to put them to work. Analyzing the 1540s and 1550s in Poitiers, Henry Heller has concluded that these were years of unusual financial difficulty for the city, and his description could be extended back to the 1530s.[65] By increasing the volume of trade in Poitiers, the hôtel de ville hoped simultaneously to solve the city's pressing social problems, improve its status as a commercial center, and thereby increase its general prestige.

The supporters of the navigation project identified all of these advantages with the public good. Jasmes de Lauzon, échevin and avocat du roi in the sénéchaussée, proclaimed the project "a public act and work better than all else"[66] and compared it favorably to recent work on the communal clock tower, that traditional symbol of urban pride.[67] Testimony in the investigation had likewise pointed to the public good that would be served, while insisting that the general benefit would greatly exceed any private injuries suffered by owners of mills and other properties along the Clain.[68] One witness, commenting on the project's "inestimable profit for the public good," even argued that the advantages to millers themselves would outweigh any inconvenience they would suffer because of the passage of boats![69]

As such references to millers would indicate, the "public good" that supporters of the project evoked ignored the particular good of many. Not only millers but also important religious establishments and seigneurs would see their proprietary rights damaged. Many inhabitants of Poitiers, too, attempted to resist impositions on their purses. Yet the supporters of the project brushed these concerns aside. In issuing their opinion that the Clain River should be made navigable, the commissioners, who were simultaneously échevins and the most important judicial officials in the sénéchaussée, explicitly enlisted the public good against any individual complaints. No private interests would be damaged, they maintained,

> and in any case, the public and common good must be preponderant and preferred. Further, that considering that the said rivers and waterways are public and by their nature disposed to be made navigable, they cannot reasonably be occupied nor hindered by private persons, with the result that the navigation project, which serves the public and common good, be interrupted or prevented.[70]

[65] Heller's work provides a good picture of Poitiers's financial plight in this period. See "The Calvinist Church in France: The Example of Poitiers," in his *Conquest of Poverty*, 176–203.
[66] ACP Reg. 20, 747 (10 June 1539).
[67] ACP Reg. 20, 719 (21 May 1539). The hôtel de ville had recently authorized repairs to the clock tower. ACP Casier 33, J1329–31.
[68] ACP Casier 9, D35, 3r–5r.
[69] ACP Casier 9, D35, 5r–7r; quotation, 6v.
[70] ACP Casier 10, D36.

Rivers, therefore, were by law and nature a part of the common domain, and their use must as a result be aimed at general benefits.

Such arguments, of course, implied that any action in the public domain fell under the authority and competence of the hôtel de ville to perform. Although the bureau de ville of Paris hired out its navigational work to the lowest bidder and paid for it with receipts from indirect taxes, the corps de ville of Poitiers supervised work on the Clain itself and collected its funding from an unwilling populace. All of this trouble and zeal had to be for a purpose. Indeed, in attempting to create this new commercial space, the hôtel de ville was acting to increase the extent of its own potential authority. Having first made the Clain River navigable, the city administration could reasonably expect to have the right to maintain it. Along with wider privileges of police within Poitiers and greater control over trade in the region, the hôtel de ville could hope to be granted access to the increased tax revenues that would accompany the growth of trade.[71] Indeed, Chartres had obtained letters granting it just these kinds of funds on the Eure.[72] Poitiers's hôtel de ville therefore shared with François I the motivation to enhance the public good at the expense of competing interests.

Such ambitions, of course, were not overtly expressed. Instead, when the hôtel de ville encountered resistance to its efforts on the Clain, members insisted that they were merely obeying the king's command. Poitiers having received numerous royal letters supporting the project, no one could deny that the king favored the scheme. In May 1541, Mayor Pierre Prevost even reported that François I had expressed displeasure with the town's lack of progress.[73] Supporters further asserted that the very idea to undertake the work had originated with the king. Thus, François Porcheron, échevin and procureur du roi in the sénéchaussée, explained to a recalcitrant clergy that during his attendance at court, François I had inquired whether the Clain had been made navigable. Hearing to the contrary, the king ordered that royal letters be immediately dispatched to the town council of Poitiers, thus prompting the subsequent investigations to be conducted and work eventually commenced.[74] Although Porcheron's account accords with the recitation in the opinion of 1538 and with Antoine du Val's subsequent narrative of events, it leaves out one important fact.[75] Back in 1534, Poitiers's town council had itself solicited royal letters granting permission to undertake the project, "but due to the opinion of some, [the mayor] did not have them ex-

[71] The privilege to collect tolls, or indirect taxes, on river transport was linked to one's responsibility to maintain the river, or so argued Mathieu Vauzelle in his 1550 *Traité des péages*. Gustave Guilmoto, *Étude sur les droits de navigation de la Seine de Paris à la Roche-Guyon du XIe au XVIIIe siècle* (Paris, 1889), 5.

[72] *Catalogue des actes de François Ier*, 6:828.

[73] ACP Reg. 23, 289–90 (18 May 1541).

[74] ACP Casier 10, D44, 7.

[75] The opinion mentions royal letters dated 6 Feb. 1538 authorizing investigations. ACP Casier 10, D36. For Val's testimony, see ACP Casier 10, D44, 7.

ecuted."[76] Clearly, François I had not conceived of the project, although he certainly followed it with interest. Jean Crouzilles even reported that the king had said that "he would never bestow any further good on the city unless it were completed."[77] Yet just as the project had been dropped in 1534, procrastination would have been a viable option in 1538. That the investigation and opinion were overwhelmingly favorable, then, reflects the town council's decision to begin the work.[78] The king's evident enthusiasm, however, allowed adherents of the project to cite obedience to the royal will to justify an endeavor that they were actively prosecuting.

"The Work of a Prince"

Despite pious references to the public good and the king's will, the hôtel de ville encountered significant opposition to its project to make the Clain River navigable. Within the corps de ville itself, several senior members urged repeatedly that the city administration steer clear of the undertaking, and numerous others tacitly withheld their support. Their doubts reveal that the reasonings of the project's adherents, and the model of royal and municipal cooperation on which they were based, represented a minority position even within the Cent. Such disagreements echoed widely diffused opposition within Poitiers. Groups of individuals who felt their property rights infringed complained about the municipality's activities. Many of Poitiers's inhabitants, moreover, refused to pay the taxes that would fund the project. Although some of this recalcitrance can be imputed to a general dislike of taxes, it also reflected widespread disapproval of the policies of the hôtel de ville. Complaints that the scheme had been undertaken without public consultation, that the tax burden had been unfairly distributed, and that the work was being incompetently handled surfaced repeatedly. Together these allegations expose not only extensive misgivings about the hôtel de ville's competence, but also a pronounced resistance to its claims for its authority.

The navigation project inspired the imagination of a limited group of supporters among the city's municipal and judicial elites. Échevins François Doyneau, lieutenant général, Jasmes de Lauzon, avocat du roi, Joachim Arembert, procureur du roi, and François Prevost, also procureur du roi, undertook the investigation and issued the favorable opinion that elicited royal permission to begin. Antoine du Val, mayor during this time, actively supported the project, offered his own wealth to initiate it, and got himself sued for his enthusiastic attempts to get it under way.[79] Pierre Rat, conseiller and

---

[76] MMP MS 51, 87v. The letters were dated 26 March 1534. See ACP Casier 10, D36 and D37.
[77] ACP Casier 10, D44, 6.
[78] ACP Reg. 20, 460–62 (11 Mar. 1538).
[79] ACP Reg. 20, 729–31 (2 June 1539).

mayor in 1539–40, later took the trip to court to obtain adequate funds. The accounts for work undertaken in the summer of 1540 also indicate the active involvement of several bourgeois: merchants Jacques Richier and Jean Goislard and avocat Jean Gaillaudon all participated by signing a significant number of work orders.[80]

Yet the project's supporters, although extremely influential individuals both within the municipality and the greater urban community, actually formed a minority within the corps de ville. Combining the votes cast in two important Mois of May 1539 in which the navigation proposal was intensely debated, only forty-two members of the corps de ville (ten échevins and thirty-two bourgeois) went on record in favor of the scheme.[81] The others, availing themselves of a common strategy in municipal politics, expressed their misgivings through absence. Within the hôtel de ville itself, there was pronounced disagreement over whether Poitiers should take on such a burden. Only two days after the judicial officials had issued their favorable opinion, échevin Maurice Vernou declared in the Mois that the city should not assume this charge.[82] In his steady objections to the project, he was soon joined by four other échevins and a bourgeois. Jean Bastard, third in municipal seniority, Raoul d'Elbenne and Guillaume Rogier, conseillers, Mathurin Roigne, conservateur, and Nicolas de Razes all repeatedly opposed their colleagues' campaign. Why? None, significantly, disputed that making the Clain River navigable would produce substantial benefits for the city. Rather, these members of the Cent questioned the model of municipal authority dictating that all measures for the public good naturally fell within the purview of the hôtel de ville.

If for Jasmes de Lauzon the navigation of the Clain represented the best public works project ever undertaken, for Raoul d'Elbenne it was "the work of a prince" (*oevrage de prince*).[83] In this assessment, Elbenne was not concurring with the viewpoint later expressed by René d'Ausseurre that the project, as the "monument of the King," must be adopted. To the contrary, he was maintaining that the responsibility to undertake such measures lay with the crown rather than the city. Financial concerns certainly underlay this attitude. In the Mois of 18 July 1539, Bastard, Vernou, Rogier, and Roigne all pronounced that the hôtel de ville should not dedicate public funds to the project.[84] At the same time, however, their disagreement reflected their competing understanding of their body's civic role. By May 1539, the corps de ville had already obtained remission of one subsidy due at least in part to the

---

[80] ACP Casier 36, K11.

[81] ACP Reg. 20, 714–23, and Reg. 21, 317–22, 359–63 (21 May 1539); Reg. 20, 725–29, and Reg. 21, 323–32, 351–57 (29 May 1539).

[82] ACP Reg. 20, 470–73 (9 Apr. 1538).

[83] ACP Reg. 20, 329 (29 May 1539).

[84] ACP Reg. 22, 3–11, 103–6.

expenses that the navigation project would entail.[85] It was for this reason that Antoine du Val insisted that the corps de ville could be called thieves (*larrons*) if they did not persevere.[86] By January 1540, of course, 3,200 livres of the second subsidy would also be dedicated to the project. To claim, therefore, that the king was not supporting work on the Clain was inaccurate.

Opponents of the navigation project, therefore, desired more than royal support and encouragement. They pointed to direct royal intervention as the only proper means to carry out the plan. Royal letters and the sénéchal's messages did not persuade them; neither did the speeches of their colleagues determined to advance the public good. The relationship of royal decree and local implementation that guided work on town fortifications did not provide an acceptable model in this case. Although general notions of what was fitting may have guided their interpretation of civic responsibilities, their dissent may also have reflected an awareness of the practical challenges inherent in the project. In either case, the result was that the ways in which both François I and the municipality acted in tandem to extend their authority in the civic realm were subject to question within the corps de ville itself.

Just as the hôtel de ville experienced division within its ranks, it met with pronounced hostility from those with competing interests. As early as 1 April 1538, before the inspection was even completed, miller Guillaume Parent accused the Mois of intending to apply tax collections to the destruction of his property.[87] Summoned to respond for his parish of Montierneuf, he responded that "the funds concerning which he [the mayor] had spoken to them [the vestrymen] the day before were for nothing but to destroy him and to have his mill broken up and to raise the price of grain for the navigation."[88] This determined opposition extended into 1539, when Parent initiated a suit in the sénéchaussée against Val for ordering alterations to his mill. The Mois eventually agreed to support Val in the case, but only after Jasmes de Lauzon fulminated against Parent, "a man full of malice since his youth" and a "Judas" to the public good.[89]

Parent, of course, was not the only owner of a mill along the Clain, and we would expect other proprietors immediately to have echoed his concerns. Yet while the clergy eventually opposed the project, their disapproval seems to have coincided with direct appeals that they contribute to its cost. Although they were vehemently to complain that the hôtel de ville had initi-

[85] The subsidy in question was the six thousand livres tournois imposed on Poitiers in March 1538. ACP Reg. 20, 479–84 (31 Mar. 1538). It was remitted by letters patent dated 22 April 1538 from La Coste Saint-André. ACP Casier 23, I17.

[86] ACP Reg. 21, 351 (29 May 1539).

[87] By 1536, Parent owned the Charruau mill, located just north of Poitiers on the main road to Châtellerault, in the chapter of St. Pierre-le-Puellier's seigneury of Fief-le-Comte. ADV G1770; 2H¹22.

[88] ACP Reg. 20, 487–99; quotation, 499.

[89] ACP Reg. 20, 739–51 (10 June 1539); quotation, 747.

ated work without their approval, all other evidence indicates that their first reactions had been positive.[90] By 1542, however, representatives of the chapters and abbeys launched a series of strong accusations against the hôtel de ville. Maintaining that the project was inadvisable from the start, they criticized the work that had already been carried out and charged that the municipality had gained royal letters to raise further funds through fraud. Challenging the motives of the project's supporters, the clerical deputies insinuated that "the enterprise . . . had possibly been begun by people who by chance sought their own glory rather than the public profit," and wondered that men of the law had sought to meddle in commercial affairs normally belonging to merchants.[91]

With these accusations, the clergy sought to expose all municipal pretensions relating to the project. They disputed not only the corps de ville's competence to complete the enterprise, but also its very motivations in beginning it. Questioning the lay officials' references to the public good, the clerics insisted that the échevins' own ambitions for glory had prompted them to entangle the entire city in a hopeless business without public consent. Their allegations that the project's supporters had transgressed their own professional sphere were not entirely true, but they did serve to highlight the extent to which the hôtel de ville was attempting to expand its sphere of authority. Although the few prestigious merchants in the Cent at this time participated in construction, and although the hôtel de ville authorized others of Poitiers's merchants to play a considerable supervisory role, this involvement fell far short of the responsibility the Merchants Frequenting the River Loire took for commercial activities on this and adjoining rivers.[92] Voiced only when direct costs were at stake, the clergy's remonstrances nevertheless went to the heart of the competing views of public action that the navigation project provoked.

There are strong indications that the clergy's assertions were not peculiar to that body but actually reflected a wider public opinion. Dissatisfaction with the hôtel de ville and its fiscal decisions proved strong in this period, and the inhabitants registered their discontent by refusing to pay their taxes and disputing the principles on which they were assigned. At issue was thus the ability of the hôtel de ville to make unilateral decisions on financial concerns impinging on individual wealth and privileges. Such questioning of municipal policies only increased once Pierre Rat had obtained the royal letters permitting conversion of tax monies from the royal subsidy to the navigation project. Tax resistance not only did not abate but also was now accompanied by complaints that both the project and its funding had been forced on the city without public consent. By linking the navigation scheme

[90] ACP Casier 10, D44, 3; Reg. 21, 7–20 (19 July 1538); Reg. 20, 684–89 (10 Mar. 1539).
[91] ACP Casier 10, D44, 3–4; quotation, 4.
[92] ACP Casier 36, K11; Mantellier and Jeanson, *Histoire de la Communauté des Marchands,* 1:80–111.

to tax collections, therefore, the corps de ville created the potential for greater hostility both to the collections and to the project.

Disputes over taxes began soon after Mayor Antoine du Val presented royal letters patent requiring a subvention of 7,200 livres tournois in April 1538.[93] When the hôtel de ville summoned the vestrymen to report on the parishes' ability to pay, it received a hostile response. The vestrymen of St. Porchaire, a wealthy parish near the Marché Vieux, reported that their parishioners would be willing to pay the tax but insisted that money first be taken from common funds. They further stipulated that "exempts"—those who claimed the privilege of nobility or freedom from taxes because of a special office—should be called on to contribute as well.[94] The parishioners of St. Porchaire thus presumed to dictate to the city council the terms of their compliance and linked their cooperation to equal sacrifices among the échevins, some of the chief individuals to claim tax exemptions. While St. Porchaire negotiated, St. Didier launched accusations against the city administration and probably refused outright to make any contributions. When summoned to report the decisions of their parishioners, the vestrymen instead presented a signed document that provoked severe displeasure in the town council. Its contents may be imagined from the mayor's sharp response that "the council is well aware that some people in St. Didier and their adherents are aiming at nothing but to provoke sedition and commotion of the people against this body and against the public good in order to defraud the king's intent."[95] For Val, therefore, St. Didier's refusal to accept the tax burden betokened conspiracy against municipal authority, the best interests of the city, and the orders of the king. Moreover, although the charges were probably overblown, they do indicate concerted action in one of Poitiers's most populous parishes to resist the policies of the hôtel de ville.

In spite of resistance, the city administration attempted to raise the subsidy over the course of the following year. Yet the complaints against unfair tax burdens and the self-interested policies of the hôtel de ville that the vestrymen of St. Porchaire and St. Didier had voiced most likely hampered the process of collection. Abandoning general collection, the corps de ville attempted to solicit "voluntary" contributions in December 1538 and January 1539.[96] Summoning groups of Poitiers's better-off inhabitants before the town council, the corps asked them to contribute liberally to ease the burdens of the populace. This call to serve the public good, however, met with miserable results. Several of Poitiers's richest merchants had to be coerced into "offering" a suit-

[93] ACP Reg. 20, 499–501 (4 Apr. 1538). Poitiers's share formed a part of the *solde de 20,000 hommes de pied*, assigned on 246 *villes closes* in 1538. Jean Jacquart, *François I* (Paris, 1981), 355. The city was already responsible for raising an imposition of six thousand livres tournois and a supply of saltpeter. Reg. 20, 487–99 (1 Apr. 1538).

[94] ACP Reg. 20, 521–26 (20 May 1538).

[95] ACP Reg. 20, 527 (23 May 1538).

[96] See ACP Reg. 20, 659–75, and Reg. 21, 143–262.

able amount, and later collection of the promised sums proved impossible. By autumn 1539, none of the subsidy had been collected from the inhabitants.[97] The public good, as defined by the city council, failed to inspire either general confidence in its decisions or compliance with orders.

Conversion of the 3,200 livres that remained of the royal subsidy to finance the navigation project did nothing to ease public discontent. On the contrary, to their former grievances against municipal taxation policies, parishioners now added accusations that certain members of the corps de ville had acted unilaterally in a case that should have been subject to communal deliberation. Although the council had early ruled that the project could not be undertaken without public approval, because it was a public act, there is no evidence that this consultation ever took place.[98] Pierre Rat's actions to obtain the royal letters of 6 January 1540 provoked similar criticism. When he attempted to quell resistance to collections in his own parish of Ste. Opportune, Rat was confronted by bourgeois Mathurin de Conzay, who scandalously insulted the mayor and accused him of damaging the financial interests of the city.[99] Conzay may have been thinking of the annual rente that Guillaume Parent owed him on the Charruau mills, but similar charges expressed in a Mois demonstrate that these allegations were not particular to Conzay.[100] Maurice Vernou here accused Rat of having obtained these letters in the name of the inhabitants of Poitiers without having gained their consent.[101] Such allegations reveal that general dissatisfaction with the corps de ville's exclusive fiscal policies had crystallized into opposition to its ability to make unilateral decisions for the city. The navigation project, these objections implied, lay beyond the authority of the hôtel de ville to adopt and to administer.

In the Face of Dissent

Given the amount of opposition to the navigation project, the determination of its supporters is impressive. In spite of internal disagreement and external resistance, these municipal officials managed to undertake a good part of the work and to obtain funding for it. Yet if this limited success indicates the extent to which a privileged minority could impose its views on the urban community, they managed to do so only with difficulty. The insistent dissent of

[97] Of the 4,000 livres tournois that had been turned over to royal officials, 2,000 had been paid out of common funds by October 1538, an additional 1,000 came from municipal funds pursuant to a decision of 29 May 1539, and the remainder was made available by a loan from Jean Goislard, bourgeois and merchant of Poitiers. See ACP Reg. 20, 627–28 (11 Oct. 1538); 725–29 (29 May 1539); Reg. 22, 25–38, 41–44, 73, 77–78, 83 (11 Aug. 1539).

[98] ACP Reg. 20, 456–57 (25 Feb. 1538).

[99] ACP Reg. 22, 308 (10 May 1540).

[100] ADV G1770 (sentence of the Grands Jours of Poitiers, 25 Oct. 1541).

[101] ACP Reg. 23, 43 (18 Aug. 1540).

important members of the corps de ville meant that the navigation project had to be continually debated, with a definitive decision lacking even once the work had begun. Moreover, although supporters managed to overrule detractors of the project within the urban administration, the supporters found their authority insufficient to impose their decisions on the inhabitants. Repeatedly, the hôtel de ville was forced to appeal to royal authority to carry out its vision of the public good, even if this support did not prove sufficient to ensure the completion of its plans.

From the beginning, the proposal to make the Clain River navigable had caused significant disagreement within the corps de ville, and the terms of debate varied little over the course of the project's existence. Raoul d'Elbenne had proclaimed the job a "work of a prince" in May 1539 and continued to insist that it was the "work of the king" as late as August 1540, at the height of the administration's involvement.[102] The persistence of such disagreement subjected the project to continual debate, since virtually every practical decision provoked controversy. During a discussion of how to implement the royal letters of 7 April 1542, authorizing the hôtel de ville to levy seventeen thousand livres tournois in Poitiers and the surrounding countryside, for example, the Mois was forced to respond to continuing doubts about the project's feasibility.[103] An exasperated Jean de Brilhac remonstrated that "if at the present time they were at the beginning," it would be appropriate "to have particular opinions on the navigation project . . . but that since the work has been begun, it is necessary to complete it."[104] Thus he sought to silence opponents, who were still attempting to obstruct the project a full four years after it had been adopted. Although the hôtel de ville frequently resorted to multiple considerations of proposals to produce eventual accord, in this case the difference of opinion proved irreconcilable.

Resistance to the navigation project within the corps de ville provoked its supporters to threaten punitive action against their colleagues. When bourgeois Laurens Chessé refused to proceed with tax collections in his parish in 1540, the échevins threatened to file suit against him in the sénéchaussée and have him declared rebellious to the king.[105] After Vernou, Rogier, and Roigne all admitted to ignoring their tax rates, the Mois ruled that all members of the corps de ville who had not paid their assessment within three days would be deprived of their office.[106] It was not just the relative ease of mak-

---

[102] ACP Reg. 20, 329; Reg. 23, 49–50.

[103] Royal letters patent dated 7 Apr. 1542 from Vauluysant, ACP Casier 10, D43. A printed version exists in [Antoine-René-Hyacinthe] Thibaudeau, *Abrégé de l'histoire du Poitou, contenant ce qui s'est passé de plus remarquable dans cette province, depuis le règne de Clovis jusqu'au commencement de ce siècle,* 6 vols. (Paris, 1782–88), 3:388–90.

[104] ACP Reg. 25, 13–46 (10 Aug., 1542); quotation, 19–20.

[105] For the dispute with Chessé, see ACP Reg. 22, 312–16, 323 (24 May 1540); 341–42 (14 June 1540); 345–50, 353–54, 317–20 (25 June 1540); Reg. 23, 13–17 (23 July 1540).

[106] ACP Reg. 23, 34–44, 49–56 (18 Aug. 1540).

ing such threats that prompted the project's supporters to insist on their colleagues' compliance. Rather, the actions of the corps de ville as individuals had a general impact on public obedience, especially when disgruntled councillors encouraged friends and neighbors to follow their example.[107]

Unable to enforce tax collections in the parishes to meet the expenses of the navigation project, the hôtel de ville resorted first to the royal courts and subsequently to the king himself in order to compel obedience to its policies. Since the royal letters of 6 January 1540 proved inadequate to ensure the levy they authorized, the municipal government turned to the sénéchaussée to obtain the confirmation of an official collation and an order of constraint against all those refusing to pay.[108] Yet these measures also failed to achieve the desired results, causing the hôtel de ville to seek recourse from the king. A Mois of August 1540 thus concluded that all resisters would be imprisoned, have their names sent to court, and be liable for all damages.[109] When royal letters of constraint were issued on 28 August, the council at last had the force to compel tax payments.[110]

As the history of these efforts shows, neither the simple command of the king nor the unaided directives of municipal councillors proved effective in the face of determined resistance. Through the interplay of city and crown, however, both could act to realize an end that advanced the interests of each. The king's support, too, extended beyond the granting of letters favorable to the hôtel de ville's efforts. By representing the benefits of the project and the motivations of its detractors in the same terms as its local supporters employed, the royal letters affirmed the latter's perspective and endowed it with greater legitimacy. Responding to complaints that the doctors of the university and officers of the mint had refused to pay their taxes on the grounds of their exemptions, the letters cited their "bad will" and explained that although such privileges pertained to royal subsidies, they did not apply in a case of the general good.[111] The royal letters, like the project's supporters, therefore identified the undertaking with the public good and subsumed all particular interests to its benefit. The result was probably just as unwelcome to privilege holders as when Jasmes de Lauzon informed the clergy in 1542 that in opposing the navigation project the clerics were denying civic unity and separating themselves from the church of the faithful.[112]

*

[107] Members of the Cent had reputedly discouraged other inhabitants from paying their tax assessments. See ACP Reg. 23, 34–44, 49–56.

[108] ACP Casier 10, D42, dated 12 May 1540; Reg. 22, 341–42 (14 June 1540).

[109] ACP Reg. 23, 49–56 (18 Aug. 1540).

[110] Letters patent dated 28 Aug. 1540 from Mauluy, ACP Casier 10, D41. A printed version may be found in Thibaudeau, *Abrégé de l'histoire du Poitou,* 3:385–90. It is possible that the hôtel de ville requested these letters as early as May 1540 (see ACP Casier 10, D42), but a second request was probably made in August.

[111] ACP Casier 10, D41.

[112] ACP Casier 10, D44, 8.

The attempt of the hôtel de ville to render the Clain River navigable, then, points to both the extent and the limitations of its authority. In spite of internal dissent and external opposition, a relatively small group of active supporters was able to begin work on an extensive project for which they had no experience. In the face of considerable popular resistance, they also succeeded in raising 3,200 livres tournois to pay for the work, although not without considerable support from the crown. From this point of view, the collaboration of the crown and municipal officials to their mutual benefit proved quite effective as a means of rule. On the other hand, however, these attempts to make the Clain River navigable ultimately failed to produce the desired results. However much the project's supporters insisted that they were acting only for the public good, this representation of their designs failed to convince people with competing interests, many average taxpayers, and even other members of the corps de ville. Their resistance to the city council's decisions reveals that there existed within Poitiers a strong opinion that ran counter to the outlook of both the urban elites and the crown. During the reign of François I, moreover, the civic political process was still capable of ensuring that this alternative approach to civic government was heard, even if it acted only through a gradual process of wearing away resolve. Although the hôtel de ville had eventually managed to collect the 3,200 livres during 1540 and 1541,[113] it soon recognized that imposing another 2,000 livres tournois on the populace in 1542 would be impossible.[114] A similar recognition that the balance of opposition had tipped against them led the project's supporters within the city government to accept the clergy's refusal to contribute to the levy of seventeen thousand livres and to neglect to attempt to raise this sum in the surrounding countryside as the royal letters of 7 April 1542 authorized them to do.[115] As the Imperial Wars resumed by 12 July 1542, moreover, the times may have seemed inhospitable for construction.[116] Municipal authority, not surprisingly, was weakest when it confronted competing corporate interests and strayed from the bounds of its urban jurisdiction. The relationship

[113] The first 1,800 livres tournois levied on the inhabitants were most likely collected by late September 1540. Afterward, no further references to outstanding sums appear in the town council registers, and various members of the corps de ville began to appeal their rates. For an example, see ACP Reg. 23, 71–72 (9 Nov. 1540). The second installment was probably assigned and collected beginning in June 1541. An incomplete copy of the tax register exists in ACP Casier 10, D40. Although Rédet's inventory assigns this document the date of 1540, it is in fact the register of the second tax assignment, for which Louis Clabat served as receveur. Reg. 23, 311–16, 279–80. Because the register indicates that Pierre Prevost was still mayor (see the records for St. Didier parish), it must have been drawn up before his term ended on 14 July 1541.

[114] Although the Mois decided to impose a tax of two thousand livres tournois on the inhabitants on 22 August 1542, the council decided to try to impose this tax exclusively on the clergy by 4 Sept. ACP Reg. 25, 27–32, 43–46.

[115] Officially declared pursuant to an assembly of the clergy on 10 Sept. 1542 and reported in the town council on 13 Nov. ADV E⁴27.5; ACP Reg. 25, 76–77.

[116] Knecht, *Renaissance Warrior*, 479.

of mutual support between king and municipal government, therefore, was strong enough to accomplish significant feats at the local level, but this relationship ultimately proved vulnerable in the face of opposition arising from a profoundly different definition of the responsibilities and jurisdiction of civic government.

6   *"Lon doibt eslire marchans"*

Political Exclusions in the Reign of Henri II

Henri II came to the throne in 1547 with a vision of the well-policed city and the conviction that he should act to ensure order, prosperity, and safety in France's many communes. These were the stated goals of his edict of October 1547, which sought to redefine who was eligible to hold municipal offices throughout the kingdom. Explaining that royal officials were not only busy with other affairs, but also less experienced than merchants and bourgeois rentiers in financial matters, the edict declared that henceforth, no judicial officials, avocats, or procureurs attached to any royal jurisdiction were to be elected to municipal office in any city in France. Merchants and other notables would be far more able to manage the cities' economic affairs, thereby ensuring their proper administration and defense. Heavy fines awaited any electoral body daring to elect proscribed individuals to city office, as well as any man of the law who tried to accept.[1] Rather than returning France's cities to their traditional order and good government, however, the edict set off a round of protest. Entrenched urban elites complained that it contravened their cities' privileges, but civic notables formerly excluded from office hailed it as the providential gift they needed to break through the solidifying bonds of political exclusion and to regain access to urban government.

The October 1547 edict had such potential to touch off conflict within French cities because it sought to legislate against one of the most controversial trends of the sixteenth century: the growing social and political domination of royal officials and men of the law. Poitiers was among the cities strongly affected by this royal directive. After all, judicial officials and lawyers had played an important role in the hôtel de ville for over a century. The city's system of life tenure in office and internal elections would also make imme-

[1] Isambert, 13:34–35.

diate compliance extremely difficult. Poitiers's electoral privileges were therefore at stake, and the corps de ville began the usual round of tactics to obtain a derogation from the edict. Yet in Poitiers as elsewhere, the edict also spoke to existing tensions surrounding municipal government, concerning both its exclusive membership and its recent financial administration. A group of merchants and other notables therefore seized on the royal directive as a means to combat municipal politics they saw as favoring the interests of Poitiers's judicial elite while excluding their own point of view and participation. Although merchants were included among the Cent in 1547, they and their allies were frustrated with a self-perpetuating electoral system that blocked access to the most obvious means of citywide authority. The edict, they believed, would help them regain influence in city government.

The merchants' efforts to have the 1547 edict enforced in Poitiers reveal the potential for dissatisfaction with municipal government to take form and to oppose dominant interests. Armed with a favorable royal directive, a small group of activists was able to challenge the municipal electoral process and eventually to force an informal compromise allowing the activists greater access to political authority. At the same time, however, these efforts uncover the basic political consensus in the city, the essential agreement over political procedures and styles of government. The merchants who used the edict to question the status quo were chiefly concerned with getting themselves or their relatives into office. They did not deny the importance of family alliance in elections but were upset that their own family groups were increasingly passed over in the selection process. Their resentment against the success of royal officials and lawyers in monopolizing municipal offices and asserting their own interests is evident, but in their statements before city and king, they never called for any actual reforms in political procedures. Instead, they charged that essentially sound practices had been corrupted to serve a single interest group. They thus did not adopt radical means to oppose perceived unfairness but used traditional tactics of coordinated litigation and electoral campaigning to get the edict enforced. In his work on the Catholic League in Paris, Robert Descimon advanced the influential thesis that the League represented the last attempt of traditional bourgeois notables to preserve a late-medieval, participatory style of government against the growing presence, habits, and concerns of royal officials.[2] Poitiers's merchant notables in the 1540s and 1550s, however, were less concerned with challenging a judicial style of government than with assuring access for themselves. That they had to rely on a royal edict to do so further confirms chapter 3's findings: By the mid-sixteenth century, royal officials certainly distinguished themselves from other civic notables, as Chevalier has argued, but they did not abandon their interests in urban government.[3]

[2] Descimon, *Qui étaient les Seize?*; "Ligue à Paris"; and "Échevinage parisien."
[3] Chevalier, *Bonnes villes*, 143–47.

Although the merchants sought to gain access to an exclusive corps without questioning the essential practices that had contributed to its formation, their protests did have implications for the nature of political authority in Poitiers. Their charges of corruption implied that the domination of particular interests had derailed proper decision making, and their attempts to gain access would necessarily lead to a broadening of the points of view that received real consideration within municipal government. When they complained about taxation procedures within the city, they implied that proper representation within the parishes had been ignored. The hôtel de ville, they believed, had failed in its responsibility to consider and to incorporate a range of civic viewpoints in its decisions, and the processes of consultation examined in chapter 2 were not being adequately observed. These wider claims led their protests to strike a chord among Poitiers's inhabitants, and the results of parish nominations show clear support for their endeavors. Yet, as the disputes over the navigation project show, concerns for popular representation in important decisions and distrust for the dominance of one source of political authority were not unique to the merchants and their supporters as a social group. Rather, ideas that corruption and unfairness would result when the interests of government became too exclusive existed side by side with an enduring agreement about the importance of municipal authority and its select governing structures. Both assumptions about civic government were available in French cities in the sixteenth century, to serve as guiding notions as individuals made decisions about urban administration or sought to defend their interests. Like Henri II, all urban notables, whether merchants and craftsmen or lawyers and royal officials, wanted a well-policed city. But there was room to dispute exactly how this ideal polity would be constituted, as well as a range of ideas on the nature and goals of urban government that did not primarily depend on professional differences.

Henri II and the Towns

In retrospect, the crown's attempt to reverse the tide of political change within French cities was a castle in the sand. Throughout France, royal officials were growing in numbers and prestige, and men of the law competed with merchants for control over city councils.[4] Yet the October 1547 edict did not come out of nowhere. Its provisions fit within a body of royal policies relative to cities and their elites, many of which had characterized the reign of François I, and others that would find expression in the major reforming ordinances of Charles IX and Henri III. As a good number of cities

[4] The contest between merchants and gens de loi is a common theme of scholarship. In addition to the discussion in chapter 3, see Robert A. Schneider, "Crown and Capitoulat: Municipal Government in Toulouse, 1500–1789," in *Cities and Social Change*, ed. Benedict, 195–220.

began to protest the edict, however, the crown was forced to examine its assumptions about urban political order. Faced with competing arguments about who could best administer French cities, royal jurisdictions repeatedly issued contradictory rulings concerning where, how, and whether the edict was to be enforced. This equivocation reflected politics as usual in a system with competing courts and councils, to be sure, but it also arose from the considerable ambiguity in thinking regarding what cities' prime functions were within the kingdom. Views that the crown could best maintain order by working with elites and promoting an efficient system of royal courts within urban centers stood in conflict with desires to tap into the commercial wealth of cities and to limit the dominance of a single set of families. The trend over time, as Annette Finley-Croswhite has shown for the reign of Henri IV, was for kings to entrust a limited group of urban elites to keep order in their name.[5] But this approach did not preclude the kings' strong desire to preserve the cities' role in trade and defense by insisting on strict accountability in administering civic resources.

Funds in the form of grants, loans, and aids flowed back and forth between the French monarchs and their cities. Kings granted urban governments the right to collect indirect taxes or to keep forced subsidies, so long as this money was used for legitimate purposes. Poitiers funded its work on the Clain River through conversion of a royal loan. Similarly, Bourges obtained permission to apply half of the money it had promised for François I's ransom from Madrid to its own desperate attempts to stave off plague and famine.[6] Usually, such royal favors were to be applied to the city's defense. For example, in 1517 the échevinage of Troyes was permitted to purchase a salt farm for ten years on the understanding that the profits would go to the city's fortifications.[7] Delegating resources to city governments to solidify defenses and thus to ensure the safety of the kingdom, the crown had a stake in assuring that these funds were spent in the right place. This was the motivation behind François I's edict of March 1514, creating *controleurs des octrois* (supervisors of royal grants) in each city and fortress in France, to prevent abuses, to make sure all fortifications were in repair, and to assure the kingdom's defense.[8] This same concern also informed Henri II's 1547 edict. The son wished to see his cities so well governed that their common funds "could suffice for the[ir] upkeep, repair, and fortification."[9] The financial vigor of French cities was vitally important to the crown. Not only did Henri II believe that the wealth of cities, if properly employed, could make them independent of royal grants,[10] but also that

[5] Finely-Croswhite, *Henry IV and the Towns*.
[6] Letters patent dated 17 May 1531 from Pont de Saint-Cloud, *Catalogue des actes de François Ier*, 2:35.
[7] Letters patent dated 27 Apr. 1517 from Paris, *Ordonnances de François Ier*, 2:46–50.
[8] Edict of March 1514 from Paris, Isambert, 12:26–29.
[9] Isambert, 13:34.
[10] This view is expressed in both the edicts of October 1547 and June 1555, Isambert, 13:34, 448.

their commercial activities, if allowed to prosper, would enable these privileged enclaves to provide needed funds to fight the Imperial Wars. Although most of France's principal cities were exempt from the taille, Henri II continued his father's policy of requesting regular subsidies from the *villes closes* of the kingdom to support troops of foot soldiers.[11] He could not have ignored the fact that the best providers were not cities like Poitiers, which had to impose these sums on the inhabitants every year, but international trading centers, such as Lyon and Paris, where subsidies could be more easily collected in the form of indirect taxes on trade, as rentes on the hôtel de ville, or some combination of the two.[12] It may have been for this reason that Henri II could contradict the economic assumptions of the previous reign and assert that "we have always seen and known by common experience that the principal means to make peoples ... rich and wealthy has been the freedom of commerce and trade that they hold with neighbors and foreigners. . . ."[13] What better way to assure the wealth of cities than to put merchants in charge of urban government?

In addition to its fiscal motivations, the October 1547 edict also had implications for judicial reform. Although these concerns were not explicitly stated in the text, the rationale that judicial officials were amply occupied with other duties reflected a long-standing royal attitude that legal personnel should not mix their functions in the royal courts with any other position. Louis XII's Ordinance of Blois (March 1499), for example, adamantly forbade royal judicial officials from acting in any advisory capacity to clerical or lay seigneurs or as judges in any subordinate jurisdictions. An edict of April 1561 reiterated these prohibitions, for fear that royal officials might reveal the secrets of their court.[14] Although the chief concern behind these directives was that officials might act against royal interests, the crown also sought to ensure that one judge could not hear the same case in first instance and on appeal. Indeed, the bourgeois of Amiens made explicit reference to the Ordinance of Blois to obtain a 1503 edict preventing any royal official from being elected to their town council. François I continued this reason-

[11] Accounts covering the years 1547–59 indicate that taxes were assessed on Poitiers's inhabitants for every year of Henri II's reign except 1549. The total amount for 1552 is not indicated. ACP Casier 23, I23. In Nantes, by comparison, records show that these loans were required in 1524, 1536, 1544, 1550–51, 1574–76, and 1578. James Collins, *Fiscal Limits of Absolutism: Direct Taxation in Early Seventeenth-Century France* (Berkeley, 1988), 46. See also Martin Wolfe, *The Fiscal System of Renaissance France* (New Haven, 1972), esp. 100, 116–17.

[12] In 1548, the bureau de ville of Paris obtained permission to raise half of the 180,000 livres tournois the city owed for the support of 7,500 foot soldiers by constituting rentes on the proceeds from taxes on luxury cloth entering the city and its suburbs. Later proceeds could then be applied to buy off the rentes. Lyon made similar arrangements to pay off its tax burden in 1549, and between 1545 and 1571 met its financial obligations to the crown without assessing any direct taxes. Instead, it raised funds via rights of entry on merchandise. See Gascon, *Grand commerce*, 1:419, and *Catalogue des actes de Henri II: collection des ordonnances des rois de France*, 5 vols. (Paris, 1979–98), 2:349–50 (Paris); 3:142–43 (Lyon).

[13] Edict of 14 Feb. 1557 from Paris, Isambert, 13:506.

[14] *Ordonnances*, 21:185; Isambert, 14:102–4.

ing in 1542, when he again forbade royal officials from being elected to city office in Amiens, because they "had the first responsibility to reform the mayors, échevins, and others constituting the political bodies of the city."[15] It is unlikely that the events in Amiens served as a direct motivation or model for the 1547 edict, but it is clear that concerns for the proper functioning of royal justice and the supervisory role of the courts influenced royal attitudes toward urban government.

The October 1547 edict had a strong impact on cities and their electoral practices throughout France. In Marseille, the overwhelming influence of merchant notables in the town council assured that it was received with approval.[16] In Bourges, the edict took effect until the 1580s, despite attempts to obtain derogations in 1554 and 1569, and in Orléans, it held sway until 1598, when royal officials with strong ties to Henri IV took advantage of changing royal strategies for maintaining urban order to have the edict overturned.[17] Other cities succeeded in acquiring exceptions, such as Toulouse in 1548, Agen in 1550, Moulins in 1560, and Amiens in 1566.[18] Poitiers was among a group of cities in which the edict caused an enduring controversy. In La Rochelle, merchant notables seized on the edict to deprive nine judicial officials, avocats, and procureurs of their municipal offices, and the resulting fierce litigation led to no fewer than five more royal decisions in an attempt to settle the issue.[19] In Paris, although a new electoral statute of May 1554 specified that ten royal officials would hold positions of conseillers, these provisions did not entirely calm the concerns raised by the edict of 1547.[20] In letters of 9 August 1554, Henri II was still insisting that the edict be obeyed, and electoral disputes of 1558 and 1559 indicate both that Parisian councils desired to appoint royal officials to office and that the Parlement and king set up obstacles against these intended nominations.[21]

As this litany of contradictory rulings indicates, the crown did not assert

---

[15] Édouard Maugis, *Recherches sur les transformations du régime politique et social de la ville d'Amiens des origines de la commune à la fin du XVIe siècle* (Paris, 1906), 105–6, 125–28; quotation, 128. Augustin Thierry, *Recueil des monuments inédits de l'histoire du Tiers État*, 4 vols. (Paris, 1850–70), 2:497.

[16] Kaiser, *Marseille*, 127.

[17] *Privileges de la ville de Bourges et confirmation d'iceux. Avec la liste chronologiqve des prvd'hommes maire et eschevins, qvi ont govverné la ville depvis l'an 1429. ivsqves a la presente année 1661* (Bourges, 1661), 3–62 (second pagination); Christopher Stocker, "Henry IV and the Échevinage of Orléans" (paper presented at French Historical Studies annual meeting, El Paso, Mar. 1992).

[18] *Catalogue des actes d'Henri II*, 2:301; 3:140 (Toulouse); 4:128 (Agen); *Catalogue des actes de François II*, 1:112 (Moulins); Thierry, *Recueil des monuments*, 2:763–65 (Amiens).

[19] Amos Barbot, *Histoire de La Rochelle*, 3 vols., ed. Denys d'Aussy, Publication de la Société des Archives Historiques de la Saintonge et de l'Aunis (Paris and Saintes, 1886–90), 2:58–61, 68–69, 72–80, 90–92, 96–99. See also Robbins, *City on the Ocean Sea*, 93–98.

[20] Descimon, "Corps de ville et les élections échevinales," 510–11. My interpretation here differs from Descimon's, which holds that the 1554 electoral statute effectively annulled the terms of the 1547 edict.

[21] *Registres des délibérations du bureau de la ville de Paris*, 4:211, 323–24; 5:3–4, 38–40.

a consistent policy on the composition of municipal governments, even within the same city. The crown's dilemma rested in the fact that although the reasoning behind the 1547 edict was convincing, so were the protests of city councils that felt their interests and privileges to be threatened. The edict ignored one fundamental reality of many municipal bodies: they exercised important judicial functions. The town councils of La Rochelle, Poitiers, and Amiens each made this privilege their prime argument for derogation from the edict. How could merchants administer justice? Because the mayor had jurisdiction over all cases involving the police of the city, delegates from Poitiers informed the royal Privy Council in 1548, a man of the robe should be elected to this position, since justice could not be "administered and exercised by merchants nor by others as expeditiously or forthrightly as by men of the robe, possessing knowledge, erudition, and experience."[22] The trend over time, of course, was to limit the judicial functions of city governments, so that in the early seventeenth century, Charles Loyseau could argue that mayors and city councillors were actually administrative, not judicial, officials.[23] Yet in the 1540s and 1550s the crown still recognized city governments as possessing important judicial functions, even as it attempted to preserve royal courts' supervisory powers over them. Just as the 1547 edict brought to the fore contradictory notions of political inclusion in cities like Poitiers, it revealed the many conflicting ideas within the royal administration of how cities maintained order and contributed to the stability of the kingdom. It was because cities still served such a protean role in the French political order that individuals could seize on these ambiguities to advance their own interests in the urban sphere.

"Lon doibt eslire marchans"

René Audebert, élu in the élection of Poitou, had personal reasons to object to the legal officials' domination of the hôtel de ville. In November 1542, he had made arrangements for bourgeois Louis Escot to resign his place in his favor, and for his father-in-law, Jasmes de Lauzon, avocat du roi in the sénéchaussée, to speak on his behalf in the Mois. But the resignation did not go smoothly. Jean Rogier, conseiller, complained that the right procedures had not been followed for an election, and Pierre Rat, also conseiller, insinuated that money had changed hands—that Audebert was attempting to buy his way into the Cent.[24] Although the majority voted to give the post to Audebert anyway, a group of legal officials hostile to the élu set about to re-

---

[22] Letters patent of Henri II, dated 24 Aug. 1548 from Lyon, ACP Casier 4, B14. For similar arguments from La Rochelle and Amiens, see Barbot, *Histoire de La Rochelle*, 2:79, and Maugis, *Recherches*, 130.

[23] Loyseau, *Oevvres*, 825.

[24] ACP Reg. 25, 83–94 (15 Nov. 1542).

verse the decision. Convincing René d'Ausseurre, *lieutenant particulier assesseur,* to propose his son, Guy, for the position that Audebert thought was his,[25] they persuaded an unusually well-attended Mois to select the assesseur's son, even though he was only "a smart kid" of around fifteen years old.[26] Audebert would get his wish and be elected to the seventy-five two years later, but only after he promised to contribute one thousand livres tournois to help pay that year's subsidy.[27] In 1547, he lost the mayoral election by a narrow margin to Charles de la Ruelle, doctor regent at the university.[28] René Audebert would be one of the most vocal members of the Cent to insist that the 1547 edict be enforced.

He was joined by Jacques Richier, bourgeois of Poitiers since 1529 or 1530 and member of an important mercantile family. Richier's father, also named Jacques but called Lorin, had also been a member of the corps de ville and was a merchant mercer with a large enough business to have at least three apprentice workers in 1527, one of whom was German. One night in 1527, this German youth defended his master in a dispute with Louis Escot, and suffered a knife wound for his pains.[29] Jacques junior was a silk merchant and may have later become an élu like Audebert.[30] Richier's public ambitions certainly went beyond his position as bourgeois. When his father died sometime in early 1532, Jacques took over his office as municipal receveur.[31] His hopes to become mayor were dashed in 1543, when he lost by only nine votes to Jean Goislard, also a silk merchant and presumably a business competitor.[32] He must have been pleased when on two occasions, Audebert insisted that he be elected échevin.[33] His connections by marriage with Pierre Pellisson and Paulin Girard, two other merchants involved in the conflict over the 1547 edict, allowed him to play a pivotal role in the controversy.[34]

Paulin Girard may have been Jacques Richier's brother-in-law. He was not as wealthy as many other merchant drapers in Poitiers,[35] but he enjoyed a high level of notability and trust throughout the city. He served as vestryman

[25] Or so Audebert claimed in a *requête* he submitted to the Mois on 28 Nov. 1542. ACP Reg. 25, 115–16.

[26] ACP Reg. 25, 109–14; quotation, 113. Audebert claimed in his requête that Guy d'Ausseurre was only fourteen or fifteen years old.

[27] ACP Reg. 25, 399–404 (19 May 1544); 408–15 (9 June 1544).

[28] ACP Reg. 28, 250–60 (1 July 1547).

[29] ACP Casier 44, 1523–63, investigation of 3 June 1527.

[30] ACP Reg. 21, 158 (18 Dec. 1538); MMP Reg. paroissial 142 (St. Jean-Baptiste, 1543–49), 23 Aug. 1548.

[31] ACP Reg. 19, 133–42 (22 Feb. 1532); Casier 59, K79.

[32] Election: ACP Reg. 25, 243–47 (29 June 1543). Goislard's profession: ACP Reg. 21, 163–64 (23 Dec. 1538).

[33] ACP Reg. 29, 169 (29 June 1548); Reg. 30, 224 (16 Apr. 1549).

[34] Paulin Girard was the husband of Françoise Richier, and Pierre Pellisson was Jacquette Richier's spouse. ADV G⁹98; G⁹106.

[35] As attested by his tax rates in 1540 and 1552. ACP Casier 10, D40 (St. Didier parish, 2r–8v); Casier 40, Reg. 1 (St. Didier parish).

for his parish of St. Didier in 1538 and was nominated to oversee the assignment of tax rates for the entire city four times between 1544 and 1548. In 1546, nine parishes, from all over the city, cast votes in his favor.[36] Girard had played an active role in overseeing construction for the navigation project, and he was one of the merchant notables summoned to a general assembly when the commune was marching toward Poitiers during the gabelle uprising of 1548, but he was not a member of the corps de ville.[37] A desire to open this body to men like himself must have driven him to take on the chief burden of litigation on the merchants' behalf, both in the sénéchaussée and the Privy Council.

One of Girard's partners in litigation was Jean de Marnef, master printer and co-owner of Poitiers's flagship print shop, the Pelican. Together with his brother, Enguilbert, Marnef took over his father's printing business in 1530 and thereafter produced works on subjects ranging from hunting and navigation to law and the Latin classics, first in Gothic and then in italic type. Both Jean and Enguilbert were tied to the Audebert family through their wives, but Jean's second marriage in 1561 to Perette Citoys, daughter of a merchant bookseller, announced an important change. By this time, Jean had become a Protestant, as his identification by the canons of St. Hilaire as one of the crowd who pillaged their church in 1562 attests.[38] Religious sympathies, in fact, may have played a role in the merchants' dispute. At least, another participant, Jean Beaucé, would become a noted Protestant in Poitiers, and a general assembly of July 1562 called to decide whether Poitiers should renounce its adherence to its Protestant captain and surrender to the king of Navarre included such merchant candidates as Jean Beaucé, Jean Cartier, and René Goupilleau.[39] It is uncertain whether these men had developed Reformed sympathies by the late 1540s, but it is possible that shared religious attitudes helped to give them a common outlook.

The October 1547 edict, then, gave a group of notables, united by a range of associational, professional, and possibly religious ties, the opening to insist on access to civic office for themselves and their peers. Of the nineteen men who played a visible role in the controversy, most were notable members of Poitiers's wealthiest central parishes of St. Didier, St. Porchaire, Notre-Dame-la-Grande, and Notre-Dame-la-Petite and exercised what in Poitiers were considered the most respectable trades of merchant draper, printer, and apothecary. Not only were several of these men united by fam-

---

[36] ACP Reg. 21, 107–13 (23 Nov. 1538); Reg. 25, 397–99 (19 May 1544); Reg. 26, 224–28 (4 May 1545); 253–54 (5 June 1545); Reg. 27, 123–32 (3 May 1546); Reg. 29, 98–106 (5 Mar. 1548).

[37] ACP Casier 36, K11; Reg. 30, 12–24 (14 Aug. 1548).

[38] La Bouralière, "Imprimerie," 72–82; Sébastien Jahan, "Réproduction professionelle et mobilité sociale: les Chesneau, notaires royaux à Poitiers (1519–1617)," *BSAO*, 5th ser., 6 (1992): 185–209; Barbier, "Chroniques de Poitiers," 195–200.

[39] Barbier, "Chroniques de Poitiers," 195–96, 198; BNF MS Fr 15876, procès verbal of 22–23 July 1562.

ily ties, but many stood as godparents for the children of their colleagues.[40]
These relations prompted them to coordinate their opposition within the hôtel de ville and the courts and to propose one another for municipal office.
Jacques Richier united with six other merchants in the corps de ville to vote
for Jean Pellisson, his relative by marriage, for mayor in 1548. René Audebert insisted that Jacques Richier and Jean Pellisson be elected échevins on
two occasions and also cast ballots for Paulin Girard, Jean de Marnef, and
Jean Beaucé, all actively pursuing the merchants' interests in the courts, in
1549. François Beaucé sought to further the interests of his son, Jean, as did
Jean Pellisson those of his brother, Pierre.[41] The men who were eager to have
the 1547 edict enforced in Poitiers clearly wished to reverse the trend toward
political exclusion of their own relations.

Desiring greater opportunities for membership in the corps de ville rather
than fundamental reform, the merchants employed tactics well within the
typical range of maneuvers that judicial elites themselves deployed. Both
sides resorted to electoral strategies to force, block, and win elections, although each side recognized that permanent victory could come only in a favorable royal ruling. The merchants were thus willing to play by all of the
established rules of political conflict, employing procedural maneuvers to
challenge authority. The elites dominating the decision process could not ignore the royal directive, but they could delay elections. From the time that
the edict was promulgated and registered by the Parlement of Paris[42] until
the next mayoral election, only one place in the Cent was filled. Although
several positions of échevin and bourgeois had fallen vacant by June 1548,
the Mois assembled solely to elect the next mayor.

This mayoral election proved the first major clash between merchants and
their judicial colleagues within the hôtel de ville.[43] The échevins maintained
that since there were no declared candidates for mayor, the election should
proceed by voice vote rather than by ballot. The merchant bourgeois disagreed, and Jacques Richier further held that all vacant positions on the
council and in the seventy-five should be filled before the election of the
mayor. Mathurin Goislard insisted that according to the king's edict, "lon
doibt eslire marchans" (we must elect merchants), cast his vote for a merchant for mayor, and urged that the other vacant positions be filled. Finally,
René Audebert directly contradicted the échevins' assertion that there were
no declared candidates for mayor, holding that there were "diverse opinions
and several candidates, from what he could understand and hear." He further insisted that the vacancies in the Cent be filled before they proceeded to
elect the mayor and required that his choices, "tous marchans" (all mer-

---

[40] MMP Reg. paroissial 142 (St. Jean-Baptiste, 1543–49); 238 (Ste. Opportune, 1539–84).
[41] ACP Reg. 29, 165–75 (29 June 1548); Reg. 30, 216–29 (16 Apr. 1549).
[42] On 28 Nov. 1547. See Isambert, 13:34.
[43] See ACP Reg. 29, 165–75 (29 June 1548), for the text of the election.

chants), be noted in a written act.[44] Despite these protests, the merchants lost the statutory debate, and thus the election. Although it was conventional to fill all empty places in the Cent before electing the mayor, outgoing mayor Charles de la Ruelle ruled that since the Mois had been convened only for a mayoral election, this would be the only vote to take place. Despite the clear disagreement over candidates, he also concluded that the election would proceed by voice vote. This decision assured the merchants' defeat, since only seven members of the Cent were willing to vote for a merchant in public view. By pretending that there were not multiple candidates for office and manipulating municipal statute, the judicial officials were able to assure the victory of their candidate.

Contention over filling the vacancies in the Mois continued long after the 1548 mayoral election. The problem, from the point of view of traditional municipal procedure, was that the 1547 edict contradicted long-standing custom in the election of échevins. Former mayors, in recompense for the pains they took in office, could normally expect to be elected to the first vacant position in the council. In 1548 and 1549, there were two such former mayors, each desiring to take advantage of this privilege, but each prevented from accepting the office of échevin by the terms of the 1547 edict. Rather than deny these men a traditional privilege, the municipality at first preferred to postpone all elections. As time went by, however, and the numerous vacancies became more glaring, it seemed more expedient to fill the uncontested positions in the Cent and to leave the places in question until further provision could be obtained from the crown. The merchants, however, continued to insist that all positions, including those of échevin, be filled at once. After numerous debates on the subject, the Mois decided to hold elections for three uncontested vacancies within the seventy-five.[45]

Three individuals whose professions did not contravene the edict had to be elected to office, and the judicial elite had clearly decided ahead of time who these men would be. Pierre Danyau, Michel Chausseblanche, and Pierre Clabat were duly summoned to appear to declare that they were of appropriate estate, and when the votes were counted, it became clear that the legal officials had voted in bloc. The proposed candidates each received around forty votes, while Pierre Pellisson, the next runner-up, obtained only six. The ballots of René Audebert and Jacques Richier had been immediately disqualified, since they had insisted on naming candidates for all seven vacancies in the Cent. The merchants' attempts to use the 1547 edict to determine municipal elections in their favor thus proved largely unsuccessful. They did manage to force the hôtel de ville to elect three individuals who

---

[44] Audebert's opinion is recorded in ACP Reg. 29, 169–70; quotations, 169.
[45] ACP Reg. 30, 137–39 (3 Dec. 1548); 196–205 (1 Apr. 1549); 207–16 (8 and 11 Apr. 1549).

complied with the edict's terms, but not the candidates they wanted. Electoral battles within the Mois could never benefit a minority. It was by coordinating activities within the hôtel de ville with persistent litigation that they sought to have the king's edict enforced.

Both notable merchants and judicial officials had recourse to the crown, in a battle of suits and countersuits to uphold or to mitigate the edict's terms. Because Poitiers's sénéchaussée still had not published the edict more than three months after the Parlement of Paris had registered it, Paulin Girard, Pierre Fourest, and Pierre Robin submitted a formal request in the court that it take effect in Poitiers.[46] The corps de ville, meanwhile, had been pursuing exemption from the edict and the following summer obtained royal letters patent permitting the corps to elect men of the robe to mayoral office.[47] Yet the merchants acted almost immediately to have the exemption rescinded and by late September had submitted a request in the Privy Council that the 1547 edict be enforced. Paulin Girard and Jean de Marnef, who appeared personally, asked that all judicial officials be required to choose between their royal office and their place in the hôtel de ville, that youths and non-residents be deprived of their positions, and that the lieutenant général be commissioned to hold an assembly of the corps de ville to elect replacements for the seven or eight vacancies then existing in the Cent. Although François Porcheron, procureur du roi in the sénéchaussée, and Gautier Rasseteau, conservateur of the privileges of the university, argued that municipal privileges required the mayor to be a man of legal training, the Privy Council decided the case in the merchants' favor.[48] Although the hôtel de ville again obtained a favorable ruling in April 1549,[49] the fact that elections proceeded as if it did not exist suggests that the merchants filed an immediate opposition against the measure.[50]

The supporters of the 1547 edict also used a series of lawsuits to question municipal proceedings. They subpoenaed municipal records of the acceptances of two former mayors as échevins, and a son of a former mayor as bourgeois. They also demanded a copy of the mayoral election of Guillaume de Morennes, receveur général, the day after it occurred.[51] They probably sought to establish that these elections were illegal and therefore void. Similarly, on

---

[46] The exact date of their request is unknown, but it was mentioned on 6 March 1548. ACP Reg. 29, 107–14.

[47] Letters patent of Henri II, dated 24 Aug. 1548 from Lyon, ACP Casier 4, B14.

[48] The Privy Council's decision was dated 24 January 1549, and the request of 29 September 1548 was mentioned in it. BNF MS Fr 18153, 59r–60r. For Porcheron's side, see ACP Reg. 30, 176–78 (22 Feb. 1549).

[49] Letters patent of Henri II, dated 28 Apr. 1549 from St. Germain-en-Laye, ACP Casier 4, B15.

[50] This was certainly the merchants' response in La Rochelle. Barbot, *Histoire de La Rochelle*, 2:74–76. In Poitiers, Guillaume de Morennes, receveur général, was elected mayor in 1549 after a debate about whether his office contravened the edict. ACP Reg. 30, 254–60 (5 July 1549).

[51] ACP Reg. 29, 177–79 (16 July 1548); Reg. 30, 261–67 (6 July 1549).

15 December 1548, Paulin Girard, Jean de Marnef, Jean Beaucé, and bourgeois Guillaume Rogier officially opposed the hôtel de ville's intention to use public funds to send a deputy to court to protest the edict.[52] By February 1549, Jacques Richier had joined his associates as plaintiffs to a suit in the sénéchaussée involving recent appointments to annual municipal administrative and police offices.[53] The merchants no doubt maintained that men of the law could not be selected even to subsidiary offices under the terms of the edict. At the same time, the group of activists began a suit in the sénéchaussée alleging unfair taxation procedures. In July 1548, the activists obtained royal letters ordering the secretary to turn over all rolls, registers, and acts concerning the assignment of taxes for the current and previous years, as well as all documentation concerning parochial nominations of tax assessors.[54] By February 1549, they had added the tax rolls from 1544 to the list and were making specific allegations of overtaxing against the assessors of 1548.[55] It could hardly have been a coincidence that Jasmes de Lauzon and his son François, relatives of René Audebert, were also protesting their tax rates.[56]

Despite all of this activity, the men who sought to enforce the 1547 edict did not seek any fundamental political change. There certainly was potential reason to do so, as elections became less open to new blood in the 1540s. The numbers of resignations of office were extremely high, and there were even attempts to use outdated statutes to limit mayoral candidates to the twenty-five échevins.[57] Unlike in La Rochelle, where a stranglehold on city offices in the early seventeenth century led to calls for a fundamental restructuring of municipal elections,[58] Poitiers's merchants never opposed resignations of office and indeed took advantage of this practice themselves. When they presented their complaints before the Privy Council in 1548, they pointed out that two former mayors could not be appointed échevins because their status contravened the 1547 edict, but they never hinted that former mayors in general should be denied the right to the first vacant position in the council. Similarly, they protested that young men under the age of twenty-five should not be given places in the seventy-five, but they did not impugn the practice by which the mayor was allowed to appoint virtually anyone he wanted to the first vacancy among the bourgeois that occurred during his watch.[59] The merchant activists, then, took advantage of the edict

---

[52] ACP Reg. 30, 140–41.

[53] ACP Reg. 30, 173 (18 Feb. 1549); 180–81 (22 Feb. 1549).

[54] ACP Reg. 29, 178–79 (16 July 1548).

[55] ACP Reg. 30, 173 (18 Feb. 1549); 186–89 (25 Feb. 1549).

[56] ACP Reg. 29, 136–42 (19 May 1548); 153–55 (25 June 1548); Reg. 30, 65–72 (27 Aug. 1548). Bourgeois François Eschinard and Guillaume Herbert also filed objections. See ADV E⁴27:3, attestation dated 22 May 1548.

[57] ACP Reg. 24, 182–86 (30 June 1542); Reg. 25, 243–47 (29 June 1543); 427–31 (27 June 1544); Reg. 36, 203–13 (30 June 1559).

[58] Robbins, *City on the Ocean Sea*, 244–74, esp. 253, 262–63.

[59] BNF MS Fr 18153, 59v.

to challenge the abuse of practices they saw as leading to the domination of particular interests and a narrowing of access to political authority. Yet they never implied that the rules themselves, the product of several centuries of corporate tradition, required any serious alteration.

"Choses monopollées"

Despite the activists' general agreement with the existing conventions of oligarchic government, the merchants inevitably possessed a different point of view from the legal personnel. Their different professional interests created areas of conflict surrounding recent municipal policy, and their relative political exclusion made them more likely to call for greater representation of a full variety of interests in decisions where consent was traditionally assumed. Their complaints against the hôtel de ville resonated with similar grievances in the parishes, so that by 1550, parochial decisions in taxation matters showed clear evidence of support for the activists. Yet we should not exaggerate the extent to which the merchants contrasted themselves with the growing body of legal personnel in Poitiers's many courts, nor their intentions to serve as leaders of popular disaffections. Clearly, the men who worked to have the 1547 edict enforced were able to tap into a strain of political opinion that ran counter to many of the hôtel de ville's recent decisions. But when it came to their imagined role in the political community, the merchant activists saw themselves as urban elites who had been unjustly excluded from their rightful place, rather than parish notables fighting for popular participation in government.

The recent policies of the hôtel de ville had the potential to ignite many areas of disagreement, and in financial matters, these policies had special power to evoke strong dissent. Although the corps de ville desired to promote trade in the city and to protect the inhabitants from excessive fiscal demands, members' need to enforce order and tendency to shore up their own interests meant that their decisions neglected rival concerns. In their attempts to have the October 1547 edict enforced, the merchants necessarily expressed a different point of view on many of these issues. In cases such as the police of cloth manufacture, the merchants had special interests that directly challenged the officials' approach. In other areas, such as taxation, the activists launched more general complaints that resonated strongly with recent popular dissatisfactions with municipal government.

The police of Poitiers provided the foremost area of contention between dominant municipal policy and commercial interests. In addition to the general supervision of the town's production and commercial activities, the hôtel de ville kept especially strong watch over the sector of cloth production and sale. Due to a tax exemption granted by Charles VIII on all cloth manufactured in Poitiers, the municipality had set production requirements for all merchant drapers, which the latter considered unreasonable.[60] The merchants therefore found themselves summoned continually before the town council to account for the discrepancies between what the échevins considered the ideal level of production and what they thought the market would bear. The conflict had begun before 1535 and had proceeded virtually unabated until 1541, when it is probable that new police ordinances promulgated during the Grands Jours of Poitiers temporarily silenced the dispute.[61] Since the group of merchant drapers receiving reproof strongly coincides with the group of merchant activists, this issue likely played a significant role in motivating their opposition.[62] The connection becomes even more evident with the renewal of the debate in 1550. In the period of compromise following the merchant opposition, the town council changed its dealings with the drapers. Rather than calling them summarily to appear with the intention of reprimand, the council decided on 28 July 1550 that the most notable merchants would be summoned, "in order to ascertain and hear from them their opinion and deliberation."[63] The council was now willing to try consultation rather than unilateral remonstrance as a way to obtain the desired results.

In their accusations of fraud in tax assignments, the merchant activists touched on much broader disaffections with urban administration. The merchants not only echoed other inhabitants in contesting tax rates but also charged that the normal procedures through which the parishes selected individuals to apportion the burden had been corrupted or undermined. To prove their allegations of unfair rates, they subpoenaed the tax rolls for 1548 and previous years, and to show that parochial choices for the group of assessors had not been respected, they requisitioned the records of parish nominations.[64] Indeed, considerable evidence indicates that their accusations of fraud over the preceding half decade were fully justified. In 1544, one of the taxation deputies reported that certain échevins and bourgeois had been left off the tax rolls, and early in 1549, René d'Ausseurre indicated that some vestrymen had intentionally hidden the names of individuals so they would not be taxed.[65] Further, examination of the tax rates imposed on the parishes for the years 1546 and 1548 reveals considerable discrepancies in the percentage of the tax burden that several parishes were assigned to bear. Al-

---

[60] Letters patent dated Apr. 1488 from Plessis-du-Parc-lès-Tours, ACP Casier 2, A31. A published version may be found in *Ordonnances*, 20:127.

[61] In his account of mayoral expenses, Jean de Brilhac records a payment to the greffier for twenty-one sentences against the merchant drapers on 10 August 1535. ADV SAHP 51, 23r. Council meetings and Mois in which the *drapperie* was discussed took place in January, July, September, and October 1537, January, July–September 1538, November 1540, and July 1541. See ACP Reg. 20, 179–81, 283–86, 310–13, 341–43, 348–61, 433–35, 563–66, 597–600, 611–25; Reg. 23, 79–86, 339–46, 349–52.

[62] ACP Reg. 20, 179–81 (28 Jan. 1537).

[63] ACP Reg. 31, 180. The phrase was actually uttered by Robert Irland.

[64] ACP Reg. 29, 177–79 (16 July 1548); Reg. 30, 173–75, 186–88 (18 and 25 Feb. 1549).

[65] ACP Reg. 25, 418–19 (18 June 1544); Reg. 30, 167–68 (28 Jan. 1549).

though the mercantile parishes of Notre-Dame-la-Petite, St. Michel, and St. Étienne were required to pay significantly more in 1548 than in 1546, other parishes, such as Ste. Opportune, Notre-Dame-la-Grande, St. Hilaire-de-la-Celle, and Ste. Radegonde, had much lighter assignments.[66] The marked differences in the percentage of the total tax that specific parishes (and thus individuals) were asked to pay could have easily led to and justified complaints of unfairness. The taxation accounts for 1548 reinforce this picture of corruption by indicating that the rolls for six parishes had inaccurate totals of the sums owed by individuals.[67]

Such accusations reflected general dissatisfactions with the taxation process and resistance to paying assigned rates. Summoned to nominate the six individuals who would be responsible for apportioning the tax burden on all the inhabitants, parish representatives responded in various ways: some simply did not appear at the assembly called for this purpose, some attempted to deny all participation in the unpopular decision by leaving the nominations up to the hôtel de ville, and others reported that the inhabitants of their parishes had refused to convene to express any opinion. Although some parishes resorted to these measures in 1544, 1545, and 1547, all three were particularly in evidence in 1548. Of the twenty-seven parishes called to nominate tax assessors in March 1548, three failed to show up, sixteen left the decision up to the city council, and three piously reported that "the inhabitants of the parish did not want to elect assessors because the commission was not signed."[68] This reluctance to participate in nominations found its complement in widespread resistance to paying. In 1547, Guillaume de Morennes, receveur général, was demanding arrears going back to 1544, and in 1552, monies were still outstanding since 1545.[69] Accounts for these years identified delinquent parishes and culpable tax collectors who had not completed their assignments.[70]

Such passive resistance, moreover, had the potential to explode into angry demonstrations against the perceived authors of Poitiers's taxation policies. Although the hôtel de ville would congratulate itself on the peace and order that reigned in Poitiers during the gabelle crisis of 1548, the city's inhabitants did not all remain quietly at home while the commune marched through western France. On 3 September 1548, Jacques Richier reported that a group of people in his parish of Notre-Dame-la-Grande were planning to sack the salt houses, and the council discussed popular rumors that Poitiers's royal officials were refusing to execute the king's orders abolishing the

[66] This comparison is possible through analysis of the total tax rates imposed on each parish as reported in ACP Casier 23, I23, account of Leon Guyvereau for 1546 and the *Mémoire et Compte* for 1548.

[67] ACP Casier 23, I23, *Mémoire et Compte*, 1548, 1–2.

[68] ACP Reg. 25, 397–99 (19 May 1544); Reg. 26, 224–28 (4 May 1545); Reg. 28, 205–13 (26 May 1547); Reg. 29, 98–106 (5 Mar. 1548); quotation, 105.

[69] ACP Reg. 29, 1–15 (22 July 1547); Reg. 32, 56 (1 Feb. 1552).

[70] ACP Casier 23, I23.

gabelle.[71] As William Beik persuasively shows for the crowd actions of the seventeenth century, the accusations of common inhabitants against urban elites usually possessed a political logic and grain of truth, even if their specific allegations were inaccurate.[72] In the gabelle crisis of 1548, as later, Poitiers's inhabitants knew that they were being taxed unfairly, and they associated these policies with the royal officials who presided both in the royal courts and in the hôtel de ville. Jean Bouchet may have been attempting to lay this idea to rest when he updated his *Annales d'Aquitaine* in 1557 to describe how Poitiers's most important legal officials had negotiated the lifting of the gabelle for much of western France.[73]

The city council's taxation policies were not the only source of popular complaint in Poitiers, and the merchant activists made use of other grievances to press their case in favor of the edict. In their oral presentations before the Privy Council in 1548, Paulin Girard and Jean de Marnef also charged that the hôtel de ville had acted irresponsibly in two other areas crucial to civic order: administration of poor hospitals and defense. "[T]he city councillors," they insisted,

> had eaten up and consumed [*mange et consumne*] all of the common funds and especially the armaments, with the result that there had not remained a single knife with which to defend oneself in case of necessity. And that they had not been content with this, but had further eaten up and dissipated the funds of the poor hospitals and had used them for their own purposes.[74]

The merchants' outrage, though, was at least in part disingenuous. Many of the merchant activists had in fact been invited to attend the important assembly convened to discuss the spreading gabelle crisis, and Paulin Girard, Jacques Richier, and Enguilbert de Marnef had been among those agreeing that a census of inhabitants and armaments should be made and the militia assembled.[75] Further, they had helped to shape Poitiers's policies of poor relief. René Audebert, for one, participated in the newly reorganized council of the poor, and many activists had promised to contribute the weekly dues that replaced occasional charity.[76] Therefore, although the activists did not really oppose these policies, they were aware that the policies drew strong criticisms within the city. This may be why the activists "proceeded by insult," as François Porcheron charged when he reported the case to the Mois. They attacked the actions of specific échevins in these areas but did not question the city's overall approach to poverty and rebellion.[77]

---

[71] ACP Reg. 30, 87–91.
[72] Beik, *Urban Protest*, 37.
[73] Bouchet, *Annales d'Aquitaine*, 572–77.
[74] ACP Reg. 30, 178–79 (29 Jan. 1549).
[75] ACP Reg. 30, 12–24 (14 Aug. 1548).
[76] ACP Casier 49, 1544–45; Casier 53, 1544.
[77] ACP Reg. 30, 178–79 (22 Feb. 1549).

Those who worked to have the 1547 edict enforced therefore disagreed with recent municipal police policies, criticized widely unpopular tax assignments, and made use of popular dissatisfactions with poor relief and defense measures. Their willingness to challenge the political status quo, even if for their own advancement, also struck a chord with many of their neighbors. The merchants' endeavors earned them support in the parishes, as manifested in the only regular political decisions that parishes made: nominations for tax assessors. Since the belief endured that the crown could tax property only with subjects' consent (Bodin made property a natural right),[78] it was common in sixteenth-century cities to involve the inhabitants in tax collections. In Poitiers, the inhabitants of each parish were supposed to gather in an assembly after Mass to nominate six men to apportion the tax rates for the entire city. The vestrymen then reported their parishes' decisions in a Mois, where the corps de ville was to appoint the six individuals who had received the most votes. This process did not differ markedly from the procedure in Paris, where notables from each quarter made the nominations, or in Limoges, where inhabitants from different "banners" elected the individuals who were to apportion the taille every year.[79] In Poitiers, the parish nominations led to the same kind of political manipulations that occurred in the hôtel de ville. Parish assemblies, with only a few exceptions, did not consistently nominate their own inhabitants and rarely chose the same individuals more than once.[80] They thus did not act with the goal to have their own parishioners well represented, but made decisions based on citywide reputations, and most likely, citywide campaigning. In 1544, for example, seven parishes made identical nominations for tax assessors, and eight other parishes reported lists that differed in only one or two individuals. The four parishes of the bourg St. Hilaire voted together (see figure 6.1).[81] Parishes also coordinated votes in 1546, when the bourg again voted in bloc, and in 1550 (discussed below).[82] Because no records for these parish assemblies survive, it is impossible to ascertain whether these results reflect a groundswell of support for a specific nominating committee, or whether key vestrymen agreed to manipulate the vote. For 1544, there were no complaints against the parishes or the vestrymen, and the hôtel de ville accepted the nominees without demure.[83] Yet of the fifteen parishes voting together, ten

[78] Bodin, *République*, 1:214, 217–23.

[79] *Registres des délibérations du bureau de la ville de Paris*, 3:30–32, 290–92 for tax assessments for 1544 and 1552. Émile Ruben, ed., *Registres consulaires de la ville de Limoges*, 6 vols. (Limoges, 1867–97), esp. 1:246–47 (specifying a new electoral regulation for 1534). See also Albert Babeau, *La ville sous l'ancien régime*, 2 vols. (Paris, 1884), 1:301–5.

[80] I have reached this conclusion from a systematic analysis of the nominees of each parish for the years 1544–50.

[81] ACP Reg. 25, 397–99 (19 May 1544).

[82] ACP Reg. 27, 123–32 (3 May 1546).

[83] ACP Reg. 26, 3 (30 June 1544).

were among Poitiers's poorest,[84] and most of these parishes routinely left the choice of tax assessors up to the hôtel de ville and "principal parishes."[85] The fact that they clearly formed a geographical bloc comprising the whole southeast of the city could argue equally for unanimity among the inhabitants or a deal struck by the vestrymen.

However the parishes made their nominations, their decisions clearly reflected political coordination, and once the activists began to protest the legal personnel's dominance in the hôtel de ville, this process worked in their behalf. In both 1548 and 1550, parish nominations favored the merchant activists or their close relatives. Although in 1548 the majority of the parishes refused to name tax deputies, those that did name candidates cast their votes overwhelmingly for merchants. Given the votes of the eight parishes, Jacques Richier, Pierre Pellisson, and Pierre Fourest would all have been appointed to the taxation committee, and, unusually, four or five of the six deputies would not have been members of the corps de ville.[86] In fact, the city council ignored the parishes' nominations and appointed a final list that did not include a single individual named by any of the eight parishes.[87]

In 1550, the results were even more revealing. Numerous parishes had again coordinated their votes, but unlike in 1544, these were not the poorest. Rather, they included such key parishes as St. Didier, Notre-Dame-la-Grande, Ste. Opportune, and Notre-Dame-la-Petite (see figure 6.2). No parish neglected to name at least one merchant activist or his close relative, and eight of these, including Enguilbert de Marnef, Pierre Pellisson, and Nicolas Audebert, received between five and ten votes.[88] The significance of these results may be gauged by the hôtel de ville's outrage against them. In the Mois of 15 April, one échevin claimed that certain vestrymen had named candidates not chosen by their parish assemblies, and another vociferated against what he called the monopolistic practices of the electors. "The said nominations and elections," he protested, "are monopolistic, rigged, and harmful matters, against the good and general profit of the commonwealth of this city and would be the means of bringing about tyranny and of causing a mutiny among the inhabitants."[89] What was at stake became clear when an échevin complained that merchants were not qualified to assess the financial means of men holding judicial office.[90] Although members of the Cent did not disdain soliciting votes for municipal elections, they refused to countenance similar behavior in the parishes when the results directly con-

---

[84] According to their total tax assessments for 1546 and 1548, ACP Casier 23, I23.

[85] See, for example, the reports of vestrymen for 1547, ACP Reg. 28, 205–13 (26 May).

[86] See ACP Reg. 29, 98–106. In previous years, the parishes' nominees had often included more members of the corps de ville—five out of six in 1547, for example. Reg. 28, 205–13.

[87] ACP Reg. 29, 123–25 (15 Mar. 1548).

[88] ACP Reg. 31, 140–43 (13 Apr. 1550).

[89] ACP Reg. 31, 143–46; quotation, 146.

[90] ACP Reg. 31, 145.

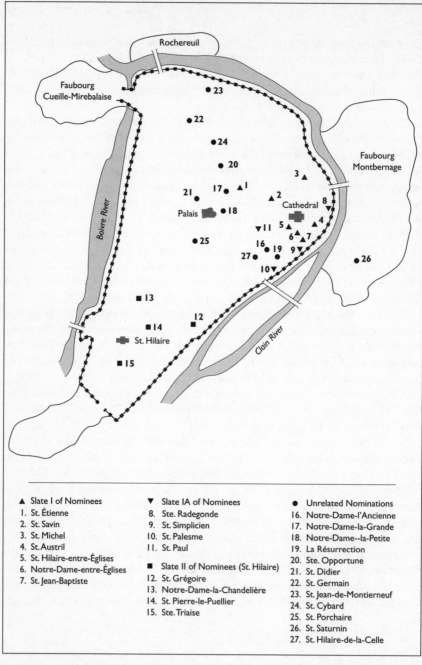

Rochereuil

Faubourg
Cueille-Mirebalaise

Faubourg
Montbernage

Boivre River

Clain River

• 23

• 22

• 24

• 20

3 ▲

21 ●   17 ● ▲ 1   ▲ 2   8 ●
        Palais ● 18   Cathedral   ▲ 4
                        5 ▲   6 ▲ 7 ▲
        ▼ 11
        16 ●   19 ●   9 ▼
27 ●   10 ▼   • 26
        • 25

■ 13

12 ■

■ 14

✠ St. Hilaire

■ 15

▲ Slate I of Nominees	▼ Slate IA of Nominees	● Unrelated Nominations
1. St. Étienne	8. Ste. Radegonde	16. Notre-Dame-l'Ancienne
2. St. Savin	9. St. Simplicien	17. Notre-Dame-la-Grande
3. St. Michel	10. St. Palesme	18. Notre-Dame--la-Petite
4. St. Austril	11. St. Paul	19. La Résurrection
5. St. Hilaire-entre-Églises		20. Ste. Opportune
6. Notre-Dame-entre-Églises	■ Slate II of Nominees (St. Hilaire)	21. St. Didier
7. St. Jean-Baptiste	12. St. Grégoire	22. St. Germain
	13. Notre-Dame-la-Chandelière	23. St. Jean-de-Montierneuf
	14. St. Pierre-le-Puellier	24. St. Cybard
	15. Ste. Triaise	25. St. Porchaire
		26. St. Saturnin
		27. St. Hilaire-de-la-Celle

FIGURE 6.1. Nominations of taxation deputies by parish, 1544. This map shows parishes that coordinated nominations for taxation deputies in 1544. All parishes listed under Slate I made identical nominations, and the parishes listed under Slate IA made nominations that differed in only one or two individuals from the first group. The four parishes in the bourg St. Hilaire also made identical nominations, and their list overlapped with Slate I in four out of six individuals. The geographical proximity of the parishes voting together is evident. Adapted from Robert Favreau, ed., *Histoire de Poitiers* (Toulouse, 1985), 193.

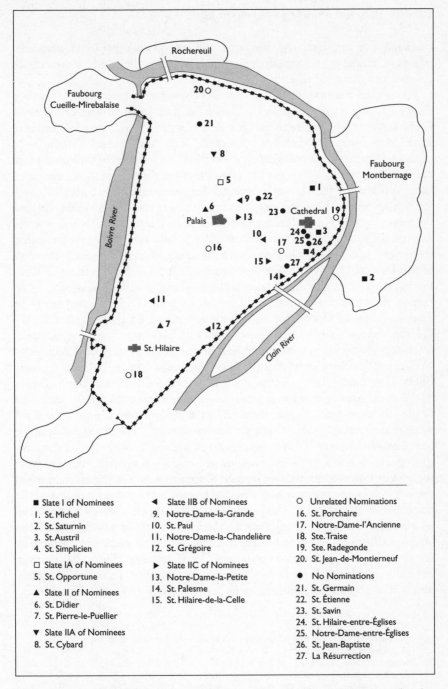

FIGURE 6.2. Nominations of taxation deputies by parish, 1550. This map shows parishes that coordinated nominations for taxation deputies in 1550. All parishes listed under Slate I made identical nominations, and Ste. Opportune, listed under Slate IA, made nominations that differed in only two individuals from the first group. Parishes listed under Slates II, IIA, IIB, and IIC similarly made nominations that were identical within their sub-groups and overlapping in three individuals or more between sub-groups. Adapted from Robert Favreau, ed., *Histoire de Poitiers* (Toulouse, 1985), 193.

tradicted their interests. The merchant activists, on the other hand, made use of every channel open to them to acquire leverage in their bid for greater access to political authority.

For whom were the merchant activists fighting? In their legal cases they claimed to represent the entire body of the merchants and inhabitants of Poitiers, but this reticence to list specific parties to the suit may have merely served as a protective measure.[91] In other cases, such as in La Rochelle in 1614 and Angers in 1650, where groups claimed to represent the entire body of inhabitants and took on the city government in the courts, their challenges led to much more fundamental demands for change and much greater disorder in the streets.[92] The results of the parish nominations may suggest that the merchants served as leaders of parochial opinion. Yet although the activists indisputably took their turns in every position of parish responsibility, they were not among the individuals distinguishing themselves through parish service. Did they rather seek to represent a unique merchant identity that withstood the dominant legal and ecclesiastical culture of the city? The person who jotted down the brief record of Jean Goislard's mayoralty of 1543–44 implied that such a consciousness existed, by claiming that the inhabitants were "fort Joyeux" (overjoyed) with his election, since it had been forty-eight years since a merchant had been elected as mayor of Poitiers.[93] Guillaume Bouchet, a merchant printer, similarly identified a separate merchant community with characteristic approaches to life. Dedicating his *Serées* to the merchants of Poitiers in 1584, he explained that the special faith and loyalty of trade made the corruptions of the religious wars especially damaging to merchants.[94] Yet in Bouchet's conversations, "full of the camaraderie of the good old times,"[95] it is apparent that sociability in Poitiers did not respect professional boundaries, since lawyers and royal officials joined in these sometimes raucous, sometimes learned dinner parties. On the evening when the law and lawyers served as the butt of humor, a magistrate was one of the chief conversationalists.[96] This impression of social permeability is reinforced by a preface written by Enguilbert de Marnef in 1556, in which he identifies his print shop near the palais as the meeting place of a motley assortment of lawyers, students, poets, and customers.[97] The activists' claims did not even obtain ascent from all of Poitiers's merchant notables. Jean Goislard early proclaimed that he had nothing to do with the legal challenges,[98] and mer-

---

[91] ACP Reg. 29, 179–89 (20 July 1548).

[92] Robbins, *City on the Ocean Sea,* 335–53; Beik, *Urban Protest,* 208–15.

[93] ACP Casier 42, Reg. 12, 573.

[94] Bouchet, *Serées,* iii–iv.

[95] Bouchet, *Serées,* iii.

[96] "Des Iuges, des Advocats, des procés, & plaideurs," in Bouchet, *Serées,* 124–72.

[97] La Bouralière, "Imprimerie," 76, 119, reproducing Marnef's "Epistre aux lecteurs" in *Discours non plus melancoliques que divers, des choses mesmement qui appartiennent a nostre France* (Poitiers, 1557).

[98] ACP Reg. 29, 110 (6 Mar. 1548).

chants such as Jacques Arnoul, Pierre Clabat, and Pierre Danyau did nothing to support the advocates of the edict after having themselves been elected under its terms.

It would be going too far, therefore, to claim that the merchant activists saw themselves as the natural leaders of parish opinion or as a group with a unique cultural identity, but their efforts to have the 1547 edict enforced did reflect a general concern with greater political inclusion. When asked to give an opinion on how to maintain order during the gabelle crisis, merchants emphasized the importance of combined actions on the part of elites and lesser inhabitants. While the avocat du roi descanted on the three kinds of government, Paulin Girard stated stoutly that "everyone is ready to march and defend themselves and that the principals should march too, and that where they put their noses, there will the people immediately follow with their feet."[99] Similar concerns are apparent in their critique of tax assessments. In examining the records of parish nominations and in acting to assure that the committee did not solely reflect the interests of the corps de ville, the activists not only advanced their own cause but also insisted on greater fairness and accountability in urban administration. There is even evidence that their endeavors in this area had some effect. By the early 1550s, the hôtel de ville firmly acknowledged that the right to appoint the tax assessors belonged to the parishes, and one bourgeois even suggested that the deputies should be elected by the majority of the inhabitants and not appointed through a process of parochial nominations.[100]

In a highly oligarchic city where judicial elites dominated urban government, ideas that emphasized the importance of popular participation and consent lived on. The activists who sought to have the 1547 edict enforced drew on these more inclusive political notions, even while they pursued exclusive positions for themselves and their relations. Their concerns thus did not extend to any fundamental reform of the system, but reflected a desire to ensure that the existing one functioned properly. The hôtel de ville's basic governing structures were sound, so long as a suitably wide range of urban notables had their chance to contribute their services and to reap civic honors. This enduring agreement about the nature of urban order led the activists to launch their attacks against instances of corruption and mishandling, rather than suing for real changes in the ways that authority was delegated. In attempting to have themselves and their associates elected to office, the merchants enacted the assumption that when city politics became vested in too few interests, corruption and unfairness would result, but as long as a variety of elite viewpoints could be aired, municipal authority would rest on a proper base. These views represented an important challenge to the attempts of entrenched political elites to legislate for the city

[99] ACP Reg. 30, 12–24 (14 Aug. 1548); quotation, 21.
[100] ACP Reg. 32, 79–82 (29 Mar. 1552); 188–89 (13 Mar. 1553); 194 (24 Mar. 1553).

unilaterally, but they were not so threatening that compromise became impossible.

In the end, the merchants were entirely unsuccessful in obtaining any long-term change in electoral qualifications for municipal office. Once the hôtel de ville had obtained a provisory ruling in May 1551, allowing elections to be conducted in accordance with Poitiers's privileges, it proceeded as if the October 1547 edict had never existed.[101] Although exactly when the final ruling was handed down is unclear, it most certainly corroborated the letters of provision.[102] Yet this is not to say that the merchants gained nothing from their opposition. By 1550, the judicial officials within the municipality had recognized that some compromise would be necessary, and certain of the merchant notables found the way clear to realize some of their personal ambitions. Thus on 6 March 1550, René Goupilleau, apothecary and former merchant candidate, was elected bourgeois, and on 27 June 1550, Jean Pellisson was finally elected échevin.[103] On 16 November 1551, the mayor remarked to the council that "he had made numerous propositions for agreement with the merchants of this town concerning the dispute over the edict."[104] If agreement had not yet been reached, the municipality had realized that negotiation was necessary. In fact, if we take a glance at the membership of the Mois in 1556, the year that the whole affair was consigned to collect dust in the trésor, it becomes clear that the municipality had reconsidered its hostility to electing merchants. By August 1556, no fewer than eleven merchants had been elected to the seventy-five, and several of these were even individuals who had been deeply involved in the earlier dispute.[105] The merchants had not gained any permanent assurances that their viewpoint would always be represented in the hôtel de ville, but a good number of individuals had at least attained the influence that lifetime membership in the Mois accorded. As Poitiers faced the hostilities of the religious wars, moreover, the concerns over proper governance and financial responsibility so evident during the reigns of François I and Henri II became inextricably intertwined with struggles over spiritual affiliations and attempts to define the religious identity of the city.

[101] Letters patent dated 26 May 1551 from Saumur, 1506 inventory, ACP Casier 42, Reg. 13, 38.

[102] Although the royal letters patent finally settling the matter no longer exist, the issue was certainly resolved by 30 November 1556, when Pierre Rat turned over all documents relative to the affair, and they were ordered to be placed in the trésor. See the 1506 inventory, ACP Casier 42, Reg. 13, 38.

[103] ACP Reg. 31, 121–33, 159–62.

[104] ACP Reg. 32, 36.

[105] The eleven were Jean Rabateau, René Pasquier, René Arnoul, Jean Beaucé, Paulin Girard, Mery Rogier, Jean Cartier, Louis Royer, Yves Rogier, Claude Regnault, and Florentin du Ruau.

PART II

Introduction

The Wars of Religion in Poitiers

On 10 March 1561 the second National Protestant Synod convened in Poitiers. By 17 August 1589, Poitiers had joined the Catholic League. In the space of a generation, the city had altered from a center of Protestant activity to a stronghold of ultra-Catholic feeling. How did this evolution occur? The process did not so much involve a radical switch in the religious loyalties of Poitiers's population, as a shift in emphasis. When Protestant influence was at its height, attempts to suppress it also occurred continually. In the last decade of the religious wars, Huguenots continued to abide in Poitiers, despite fiscal penalties and all of the efforts to prevent the Huguenots' worship. Indeed, the exact composition and relative strength of the Poitevin Protestant community is difficult to gauge, since extremely few sources have survived. Because the municipal government also kept silent concerning religious differences, conflict is also difficult to track through the municipal registers. During certain periods, this silence may reflect a stance of neutrality or cooperation between the adherents of the two religions. After all, throughout the period, Protestants in smaller or greater numbers attended meetings at the hôtel de ville. At the same time, this reticence to record divisions in faith may have looked more toward preserving Poitiers's external image of order.

The two communities of believers were certainly in conflict, and the fight proceeded on several levels at once. First, the conflict involved public worship of the Reformed faith, since after the early 1560s, Protestants were unable to obtain an official location to practice their cult. Another source of conflict was the issue of political and military dominance within the city. Protestants were strong and numerous enough to take control of Poitiers in 1562 but lost their advantage with the end of the first religious war. Finally, the conflict involved the representation of events, both in the past and as they were occurring. Why was the siege of 1569 an example of heroic resistance to enemy troops, while a similar resistance to Catholic forces in 1562 was nothing but subjection to a foreign captain? Interpretations of Poitiers's recent past were part of the struggle over its religious identity. They contributed as much as actual physical conflict toward the development of a politically influential group of militant Catholics and the articulation of an ultra-Catholic identity for the city at large.

The Reform took early root in Poitiers, and by the late 1550s, not only was the Protestant community considerable and formidable, but Poitiers also served as a center for the dispersion of Reformed belief.[1] The Reformed community owed its beginnings to none other than Jean Calvin, who spent a short time in Poitiers in 1534 and took advantage of his stay to impart his ideas to individuals in university and judicial circles.[2] Despite some early preaching in Poitiers, repression kept Reformed practice underground.[3] Finally, a Protestant church was officially established in 1555, one of the first in France. It is possible that the idea of organizing a national Protestant synod was first developed in Poitiers, and the provincial capital was the site of its second meeting.[4] Before the outbreak of the first religious war in 1562, Catholics complained about the visibility of, and large attendance at, Protestant sermons, and the presence of Protestant nobles in Poitiers, particularly the queen of Navarre, encouraged Reformed worship.[5] Usually meeting in secret in private houses, the Reformed community was occasionally able to hold services in a recognized location. In the fall of 1561, it seized the Augustinian convent for such a purpose.[6] When François II convoked provincial assemblies to draw up *cahiers* for the Estates General of 1560, the Protestants formed a strong enough presence to argue that demands for religious tolerance be inserted in the remonstrances for the Third Estate.[7]

---

[1] On Protestants in Poitiers, see generally Pierre Dez, *Histoire des protestants et des églises réformées du Poitou* (La Rochelle, 1936), and Jacques Marcadé, "Les Protestants dans le Centre-Ouest de 1534 à 1660," *BSAO*, 5th ser., 1 (1987): 99–115. Much of the information on Poitiers's early Reformed community comes from Théodore de Bèze, *Histoire ecclésiastique des églises réformées au royaume de France*, 3 vols. (Paris, 1883–89).

[2] Barbier, "Chroniques de Poitiers," 2. It should be noted that Bèze does not mention that Calvin spent time in Poitiers, although he discusses his travels of 1533–35 (1:80–82). On the other hand, local tradition asserted that Calvin had indeed spent time in Poitiers: in 1589, Jacques de Hillerin heard about it from a canon of Notre-Dame-la-Grande, who had it on the information of another canon who had died twenty years earlier. Hillerin, *Chariot chrestien*, 29–30.

[3] Much of the evidence for repression comes from sources external to Poitiers. See Bèze, *Histoire ecclésiastique*, 1:81, and the journal kept by Guillaume Le Riche, avocat du roi at nearby Saint-Maixent, published in Le Riche, 15, 34–35, 50.

[4] Bèze, *Histoire ecclésiastique*, 1:122, 199–200.

[5] Bèze, *Histoire ecclésiastique*, 1:364, 846; Barbier, "Chroniques de Poitiers," 10, 19, 96; ACP Reg. 38, 8–12 (25 July 1561).

[6] Bèze, *Histoire ecclésiastique*, 1:846–47.

[7] For an account of the first meeting of all three estates, see *Remonstrances du clergé et du tiers-état de Poitou, 1560–1588*, AHP 20 (Poitiers, 1889), 326, 330. For the Protestants' arguments, see Bèze, *Histoire ecclésiastique*, 1:364, and Barbier, "Chroniques de Poitiers," 95.

The growth of the Protestant community did not occur without opposition. Several of Poitiers's judicial officials were zealous in their attempts to repress the movement, and several Reformed believers were executed.[8] Others left for Geneva.[9] When Louis Régnier de la Planche, a well-known Protestant historian of the early 1560s, wished to describe policies of judicial repression in the provinces, he lighted on the actions of Poitiers's sénéchaussée as a particularly telling example.[10] In 1557, the municipality began a campaign against illicit private teachers in the city, and its targets were most certainly Protestant catechists.[11]

Despite attempts to keep the Reformed presence to a minimum, events in Poitiers convinced inhabitants and external authorities that Protestants were indeed a potent force. In an incident resembling the conflict at St. Médard church in Paris in 1560, Protestants and Catholics came to blows on 27 March 1559 at the Jacobins convent in Poitiers. Accounts differ concerning whether Protestants or Catholics provoked the conflict, but violence between individuals of the two faiths ensued, and the Jacobin preacher was endangered.[12] The incident was particularly significant since it occurred on Easter Monday, the day when Poitiers celebrated its delivery from English attack through saintly intervention in the Miracle of the Keys (see chapter 7).

The Catholic judicial officials had been able to suppress the outbreak of violence at the Jacobins and to punish the individuals whom they held responsible, but by 1562 the balance of control had shifted considerably. On 13 April 1562, the Reformed community in Poitiers received a copy of the prince de Condé's declaration of 8 April, explaining why he had taken up arms and soliciting military support.[13] Simultaneously, the Edict of January was finally promulgated in Poitiers.[14] Catholic and Huguenot leaders of the city initially settled on a policy of cooperation, with individuals from both

François II had been informed that such a request would be made and took steps to forestall it: Ledain, ed., *Lettres adressées*, 13:94–95.

[8] Le Riche, 34–35.

[9] In the periods of 1549–60, 1572–74, and 1585–87, thirty-two individuals from Poitiers (some probably with their families) were registered in Geneva's *Livre des habitants*. Of these, eleven were recorded in 1559. One native of Poitiers was also admitted as a bourgeois of Geneva in 1562 without the customary payment, since he was serving as a minister. See Paul-F. Geisendorf, ed., *Livre des habitants de Genève*, 2 vols. (Geneva, 1957–63), and Alfred L. Covelle, ed., *Le livre des Bourgeois de l'ancienne République de Genève* (Geneva, 1897), esp. 271.

[10] Éd. Mennechet, ed., *Histoire de l'estat de France, tant de la république que de la religion, sous le regne de François II: par Régnier, sieur de la Planche* (Paris, 1836), 40–41.

[11] ACP Reg. 34, 175–83 (11 Jan. 1557); 209–10 (15 Feb.); 237–50 (15 Mar.); 314–19 (29 Mar.); 323–37 (5 Apr.); 376–89 (29 Apr.); 398–402 (3 May); 402–9 (10 May); 438–44 (14 June); Reg. 35, 154–58 (13 Dec. 1557).

[12] Barbier, "Chroniques de Poitiers," 4 n. 1; Le Riche, 79–80; Bèze, *Histoire ecclésiastique*, 1:227–28. Bèze's account represents the incident as unplanned, even begun by the Jacobin preacher himself. For an account of the incident at St. Médard in Paris, see Jacques-Auguste de Thou, *Histoire universelle de Jacques-Auguste de Thou, avec la suite par Nicolas Rigault*, 11 vols. (La Haye, 1740), 3:100–1.

[13] Bèze, *Histoire ecclésiastique*, 2:701; De Thou, *Histoire universelle*, 3:138–42.

[14] Barbier, "Chroniques de Poitiers," 96; De Thou, *Histoire universelle*, 3:143.

religions guarding the gates.[15] Yet when Catholics attempted to deny a Protestant noble entry to the city, Protestants gained control of the Tranchée gate and admitted Reformed troops.[16] Although the Protestants were now an effective military presence in Poitiers, attempts at compromise still occurred.[17] Granted, iconoclastic incidents broke out, and rowdy students of Reformed sentiment formed guard units and noisily paraded on the Marché Vieux.[18] At the same time, though, individuals from both sides assembled and swore to preserve the peace.[19] The main preoccupation of the municipality at this time concerned the actions of two Protestant financial officials and measures to preserve royal tax monies. While each side claimed to be acting solely in the king's interest, they were both also maneuvering to assure control of Poitiers's château. By early May, receveur général François Pineau was firmly ensconced in the fortress, and the Protestants seemed to have gained charge of all access to the city.[20]

The situation changed dramatically with the arrival of Lancelot du Bouchet, sieur de Sainte-Gemme, to act as governor for Condé in Poitiers. Within days of his arrival, Sainte-Gemme had confiscated the keys to the town gates, required that all Catholics turn over their arms, and confiscated all Church valuables.[21] When Gascon troops under the leadership of the seigneur de Grammont passed through the area on their way to Orléans, they were admitted to the city, and many of Poitiers's churches were sacked.[22] The body of Ste. Radegonde was removed from her sepulchre and her bones scattered.[23] By the summer of 1562, Poitiers had become a haven for Protestant troops from the entire region.[24] Yet Sainte-Gemme did not have complete control of the city: Pineau, the receveur général, was still ensconced in the château despite repeated attempts to remove him. His presence there would prove crucial. When royal forces under the command of the duc de Villars and the maréchal de Saint-André attacked the city, Pineau trained the

---

[15] Bèze, *Histoire ecclésiastique*, 2:702; Barbier, "Chroniques de Poitiers," 96.

[16] Bèze, *Histoire ecclésiastique*, 2:702–3; De Thou, *Histoire universelle*, 3:195; Barbier, "Chroniques de Poitiers," 97; Ledain, ed., *Lettres adressées*, 13:104–5.

[17] Barbier, "Chroniques de Poitiers," 166.

[18] Bèze, *Histoire ecclésiastique*, 2:703–4; Barbier, "Chroniques de Poitiers," 98.

[19] Barbier, "Chroniques de Poitiers," 184. See also Ledain, ed., *Lettres adressées*, 13:109–10.

[20] Bèze, *Histoire ecclésiastique*, 2:703; De Thou, *Histoire universelle*, 3:195; Barbier, "Chroniques de Poitiers," 97, 162–65, 167–68, 170–77; Ledain, ed., *Lettres adressées*, 13:103; Bélisaire Ledain, ed., *Lettres des rois de France, princes et grands personnages à la commune de Poitiers*, parts 1 and 2, AHP 1, 4 (Poitiers, 1872, 1875), 1: 143–201; 4: 275–340, esp. 329–30.

[21] Bèze, *Histoire ecclésiastique*, 2:704; De Thou, *Histoire universelle*, 3:195; Barbier, "Chroniques de Poitiers," 26, 180–84, 197–98.

[22] Bèze, *Histoire ecclésiastique*, 2:704; Barbier, "Chroniques de Poitiers," 191–210; "Inventaire des Lettres tiltres Et enseignemens de la fabrice de leglize parroischialle de Sainct porchaire," ADV G⁹114, 16v; "Memoyre so [gap] A tous p[rese]ns et advenir," ADV G⁹114, 2v.

[23] Barbier, "Chroniques de Poitiers," 200; ADV G1589, 3r (10 Aug. 1562).

[24] Bèze, *Histoire ecclésiastique*, 2:706; De Thou, *Histoire universelle*, 3:196; Barbier, "Chroniques de Poitiers," 99–100, 199, 201.

guns of the château on the Protestant defenders rather than on the Catholics and helped to bring victory to the royal forces. Catholic troops then entered the city and sacked it, ironically doing far more damage in relieving it than it had suffered at the hands of the Protestants.[25]

What was the stance of Poitiers's Reformed community throughout this episode? Several sources tell of their growing disaffection with Sainte-Gemme, their opposition to seizing the château from Pineau, and their progressive abandonment of the city under outside domination.[26] Yet the Protestants of Poitiers may very well have requested the captain's presence to begin with,[27] and inhabitants certainly participated in the iconoclastic violence that occurred with the entry of the Gascon troops. It seems likely that during his stay in Poitiers from May to July 1562, Sainte-Gemme enjoyed the support of the town's Protestants. Indeed, the version of the events of 1562 that Jacques-Auguste de Thou presents in his *Histoire universelle* is decidedly favorable to the captain and bears evidence of having been communicated to him by a Protestant of Poitiers.[28] Sainte-Gemme's characterization as a fanatic outsider who temporarily took control of the city is most probably a product of the Protestants' weak position after the town returned to Catholic hands. Hoping to retain some rights of worship, they would attempt to downplay their role in the violent overturning of Catholic order. In this way, Poitiers's Catholics won the first religious war on two fronts. They not only regained control of the city, but they also dictated the version of events that would be retained. Memory of the havoc inflicted by royal, Catholic troops persisted, to be sure. But as time passed the story became confused, and inhabitants were sure that the violence had been perpetrated by the *Protestants*.[29]

The 1560s were a time of continual unrest in Poitiers and the region of Poitou. After the Edict of Amboise (March 1563), Catholics refused to honor the peace on numerous occasions.[30] There was a general movement to take up arms among the Poitevin nobility in 1564 and continual disagreement over whether the edict allowed for Protestant worship in Poitiers.[31] During the second religious war (September 1567–March 1568), there was concern over Poitiers's safety, and in the peace that followed (March–September 1568), Protestants were allowed to return to their homes, but only under

---

[25] Bèze, *Histoire ecclésiastique*, 2:708–10; De Thou, *Histoire universelle*, 3:197; Barbier, "Chroniques de Poitiers," 211–13.

[26] Bèze, *Histoire ecclésiastique*, 2:705–7; Barbier, "Chroniques de Poitiers," 100, 186–89.

[27] Barbier, "Chroniques de Poitiers," 193.

[28] De Thou, *Histoire universelle*, 3:197.

[29] De Thou reports that during the siege of 1569 at the hands of Protestant forces, the inhabitants of Poitiers feared the coming of 1 August, remembering the sack that had occurred on this day in 1562 (4:207).

[30] The comte du Lude, gouverneur de Poitou, received several letters instructing him to release prisoners: Ledain, ed., *Lettres adressées*, 13: nos. 97, 100, 103, 106.

[31] Ledain, ed., *Lettres adressées*, 13: nos. 103, 106, 113, 117, 119, 124, 126–27.

close guard.[32] The situation in Lower Poitou, an area of strong Protestant presence, remained extremely unsettled, and Catholics formed a league among themselves for protection.[33] With the third religious war (September 1568–August 1570), Poitiers found itself in the middle of the area under dispute.

On 24 July 1569, Protestant troops under the command of Gaspard de Châtillon, amiral de Coligny, laid siege to Poitiers. Training their cannon on the city from the surrounding heights, they attacked intermittently for seven weeks and almost succeeded in taking it. Yet by early September, Coligny judged the siege not worth the effort and lifted it, only to be defeated at the battle of Montcontour shortly afterward.[34] Poitevin accounts of the siege represent it as a great moment in the town's history. Alerted to the possibility of attack, the comte du Lude, governor of Poitou, entered the town for its defense, as did the young Henri de Lorraine, duc de Guise, his brother, Charles de Lorraine, duc de Mayenne, and a company of Italian soldiers.[35] With the inspiration of such noble company, Poitiers's inhabitants were able to withstand the siege, even when events looked bleak. When bombardments had created a breach in the walls, they labored all night to fix them.[36] When it looked as if troops would enter the city, they flooded the means of access.[37] Several of Poitiers's leaders also served valiantly as militia captains and actively engaged the enemy.[38] Marin Liberge particularly bestowed his praise on Jean de la Haye, lieutenant général, and Joseph Le Bascle, mayor, for their martial valor, inspirational example, and organizational skill during the siege.[39]

For Liberge and for Catholics looking back on the early religious wars, the siege of 1569 was as significant a victory as the siege of Metz in 1552.[40] It was also a testament to the city's special relationship with God: Poitiers's Catholics had acted in unison against heretic attack and had preserved the city in a manner recalling the Miracle of the Keys.[41] Yet such an interpreta-

---

[32] Ledain, ed., *Lettres adressées,* 13: nos. 138, 143–44; *De par le roy et monseigneur le conte du Lude cheuallier de l'ordre dudict seigneur, gouuerneur & lieutenant general pour sa maiesté en Poictou. Il est ordonné que toutes personnes obeiront au contenu en ceste presente sur peine d'estre penduz & estranglez, & porteront croix blanche en la forme y contenue* (Poitiers, 1567).

[33] Ledain, ed., *Lettres adressées,* 13: nos. 146, 151.

[34] On the siege of 1569, see *Siége de Poitiers;* De Thou, *Histoire universelle,* 4:205–14; Agrippa d'Aubigné, *Histoire universelle,* ed. Alphone de Ruble, 10 vols. (Paris, 1895), 3:103ff (chap. 15); *Discovrs dv svcces des affaires passez au siege de Poictiers, despuis le dixneufiesme iour de Iuillet, 1569. iusques au vingtvniesme de Septembre audict an: Enuoyé à Mo[n]seigneur de Mandelot Gouuerneur de Lyon* (Paris, 1569).

[35] *Siége de Poitiers,* 22, 27–28.

[36] *Siége de Poitiers,* 47–49.

[37] *Siége de Poitiers,* 61.

[38] *Siége de Poitiers,* 22.

[39] *Siége de Poitiers,* 20–21, 49–51.

[40] Liberge makes the comparison explicit; *Siége de Poitiers,* 56.

[41] Jean de la Haye reminded his soldiers of the miracle during a speech preparatory to battle. See *Siége de Poitiers,* 86.

tion conveniently reinterpreted the actual course of events. From Liberge's own account, it is clear that many inhabitants of Poitiers were not in favor of holding out against Coligny; some saw no reason to make a firm stand either way.[42] The opinions of property owners who saw their dwellings and fields razed for defense purposes were also not likely to be favorable.[43] Liberge's account, therefore, was as much an argument for the advisability of continuing the defense as a relation of the glorious defeat of the Protestants. Opinion in Poitiers was divided, and it fell to a group of committed ultra-Catholics to convince everyone else that defense was better than negotiation. These Catholic activists found their task facilitated by the fact that many of them held positions of authority within the city; many were judicial officials and members of the hôtel de ville. At the same time, the enormous prestige of the duc de Guise helped them to carry their point. Yet the siege and its memory were also important components in the elaboration of an ultra-Catholic viewpoint in Poitiers. Because of the ultimate withdrawal of Coligny's troops, Guise could be remembered as a hero full of youthful ardor and concern for the town, rather than as a brash outsider seeking power, as Sainte-Gemme had been in 1562. As a picture of cooperation and unity during the siege replaced the reality of disagreement, the event became yet another argument for the necessity of preserving Poitiers's Catholic identity, hallowed by history and confirmed by providence.

After 1569, Poitiers retired from the center of national events. The Saint Bartholomew's Day Massacre provoked a belated reaction when, on 27 October 1572, lieutenant général Jean de la Haye ordered the death of several Protestants. A bourgeois of nearby Parthenay reported that more would have been killed had they not sought protection with their Catholic friends.[44] Despite these deaths, Poitiers does not seem to have participated in the siege of Protestant La Rochelle, which formed the prime theater of conflict during the fourth religious war (February–August 1573). Poitiers's main contribution to the war effort consisted of welcoming the duc d'Anjou (future Henri III) when he passed through the country on his way west.[45]

It was during the fifth religious war (November 1574–May 1576) that Poitiers again found itself in the midst of strife, thanks largely to the activities of its lieutenant général, Jean de la Haye. This outbreak of hostilities was more complicated than the ones preceding it. Not only did Protestants and Catholics oppose each other, but a third group, Malcontent Catholics, joined their Reformed compatriots in the fight against the crown. Struggles in court had strong reverberations in Poitou. François de la Noue allied himself with

[42] *Siége de Poitiers*, 25, 96–98.
[43] *Siége de Poitiers*, 34–35.
[44] Bélisaire Ledain, ed., *Journal historique de Denis Généroux, notaire à Parthenay 1567–1576* (Niort, 1865), 95–96.
[45] Ledain, ed., *Lettres adressées*, 13:332–33; Le Riche, 126; ACP Reg. 41, 58–59 (11 May 1573).

the Malcontents and persuaded La Rochelle to join the Union.[46] Farther east, another lesser noble declared himself the head of a party of publicains demanding judicial and religious reform from the crown. This individual was none other than Poitiers's Jean de la Haye.[47]

Unlike la Noue, la Haye met with intense criticism for his actions in the 1570s, and his reputation has passed down to us as a grasping, insincere manipulator. This judgment is no doubt a product of la Haye's uncertain loyalties, which seemed to shift with the situation. In his *Les memoires et recherche de France* and in assemblies with various nobles and officers, he pointed the way to religious reform and peaceful reconciliation, as well as urging reform of justice and royal administration through calling the Estates.[48] Yet when he was summoned to court for his activities favoring the Malcontents, he argued that he was merely gaining their confidence in order to deliver them over to royal justice.[49] That he remained at liberty so long is testament to the uncertainty of information during the religious wars.[50] Until Poitiers' hôtel de ville itself sent a deputation to court, la Haye was able repeatedly to convince Catherine or her advisors that he was working on her behalf, or at least could be useful to her.[51] In Poitou, either the prestige of his office or the wavering support of the crown was sufficient to maintain doubt over the purpose of his actions. Indeed, such a judgment is as difficult to make now as it was then. Was la Haye following a Machiavellian course to advance his personal position? Was he sincerely working toward Malcontent success? Was he acting out an elaborate plan to gain the confidence of the Protestants so that he could eventually deliver them over to the crown? It is impossible to be sure.

In Poitiers, though, a group of ultra-Catholics increasingly came to see la Haye as a threat. If the inhabitants were uncertain why the lieutenant général

[46] On la Noue's actions during the fifth religious war, see Barbot, *Histoire de La Rochelle*, vol. 3; Pierre Brisson, "Chronique des guerres civiles en Poitou, Aunis, Xaintonge et Angoumois, de 1574 à 1576," in *Chroniques fontenaisiennes, contenant 1. La chronique d'une commune rurale de la Vendée (Le Longon, près Fontenay-le-Comte); 2. La chronique des guerres civiles en Poitou, Aunis, Xaintonge et Angoumois, de 1574 à 1576; 3. Et la chronique de la guerre des trois Henri, en Bas-Poitou; où se trouvent des détails curieux sur les desséchements des Marais et sur les guerres de Religion*, ed. [Armand-Désiré] de la Fontenelle de Vaudoré (Fontenay-le-Comte, 1841); De Thou, *Histoire universelle*, 5:33–42; François de Crue, *Le parti des politiques au lendemain de la Saint-Barthélemy: La Molle et Conconat* (Paris, 1892), chaps. 7–8.

[47] For a summary of facts and sources regarding Jean de la Haye, see Charles de Chergé, "Notice bibliographique sur Jean de la Haye, lieutenant général de Poitou," *MSAO*, 1st ser., 8 (1842): 173–220.

[48] Jean de la Haye, *Les memoires et recherche de France, et de la Gaule Aqvitaniqve* (Poitiers, 1643). For a description of la Haye's ideas on reforms, see Brisson, "Chronique," 249–52, 274–77.

[49] Brisson, "Chronique," 248–49, 360–61, 374–81; Ledain, ed., *Lettres adressées*, 14:9–12; De Thou, *Histoire universelle*, 5:119–20.

[50] Michel Le Riche, for example, was unsure of la Haye's intentions until October 1574, when he described him as "capitaine du bien public élévé" for the first time. Le Riche, 204.

[51] For Poitiers's deputation, see ACP Reg. 42, 71–81 (18 and 20 Oct. 1574); 181–85 (26 Apr. 1575).

set up patrols in Poitiers on his own authority in late November 1573,[52] his attempt to capture the château on Mardi Gras 1574, the day planned for a general Malcontent uprising, convinced many that he was a danger to the security of the town.[53] In fact, the protracted struggle with la Haye and his adherents contributed to a definitive elaboration of a militant Catholic stance in Poitiers. When la Haye first introduced his supporters into the city in November 1573, the duc de Montpensier arrived in town to combat the threat and entrusted the guard of the château to the mayor and échevins of Poitiers.[54] From that point until the château returned to royal hands in 1577, the municipality had a greater role and responsibility to defend the city than it had ever exercised before. La Haye's attempt to gain control of the château in February 1574 then brought hostilities out into the open. Had it not been for the armed opposition of Joseph Doyneau, sieur de Sainte-Soline, son of the late lieutenant général François Doyneau and friend of la Haye's rival, président Pierre Rat, la Haye might have gained military control of the city.[55] That spring, a special war council was set up in the Cordeliers convent,[56] and in May 1574, la Haye's third attempt to seize Poitiers was discovered and defeated.[57] While the duc de Montpensier laid siege to the nearby fortress at Lusignan, the hôtel de ville sent deputies to the crown to produce incriminating evidence against the head of its sénéchaussée.[58] La Haye remained at liberty, however, and again attempted to gain control of Poitiers and Fontenay in March 1575.[59]

Despite these attempts, la Haye's intentions and loyalties remained uncertain. On 30 May 1575, therefore, the municipality arranged a procession on the pattern of the Miracle of the Keys, celebrating the failure of one of la Haye's maneuvers the year before.[60] Members of the corps de ville used the occasion to represent la Haye and his supporters as a threat to Poitiers's political and religious integrity along the lines of the English threat in the year 1200 and the Protestant menace in 1569. That they felt called to do so indicates both the strength of their conviction and the continuing support for la Haye in Poitiers. Not only were many people uncertain about the reasons behind his actions, but the kinds of complaints that he claimed to represent also continued to elicit a sympathetic following. As lieutenant général, no doubt, he had also built up a substantial following, and he offered one al-

---

[52] Le Riche, 149; Ledain, ed., *Lettres adressées*, 13:342–45; Brisson, "Chronique," 233.

[53] Ledain, ed., *Journal historique*, 114; Brisson, "Chronique," 237–38, 242–45.

[54] Ledain, ed., *Lettres adressées*, 13:342–45.

[55] Brisson, "Chronique," 244–45; Ledain, ed., *Lettres adressées*, 13:354–56.

[56] These councils are recorded in ACP Reg. 42. Between May and July 1574, separate secretaries recorded the meetings at the Cordeliers and at the hôtel de ville (Reg. 41).

[57] Le Riche, 172; Ledain, ed., *Journal historique*, 119; Brisson, "Chronique," 254–56; ACP Reg. 42, 61–62 (21 Sept. 1574).

[58] ACP Reg. 42, 71–81 (18–20 Oct. 1574).

[59] Brisson, "Chronique," 361–74; ACP Reg. 42, 158 (10 Mar. 1575); Le Riche, 220–21.

[60] ACP Reg. 42, 199–204 (30 May 1575).

ternative in the system of political oppositions that developed within city walls. Local loyalties and the larger political scene thus had an impact on one another: la Haye's activities confused the divisions between Protestants, Malcontents, and ultra-Catholics, but they also allowed a coterie of his committed opponents to elaborate an uncompromising Catholic stance and to represent it as the natural outcome of Poitiers's historic identity.

La Haye did not remain a threat to his opponents for long. A new plot to capture Poitiers in July 1575 convinced both the king and the inhabitants that the lieutenant général was a traitor.[61] The sénéchaussée duly condemned him for lèse-majesté, and a group of several hundred inhabitants, led by the sieur de Sainte-Soline, rode out to his country estate and killed him. His body was brought back to Poitiers and hacked to pieces by the crowd.[62]

From the end of the fifth religious war until the crisis of the Catholic League, Poitiers took a consistently Catholic position, but refrained from any overt challenge to Henri III and his court. In 1576, the municipality refused to join the League of Péronne, even though the governor of Poitou urged it to do so.[63] Henri III spent much of the summer of 1577 in Poitiers, whence much of the peace of Bergerac was negotiated.[64] In 1579, an important session of the Grands Jours sat in Poitiers, during which magistrates not only amused themselves with the sophisticated company of the dames des Roches, but also condemned to death many nobles and others who had committed violent acts during the religious troubles.[65] In 1585, Poitiers's royal officials enforced with alacrity the stipulations of the Treaty of Nemours, which ordered all Protestants to convert or to leave the kingdom.[66]

Over the course of approximately fifty years, therefore, Poitiers witnessed a considerable change in religious conditions and political relations within its walls. Early constituting one of the most important Reformed communities in France, the Protestants of Poitiers succeeded in gaining control of the city for a short time, only to watch their relative advantage disappear over the next few decades. Catholic sentiment had always been strong in Poitiers, but the challenges of the religious wars slowly encouraged a rigidification in militancy, until the city finally declared for the Catholic League in 1589. The siege of 1569 and the experiences of the mid-1570s were especially important in creating both an ultra-Catholic view of the city's history, and a de-

[61] ACP Reg. 42, 240–41 (11 July 1575); Brisson, "Chronique," 381–85; Le Riche, 228.

[62] Brisson, "Chronique," 386–89; Le Riche, 229–31; Brilhac, 11; ACP Reg. 42, 260–61 (25 July 1575); MMP MS 574, 37r.

[63] ACP Reg. 42, 565–72, 574–77 (26–31 Jan. and 13 Feb. 1577).

[64] ACP Reg. 42, 647–51 (2–3 July 1577); Brilhac, 12–14.

[65] On the Grands Jours of 1579, see Brilhac, 15–17; ACP Reg. 42, 840–42 (11 Sept. 1579), 999–1008 (24 Aug.–4 Sept.); 1010–12 (14 Sept.); the numerous *arrêts* published during the session (see Bibliography); ADV F8, "Grands Jours de Poitiers, 1531–1635," vol. 50; AN X^{1A} 9205, "Registre des Ordonnances Civils des Grands Jours à Poitiers, 1579;" X^{1A} 9208, "Registre du Grands Jours de Poitiers."

[66] Le Riche, 410.

termined group of activists set upon preserving the purity of religion in Poitiers. Ironically, one of the Catholic heroes of the siege ended by drawing his former companions together against him in 1574–75.

By the 1580s, many of Poitiers's notables and lesser citizens had obtained considerable experience in the manifestations of religious war. The militia had developed its organization over the last few decades; the municipality had instituted a system of emergency councils to discuss military and political matters; the town had witnessed the importance of sympathetic governors and control of the château. Yet by the last years of the reign of Henri III, there was still considerable disagreement about what Poitiers's history meant, what the city's relationship with the crown should be when the king seemed remiss in supporting the Catholic faith, and what groups would ultimately gain the upper hand. In part II, therefore, we will look in depth at Poitiers's historical tradition, its perceived relations with the kings of France, and how the crisis of the Catholic League temporarily altered the lines of authority within the city and affected its relationship with the kingdom at large.

7 The Miracle of the Keys and the Urban Historical Tradition

Throughout the medieval and early modern periods, the following story was told: In the year 1200, the mayor of Poitiers sent his trusted clerk on an errand to Périgueux. There the traitorous servant was approached by the English, enemies of the king, who offered him a large sum of money to deliver Poitiers into their hands. The clerk accepted, and they agreed that the following Easter he would steal into the mayor's bedroom and take the keys to the town gates, which he would then open to the waiting English. Easter arrived, and the enemy was assembled as planned, but when the clerk went to look for the keys, they were nowhere to be found. He immediately went to alert his coconspirators, and the English were taken with such fear that they began to slaughter themselves. What so frightened them was the apparition of a great queen, surrounded by infinite numbers of armed men and accompanied by a bishop, ready to descend upon them like a lion on its prey. The queen was the Virgin Mary. The bishop was St. Hilaire of Poitiers, whose bones lay within the town walls. The carnage awoke the inhabitants and the mayor, who was distraught at not being able to find the keys. They then began a general search, and, finally arriving at the church of Notre-Dame-la-Grande, what did they find within the hands of the Virgin but the very keys they sought. The town then swore to hold a procession every Easter Monday in commemoration of this miracle.[1]

This miracle, the Miracle of the Keys, was a fundamental event in Poitiers's historical tradition: it established a firm and venerable relationship of loyalty between the town and the kings of France and invested it with divine

---

[1] For this recounting of the miracle, I rely on the version to be found in MMP MS 51, 22r, and reproduced in Lecointre-Dupont, "Mémoire sur le miracle des clefs et sur la procession du lundi de pâques," *MSAO*, 1st ser., 12 (1845): 210–13.

approval. This version of the miracle was copied into the municipal statute book in 1463, and the town government would make continual reference to it throughout the rest of the fifteenth and sixteenth centuries and beyond. For the hôtel de ville, history was more than a subject of urban pride. Integral to the town council's conception of its own authority, the past explained and justified current relationships within the urban sphere. If the municipality could claim a seigneurial relationship over the inhabitants, it owed this right as much to its staunch fidelity to the kings of France as to sworn oath. If Poitiers could boast an impressive collection of liberties and take pride in a broad assortment of legal, academic, and religious institutions, these advantages were also the fruits of obedience. Indeed, the municipal conception of the urban past was organized around a series of such exchanges: every privilege granted had been a mark of special royal favor merited by the town's support of the French king and of what was due him as such.

This view of the town's history meant that not only did the past affect the present, but that the present also exerted influence over the past. On the one hand, the hôtel de ville evoked the town's historical tradition in its continual negotiations with the French crown. Both city and king resorted to a model of past cooperation, loyalty, and affection as a basis for establishing accord. The town council also used the language of historical tradition as a means of political argument within the city. References to events, miraculous or otherwise, in Poitiers's past served as guides for present activity. Current situations were regarded as analogous to previous ones and thus called for similar means of resolution. Yet history also set the parameters of appropriate and desirable action, and the municipality viewed any contradiction of its historical interpretation as a rejection of the entire tradition. Any actual or symbolic denial of a privilege, for example, immediately put into question the whole structure of the town's special liberties and place within the kingdom. In this way the present exerted power over the past; any refusal to follow the course that the municipal government had painstakingly identified altered the very terms of the tradition. This is not to say that Poitiers's historical tradition was immutable. On the contrary, the past underwent constant revision and adjustment to suit the circumstances of debate. Indeed, the very emphasis on Poitiers's relationship of obedience to the kings of France had received particular elaboration only since the time of Charles VII. Yet however it adapted tradition, the hôtel de ville sought to remain its primary interpreter.

As important as Poitiers's history was for the municipality, it also formed an integral part of the town's wider identity. If the urban past could be used to make arguments about present concerns, this was only because it constituted a general language comprehensible beyond the walls of the hôtel de ville. Historians of urban identity such as Claire Dolan, André Sanfaçon, and Philippe Guignet have tended to see historical traditions as the product of elite concerns or manipulation. Indeed, Guignet has argued that the general populations of Tournai, Cambrai, and Lille were not very interested in the historical traditions, classical origins, or foundation myths of their cities, but participated in urban culture through the less intellectual medium of religious festivals.[2] Yet as Poitiers's experiences show, government was a complicated process, in which interactions always contained a threat of force but where persuasion was a necessary element. The ways in which civic memory was preserved and transmitted certainly varied, but to be an effective political medium, the historical tradition had to be shared. As the Miracle of the Keys reveals, too, these historical traditions could be embedded in religious beliefs, rather than existing in opposition to them. Yet since history belonged to a sphere of public discourse, debate was sure to arise over its interpretation and application.

At the same time, alternative visions of the past existed that the municipality did not ultimately adopt. If the city government had finally turned its gaze on the French crown and chosen to emphasize ties of loyalty and dependence, it had also experimented with traditions underscoring the great age of the city and its importance in a period predating the French kings. Existing in tandem with the view of Poitiers as the ideal bonne ville were notions of the county of Poitou as an ancient and independent region with its own traditions and concerns. Each of these views grew out of a particular selection of elements available from Poitiers's past, but each had different implications for the town's prescribed political identity. History was indeed adaptable to event, but only within the confines of a particular tradition. The limitations of the version favored by the hôtel de ville would become apparent with the religious wars and the Catholic League. Until that period, that version appeared the best suited to the twin goals of bolstering the authority of the municipality within Poitiers and of winning further favors from the crown.

A Developing Historical Tradition

The Miracle of the Keys became an official municipal text in the mid-fifteenth century because it expressed persuasively a central aspect of a developing historical outlook. In situating Poitiers's divinely sanctioned and celestially aided loyalty to the kings of France as far back as the year 1200, it represented and reinforced a vision of the past that accorded well with the tradition that the municipality favored. Although scholars are uncertain when the miracle was first written down and whether it was celebrated continuously since the thirteenth century, evidence indicates its increased im-

[2] Dolan, "Images en action"; André Sanfaçon, "Traditions mariales et pouvoir ecclésiastique à Chartres sous l'Ancien Régime," in *Productions symboliques,* ed. Laurier Turgeon, 45–64; Guignet, *Pouvoir dans la ville,* 79–81.

portance by the fifteenth.[3] It was at this time at least that statuary was added to the façade and lateral porch of Notre-Dame-la-Grande in commemoration of the miracle.[4]

Poitiers's municipal government in the sixteenth century rarely acknowledged that the town's past extended beyond the thirteenth century. Unlike the citizens of Toulouse, Bordeaux, and Lyon, members of Poitiers's corps de ville neither emphasized their city's origins in classical antiquity nor eagerly claimed their own descent from Roman consuls.[5] Although Poitiers had been an important center in the Gallo-Roman period, an essential part of the kingdom of Aquitaine, and the capital of the powerful counts of Poitou, official history began with the oldest surviving charters granted by Eleanor of Aquitaine in 1199. Since Poitiers entered the dominion of Philip Augustus in 1204, when the French king confirmed Eleanor's grants and sent the town a copy of the *Établissements de Rouen,* this partial historical amnesia encouraged the idea that Poitiers had been loyal to the kings of France throughout its history. Indeed, the story of the Miracle of the Keys made even further claims concerning this relationship: in the year 1200, Poitiers belonged to the count of Poitou, who was none other than King John of England, the very enemy against whom the town's patron saints afforded their protection. The story therefore implied that the town had recognized the superior claims of the French king even before he had confiscated the county from his rival.[6]

The historical tradition of obedience and favor organized the town's past around a series of exchanges between Poitiers and the French kings. Important privileges marked the course of this history as the natural products of an ideal relationship between sovereign and city. Because so many of the preceding years had been marked by warfare between France and England, obe-

---

[3] The uncertainty is due to a problematic attribution within the text of the miracle. The version recorded in MMP MS 51 identifies its source as Vincent of Beauvais's *Speculum morale.* Yet not only is the *Speculum morale* now generally considered an apocryphal text, but the narration of the miracle appears nowhere within the standard Douai version. If the miracle was copied from this text, therefore, it was from an interpolated version existing in Poitiers in 1463, but now unidentifiable. See Lecointre-Dupont's discussion of this problem, 215–16. On the *Speculum morale* see Serge Lusignan, *Préface au Speculum Maius de Vincent de Beauvais: réfraction et diffraction* (Montréal and Paris, 1979), 77–90.

[4] Lecointre-Dupont, "Mémoire sur le miracle des clefs," 237–38.

[5] Toulouse: La Faille, *Annales,* 2:261–62; Henri Ramet, *Le Capitole et le Parlement de Toulouse* (Toulouse, 1926), 11–12. Bordeaux: Lurbe, *Chroniqve bovrdeloise,* 3v, 52r–v, 60r, 61r–v; Elie Vinet, *L'antiqvité de Bovrdeavs, et de Bovrg,* ed. Henry Ribadieu (Bordeaux, 1860). Lyon: Rubys, *Privileges,* 20–26.

[6] Evidence indicates that this dating disturbed several expounders of the miracle. When Jean Bouchet told the story in his *Annales d'Aquitaine,* he situated the event in the year 1202, presumably to coordinate it with the conflict occurring between Philip, John, and Arthur of Brittany in this year. Bouchet, *Annales d'Aquitaine,* 159–61. For a detailed account of the relations between John, Philip Augustus, Arthur, and the barons of Poitou at this time, see Warren, *King John,* 54–119; Maurice Powicke, *The Loss of Normandy 1189–1204: Studies in the History of the Angevin Empire,* 2d ed. (Manchester, U.K., 1960), 145–69; and Alfred Richard, *Histoire des comtes de Poitou, 778–1204,* 2 vols. (Paris, 1903), 2:334–453.

dience was often equated with rejection of the English cause and with military or symbolic defense of the French crown. The result was to accentuate the importance of certain privileges and benefits and to consign others to obscurity. The town walls, which made Poitiers the largest town in France after Paris, had been built during the dual reign of Henry II of England and Eleanor of Aquitaine.[7] In an era when the emphasis was on resisting the English, this fact was conveniently ignored. Equally forgotten were the circumstances under which Poitiers was first accorded its commune—again, almost certainly by the counts of Poitou.[8] Finally, the municipality was forced to recognize that its right to administer civil and criminal justice had been granted by the Black Prince in 1369. Essential to the jurisdictional rights of the town government, the privilege was sure to be evoked whenever these rights were threatened. Yet the privilege did not belong to the litany of grants often recited to illustrate the bonds between Poitiers and its sovereigns.

By the sixteenth century, the municipality had identified a canon of important privileges as essential to its authority and historical identity. Most of these had been granted by the kings of France, many of them in recognition of important services that the town had rendered against the English. When Poitiers sent its privileges to be confirmed by the new king Henri III in 1575, it saw fit to send all of those confirmed by Louis XI in 1461, supplemented by others granted subsequently.[9] The collection of charters was far from complete and gave a selective view of Poitiers's history. Anyone consulting it in isolation might have concluded that the town had become a commune in 1222, and Jean Le Roy was in fact under this mistaken impression.[10] Even more important, four out of a total of nine privileges had been granted by either Charles V or Charles VII in recognition of Poitiers's signal services rendered during the most difficult periods of the Hundred Years' War.

Poitiers never forgot the period of the "Kingdom of Bourges," when the town served as the de facto capital of the dauphin, later to become Charles VII. Forced to quit Paris, Charles found his welcome in the Poitevin capital, where he reconvened the Parlement of Paris in 1418. The Parlement was to sit in Poitiers until 1436, and when Joan of Arc came to announce her famous vision, it was here that she met the dauphin. Jean Bouchet could still point to the stone from which she mounted her horse to embark on her mil-

---

[7] Bouchet, *Annales d'Aquitaine*, 145; Favreau, *Ville de Poitiers*, 50.

[8] See chapter 1.

[9] The collection included two charters granted by Philip Augustus in 1204 and 1222; the 1369 grant of legal jurisdiction; a charter of Charles V granting the mayor and échevins noble status in 1372; the 1431 founding of the university; two charters of Charles VII permanently attaching Poitou to the royal domain and establishing a royal court in Poitiers dating from 1436; a privilege of freedom from military service of 1472; and a charter granting freedom from royal taxes on cloth production in 1488.

[10] The origins of his mistake are uncertain, but he declared in his *Recueil Au vray* that he had begun his text in 1200 despite the fact that there was no evidence of any mayors of Poitiers before 1222; MMP MS 574, 2v.

itary campaign.[11] The period was important for several reasons. Not only did it establish a special relationship of service and gratitude between the city and the king, but it also offered the hope of further honors. For its support of the claimant to the crown of France in the early fifteenth century, Poitiers had received a group of privileges that had significantly enhanced its urban status and that would continue to have a profound impact on its civic life. Sixteenth-century Poitiers derived much of its prestige and a good part of its wealth from its renowned university and important royal courts, and it owed the establishment of both to Charles VII. The university's foundation dated from a grant of 1432, and a privilege of 1436 identified Poitiers's sénéchaussée as the principal court of the region, to which appeals from other jurisdictions could be addressed. This same privilege echoed the provisions of a contemporary grant, which had enormous symbolic importance: Poitou was henceforth permanently attached directly to the royal domain and could no longer be given out in fief, even to members of the royal family.[12]

Because these privileges had been granted and the special relationship with the kings of France had been forged in a time of conflict with England and its French allies, the theme of resistance against the English became a special narrative thread connecting the important moments of Poitiers's past. In retrospect, a privilege very dear to the members of the town council could be woven into the long-standing tradition of loyalty: in 1372, Charles V had granted the privilege of nobility to the mayor and échevins of Poitiers, in recognition of the town's rejection of English dominion and actions to deliver itself over to Bertrand du Guesclin. By the sixteenth century, the role of Jean, duc de Berry, in obtaining the grant had been all but forgotten, and the city council was pleased to be able to associate a privilege so beneficial to themselves with the town's heroic past.[13]

Poitiers's historical tradition was so powerful because it held as many implications for the future as it did for the past. Ever since the Parlement of Paris had returned to the French capital, Poitiers had been attempting to obtain its own sovereign court. In this endeavor, the town met with opposition not only of the existing institution, but also of Bordeaux, which had been Poitiers's successful rival in soliciting this boon. In the competition with Bordeaux to be the principal administrative city of western France Poitiers obviously lost out, but the rebelliousness of the capital of Guyenne in the second half of the fifteenth century made this outcome temporarily uncertain. In the eyes of the hôtel de ville, Poitiers's tradition of loyalty offered a firm contrast to Bordeaux's disobedience. The town government was eager to take advantage of any of the failings of its southerly rival, and in the early

[11] Bouchet, *Annales d'Aquitaine*, 246.

[12] For printed versions of these ordinances, consult *Ordonnances,* 13:179–81 (16 Mar. 1431 [o.s.] from Chinon); 13:226–27 (Aug. 1436 from Tours); 15:677–79 (Aug. 1436 from Tours).

[13] For the text of the privilege, see Audouin, ed., *Recueil de documents,* 46:251–53. On the role of Jean, duc de Berry, see la Haye, *Memoires et recherche,* 48.

1450s recorded almost as much detail concerning Bordeaux's espousal of the English cause and subsequent reconquest by Charles VII as concerning events occurring in Poitiers itself.[14] These efforts met with temporary success in 1469, when the Parlement of Bordeaux was transferred to Poitiers, only to be returned to its original home three years later.[15] The gabelle uprisings of 1548 reinforced Poitiers's sense of difference from Bordeaux. While the capital of Guyenne joined the disturbances occurring throughout the region, Poitiers resolutely opposed any agitations. The mayoral chronicle for 1548–49 took advantage of the discrepancy. In an extremely partial account, it recorded merely that a rebellion had occurred in Bordeaux and Saintonge and that the king had sent an army to put it down.[16]

Despite its best efforts, Poitiers never succeeded in obtaining a permanent parlement.[17] The town also had constantly to guard against being included in the government of Guyenne. The danger was still present during the Estates General of 1588, where the question arose whether the noble deputy of Poitou would sit with the assembly of Guyenne or of Orléans. The town council instructed its deputies on no account to join the Guyenne assembly, since this participation would damage the right of Poitou to exist as a separate government under the direct dominion of the kings of France.[18] For a brief time, Poitiers had experienced the hope of becoming the judicial capital of western France. In the narrative of its past virtues and Bordeaux's previous perfidy, resistance to the English played an important part. The tradition thus met two concerns at once: to provide the essential context for Poitiers's notable array of privileges and to offer sufficient persuasion for their ever desired extension.

A vein of political discourse emphasizing Poitiers's loyalty and obedience suited the French crown as much as it did the hôtel de ville. Without royal complicity, the tradition could never have been elaborated. Once the tradition was formed, the kings of France relied on it and its underlying logic to mediate their relations with the town, in the same way that the hôtel de ville made reference to it in interactions with the monarch. In establishing a model of an ideal past, the tradition ensured that both town and king agreed on

[14] An account of the entry of the count of Dunoys into Bordeaux dated 30 June 1451 is recorded in MMP MS 51, 88r–89r. ACP Casier 42, Reg. 11, also testifies to Talbot's taking of Bordeaux in 1452 with the help of the inhabitants; letters announcing Talbot's death at Castillon and the victory of the French in 1453; the text of royal letters patent dated 27 Oct. 1453 in which Charles VII reported on his actions in Guyenne since the victory; and the king's sojourn in Poitiers for eight days in 1454. During this visit Poitiers argued that the disloyalty of the Bordelais should cause them to forfeit their parlement in Poitiers's favor. ACP Casier 42, Reg. 11, 4v–5v.

[15] ACP Casier 42, Reg. 13, 117; Bouchet, *Annales d'Aquitaine,* 275.

[16] ACP Casier 42, Reg. 12, 574.

[17] A deputation to Louis XII in 1497 petitioned for a parlement, and the subject was revived once more (perhaps for the last time) in 1573. See Bouchet, *Annales d'Aquitaine,* 318–19; Le Riche, 139 (entry for 2 June 1573).

[18] ACP Reg. 48, 132 (24 Oct. 1588).

their respective rights and obligations and offered a solid precedent for successful interaction. Common interpretation of the past was the best way to ensure future cooperation and benefit. The desire for and belief in a common means of expression was so pronounced that as tensions mounted between the town and the king in the last quarter of the sixteenth century, resort to it became more insistent rather than less so. This increased use of a common historical discourse in a time of friction was not the result of hypocrisy. Rather, it testified to the power of an historical model to act as a means of political negotiation between two entities that were drawing ever further apart.

The evolution of Poitiers's historical tradition is evident in the preambles of royal privileges. Until 1436, general references to the town's loyalty and service predominate. Beginning with the two privileges granted in this year, however, the texts impart a historical context, which by the sixteenth century would become a developed historical narrative. In the charter by which he permanently attached the county of Poitou to the royal domain, Charles VII recited the exploits of the English, his reception in Poitiers, and the support and duty that he had received in the city.[19] A second charter granted in the same month repeated much of this narrative and added specific details concerning the tenure of the Parlement of Paris in Poitiers. According to the preamble, the Parlement had sat for eighteen years in Poitiers, "highly honored and well obeyed."[20] It was in recompense for such services, explained Charles, that he was establishing a permanent royal court at Poitiers with special rights.[21]

After 1436, the recital of Poitiers's special loyalty to the crown became a common element of royal privileges. In a charter granting the crafts of Poitiers exemption from royal taxes on cloth production, for example, Charles VIII recounted the town's reception of his grandfather during the time of the English occupation as a consideration informing his generosity.[22] Yet nowhere was the narrative of the historical relations between the Poitevin capital and the French crown as developed as in a privilege granted by Henri III in 1576, by which he conferred special judicial rights upon the mayor and échevins. Beginning with the town's refusal to swear obedience to King John after the death of Eleanor of Aquitaine, the text went on to describe Poitiers's continuing perfect fidelity to the French crown after the capture of Jean le Bon, its vigor in aiding Bertrand du Guesclin, constable of France, to deliver the town from its English captivity into the dominion of Charles V, and the well-known reception of Charles VII at the height of English success. Recent testimonials to the city's notable loyalty were also included, with special

---

[19] Letters patent of Charles VII, dated Aug. 1436 from Tours, *Ordonnances*, 15:677–79.
[20] *Ordonnances*, 13:226.
[21] Letters patent of Charles VII, dated Aug. 1436 from Tours, *Ordonnances*, 13:226–27.
[22] Letters patent of Charles VIII, dated Apr. 1488 from Plessis-lès-Tours, *Ordonnances*, 20: 127–28.

mention being given to Poitiers's resistance against the Protestant siege of 1569, active guard of the château, and financial sacrifices to fund the royal armies fighting the Huguenots in Poitou. The privilege therefore offered a kind of official history of the relations between Poitiers and the French kings to which both parties could ascribe. The text, moreover, did not leave the assessment of the historical record to chance, but provided its own interpretation of the purport of such relations. The inhabitants of Poitiers had acted with "the fidelity [and] natural affection that all good subjects owe to their true and legitimate king," and they "intended to continue such services . . . and increase them by every means in their power in order to retain this important and honorable name and title of good and loyal Frenchmen, devoted and entirely dedicated to the conservation of the kingdom, which is their own native country. . . ."[23] The conclusion was clear: the town's exemplary loyalty to the kings of France in the face of English aggression had ensured a harmonious relationship to the benefit of each. The continuation of such a rapport, this time in alliance against the Protestants as current disturbers of the French peace, would afford further assurances of honors and security.

References to Poitiers's tradition of special loyalty are not surprising in texts of royal privileges, which were in some sense rewards for past amicable relations. Yet the tradition could also be used as an active device, to remind each side of the positive results of successful interaction and to ensure its continuation according to the dictates of the established model. As Poitiers's unquestioned obedience to the crown became less assured, therefore, references to past loyalty and harmonious relations increased and took on added importance. Each side sought to convince the other that it risked rupturing the pattern of their accord and sought to recall it within the bounds of past agreement. At no time did the corps de ville more clearly express its conception of the duties that it owed to the king as when it refused to contribute to a voluntary subsidy to relieve the embarrassment of the king's affairs. Poitiers's past sacrifices and trials, the mayor argued, had made little impact on the king, so that its resistance to the Protestants in 1562 and 1569 should now dispense the town from monetary contribution. The city, suggested the mayor, had acquitted all of its responsibilities, only to see the crown ignore its own essential duties.[24]

Henri III, in his turn, referred to urban tradition in a desperate attempt to preserve the essence of his authority. In a letter of 12 March 1589 he cited Poitiers's tradition of "particular fidelity" and the benefits that it would continue to inspire both as a reason leading him to have confidence in its continuation and an argument against its contravention.[25] Such language was important. Just two months before Poitiers refused Henri III entry through

---

[23] Letters patent of Henri III, dated May 1576 from Paris, ACP Casier 3, A43.
[24] ACP Reg. 44, 122–24 (10 Jan. 1583).
[25] ACP Reg. 48, 356–57 (17 Mar. 1589).

the town gates, the municipal government ordered that the letter be printed, posted, and cried aloud, so that everyone would be aware of the king's good opinion of the city.[26] The language of loyalty and favor was certainly not strong enough to prevent rupture during the mounting tensions of the civil wars. Yet such examples reveal that the urban historical tradition was one medium, and a powerful one, to which town and king resorted in an attempt to resolve differences and to reunite divergent interpretations that current events aroused.

The Miracle of the Keys

As important as the historical tradition was for the municipal government as an interpretation of the past and as a guide for the future, it did not fall within the unique preserve of the hôtel de ville. Just as history served as an essential means of communication between the municipality and the king, it formed a central aspect of the town's greater identity. Not only were all elements of the population familiar with Poitiers's historical tradition, but they each recognized history as an effective means of representation. Whether the object was to persuade a public audience or to convince oneself, the past provided a trove of references that could be enlisted to prove a point. Past practice had long been the standard of present behavior. Not only did age lend law or statute particular authority, but custom frequently determined contemporary procedure. Until 1559, memory of the past served as a prime means to settle current disputes, so that educated and uneducated alike turned to history as a proof of law.[27]

History could thus be employed as a medium of political debate within the civic realm, just as it served as a means of negotiation with the crown. Of course, the same methods could not be applied in both cases. Whereas city and king communicated largely through written texts, the means of political representation within the urban sphere were mostly oral and ceremonial. In particular, the municipal administration relied heavily on annual processions to convey a particular point of view concerning Poitiers's past and its implications for present action. Yet processions, like all urban spectacles, were extremely complicated events that did not always lead to the desired ends of their organizers. Although members of the corps de ville would

[26] ACP Reg. 48, 356.
[27] Until the redaction and reform of much of France's customary law at the hands of Christofle de Thou and his fellow commissioners from 1555 to 1581, one proved customary law stipulations through the testimony of individuals assembled in groups called *turbes*. If it could be proven that a practice had existed continuously for forty years, it would be incorporated into custom. The customary law of Poitou was officially recorded in 1514 and reformed in 1559. On the reformation of customary law, see René Filhol, *Le premier président Christofle de Thou et la réformation des coutumes* (Paris, 1937). For a discussion of the place of customary law in the structure of royal legislation, see Church, *Constitutional Thought*.

no doubt have approved the theories of many current scholars, who hold
that spectacles reinforced a particular view of the social and political order
and united the whole community in common feeling, the very efficacy of ceremony to convey a point of view belies the unidirectional nature of the argument.[28] If everyone accepted that history could express ideas important
to the present and that processions could relate or reflect historical arguments, it did not follow that everyone interpreted history or its representation in the same way. Different aspects of the same story could receive
varying emphases, and symbols in particular were always open to divergent
construction. Processions could thus never be simple reflections of public order as envisioned by their organizers, but depended on the cooperation of
each participating group, including the audience. They were concentrated instances of political debate, in which all groups participated in the construction, acceptance, or rejection of a particular type of political language, even
if the danger of misunderstanding was always present. What was true of
spectacle as a means of argument was also true for history. Historical actors
and events could be arrayed in a well-ordered narrative, with the goal of involving the audience in a particular conception of civic identity. Yet even if
inhabitants consented to participate and were willing to play the roles assigned to them, they did not always agree concerning what parade they were
watching.

History, from the hôtel de ville's point of view, offered an important way
to try to assert its own construction of its role and authority within the town.
At the same time, the medium provided a fertile field for reinterpretation and
recombination of events, which meant that it could never be assumed to provide a static or assured means of representation. Like the political forum that
it helped to define, historical expression was shared but also offered the possibility for radically different viewpoints. Despite the dangers of misinter-
pretation or reinterpretation, however, the municipality turned to Poitiers's
past to advocate a specific point of view concerning events that were un-
folding within the town and the kingdom. In the sixteenth century, the municipal government made ample use of the Miracle of the Keys and the
ceremonial traditions that had grown up around it to make arguments concerning proper allegiance and religious identification—both of which the
civil wars had called into question.

The Miracle of the Keys, of course, did not speak uniquely to issues of po-

[28] For a range of interpretations of the purposes of spectacle in the urban sphere, see Hanawalt and Reyerson, eds., *City and Spectacle*. The essays in this collection vary in seeing ceremony either as expressing unity or including conflictual elements and in interpreting it as purely
representational or as a process of political debate. Not surprisingly, unity and representation
are allied as interpretive concepts, as are conflict and process. My interpretation of urban spectacle differs from these in that I see the phenomenon as a means of political debate within the
urban sphere, among the participants; the other authors tend to see political arguments as occurring only between cities and their rulers, acting as organizers and audience for ceremonial
event.

litical allegiance. It also formed a significant element in the town's religious identity. The miracle illustrated beyond doubt the special care of Poitiers's patron saints: the Virgin Mary, St. Hilaire, and Ste. Radegonde. The municipality was therefore not the sole body to make reference to it, and the chapter of Notre-Dame-la-Grande was as eager to preserve its memory as the city government. The miracle was incorporated into the church's liturgical calendar, where it was recounted as the second lesson of the nocturnes of the day after Quasimodo Sunday. The text of the miracle could thus be found in Notre-Dame's *Proprium sanctorum ac festorum,* in a version almost identical to that of the municipal statute book.[29] In addition to emphasizing the town's special relationship to the Virgin Mary, the church's patronage of the miracle may have contributed to its preservation and enhanced its familiarity.

The event must have been well-known to the general inhabitants of Poitiers. Whether the commemorative procession had been carried out since the time of the miracle is unclear, but it was certainly performed every year from the beginning of the fifteenth century. The first mention of municipal expenses associated with the procession dates from 1416,[30] and the town council registers for the sixteenth century mention it periodically.[31] That the inhabitants of Poitiers would have been ignorant concerning the purport of the procession is hard to imagine. The corps de ville, royal officers, chapters, convents, and inhabitants all participated in it, following the reliquary of the Virgin and other saints from Notre-Dame-la-Grande around the entire extent of the fortifications.[32] As with many early modern processions, the event could lead to discord: in 1580, the subdeacon of the chapter of St. Hilaire complained that he had been prevented from marching to the left of the bishop at the end of the procession, as was customary.[33] The entire company then paused to hear a sermon either in the Pré l'Abbesse, a large field near the town walls, or in the buildings belonging to one of the religious orders.[34]

[29] Unfortunately, the *Proprium* has disappeared from view, but Lecointre-Dupont was able to compare the two versions in 1847. He concluded that the municipality's account was copied from the church lesson. This view is impossible to substantiate without the *Proprium,* but the reported differences in wording make this far from certain. For a description of the *Proprium sanctorum ac festorum ad usum ecclesiae B. Mariae Majoris Pictaviensis,* I rely on Lecointre-Dupont, "Mémoire sur le miracle des clefs," 209 n. 1.

[30] Lecointre-Dupont, "Mémoire sur le miracle des clefs," 221. For municipal expenses related to the procession, see Rédet, "Extraits des Comptes," 399–401.

[31] Notably in 1537 (ACP Reg. 20, 211–13), 1559 (Reg. 36, 125–27), 1579 (Reg. 42, 819–20), 1589 (Reg. 48, 489–92), 1592 (Reg. 51, 158–64), 1593 (Reg. 53, 71), and 1595 (Reg. 54, 155–57).

[32] An eighteenth-century document details each church at which the procession paused and the chants sung by each religious body, but whether these specifications reflect sixteenth-century practice is uncertain. See Lecointre-Dupont, "Mémoire sur le miracle des clefs," 225–27.

[33] ADV G505, notarial minute dated 4 Apr. 1580.

[34] Poitiers's Easter Monday procession resembled numerous other processions of celebration or supplication performed in other cities in the name of other patron saints. For the parallel example of Paris's invocation of Ste. Geneviève, see Moshe Sluhovsky, *Patroness of Paris: Rituals of Devotion in Early Modern France* (New York, 1998); for a discussion of the capital's reli-

Other testaments to the miracle reminded Poitevins of the event year-round. Statues of Poitiers's three patron saints, dating from the late fourteenth or early fifteenth century graced the façade of Notre-Dame-la-Grande, and further statuary was added to its lateral door in the late fifteenth century.[35] A statue of the Virgin holding the keys surveyed the church's altar. Her replacement, dating from the second half of the sixteenth century, remains there still (see figure 7.1). A book of hours published in Poitiers in 1576 even reminded devotees that "On this day, [occurred] the miracle of Our Lady . . . for which we make the general procession the Monday after Easter around the walls of the town of Poitiers."[36]

In fact, accounts of the miracle must have been circulating that differed in some respects from the version in the municipal statute book. When Jean Bouchet included the miracle in his broadly circulating *Annales d'Aquitaine,* first published in 1524, his story showed signs of having profited from a more greatly elaborated version.[37] Some of the differences were probably introduced by the author himself. An expert storyteller, Bouchet most likely changed the order of events and introduced certain details to enhance the story's logic and verisimilitude. One such extremely important change was to alter the date of the Miracle from 1200 to 1202, in order to account for Poitiers's resistance to King John. Other aspects of Bouchet's version may derive from an enriched oral tradition. He specifies, for example, the amount of money that the English offered the mayor's clerk to betray his town and recounts that the traitor was well received in Périgueux because he had an uncle there. More important, the annalist adds the figure of Ste. Radegonde to the heavenly apparition that struck such terror into the hearts of the English. Although Ste. Radegonde was not included in the 1463 version of the miracle story, a stained glass window dating from the mid-thirteenth century, portraying her with the Virgin and possibly a set of keys, suggests that she was associated with it from very early on.[38] Having left her regal station as wife of Clotaire I to found the abbey of Ste. Croix just outside Poitiers, Ste. Radegonde was an influential saint within the city. Bouchet, for one, expressed his devotion to her by writing an account of her life.[39] It was therefore natural to include her in this important miraculous event.

---

gious calendar, consult Barbara B. Diefendorf, *Beneath the Cross: Catholics and Huguenots in Sixteenth-Century Paris* (Oxford, 1991). Natalie Zemon Davis discusses the importance of processions in defining civic and religious space in "The Sacred and the Body Social in Sixteenth-Century Lyon," *Past and Present* 90 (1981): 40–70.

[35] Lecointre-Dupont, "Mémoire sur le miracle des clefs," 237–38.

[36] *Heures de Nostre Dame, à l'vsage de Poictiers* (Poitiers, 1576), A8v.

[37] Bouchet recounts his version of the miracle in *Annales d'Aquitaine,* 159–61.

[38] Meredith Parsons Lillich advances this interpretation of the window's subject in *The Armor of Light: Stained Glass in Western France, 1250–1325* (Berkeley, 1994), 93–94.

[39] *Lhistoire et cronicque de Clotaire Premier de ce nom. vii. roy des fra[n]cois. et monarque des gaulles. Et de sa tresillustre espouse: madame saincte. Radego[n]de extraicte au vray de plusieurs croniq[ue]s antiq[ue]s & modernes* [Poitiers, 1518].

FIGURE 7.1. Notre-Dame-des-Clefs. This statue of the Virgin of the Keys, dating from the second half of the sixteenth century, is located in the church of Notre-Dame-la-Grande, Poitiers. Phototype Inventaire Général/Alain Dagorn 1995 © A.D.A.G.P. Reprinted with permission.

The miracle's numerous sources ensured that it was widely known and allowed it to be enlisted as a means of public persuasion. When, for example, Poitiers received report of the uprisings of the commune sparked by the gabelle in 1548, François Doyneau, senior échevin and lieutenant général, reminded the extended Mois at which clergy, vestrymen, and merchants were present of the traditions of obedience and unity that had always reigned in the city. They had always assured that Poitiers was well guarded, "even divinely and by miracle, referring on this subject to the miracle of the English in memory of which the procession of Easter Monday was performed every year around the walls of this city."[40] Doyneau thus invoked the miracle and its annual celebratory procession to illustrate the loyalty that Poitiers had always shown the French kings in the past and which it owed now in the face of popular rebellion. In doing so he assumed not only that the miracle would be familiar to his hearers, but also that they would recognize its place within the greater historical tradition.

If Doyneau's intention in recalling the Miracle of the Keys was clear, most of the references to it in the sixteenth century were ceremonial, and thus subject to broader interpretation. The Easter Monday procession served as a model for further expressions of thanksgiving that, although represented as general to Poitiers, always involved a specific definition of the civic community. Divine protection against the enemy had always been an essential aspect of the miracle. In the sixteenth century, the direct threat from the English was of course much decreased, but the growth of Protestantism and the conflict of the religious wars suggested a new danger in religious difference. The staunch Catholics of Poitiers came to identify the Huguenot armies as the victims of the Virgin's wrath. The transfer was all the easier to make since England was also Calvinist, and the saints could be expected to act against those who denied their efficacy. The Reformed of Poitiers, however, could certainly never agree to this characterization of themselves as a threat to the urban community; nor did they credit a miracle story. Celebrating the Miracle of the Keys, therefore, asserted a definition of legitimacy that excluded a significant sector of the population. The Protestants, in turn, were deeply angered by all that the miracle represented. In 1559, they expressed their disavowal of such constructions by attempting to assassinate the preacher during the annual processional sermon of Easter Monday.[41] Even more significant, when Reformed Gascon troops entered Poitiers in 1562, a group of Protestants found the statue of the Virgin that had been hidden away, paraded it around the city, and finally burned it, together with a crucifix from the church of St. Hilaire and an image of Ste. Radegonde.[42] Their rejection

---

[40] ACP Reg. 30, 16–17 (8 Aug. 1548).
[41] ACP Reg. 36, 125–27 (28 Mar. 1559). For a copy of the letter that François Aubert, lieutenant général, wrote to Henri II on this attempt, see Barbier, "Chroniques de Poitiers," 3–5 n. 1.
[42] Bèze, *Histoire ecclésiastique*, 2:705.

of the miracle and of Poitiers's religious identity could not have been more explicit.

Adaptations of the Easter Monday procession also gave expression to the conflict. After Coligny and his Reformed troops lifted their seven-week siege of Poitiers in the summer of 1569, the town engaged in a general procession of thanksgiving.[43] From that time forward, the procession of 7 September figured in the calendar of civil and religious observance, and each year the Catholics of Poitiers celebrated their special resistance to the Protestant enemy.[44] The procession was explicitly modeled on that of Easter Monday: in 1587, Jean Palustre, senior échevin, explained that "it is the praiseworthy custom that every seventh of September . . . , we make a tour of the walls of Poitiers and a general visitation to each of the churches, following the example of the Easter Monday procession, to celebrate having been delivered from the enemy and the siege of this town in the year 1569, which was raised by miracle. . . ."[45] The inauguration of the procession of Notre-Dame-de-Septembre forcefully expressed the hôtel de ville's commitment to a Catholic definition of the polity. As the defeat of the siege itself became a notable event in the town's history, religious belief, political exclusion, and Poitiers's tradition of indefatigable loyalty all merged to form a powerful argument for the nature of its civic identity.

Recourse to the model of the Easter Monday procession for the purposes of political persuasion could be even more explicit. When Jean de la Haye forged an alliance with the Protestants and formed an alternative publican party in the 1570s, the staunch Catholics of Poitiers opposed his activities and defeated his attempts to gain control of the town at Pentecost 1574. One year later, the city council decided to commemorate this resistance and held a general procession on the model of Easter Monday. The participants visited the scene of la Haye's defeat, displayed relics, and attended a sermon thanking the Virgin, St. Hilaire, and Ste. Radegonde, "patrons and defenders of the town," and the other saints for their miraculous protection. Thanks to their aid, "the conspiracy was miraculously discovered and revealed through God's grace, allowing it to be prevented and resisted."[46] The terms of the decision and the performance of the procession thus linked la Haye's actions with the two previous occasions in which an outside enemy had threatened the town's security. The implications of the argument were clear: although represented as a celebration of past success, the procession was

[43] *Siége de Poitiers,* 115–17.

[44] Deliberations concerning the procession of 7 September appear periodically in the registers of deliberation: ACP Reg. 40, 48–50 (3 Sept. 1571); Reg. 42, 526–28 (3 Sept. 1576); Reg. 47, 96–97 (31 Aug. 1587); Reg. 48, 65–70 (5 Sept. 1588); 297–300 (6 Feb. 1589); Reg. 51, 49–50 (2 Sept. 1591); 50–54 (6 Sept. 1591); Reg. 53, 26 (31 Aug. 1592); Reg. 54, 70–72 (5 Sept. 1594). The procession was also listed in the *Heures de Nostre Dame* as the "Procession generalle vouee à Poictiers, pour le siege des Rebelles, l'an 1569," B6r.

[45] ACP Reg. 47, 96–97 (31 Aug. 1587).

[46] ACP Reg. 42, 199–204 (30 May 1575); quotations, 202.

clearly conceived in the attempt to convince the inhabitants of the perfidy of la Haye's actions and of the strength of his opponents. The publicains still had considerable support in Poitiers, as an attempt to gain control of the city only one month later would show.[47] The procession's short career also confirms its specific political use. Although conceived as an annual commemoration, after the crisis had passed, the procession of the Monday of Pentecost was noticeably absent from municipal records.

History, whether referred to directly in speech or evoked through ceremonial representations, was thus an important resource for political expression. To turn to the Miracle of the Keys and the ceremonial practices that grew up around it in order to make arguments about current events was not unusual—history frequently served as a model or a metaphor for the present. The miracle was particular only in its great familiarity among all social segments of the city and in the development of a whole historical tradition with which it was associated. That the miracle was embedded within an elaborate historical narrative and that it occupied such an important place within Poitiers's ceremonial calendar certainly increased its power to persuade. Yet the tradition of loyalty to the kings of France of which it formed a part was not the only possible interpretation of Poitiers's past available in the sixteenth century. Other narratives, privileging other periods or aspects of the town's history, existed simultaneously. And although the logic of these alternative historical interpretations was never exploited to the same degree as the tradition we have been studying, their very existence allowed for possible competing viewpoints concerning Poitiers's historical identity, relationship with the kings of France, and place within the kingdom.

Alternative Histories

The Miracle of the Keys, with its emphasis on resistance to the English enemy, downplayed Poitiers's long, distinguished past. During the Gallo-Roman period, Poitiers may have been the largest town in western Gaul. Only a few centuries later, St. Hilaire, bishop of Poitiers, established a flourishing set of schools and made the town an important religious center. The city later served as one of the capitals of the kingdom of Aquitaine, and Charles Martel's defeat of the Saracens occurred not far from its site. Sixteenth-century inhabitants were certainly familiar with Poitiers's late antique and early medieval history. Even if they were inclined to forget, physical remains—such as the monumental Roman arena still largely intact at the time—must have reminded them. The hagiographies of St. Hilaire and Ste. Radegonde also

---

[47] Brisson, "Chronique," 360–67.

recalled the distant past. The publication of Jean Bouchet's *Annales d'Aquitaine* in 1524 provided a detailed account of the full span of Poitiers's history. Ostensibly writing the history of Aquitaine, Bouchet particularly favored the experience of his native city. In a style consonant with the developing historical genre and providing a content reflecting the interests of the French Renaissance, he traced Poitiers's august past from its mythical foundation by the offspring of Hercules, through the varying periods of its medieval history, up until the time of publication. The work was extremely popular and was reissued in revised editions no fewer than four times during the author's lifetime.[48]

However familiar Poitiers's ancient past, the hôtel de ville made scant reference to it in its numerous representations of the town's identity and ideal course of action. This neglect was more the product of choice than of ignorance. If any member of the corps de ville was unfamiliar with the long course of Poitiers's history, Jean Bouchet, bourgeois since 1517 and municipal secretary from 1531 to 1533, could have remedied this deficiency.[49] In fact, thanks to Bouchet, the hôtel de ville once indulged in a greatly elaborated reference to Poitiers's heroic past in its relations with François I. When the new French king made his official entry into Poitiers in January 1520, the town's ancient character served as the theme uniting entry stations, declamatory speeches, and gifts. Through a complicated series of interrelated allusions, the entry program evoked Clovis's defeat of the Arian Visigoths and associated Poitiers with the stag that showed France's first Christian king where to ford the Vienne River. Further references to antique figures, the Picts, and Ste. Radegonde reinforced the venerable age of the relationship between the town and the kings of France.[50] The character of this tie was, moreover, quite different from that to emerge from the tradition beginning with the Miracle of the Keys. There, the relationship was defined by a series

---

[48] On Jean Bouchet and his works, consult Hamon, *Grand rhétoriqueur*. The scholarship on the French historical tradition is large, but see Donald R. Kelley, *Foundations of Modern Historical Scholarship: Language, Law, and History in the French Renaissance* (New York, 1970); George Huppert, *The Idea of Perfect History: Historical Erudition and Historical Philosophy in Renaissance France* (Urbana, 1970); Claude-Gilbert Dubois, *Celtes et Gaulois au XVIe siècle: le développement littéraire d'un mythe nationaliste* (Paris, 1972); Claire Dolan, "L'identité urbaine et les histoires locales publiées du XVIe au XVIIIe siècle en France," *Canadian Journal of History* 27 (1992): 277–98; and Myriam Yardeni, "Histoires de villes, histoires de provinces et naissance d'une identité française au XVIe siècle," *Journal des savants* (Jan.–June 1993): 111–34.

[49] He was elected on 27 April. ACP Reg. 15, 290–96.

[50] Different but complementary accounts of the entry of François I may be found in ACP Casier 42, Reg. 11, 61v–62r, and Bouchet, *Annales d'Aquitaine*, 363–66. Neither text identifies Bouchet as the author of the entry's imagery, but the town council register makes it clear that Bouchet exercised responsibility for it, in conjunction with two colleagues. See ACP Reg. 17, 68 (25 Dec. 1519); 72 (27 Dec. 1519); 83 (30 Dec. 1519). Hamon argues likewise that the annalist was responsible for the symbolic program of the entry, based on the level of detail of its description; *Grand rhétoriqueur*, 124–27, esp. 127 n. 1.

of exchanges that reinforced mutual obligations; here, the bond was mystical[51] and based on the judicial qualities of a Christian monarch.[52]

Poitiers's welcome of François I thus enlisted a full battery of Renaissance themes and imagery and showed beyond doubt that such references were fully available for the purposes of political representation. That the municipality chose to emphasize a different tradition therefore indicated that it preferred the implications of one interpretation of the past over another. Both symbolic systems posited a close relationship between the town and the kings of France. Yet although one—that which the municipality favored—provided a context for the particular privileges and authority of the town government, the other went much further. It did nothing less than to assign both town and king a place within the wider framework of France's Christian past.

The imagery used in the entry of François I and the terms of the tradition of loyalty associated with the Miracle of the Keys lent themselves to extremely different, but not mutually exclusive, interpretations. If the hôtel de ville did not ultimately adopt the system of references that it displayed in 1520, it could nevertheless try it out without evident contradiction. Other strands in Poitiers's history, however, posed more of a challenge to the centrally oriented tradition of fidelity and service. Poitiers had once been the capital of the large and important county of Poitou, which had frequently been ruled by someone other than a member of the French royal family. No one in the sixteenth century would seriously have suggested that Poitou should once more be separated from the royal domain, but strands of provincial consciousness endured, and sometimes in surprising places.

---

[51] The text of the speech with which the mayor's son presented Poitiers's gift to François I is recorded in ACP Casier 42, Reg. 11, 61v:

> Comme le cerf desire La fontaine Ceulx de poictiers par amo[ur] treshumaine
> Roy triumphant ont desire vous voir Et recordans que guyde trescertaine
> Fut a clovis le cerf en Rive pleine Forte a passer pour seur chemin avoir
> Quant pres poictiers par ses forces belliq[ue]s Ce petit cerf vo[us] presentent cher sire
> Prenez en gre le don des pictoniques. Paouvres de biens en vouloir magnifiques
> Ch[ac]un desqueulx voustre grace desire.

In addition to the historical references, the poem implies a sacred relationship between town and king. The opening line is an adaptation of the Vulgate Psalm 41:2: "Quemadmodum desiderat cervus ad fontes aquarum, ita desiderat anima mea ad te, Deus" (Revised Standard Version, Psalm 42:1). Poitiers is therefore drawn to the royal presence in the same way that the soul thirsts after God.

[52] A fountain flanked by shepherds constituted one of the stations of the entry and, in accordance with standard Renaissance imagery, could be associated with the fountain of royal justice. This interpretation was all the more apposite since the Grands Jours had come to sit in Poitiers earlier that autumn, at which time the mayor had described the président and the other officials of the Parlement of Paris as "La so[ur]ce et fons de Justice." The reference would acquire further levels of meaning in the presentation speech quoted in n. 51. For the fountain, see Bouchet, *Annales d'Aquitaine,* 364–65, and Hamon, *Grand rhétoriqueur,* 125. For the Grands Jours, consult ACP Casier 42, Reg. 11, 61r.

The municipality all but ignored the town's comital history. It rarely made reference to privileges granted or confirmed by the counts of Poitou and preferred to ignore the time when it was forced to bow to prévotal justice. Although Jean, duc de Berry, could claim much of the credit for Charles V's granting the municipality's prized privilege of échevinal nobility, the town government never made reference to this debt to Poitou's last count.[53] Despite such institutional lapses of memory, references to Poitou's independent past persisted. These were never articulated within the administrative context but found their utterance within the history writing germane to the province.

Both of Poitiers's sixteenth-century historians were members of the corps de ville. We have already seen the first, Jean Bouchet, acting as author of an entry program thanks to his position as bourgeois. The second, Jean de la Haye, served as mayor in 1562–63 and was accordingly received as an échevin.[54] Each, however, in writing his historical account, gave considerable importance to the status of Poitou as a separate and largely independent region. Bouchet, after all, had originally conceived his project as a history of the region of Aquitaine, and if its historical fate eventually became incorporated with that of France, the very act of relating its separate existence recalled a time when the French kings could not boast the power that they currently possessed.[55] It is unlikely, however, that this servitor of Louis XII and François I was advocating less dependence on the kings of France. Rather, his special pride in his city and region prompted an historical account that could be enlisted in the cause of a separate provincial identity.

Jean de la Haye set out more consciously to relate Poitou's special history and to preserve its unique past from obscurity. Explaining that Bouchet had done much important work but had tended to misrepresent the past where the experience of his clients was concerned,[56] the lieutenant général presented a more inclusive history of the great families of Poitou, paying particular attention to their genealogies and arms. He was explicit in the subject matter and goals of his work:

And I will relate little concerning the nobles of the region, except where those who are descended from our princes are concerned. And I will succinctly share

53 La Haye, *Memoires et recherche*, 48.
54 La Haye replaced Jacques Herbert, elected mayor in 1562, after the latter had been executed for his role in abetting the Protestant takeover of Poitiers that spring. The exact date on which la Haye was elected échevin is unknown, since the register of deliberations for this mayoral year no longer survives.
55 In her examination of French national identity through the genre of provincial history writing, Yardeni remarks that often current loyalty to the crown was presented as counterbalancing the long anti-French tradition of a province. Bouchet's work may be interpreted in this vein, and it is noteworthy that from the time that Aquitaine became a part of the French domain, its history was conflated with that of France. On the other hand, the very decision to write a provincial history was a significant act. See Yardeni, "Histoires de villes," esp. 116, 133.
56 Bouchet acted as official counsel and habitual poet to the family of La Trémoille beginning in 1510. Hamon, *Grand rhétoriqueur*, 39–70.

with posterity as occasion arises what rare and true facts I have uncovered, serving the history of Poitou, in this way revenging the region against those who have condemned and subjected it to death and oblivion.[57]

His acknowledged sources were also uniquely Poitevin: the first was an early thirteenth-century chronicle kept by a monk of Poitiers's abbey of Montierneuf; the second was a manuscript found with the papers of the duc de Berry composed in the late fourteenth century.[58] La Haye was not a native of Poitiers, but by his own admission came from a minor noble family of the region.[59] The city government, however, rejected la Haye's point of view as it resisted his politics. Representations of the age and importance of the region met with few objections, but any account that glorified Poitou's great noble families at the inevitable expense of municipal self-importance was not likely to appeal to Poitiers's recently ennobled citizens.[60]

If the town government was firm in rejecting this particular historical outlook, however, its articulation in the 1570s and publication in the 1580s meant that it was generally available as a point of counter-reference against the municipality's preferred representation of Poitiers's past.[61] Historians, moreover, were not the only individuals to offer alternative visions of the past in an attempt to influence contemporary circumstances. During the legal proceedings between the chapter and parishioners of Ste. Radegonde concerning which group had the right to name a bell ringer, both sides made reference to the church's past as a means to support their own pretensions. The chapter, on the one hand, invoked the circumstances of Radegonde's life and the act of royal foundation in order to justify its claims to seigneury over the church and the parish. The parishioners, on the other hand, resorted to an alternative ancient tradition and the dictates of custom to prove their claims. The church, they asserted, had been founded by its parishioners long before the time of Ste. Radegonde and had been known as the church of Our-Lady-outside-the-Walls (Notre-dame-derrière-les-murs). Since that time, a prince or seigneur had established a chapter to serve and to maintain the church, but the parishioners had always retained certain rights, including the ringing of the parish bell. The canons, moreover, had recognized these rights for so long that they could not now dispute them.[62]

History, therefore, could serve as a medium for contemporary argument

[57] La Haye, *Memoires et recherche*, 6.
[58] La Haye, *Memoires et recherche*, 10–11.
[59] La Haye, *Memoires et recherche*, 3.
[60] As chapter 1 shows, this concern was not an idle one: during the Estates General of 1588, the municipality was forced to make protracted representations to the Noble Assembly and the king's Privy Council in order for their deputy for the second estate to be recognized along with the candidate of the provincial nobility.
[61] La Haye's *Memoires et recherche* was published as early as 1581 by the Parisian publisher J. Parant.
[62] ADV G1346, audience dated 30 Dec. 1503.

in many spheres. Against the official history advocated by an institution, the parishioners proposed their own version of the past better suited to their own purpose. Like the hôtel de ville, the chapter of Ste. Radegonde rooted its prerogatives in special privileges accorded it because of the circumstances of its foundation and looked to history, in this case the life of its patron saint, to enhance its prestige. The inhabitants who depended on the church as a place for the expression of their religious life, however, felt free to cast their own net into the broad range of Poitiers's history and to counter the chapter's privileges not only with a more ancient historical tradition but also with the practices of living memory. Normally eager to claim a part in the prestige that their patron saint accorded and that the chapter obtained for the parish, the inhabitants here resorted to alternative visions that existed as a potential defense against this very authority.

What was possible for the parishioners of Ste. Radegonde held for Poitiers's inhabitants in general. Although they were often willing to countenance the version of Poitiers's past that the hôtel de ville advocated, history and its means of expression always offered the potential for disagreement. The tradition that began with the Miracle of the Keys and that was enlisted to explain many of the most traumatic events of the sixteenth century may have been universally familiar and even generally understood, but it was not the only possible historical outlook. Reference to the past constituted a common and accepted way to make arguments about the present and the future, but choices of historical interpretation inevitably affected the range of possible conclusions and potential actions. The municipality clearly favored a tradition that highlighted its own close relationship with the kings of France and that cast its privileges, rights, and authority in terms of a successful series of exchanges. Yet other traditions existed simultaneously that suggested different bonds between city and king and different ties between provincial and royal history. The municipality was successful in ensuring that its own particular interpretation was known and feted, but it could never gain exclusive control over the implications of the past or the terms of political argument. Poitiers's town government certainly spoke with an authoritative voice, but it could never reduce claimants of other points of view to silence.

8   *The Tradition Overturned?*

Poitiers Declares for the Catholic League

Human society, explained Pierre Humeau, avocat in the presidial court of Poitiers and deputy to the procureur général, is composed of four degrees or offices, arranged in a hierarchy of importance. Subvert their natural order, and tragedy results; acquit the duties of each in their proper turn, and society and the state are maintained. The first degree, fundamental to the whole structure, comprises the duty one owes to God and the church. If Christian discipline is neglected, then society is undermined in its very foundations. Second in the hierarchy comes duty to country, including obedience to monarchs, governors, and magistrates. Although placing love of country and obedience to its rulers before religious conviction can only lead to disaster, the concerns of justice and obedience to the law play an essential part in assuring a well-ordered Christian society. On the third rung of the ladder, we encounter duties owed relations, friends, and allies—namely, to equals. The fourth and final level comprises responsibilities to clients, vassals, and subjects. Inferiors, exhorted Humeau, should be assured protection, charity, and judiciousness as the proper rewards for their obedience and submission to their governors.[1]

Such was the social vision expounded in the presidial court on 17 August 1589, the day Poitiers finally registered its adherence to the Catholic League. Support for the movement had reputedly been growing since 1585, but this traditionally loyal city waited for the death of Henri III to make its adhesion official. The presidial court read and registered the *Règlement de l'Union*,

---

[1] Pierre Humeau, *Devx harangves ov remonstrances faictes en la cour ordinaire de la seneschavcee de Poictou & siege presidial à Poictiers, Sur la publication du reglement general faict pour remedier aux desordres aduenus à l'occasion des troubles presens* (Poitiers, 1590), 43–98.

previously drafted in Paris and sent to Poitiers by the duc de Mayenne, and put it into execution four days later. On 21 August, therefore, the court assembled once again to swear the Oath of Union. The corps de ville had already declared its adhesion by swearing the oath in a Mois convened three days earlier.[2]

The Sacred Union, continued Humeau in the second assembly, was both a manifestation of, and a means to promote, harmonious society. The dictates of Christian liberty rejected willful independence and a false reliance on self; this course ended only in heresy and atheism. Rather, liberty consisted in an oath of piety, ensuring a proper respect for the law and performance of Christian duties. "Let a salutary zeal, which is the true father and nurse of this sacred unity and concord of true religion, therefore, embrace and emblaze each one of us to such an extent," exhorted Humeau,

> that we each have the courage to advance and to surpass our fellow in virtue
> and diligence, so that we may the more quickly return to our pristine health
> and Christian liberty, through the maintenance of this sacred union and mu-
> tual accord of living faith and charity in one, sole Church, unique spouse of
> our God.[3]

An act of Christian zeal uniting the people in one sacred body, the Oath of Union still did not call for any innovations in the social order. Just as Mayor Maixent Poitevin, in his introduction to the police measures of 1566, had portrayed a model of civic harmony assured by the unity of Poitiers's inhabitants in obedience to the law,[4] Pierre Humeau, two decades later, represented the oath as constituting a society in which members devoutly respected the obligations of a hierarchy of religious, social, and political relationships. In the sixteenth century, after all, swearing an oath did not necessarily establish equality among the parties; it merely assured that each would be upheld in its rights and responsibilities. Such a message was sure to appeal to the audience of magistrates and lawyers who, in Poitiers, joined their administration of royal justice with participation in municipal government. Indeed, Humeau combined his reverence for the law with an explicitly paternalistic vision of the city's governors, who should act as "fathers toward the inhabitants."[5] In this way, the League did not necessarily challenge the assumptions of civil society and political authority internal to the urban community; it actually lent them support.

Since Henri Drouot's influential *Mayenne et la Bourgogne*, historians have been attempting to come to grips with the nature and implications of

---

[2] Humeau, *Devx harangves*, 123, [113] (numbers in brackets refer to a second pagination); ACP Reg. 49, 16–20 (17–18 Aug. 1589).

[3] Humeau, *Devx harangves*, [80–110]; quotation, [103].

[4] See chapter 1.

[5] Humeau, *Devx harangves*, 94.

the urban Catholic League. Although all agree that religious convictions were fundamental to the movement, many argue about the social character of its appeal and leadership, as well as about how radical a challenge it posed to political authority embodied in the monarchy and urban institutions. Indeed, these two questions are related: the more the Sacred Union has been seen to overturn patterns of social hierarchy, the more elemental its challenge to the political structures of the Valois monarchy. Those who describe the League as allowing new social or corporate groups to claim unaccustomed power over urban life therefore tend to argue that these militant Catholics also envisioned a different political order, generally rooted in local control at the expense of the developing royal administration. Yet others who focus on the many provincial cities that declared for the League without overturning the influence of existing elites have frequently portrayed a Sacred Union less threatening to existing political assumptions and more rooted in local rivalries.

Paris, with its Seize, high-profile executions, and militant clergy, has long provided the model for the radical League, and its two best known historians, Elie Barnavi and Robert Descimon, each in his own way points to social tensions as a defining characteristic of the movement. Each confirms for Paris what Drouot found in Dijon: merchants, lawyers, and petty officials took advantage of the deep religious and political rift in the kingdom to express their hostilities against the royal officials who dominated royal office and presumed to dictate to the rest of the urban community.[6] For Barnavi, the Seize and their supporters constituted a revolutionary party committed to a campaign of propaganda and terror.[7] For Descimon, these activists reflected a fervent commitment to an older model of municipal government that royal office holders rejected. Leaguers attempted to preserve a relationship with the French crown that favored urban privilege and assured the distribution of municipal honors. They disavowed one in which royal office, and thus political authority, was subject to ownership and exclusive control. The League was thus the last gasp of the medieval world: it opposed the growing absolutist tendencies of the French state with the traditional worldview of municipal honor and sacrality.[8] More recently, Jean-Marie Constant has united the views of Barnavi and Descimon with Denis Crouzet's emphasis on the intense anxieties fueling militant Catholicism. He portrays the

---

[6] Henri Drouot, *Mayenne et la Bourgogne: étude sur la Ligue (1587–1596)*, 2 vols. (Dijon, 1937), esp. 1:51–55, 160–61, 235–38, 257–90, 340–41.

[7] Elie Barnavi, *Le parti de dieu: étude sociale et politique des chefs de la Ligue parisienne, 1585–1594* (Brussels and Louvain, 1980).

[8] Descimon, *Qui étaient les Seize?*; "Ligue à Paris"; "Prise de parti, appartenance sociale et relations familiales dans la Ligue parisienne (1585–1594)," in *Les réformes: enracinement socio-culturel*, ed. Bernard Chevalier and Robert Sauzet (Paris, 1985), 123–36; "Les assemblées de l'Hôtel de Ville de Paris (mi-XVIe–mi-XVIIe siècles)," *L'administration locale en Île-de-France. Mémoires de la Fédération des Sociétés historiques et archéologiques de Paris et de l'Île de France* 38, 1 (1987): 39–54; "Échevinage parisien."

Seize and their adherents as driven by resentment of royal institutions, a fervent belief in an imminent apocalypse, and a radical attempt to redefine the French monarchy, all to create an urban movement with truly revolutionary overtones.[9]

Studies of the League in the provinces have not confirmed the social tendencies of the capital. Rather, they have emphasized the extent to which the League depended on and encouraged traditional rivalries and did little to innovate beyond existing patterns of authority. Philip Benedict describes the League period in Rouen as opposing two elite factions with experience in the Parlement and the hôtel de ville and revealingly relates that in 1589, the "people" were forced to choose their representatives under the close supervision of armed men. Penny Roberts and Christopher Stocker echo his conclusions for Troyes and Orléans, where "a small and definable cluster of notables was supplanted by another discernable grouping . . . well connected within the established political elite."[10] In Rennes, Nantes, and Angers, Robert Harding concluded, no set of social characteristics consistently determined League activity, and royal officials played a leading role in Nantes and Rennes.[11] Although none of these authors deny an innovatory character to the League, they identify it as arising from a new and fervent Catholic activism, disgust with religious corruption, and theoretical redefinition of the origins of political authority rather than from a rejection of urban governing procedures or royal authority per se.[12] Wolfgang Kaiser's study of Marseille further emphasizes the ways that religious sensibilities operated within an established medium of social alliances and factional politics. In his view, the religious wars added the elements of religious outlook and political style to the previously existing nexus of family alliance, business interests, and political activity. The first phase of the League in Marseille therefore marked a struggle between two elite factions, to be followed by a more radical period of social tension, in which one family and its network gained the upper hand.[13] Annette Finley-Croswhite similarly shows the importance of alliances to the League in Amiens by tracing the relationships between the duc d'Aumale and the city's elite families from 1588 to 1594.[14] An important exception to this pattern, though, is Yves Durand's contention that during the

[9] Jean-Marie Constant, *La Ligue* ([Paris], 1996); Denis Crouzet, *Les guerriers de dieu: la violence au temps des troubles de la religion vers 1525–vers 1610*, 2 vols. ([Paris], 1990), chaps. 17–20.

[10] Benedict, *Rouen*, 179–89; Roberts, *City in Conflict*, 176; Christopher W. Stocker, "Orléans and the Catholic League," *Proceedings of the Annual Meeting of the Western Society for French History* 16 (1989): 12–21; quotation, 14.

[11] Robert Harding, "Revolution and Reform in the Holy League: Angers, Rennes, Nantes," *Journal of Modern History* 53 (1981): 384–89.

[12] Benedict, *Rouen*, 188–89, 190–208; Harding, "Revolution and Reform," 401–5; Stocker, "Urban Police," 10, 12.

[13] Kaiser, *Marseille*.

[14] Finley-Croswhite, *Henry IV and the Towns*, 29–37.

League period provincial cities took advantage of the breakdown of order to establish themselves as independent republics. Yet it is revealing that his analysis rests on three maritime cities—Marseille, Saint-Malo, and Morlaix—where merchants rather than royal officials enjoyed elite status and set urban policies.[15]

Poitiers's experience during the Catholic League era tends to confirm what has been found in many other provincial cities: royalists and supporters of the Sacred Union came from the same privileged institutions, the same social groups. The hôtel de ville, the presidial court, the financial institutions, the university, and the church chapters all produced adherents of both sides, although the trésoriers généraux had a greater tendency to be royalists.[16] Indeed, the kinds of divisions that Drouot and Descimon noticed for Dijon and Paris were unlikely in towns such as Poitiers, where royal officials were thoroughly integrated into municipal government. Their continued ascendancy under the Union also limited the possibilities for League activists to pursue a new social or political vision. Urban elites could be just as motivated by a profound religious consciousness as "the people," and they could be just as adamant that a heretic should not govern France. But they were much less likely to envision or to desire a fundamental alteration in the lines of authority underlying their own privileges and assuring their own status. They might harbor ambitions to accumulate even more control over their own civic environments, but they were not likely to erode the very structures that placed them at the head of their local communities in the first place. For Poitiers's royal officials and corps de ville, the considerations prescribing continued obedience to Henri III were numerous and compelling. Poitiers, as we have seen, gloried in its self-image of notable loyalty to the kings of France, and its governing institutions all owed their special privileges to this relationship. These preexisting sources of legitimacy tempted even militant Catholics to temporize with a tyrant. Several of Poitiers's League leaders adamantly opposed the idea of Henri de Navarre becoming king and waited until July 1594 to recognize him as Henri IV. Yet these same men attempted in the spring and summer of 1589 to retain ties to Henri III, despite complaints about his rule and in the face of events strongly indicating their city's rebellion.

---

[15] Yves Durand, "Les républiques urbaines en France à la fin du XVIe siècle," *Société d'Histoire et d'Archéologie de l'Arrondissement de Saint-Malo, Annales 1990* (Saint-Malo, 1990): 205–44. For further works on the League in cities, see J. H. M. Salmon, "The Paris Sixteen, 1584–1594: The Social Analysis of a Revolutionary Movement," *Journal of Modern History* 44 (1972): 540–76; Michel Cassan, "Mobilité sociale et conflits religieux: l'exemple limousin (1550–1630)," *La dynamique sociale dans l'Europe du Nord-Ouest (XVIe–XVIIe siècles): colloque, 1987,* Association des historiens modernistes de l'Université 12 (Paris, 1987), 71–92; "Laïcs, Ligue et réforme catholique à Limoges," *Histoire, économie et société* 10, no. 2 (1991): 159–75; Martin, "Escamotage d'une réforme."

[16] Self-interest may have encouraged their royalism. During the Estates General of 1588, League advocates attempted to reduce the number of trésoriers généraux in each bureau from ten to two, in an attempt to limit the political influence of the financial officials. De Thou, *Histoire universelle,* 7:318.

Elites by themselves, of course, did not make the League, and in Poitiers there is evidence of the same kinds of inflammatory preaching, popular animus against Henri III, and enthusiasm for taking up arms for Catholicism that occurred in Paris, Brittany, and Orléans. Indeed, without the insurrections of the inhabitants it is doubtful that the Sacred Union would ever have been sworn in Poitiers. There is also some evidence that the League period gave vent to social hostilities that lay just beneath the surface, but cooperation between radical League leaders and their social inferiors is more striking in the stream of events than actions specifically aimed against the elite. Throughout, the traditional governors managed to maintain their dominance, not only in previously existing political institutions, but also in the new structures created under the Union. From August 1589 until the fall of 1592, Poitiers possessed a fully functioning Conseil de l'Union (Union Council), but as at Rouen and Toulouse, this new political body afforded the general inhabitants little chance to influence the terms of urban government.[17] The League, to be sure, politicized many aspects of daily life, but the city's traditional leaders never ceded their governing prerogatives to the "people," usually more eager to learn what had been decided than to make the decisions themselves. Despite increased popular activity, therefore, Pierre Humeau's vision of the four levels of obedience and authority, based simultaneously in an official's reverence for the law and a notion of a communitarian bond rooted in Catholic worship, could survive more or less intact.

This first chapter on the League in Poitiers evaluates the long process through which the city debated renouncing its allegiance to Henri III and adhering to the Holy Union, as well as the social dynamics informing this decision. The following chapter analyzes the changes in authority arising from a new configuration of governing institutions in the city. It also assesses the extent to which League advocates envisioned a new political order by promoting urban independence over the structures and assumptions supporting the French monarchy.

The Rise of the League in Poitiers

Poitiers swore the Oath of Union some two weeks after the death of Henri III, but the process of adhering to the Catholic League was a long one. Struggles between elites, cultivation of popular support, negotiations with the crown, and armed encounters all marked the gradual escalation of the dispute. Tensions increased and the ambiguities of political life became more striking, as each succeeding crisis seemed to lead only to further uncertainty.

---

[17] Benedict, *Rouen,* 180–81; Mark Greengrass, "The Sainte Union in the Provinces: The Case of Toulouse," *The Sixteenth Century Journal* 14 (1983): 481.

The town council registers and municipal ordinances reveal their usual predisposition to portray a situation of order and obedience, even as expressions of disloyalty and violent disputes were occurring in the town. Their story reflects a profound ambivalence: for all of the Leaguers' religious conviction, hostility to the royal governor, and distrust of the king, the town never directly disavowed royal authority as long as a Catholic sat on the throne. As other cities reacted during the winter of 1589 to the royal assassinations of the duc and cardinal de Guise, neither royalists nor Leaguers in Poitiers could gain the upper hand. After the tumultuous events of May 1589 had forced the king's principal supporters to depart, important members of the League faction who opposed the break remained. Even in the face of deep disaffection with royal policy and a profound sense of religious threat, they were loath to abandon the tradition of fidelity that had assured Poitiers's importance as a provincial capital and their own predominance in the urban political arena, all of which rested on a notable system of privileges. Yet although these concerns were important enough to prevent an irreparable rupture with Henri III, they evaporated when confronted with the calamitous reality of a Protestant's claiming the French throne.

"Gaigner et pratiquer les hommes," 1585–88

News of the resumption of League hostilities reached Poitou quickly in April 1585,[18] and Henri III was soon being reassured from all sides that its capital city remained loyal and actively on the defense.[19] Poitiers lost no time in putting into effect the Edict of Nemours, and the presidial court even ordered that its provisions for disarming Protestants be carried out two days before the Parlement of Paris was forced to register it on 18 July.[20] Nevertheless, the city continued to combine its categorical religious policies with tolerance of individuals of the Reformed faith. Although the hôtel de ville taxed and restricted current and former Protestants,[21] it also remitted the tax of the well-known Huguenot Jean Boiceau and selected him to serve as one of the council's consulting avocats.[22] As religious tensions heated up in 1588, someone even voted that he become an échevin.[23]

Since many of the military campaigns of this eighth religious war were

---

[18] Michel Le Riche, lieutenant criminel of Saint-Maixent, received a royal declaration prohibiting all leagues from Poitiers on 2 April 1585 as well as news from Paris of the hostilities on 8 April. Le Riche, 397–98. See also BNF MS Fr 15569, 37r, 52r (letters from La Frézelière to Henri III dated 4 and 9 Apr. 1585); 113r (letter from Sanzay to Henri III dated 24 Apr. 1585).

[19] BNF MS Fr 15569, 20r (letter from Chemerault to Henri III dated 28 Mar. 1585); 32r (letter from Pierre Rat to Henri III dated 3 Apr. 1585); 43r (letter from the corps de ville of Poitiers to Henri III dated 6 Apr. 1585).

[20] The edict was registered in Poitiers on 27 June. Le Riche, 410, 413.

[21] ACP Reg. 47, 56–57 (6 Aug. 1587); 108–11 (10 Sept. 1587); 280–86 (28 Dec. 1587).

[22] ACP Reg. 46, 14–26 (25 July 1586); Reg. 47, 144–50 (28 Sept. 1587).

[23] ACP Reg. 48, 92–98 (21 Sept. 1588).

waged in Poitou and the West, Poitiers suffered continual rumors of attack and was compelled to supply royal armies in the field to combat the forces of Henri de Navarre.[24] The town grudgingly fulfilled its responsibilities in the war effort, but there were already signs of division within it. According to an anonymous account of events in Poitiers in 1588–89, the duc de Mayenne had solicited support for the League in Poitiers as early as his campaigns in Guyenne in 1585, and when he left, his wife remained behind to give birth to their child and to sow division.[25] Michel Le Riche, lieutenant criminel in nearby Saint-Maixent, reported a quarrel at a dinner party in Poitiers between René Boisson, mayor, and François Palustre, conseiller (Le Riche's relative by marriage), where Palustre slapped the mayor for calling him stupid.[26] Since Palustre would later be an ardent Leaguer, could not this quarrel attest to Mayenne's success? In any case, in April 1585 the corps de ville was already protesting to the king that there were no divisions in Poitiers, and by February 1586 Jean de Chourses, sieur de Malicorne, lieutenant général for the king in Poitou, was instructing the mayor (now François Palustre!) that he was to identify and to imprison the people of quality in Poitiers suspected of opposing the king.[27]

Future communications between the governor and the hôtel de ville would repeat these patterns of warnings and denials, indicating that Malicorne and Henri III were justified in their concerns. In April 1587, the governor forwarded royal letters that exhorted unity against troublers of the state at the same time that they promised rewards for continuing loyalty, prompting the council and then the Mois to take all measures to assure both the governor and the king of their complete fidelity.[28] Yet by the winter of 1587 the governor himself had reason to complain. Having informed the corps de ville that he intended to spend the winter in Poitiers, Malicorne was seriously displeased to learn that the Mois refused to locate and to subsidize lodgings for him. Poitiers had developed a poor relationship with its governor ever since his first entry into the town in September 1585, but he clearly interpreted this recalcitrance as a serious sign of disobedience.[29] In January 1588 he

[24] BNF MS Fr 3310, 39v (letter from Henri III to the inhabitants of the cities of Poitou dated 28 Jan. 1586); BNF MS Fr 15572, 144r (letter from François Palustre, mayor, to Henri III dated 9 Apr. 1586). ACP Regs. 46 and 47 provide much information on royal troops in Poitou. See also Léo Desaivre, ed., *Lettres missives de Jehan de Chourses, seigneur de Malicorne, gouverneur du Poitou de 1585 à 1603: lettres missives à lui adressées et autres documents relatifs à l'histoire du Poitou pendant cette période*, AHP 27 (Poitiers, 1896), 287–411.

[25] BNF MS Fr 20157, "Discours de ce qui s'est passé en la ville de Poictiers es annees 1588 & 1589," 153r–164r, at 153r. See also De Thou's summary of this text, *Histoire universelle*, 7:459; and Henri Ouvré, "Essai sur l'histoire de la Ligue à Poitiers," *MSAO*, 1st ser., 21 (1854): 121–22.

[26] Le Riche, 405.

[27] BNF MS Fr 15569, 110r (letter of mayor and échevins of Poitiers to Henri III dated 24 Apr. 1585); Desaivre, ed., *Lettres missives*, 300–302.

[28] ACP Reg. 46, 262–75 (9–10 Apr. 1587).

[29] Ouvré, "Essai sur l'histoire de la Ligue," 121. René de Brilhac describes the entry in Brilhac, 19.

characterized the refusal as "a witness of poor will, which must not extend to those who have the king's authority, his majesty's service, the duties of their charge, and [the town's] own good in recommendation. . . ."[30] In the end, he chose his own lodgings.

Poitiers's reaction to the Day of the Barricades in May 1588 points to further uncertainties of political allegiance. Officially, the town's response was anything but ambivalent. Having received letters from Henri III relating the events of 13 May in Paris, Jean Jay, sieur de Boisseguin, governor of Poitiers and its château, and Mayor Jacques Clabat convened a general assembly of all the corps of the town. There they were joined by Geoffroy de Saint-Belin, bishop of Poitiers, and Pierre Rat, lieutenant général of the sénéchaussée, in remonstrating the obedience that the town owed to the king. The assembly commissioned letters assuring Henri III of its unwavering fidelity and of its determination to hold fast just as its predecessors had done when it seemed that the English would overrun the entire kingdom.[31] It then dispatched René Fumé, avocat du roi, as a deputy to travel to Chartres to present the letters and Poitiers's obedience in person.[32] All of the letters to and from the king and other individuals in court were recorded in their entirety in the town council register.[33] Finally, Boisseguin turned over the king's account of events to a local printer, and a race to get the first copies out indicates that sales were expected to be brisk.[34]

Despite all of these protestations of obedience, there were further signs that Poitiers's loyalty was not completely assured. A letter reputedly sent from a bourgeois of Poitiers to his friend in Paris thanked his correspondent for a "true" account of the duc de Guise's blameless actions during the Day of the Barricades, instead of the praise for the duc d'Épernon, a "demy Béarnois," that was being circulated in Poitiers.[35] While the town was drafting its response to the event, Malicorne dispatched letters that combined references to the town's ancient loyalty with warnings against the particular passions and divisions that could trouble its tranquility.[36] In early June, moreover, the council found itself obliged to respond to royal suspicions and to protest that certain individuals' recent trips to Paris had been made for

[30] ACP Reg. 47, 236–37 (26 Nov. 1587); 240–48 (30 Nov.); 267–78 (24 Dec.); 306–11 (22 Jan. 1588); quotation, 308.
[31] BNF MS Fr 15574, 170r (letter from the mayor, échevins, bourgeois, and inhabitants of Poitiers to Henri III dated 19 May 1588); 175r (letter from Pierre Rat to Henri III dated 19 May 1588); ACP Reg. 47, 445–55 (21 May 1588).
[32] ACP Reg. 47, 458–68 (25 May 1588); BNF MS Fr 15574, 170r.
[33] ACP Reg. 47, 446–55, 457, 460–65.
[34] ACP Reg. 47, 455–56 (22 May 1588); the competitor's text still survives: *Lettres dv roy, addroissantes a monseigneur de Boisseguin, gouuerneur pour sa Majesté en sa ville de Poictiers, sur l'esmotion aduenuë à Paris* (Poitiers, 1588).
[35] *Copie des lettres escrites par le dvc d'Epernon av roy de Nauarre, touchant les affaires de ce temps, enuoyees par vn bourgeois de Poictiers, à vn sien amy estant en ceste ville de Paris* (n.p., 1588), 3–5. It is possible of course that this letter was entirely fabricated.
[36] ACP Reg. 47, 457 (23 May 1588).

their own affairs. Since one of the travelers in question was François Palustre, one of the most ardent supporters of the League in Poitiers, it seems likely
that the king's misgivings were well founded and that Palustre had been at
least partially engaged in consulting with the Paris League.[37]

Such discrepancies between official representations and uneasy rumor
point to divisions within Poitiers itself. It is impossible to know whether
Poitiers developed any organized groups dedicated to the propagation of the
League similar to those that had acted in Paris since 1585.[38] Our only direct
testimony indicates that Mayenne had attempted to sway both men in command and popular elements to the cause, but it comments not at all on how
these League advocates were organized or worked to spread their ideas.[39]
By spring 1588, however, there were clearly individuals in Poitiers, such as
François Palustre and his father, Jean Palustre, a trésorier, who favored solidarity with the radical actions taken in the capital. They may have been
joined by the lieutenant criminel, François de Brilhac, who would later prove
himself one of the radical supporters of the League. On the other hand, many
other militant Catholics did not yet envision a break with Henri III. Both
Louis de Sainte-Marthe, lieutenant civil, who was deputed to draw up the
pledge of loyalty to the king, and René Fumé, avocat du roi, commissioned
to deliver it, would later show their commitment to the League by taking an
active part in civil government after the swearing of the Oath of Union. Geoffroy de Saint-Belin, bishop of Poitiers, who remained an important League
leader throughout the city's adhesion to the Sacred Union, nevertheless exhorted obedience at this time. In the spring of 1588, therefore, an important
contingent among League sympathizers preferred Poitiers's tradition of loyalty to a Catholic king to the adventure of associating with the League
princes. The League movement in Poitiers had therefore to overcome a predisposition to royalism that characterized not only the town's future politiques, but also those who would later place the exigencies of the Catholic
faith above the inviolability of royal succession.

"Infinis iuremens et protestations," December 1588–April 1589

Although unrest in Poitiers continued throughout the summer and autumn
of 1588, tensions began seriously to escalate at the end of December. The assassinations of the duc and cardinal de Guise intensified hostilities to Henri
III all over France, and cities such as Orléans, Rouen, Toulouse, and Le Mans
experienced revolts and declared for the League in the weeks that followed.[40]

[37] ACP Reg. 47, 470–74 (6 June 1588).
[38] Barnavi, *Parti de dieu*, 61–64, 75–78; Constant, *Ligue,* 116–22, 146–55.
[39] BNF MS Fr 20157, 153r.
[40] Christopher Stocker, "The Governance of Orléans under the Catholic League" (paper presented at Sixteenth Century Studies conference, St. Louis, Dec. 1993), 7; Benedict, *Rouen,* 179;
Greengrass, "Sainte Union," 480–81; Constant, *Ligue,* 300.

In Poitiers, the news arrived just as other significant events were occurring. On 28 December, Henri de Navarre's forces captured Niort and Saint-Maix-ent, two important towns in Poitou.[41] François de Barbezières, sieur de Chemerault, was soon circulating an account that blamed Malicorne for the loss of Niort.[42] Just as Poitiers was digesting this information, Scévole de Sainte-Marthe arrived from Paris on 30 December to relate the murder of the Catholic princes one week before.[43] It was also at this time that Joseph Le Bascle, who was a hero of the siege of 1569 and who had been elected mayor six months before to maintain Poitiers in unity and obedience, died in office. He was replaced "unanimously" by Jean Palustre, ardent League supporter, after a dispute in the Mois concerning the method of succession had been resolved.[44]

We are fortunate to have two opposing accounts of political tensions as-sociated with the League, beginning at this time and continuing until the summer of 1589. The first, a manuscript account written by an anonymous royalist (probably an échevin) who left Poitiers in May 1589 and who recorded his memories sometime in 1590, most certainly provided the basis for De Thou's summary of events in Poitiers in his *Histoire universelle*.[45] This author, who blamed everyone *except* the city's royalists for Poitiers's de-fection, describes the assassinations as causing "astonishment and terror" among the League supporters until they realized that their views were spreading in other cities.[46] The second, an anonymous pro-League pamphlet written in September 1590, may have been a response to the royalist account or to one like it. This pamphlet maintains that Poitiers was so firm in its loy-alty to Henri III that the Catholics had no idea of reacting against the roy-alists until they received news of the "massacre" at Blois.[47] Whatever the

---

[41] For a detailed account of the siege of Niort, see Pierre Victor Palma-Cayet, *Chronologie novenaire, contenant l'histoire de la guerre sous le règne du tres-chrestien roy de France et de Navarre Henry IV, et les choses les plus memorables, advenues par tout le monde, depuis le commencement de son règne . . .* , in *Nouvelle collection des mémoires pour servir à l'histoire de France depuis le XIIe siècle jusqu'à la fin du XVIIIe*, ed. Michaud and Poujoulat, 1st ser., 12 (Paris and Lyon, 1850), 84–86; De Thou, *Histoire universelle*, 7:362–63; Aubigné, *Histoire universelle*, 8:1–8. Poitiers's corps de ville reported the news to the duc de Nevers and asked for special protection. See BNF MS Fr 3405, 74r (letter from the mayor, *pairs,* and échevins of Poitiers to Nevers, dated 30 Dec. 1588); 3614, 1r (letter from mayor and échevins of Poitiers to Nevers, 1 Jan. 1589).

[42] Desaivre, ed., *Lettres missives,* 458–60.

[43] ACP Reg. 48, 215–20, 223–24 (29–30 Dec. 1588).

[44] Le Bascle died on 18 January (ACP Reg. 48, 259–64). The town council register does not mention the electoral dispute, but René de Brilhac recorded the event in his journal. See Reg. 48, 281–89 (27 Jan. 1589); Brilhac, 22.

[45] See BNF MS Fr 20157, 151r–162v; De Thou, *Histoire universelle*, 7:459–62. I speculate that the author was an échevin, since the text reproduces arguments that the corps de ville pro-duced concerning noble deputies to the Estates General of 1588 (see chapter 1). Internal evidence also makes it likely that the author left Poitiers shortly after the events of 2–3 May (see below).

[46] BNF MS Fr 20157, 152v–154r.

[47] *Response d'vn catholiqve citoien de Poictiers à la lettre d'vn sien ami cy deuant son conci-toien & catholique, mais a present partisan des heretiques & mescreans* (n.p., 1590), 8. The text is dated 22 September 1590 from Poitiers.

Leaguers' attitudes toward the king before the assassinations, the news clearly intensified divisions. Poitiers sent deputies to Paris in February 1589 to attend an assembly that resolved that the murders absolved all French subjects of obedience to the king, and the delegates returned home armed with instructions, *memoires*, and money to bolster the cause.[48]

The immediate and most characteristic sign of increased League activism in Poitiers was the increased volley of mutual assurances of loyalty and service that passed between king and municipality in the succeeding months. The town's protestations of loyalty represented a desperate attempt of royalists and moderates to retain the upper hand against radical Leaguers, while the king's promises of favor sought to retain the town within the confines of its traditional relationship. Immediately after Poitiers had heard the news of the Guises' death, the municipality dispatched letters assuring the king of its unwavering loyalty.[49] Henri III responded with a message of continuing good will but by 22 January had instructed the hôtel de ville to keep him minutely informed of the situation in Poitiers through weekly reports.[50] The Mois commissioned further protestations of fidelity on 10 March, in response to an undescribed crisis in Poitiers on that day, and by the 17th, it had received royal praise for its notable loyalty and promises of great benefits to come.[51] As in May 1588, not only were the texts of these letters recorded in the town council register, but they were also printed and cried aloud in the streets to publicize the town's continuing stance of obedience.[52]

Henri III surely knew what was happening in Poitiers, since in addition to the municipality's assurances of tranquility he also received the troubled reports of the governor of Poitou. Our royalist author complains that although Malicorne came to Poitiers on the urgent request of the king's supporters, the governor was fooled into believing that "for the most part, [the Leaguers] were not poorly disposed to their duty."[53] This accusation is very unlikely. By early January 1589, Malicorne was aware that recriminations were spreading against him for the loss of Niort, and in a letter of 6 January, he felt obliged to defend himself against "the passions and false reports that some of those who deserve the most blame were spreading."[54] It is clear that Malicorne subsequently complained to the king about the town's attitude toward him, since in his letter of 18 January, Henri III specifically enjoined the corps de ville to recognize and to honor him as it ought.[55] Rather

[48] *Registres des délibérations du bureau de la ville de Paris*, 9:297–99; BNF MS Fr 20157, 154r.

[49] ACP Reg. 48, 232–38, 253–56 (6 and 16 Jan. 1589).

[50] ACP Reg. 48, 276–80, 291–92 (23 and 30 Jan. 1589). Henri III made the same requirement of Châlons-sur-Marne. See Konnert, *Civic Agendas*, 60.

[51] ACP Reg. 48, 343, 356–57 (10 and 17 Mar. 1589).

[52] ACP Reg. 48, 290–91 (30 Jan. 1589); 354–55 (17 Mar.).

[53] BNF MS Fr 20157, 154v.

[54] ACP Reg. 48, 238–44 (9 Jan. 1589); quotation, 239. Malicorne had been in command of the château of Niort at the time of the siege and was allowed to quit it shortly after Navarre's victory, with no threats to his personal safety.

[55] ACP Reg. 48, 280.

than showing ignorance, Malicorne was no doubt responding to the same uncertainties that prompted many of Poitiers's royalists to wait and see. Jean Jay, sieur de Boisseguin, governor of Poitiers and its château, was in the process of transferring his allegiances from a lifetime of royal service to support for the League. Half of the militia captains reputedly favored the Holy Union.[56] On 10 March the Mois decided that the guard of the city would be assured by Malicorne, Boisseguin, Chemerault, the bishop (who had become a League supporter), and Joseph Doyneau, sieur de Sainte-Soline (a leading royalist)—meaning, by an uneasy combination of advocates and opponents of the League.[57] It would take more than an aged provincial governor with a traditionally poor relationship with the capital city to assert the king's authority unequivocally.[58]

Evidently aware that the presence of Malicorne was not enough to assure the town's allegiance, Henri III sent a series of representatives to Poitiers to preserve it within the royal camp. Scévole de Sainte-Marthe had been his first emissary.[59] In early February, René, comte de Sanzay, appeared in the Mois to deliver a message from the king enjoining the town to remain unified in the service of his majesty.[60] This nobleman had represented Poitiers's échevins at the Estates of 1588 and therefore should have held some influence with the municipality. Yet the Leaguer pamphlet derisively described his message as a piece of sophistry in which he held that one could draw a distinction between heretics and heresy and between the League and the Sacred Union.[61] More concretely, League advocates posted an armed group of men outside Sanzay's lodgings to discourage him from taking any decisive action.[62]

Soon afterward Aymeri de Barbezières, sieur de la Roche-Chemerault, and François du Plessis de Richelieu appeared on the part of the king. Each enjoyed good relations with many inhabitants of Poitiers, and Henri III no doubt hoped that La Roche-Chemerault could convince Chemerault, his older brother, to quit his encouragement of the League in Poitiers.[63] Although the later League account would describe their arrival as *gracieuse,* the council early showed its distrust of their mission by deciding that it would not greet them outside the walls.[64] Advocates of the League indeed had much to fear, for no sooner had they arrived in Poitiers than the two envoys un-

[56] BNF MS Fr 20157, 154r–v.

[57] ACP Reg. 48, 347–48.

[58] Malicorne was around sixty-five years old in 1589. Desaivre, ed., *Lettres missives,* 253.

[59] Gabriel Michet de Roche-maillet, "La vie de Scévole de Sainte-Marthe. A Paris, Chez Iacqves Villery, au Palais. M. DC. XXIX. Avec Privilege dv Roy," in Scévole de Sainte-Marthe, *Opera Latina et Gallica,* 2 vols. (Geneva, 1971–72), 2:213.

[60] ACP Reg. 48, 301–9 (10 Feb. 1589).

[61] *Response d'vn catholiqve,* 9–10.

[62] BNF MS Fr 20157, 155r.

[63] BNF MS Fr 20157, 155v.

[64] *Response d'vn catholiqve,* 10; ACP Reg. 48, 386–90 (17 Apr. 1589).

dertook to gain control of the extraordinary council and to reorganize the guard. The day after their arrival, a general assembly passed measures specifying that only individuals chosen from a list composed by the governors and mayor would be selected each day to guard the gates.[65] The two royal commissioners exerted an authority that temporarily made their measures effective, but their attempts to bring Poitiers firmly into the royalist camp led only to open confrontation between Leaguers and royalists.

The spring of 1589 was a period of great unrest and confusion in Poitiers. Many normal activities ceased. The dominicale stopped meeting after 16 April, and collections in many parishes were left unfulfilled.[66] The chaplains of Ste. Radegonde suspended their meetings between 8 May and 6 September.[67] As early as the previous September, moreover, Malicorne had forbidden all inhabitants from provoking or insulting one another, but by March, hostilities had reached a new pitch. New ordinances prohibited all inhabitants

> from harming each other by word or deed in any way or manner whatever, and
> from provoking or insulting each other either by saying that they belong to the
> League, counter-league, [or are] politiques, heretics, traitors, atheists, machi-
> avellians, partisans, tax collectors, seditious or rebels, and other seditious and
> factious names that lead to divisions among the people.[68]

Accusations were flying in Poitiers, and the inhabitants were making the same kinds of associations between political loyalties and religious sensibilities as could be found in the pamphlets no doubt also making the rounds. The local League also drew on the same hostilities toward the royal financial administration that could be found in Rouen, Brittany, and the Estates of 1588.[69] Yet as disturbing as such vituperations were, the divisions did not stop here. The same ordinances went on to forbid that anyone "hold any private assemblies, court supporters [*Praticquer hommes*], or put them in arms, either in this town or elsewhere."[70] Both sides were preparing for a clash.

"Changement et revolution," May 1589

The royalist author of the 1590 *Discours* saw the events of 2–3 May as the real turning point in the history of the League in Poitiers. These were liter-

[65] ACP Reg. 48, 390–95 (18 Apr. 1589).

[66] On 6 August 1589 it was noted that collections had ceased in Montierneuf seven months before; on 20 August, it appeared that they had not been carried out in St. Porchaire since April; and on 19 November it was noted that Ste. Radegonde had refused to pay for the last eight months. ACP Casier 53, 1587–90.

[67] ADV G1694, 51r–v.

[68] ACP Reg. 48, 77–79 (12 Sept. 1588); 369–70 (29 Mar. 1589); quotation, 369.

[69] Benedict, *Rouen*, 172–74; Harding, "Revolution and Reform," 403–5; Constant, *Ligue*, 165–201; BNF MS Fr 20153, 327–28.

[70] ACP Reg. 48, 370.

ally Poitiers's days of the barricades. Both royalists and Leaguers had been assessing their support and preparing to seize the upper hand, but their opposition had not yet erupted into open disorder. An argument would now provide the excuse. Accounts of the exact course of events vary with the sympathies of the reporter. The League pamphleteers and the royalist memorialist each blamed the other side for sparking the violence through a plot to capture and kill their opponents' leaders. Jacques de Hillerin, a student of royalist sympathies studying in Poitiers at the time, merely reported what he saw or heard and was not aware of any premeditated hostilities.[71] Yet whether a confrontation was planned for this particular day or not, both sides had reason to expect that Poitiers's allegiances would soon be decided through violent means. The royalist leaders had requested that the king send troops led by the prince de Dombes to support them, and the maréchal de Biron, similarly sent to aid the royalists, had been unceremoniously chased out of Poitiers only two days before.[72] The League adherents, for their part, had summoned the aid of troops led by Georges de Villequier, vicomte de la Guierche, son-in-law of Boisseguin.[73] Since the truce between Henri III and Henri de Navarre, first concluded on 3 April and put into effect on 26 April, was registered in the presidial court of Poitiers on 2 May, the League faction may have decided that with Navarre's forces in control of much of Poitou and the king ensconced at Tours, it was now imperative to secure its position by gaining complete control of Poitiers.[74]

An argument between François Palustre and Jean Martin, the sergeant-major of the militia, set events in motion. An assembly involving all sides was called to meet in the episcopal palace to work out a compromise, but the "people" became so alarmed that they rose up in arms and set up barricades throughout the city.[75] Their concern was understandable if, as the League pamphlets claimed, the royalists intended to execute their principal opponents at this assembly.[76] Exiting the meeting, Sainte-Soline, an important royalist leader, encountered the barricades and began to put their defenders to flight. In the middle of the confusion, he came upon Mayor Jean Palustre, who, depending on the point of view, was either riding through the streets to quiet the disorder or reviling Sainte-Soline for his own attempts to do so.[77] A dramatic confrontation resulted, in which the royalist gentil-

[71] Hillerin, *Chariot chrestien*, 31–32.

[72] Hillerin, *Chariot chrestien*, 31; Aubigné, *Histoire universelle*, 8:32; Brilhac, 24. Palma-Cayet, *Chronologie novenaire*, 140, explains that Biron had arrived from Guyenne on the summons of Henri III, who was preparing to enter Poitiers in the near future. For the prince de Dombes, see BNF MS Fr 20157, 156r.

[73] *Response d'vn catholiqve*, 13–14; BNF MS Fr 20157, 158v. Royal letters dated 5 May 1589 from Tours mention the presence of La Guierche. ACP Reg. 48, 418–19 (6 May 1589).

[74] ADV C74, 102v.

[75] BNF MS Fr 20157, 156r–v.

[76] *Response d'vn catholiqve*, 11–12; *La grande trahison descouverte en la ville de Poictiers, sur les entreprises de Richelieu, & Malicorne* (Paris, 1589), 4.

[77] *Grande trahison*, 5; *Response d'vn catholiqve*, 12–13; BNF MS Fr 20157, 156v.

homme threatened the Leaguer mayor. Sainte-Soline "put his sword to [Palustre's] throat and forced him thus to withdraw, reproaching him that he alone and his son were the instruments and cause of all the evil."[78] The quarrel under control and the uprising calmed down, the leaders met in a second assembly to reconcile the parties. But that night, the royalist *Discours* maintains, the Leaguers spread out over the entire city and took control of the bell towers, including one within shot of Sainte-Soline's hôtel. Meanwhile, François Palustre filed a complaint with the governors against Sainte-Soline for his insults against him and his father. The following day saw a continuation of the hostilities. Royalist militia bands found themselves at a disadvantage, since they were posted at the gates most distant from the fighting, but they managed to group their forces and set up barricades between the Marché Vieux and the Cordeliers. The tocsin rang out continually. Sainte-Soline was besieged in his hôtel, and his absence seriously weakened the royalists. Finally, the governors and royal envoys determined to calm the uprising by acceding to the Leaguers' most insistent demand: that Sainte-Soline quit Poitiers. Asked to do so by friends and relations, he complied almost immediately, accompanied by several other supporters of the king.[79]

Despite the dramatic nature and conclusion of these clashes, neither side could claim full control of the city. Malicorne called an extraordinary council that passed stringent measures for the guard of the town.[80] Meanwhile, League advocates in Poitiers were gaining the support of the surrounding communities. In a secret assembly of 4 May, Leaguers from Poitiers and other towns decided unanimously to maintain the Catholic party against the troops of the tyrant, Henri de Valois, headed by Richelieu and Malicorne. League delegates continued to arrive, and a meeting of 9 May confirmed the conclusions of the earlier gathering. Having discovered the existence of these assemblies, Malicorne and Richelieu reputedly responded by having six notable Catholics killed. The action prompted a popular uprising, in which Poitiers's inhabitants seized the murderers and killed them in their turn.[81] The group also captured Malicorne, "whom they marched through their town with their halberds at his throat, with all the bells ringing," as well as Richelieu, and imprisoned them.[82] The governor was ultimately allowed to leave Poitiers and to set up his base of operations at Parthenay.[83]

Significantly, none of these actions constituted a break with the king, and Henri III now determined to follow through on previous plans and go to

[78] BNF MS Fr 20157, 156v.

[79] BNF MS Fr 20157, 156v–158v; *Response d'vn catholiqve*, 11–13; Hillerin, *Chariot chrestien*, 31–32.

[80] ACP Reg. 48, 412–15 (4 May 1589). These ordinances were evidently printed and posted publicly, since the council ordered that Aymé Mesnier, printer, be paid on 8 May. Ironically, the receipt was dated 12 May, after Malicorne had lost control of Poitiers. ACP Casier 37, K28.

[81] *Grande trahison*, 5–9.

[82] Aubigné, *Histoire universelle*, 8:32; *Grande trahison*, 9.

[83] *Response d'vn catholiqve*, 16; Aubigné, *Histoire universelle*, 8:32.

Poitiers in person. As early as February 1589 there had been rumors that the monarch would retire to Poitiers, and people returning from Tours reported the king's desire to leave that city. After the duc de Mayenne almost succeeded in ambushing the king in a suburb of Tours on 8 May, speculations ran high that Henri III, like his predecessor Charles VII, would seek refuge against traitors to the crown in the Poitevin capital.[84] The king's arrival was discussed when deputies went to Tours after the disorders of 2–3 May to assure Henri III of Poitiers's continuing loyalty.[85] Some League sympathizers, such as Louis de Sainte-Marthe, joined royal supporters in requesting his visit, but given the recent events in Poitiers, the prospect of the king's presence incited general fears.[86] The council therefore decided on 15 May to supplicate that he delay his visit. Two conseillers of the presidial court also found themselves menaced by a group of armed inhabitants when they thought to quiet their concerns by informing them that the forces they spied in the area belonged to the king. Far from desiring the king's arrival, the group threatened to admit League troops by one gate, should royal ones seek entrance by another.[87] For some of Poitiers's inhabitants, the model of Poitiers's historic reception of Charles VII clearly held little appeal.

Speculations about the king's arrival finally materialized on 17 May, when Henri III and his soldiers appeared outside Poitiers early in the morning. His presence precipitated a general crisis. The palais halted its business, and people gathered in the streets, crying that they would rather die than let him enter the town. There was a general call to arms, and those determined to deny the king entry called to inhabitants to ignore the representations of certain conseillers and trésoriers who were equally desirous to open the gates. The king's appearance caused a genuine rift in the League. Jean Palustre, Chemerault, and François de Brilhac sent deputies to Henri III to assure him that they would soon arrange to admit him via Poitiers's château. They found themselves, however, unable to make good on their offer. A general pause occurred around midday, as the king retired for dinner, but the alarm and confusion became more intense in the afternoon, as royal troops appeared at the St. Ladre and Pont-à-Joubert gates. Someone rang the tocsin, all the shops were closed up, and inhabitants streamed out of their houses with arms. Shots were fired at the royal forces from the château, and cries that the king was in Poitiers were countered by assurances that he was still out-

---

[84] Hillerin, *Chariot chrestien,* 10, 34–35, 38–39.

[85] ACP Reg. 48, 423–25 (15 May 1589); *Response d'vn catholiqve,* 14–15; Aubigné, *Histoire universelle,* 8:32; BNF MS Fr 20157, 159r.

[86] Étienne Pasquier, having left Paris for Tours, was informed by Sainte-Marthe himself of the errand of the Poitevin deputies. *Les oeuvres d'Estienne Pasquier . . . ,* 2 vols. (Amsterdam, 1723), 2:392.

[87] ACP Reg. 48, 423–25; Hillerin, *Chariot chrestien,* 35–37. It is possible that this incident took place on 15 May, since the register of the bureau of the trésoriers généraux at Poitiers mentions that the regular meeting was canceled on this day because of "troubles" and the king's army being near Poitiers. See ADV C74, 104v.

side the walls. The confusion gradually subsided two or three hours later. Even now the king sent articles of agreement designed to achieve a compromise, but they were returned with so many disrespectful alterations that no compromise was possible. Repulsed so rudely by this traditionally loyal city, Henri III retreated to Tours the following day.[88]

The League and Popular Politics

Contemporary narrators of the League in Poitiers put emphasis on its elite leaders. Agrippa d'Aubigné, for example, pointed to the vicomte de la Guierche; François de Brilhac, lieutenant criminel; Palustre (it is unclear whether he meant the father, Jean, or the son, François); and Geoffroy de Saint-Belin, bishop of Poitiers, as denouncing the assassinations of 1588, praising the Guises, and reviving memories of the siege of 1569, all in an attempt to encourage sedition.[89] Narrators equally focused on elite supporters of the crown, including Malicorne, Scévole de Sainte-Marthe, Sainte-Soline, and his friend, Pierre Rat, lieutenant général.[90] But as the complicated history of the League in Poitiers shows, popular convictions and active support were essential to the Holy Union's success. Without the detailed sources for the movement in Poitiers such as exist for Paris, the internal dynamics of League organization in this provincial city must remain obscure. If we assess the role that the inhabitants played, however, it is clear that repeated crowd actions were neither the spontaneous uprisings that League advocates represented, nor the manipulated events that royalists claimed. For the events of 17 May, it is even possible that general opinion turned against the negotiations that the supposed leaders were trying to conduct. From the point of view of Poitiers's inhabitants, the League movement provided avenues for greater political expression and even for the kind of deep-seated hostility toward elites that characterized the radical League in Paris. Yet if the League movement integrated popular activity more thoroughly into the permissible boundaries of politics, it still retained limitations on how central a part nonelite inhabitants could play. Traditional political hierarchies were preserved to such an extent that it fell to elites to determine

[88] Hillerin, *Chariot chrestien*, 39–40; BNF MS Fr 20157, 159v–161r; MMP MS 574, 39v; Aubigné, *Histoire universelle*, 8:32; De Thou, *Histoire universelle*, 7:461–62; Palma-Cayet, *Chronologie novenaire*, 140.

[89] Aubigné, *Histoire universelle*, 8:31–32.

[90] Aubigné, *Histoire universelle*, 8:32–33; BNF MS Fr 20157, 157r–158v; Brilhac, 24. On the friendship between Rat and Sainte-Soline: when Sainte-Soline was arrested in 1584 by the king's orders and fell sick in the prisons of the presidial court, he was removed to Rat's hôtel. Henri III was severely angered and summoned both men to Paris. Le Riche, 395–96; BNF MS Fr 3310, 4v. When the chapter of St. Hilaire was embroiled in legal proceedings, it decided to recuse Rat as judge of the case because of Rat's support of Sainte-Soline, his "Inthime amy." ADV G533, 391r–v.

when Poitiers would officially break with the crown and formally declare for the Holy Union.

Although there is no evidence that Poitiers witnessed the same kind of penitential piety that occurred in cities such as Paris, Rouen, and Marseille, an atmosphere of Catholic devotion conducive to League sympathies prevailed.[91] Miracle stories, revealing how mockers of the Catholic religion were literally struck dumb, may have circulated here before making their way to Paris.[92] When Hillerin arrived in Poitiers from Angers in March 1589, he was struck by the piety of the people, growing more marked with each passing day.[93] Jean Porthaise, Franciscan friar and *théologal* at the cathedral, delivered a sermon there each Sunday to a large audience including the lieutenant général, lieutenant civil, and other conseillers of the presidial court.[94] League forces, judged Hillerin, would certainly gain the upper hand, since they had the advantage of reference to the Catholic religion, so strongly regarded among the people.[95] As the political situation became more intense, moreover, so did the efforts of the preachers. Shortly after Poitiers's refusal to admit Henri III, Hillerin remarked that they no longer exhorted their congregations to pray for the king and often departed from their assigned texts to discourse on politics. This must have represented a significant change in style and subject matter, since only a month earlier the royalist lieutenant général had attended public sermons. In addition to preachers, such as Porthaise, who had been in Poitiers for some time, there were some recent arrivals, the most popular of whom did not mince their words. By June, even the friars had begun to take liberties, and had abandoned the terms of the church fathers, who teach obedience to constituted authority.[96] In Poitiers as in Paris, therefore, inhabitants could hear a message of militant zeal in the sermons of their parish clergy supplemented by the eloquent efforts of new arrivals. Such exhortations seem to have had a strong impact on popular opinion, as active participation in League uprisings would attest.[97]

[91] The one hint of the presence of penitential societies was a mention of a "procession noire" in which the canons of Ste. Radegonde took part. ADV G1347, legal memoir, 1580. Denis Crouzet, "Recherches sur les processions blanches, 1583–1584," *Histoire, économie et société* 1 (1982): 511–63; Benedict, *Rouen*, 190–92, 200–2; Kaiser, *Marseille*, 182–90, 216–18, 319–20.

[92] *Discovrs miracvlevx advenv en l'an M.D.LXXXVI. pres la ville de Potiers, en la personne d'vn nommé Bernardeau, aduocat au siege presidial de Poictiers* (Paris, 1586).

[93] Hillerin, *Chariot chrestien*, 24.

[94] Hillerin, *Chariot chrestien*, 27–28.

[95] Hillerin, *Chariot chrestien*, 35.

[96] Hillerin, *Chariot chrestien*, 40–41, 45.

[97] On the importance of preaching in forming public opinion during the League, see: Charles Labitte, *La démocratie chez les prédicateurs de la Ligue* (Paris, 1865); Arlette Lebigre, *La révolution des curés: Paris 1588–1594* (Paris, 1980); Crouzet, *Guerriers de dieu;* Harding, "Revolution and Reform "; Megan Armstrong, "The Franciscans and the Catholic League: A Question of Civic Ties and Spirituality," *Proceedings of the Western Society for French History* 24 (1997), 134.

Crowd action, as we have seen, played an essential role in the League's rise in Poitiers. Contemporaries recognized this fact at the same time that they derided any popular involvement as inherently seditious. Hillerin, who would eventually become a *conseiller-clerc* in the Parlement of Paris, was typical in this respect. Speculating on whether Poitiers would adhere to the League shortly after 3 May 1589, he surmised that victory would go to the faction led by Jean and François Palustre, "who, since they are more greatly loved by the people, will come out the strongest."[98] Yet he also did not hesitate to label popular interventions as rebellious. Repeating a truism of the age, he commented: "I have always heard it said that it is the poorest and lowest among a people who ordinarily incite seditions . . . who, each exciting the other, bring themselves to passion and cruelty extremely easily, if one attempts to talk to them to calm them down."[99]

This ambivalence toward popular participation in important events explains why political opponents were sure that it was the result of elite manipulations while supporters attempted to pass it off as spontaneous. When describing the incident in which the maréchal de Biron was threatened by a royal sergeant and some of his fellows and forced to leave Poitiers, for example, our anonymous royalist commented knowingly that such men would never have dared to act in this way had they not been brought to it by greater men, who wished to carry out evil without receiving the blame.[100] By contrast, League pamphleteers represented each of the important crowd actions of May 1589 as impulsive and unprompted. The author of the *Response d'vn catholiqve* credited divine agency for spreading rumors of a plot against leading Catholics and bringing the inhabitants suddenly to arms on 2 May and blamed Poitiers's refusal to admit Henri III uniquely on the king, who he said should have been more sensitive to the doubts and fears of the people. Henri III should not have tried to gain entrance to Poitiers,

> because the too recent disorder, the fire yet to be extinguished, the complaints
> of the absent turning the particular into the general, the numerous opinions of
> his Majesty's anger . . . , these were all pertinent reasons for delay, during which
> it would have been possible to reassure the people, calm public opinion, and
> retain all allegiance in its accustomed path.

But the king had foolishly appeared suddenly at the town walls, causing a general panic. "What could the speed and ardor of such a voyage, made under such exhausting conditions by an angered king, immediately cause a people, troubled by all this, to imagine? What could anyone hope from this but

---

[98] Hillerin, *Chariot chrestien*, 31.
[99] Hillerin, *Chariot chrestien*, 36. Decimon has pointed to the tendency of prominent royalists to identify all active opposition as originating in the lower levels of society. *Qui étaient les Seize?* 19–20, 27–33.
[100] BNF MS Fr 20157, 159r–v.

defiance, tumults, alarms and resistance?"[101] It is revealing that a League adherent in 1590 would desire to represent Poitiers's rebuff of Henri III as an impromptu result of popular fears, especially since Hillerin's testimony contradicts this view. When news reached Poitiers that Henri III was at Châtellerault, Hillerin was shocked by agitation among the people, "in which Monsieur the Mayor, and several others from the palais are very involved." Accompanied by certain members of the nobility, they were circulating throughout the town, "in order to incite the people to sedition."[102] Yet it is also possible that the League pamphleteer was reflecting a very real sense that League leaders had lost control of the situation. It is hard to understand why the mayor, the lieutenant criminel, and a prestigious gentilhomme sent deputies to arrange for the king's entry, only later to fire on his troops from the château. The royalist narrator speculates that their intentions were feigned or that they subsequently changed their minds, but it is equally possible that the dominant opinion, enforced by a people in arms, was against admitting Henri III into the city.[103] Popular hostility to the king was therefore not, or not entirely, the product of a sudden confusion or *émotion*. On the contrary, it stemmed from a militant religious outlook cultivated by League preaching that coincided with, or even surpassed, the sympathies of the most zealous among the elite. It was also instrumental in promoting the success of the League in Poitiers.

However elites felt about and represented forms of popular activism, the League period provided greater opportunities for Poitiers's inhabitants to form and to express their opinions in a significant way. Interest in the deliberations of Poitiers's extraordinary councils—first held in the Cordeliers convent and then converted to the Union Council—was intense, and this eagerness to know and to influence what was being decided explains why membership had so often to be limited and secrecy reinforced. Ordinances continually forbade attendance of anyone not specifically elected, and guards were posted at the entrance to the Union Council to prevent unauthorized admittance.[104] The distribution of guard assignments excited the same kind of curiosity.[105] Artisans developed the same strong political sentiments that led elites to support the League or to quit Poitiers for royalist territory, and they showed the same concern to ensure responsible administration of their property and businesses in times of war. As husbands fled or were banished to royalist strongholds, therefore, wives took on administration of family

[101] *Response d'vn catholiqve*, 15–16. Jean Le Roy also describes Poitiers's resistance as a response to royal actions, MMP MS 574, 39v.

[102] Hillerin, *Chariot chrestien*, 39.

[103] BNF MS Fr 20157, 160r.

[104] For example, ACP Reg. 48, 465–67; Reg. 52, 1–3.

[105] Ordinances dated 20 June 1589 forbade anyone, except those going on duty, to be present at the place Notre-Dame when the guard assignments were being handed out. ACP Reg. 48, 465–67.

concerns. On 17 May 1589, for example, Marie Babynot, wife of Helie Cymetiere, hatter, terminated a contract of apprenticeship, since "the said Cymetiere had absented himself and left the said town of Poitiers two days ago leaving the said Pierre without a master. . . ."[106] The wives of Pierre Bugean, a chamois merchant, and Jean Frappier, merchant, similarly took over the family's affairs.[107] The divisions in political opinion and hostile confrontations that occurred in all sectors of society further required more than general police ordinances forbidding name-calling and mutual provocations. For this reason the militia hierarchy was invested with the role of conflict resolution. No other institution incorporated so many of Poitiers's inhabitants within one administrative structure. Ordinances of September 1588 therefore instructed the inhabitants to bring all disagreements to their militia captain.[108] By 1592, the captains and the mayor met in a separate body designed to resolve the large number of problems arising from the administration of the militia and the discipline of its soldiers.[109]

In cities such as Paris and Marseille, the militia has been identified as an important organizational structure, through which members formed social and political ties, created a particular understanding of bourgeois identity, and took violent action into their own hands.[110] Sources on Poitiers's militia are poor, but it is clear that by the League period, the six companies had developed new administrative structures and representative functions. Concerns that all citizens fulfill their military responsibilities had encouraged record keeping, so that the companies now boasted their own secretaries. When in 1591 the Union Council decided to expel all Protestants and wives of absentees from Poitiers, it instructed the captains to deliver the rolls of individuals concerned to the *syndic* of each quarter. The syndics could then question the curé of each parish concerning the faith of suspect parishioners.[111] This approach reversed traditional procedure, in which the parishes would have provided a list of inhabitants to the companies. The militia also came to be seen as the body most directly expressing the concerns of average inhabitants. By June 1589, each company was permitted to elect a representative, who was to present all complaints arising among his peers for adjudication in the Cordeliers council.[112] There is evidence, too, that the militia provided a real medium through which residents could act

---

[106] ADV E⁴26.14: termination of contract between Mathieu Balloneault and Marie Babynot.

[107] ADV E⁴24.19, act between Pauline Bezanceau and Ysaac Torses, dated 15 July 1589; E⁴27.27, contract between François Chartreau and Jacquette Cailleteau, 17 Jan. 1591. Women's acts of political expression during the League era are often difficult to uncover. See Annette Finley-Croswhite, "Engendering the Wars of Religion: Female Agency during the Catholic League in Dijon," *French Historical Studies* 20, no. 2 (1997): 127–54.

[108] ACP Reg. 48, 77–79 (12 Sept. 1588).

[109] ACP Reg. 53, 5–10 (20 July 1592).

[110] Descimon, "Milice bourgeoise"; Diefendorf, *Beneath the Cross*; Kaiser, *Marseille*, 286, 305–18.

[111] ACP Reg. 52, 133–35 (30 Dec. 1591).

[112] ACP Reg. 48, 436–37 (2 June 1589).

out their sense of commitment. Many of the "disorders" of the League period were due to the independent actions of the *écouades*, small detachments of the militia based in particular neighborhoods. In June 1589, in response, all soldiers were enjoined to obey their captains, and "to undertake nothing on their own private authority, either through threats, intimidations, insults, or anything else, and especially while on guard."[113] These militia groups could also take action against the abuses of their superiors. In 1592, the soldiers of the écouade of St. Pierre presented a complaint in the Union Council against a canon of Ste. Radegonde for violence against his corporal and other soldiers. They obtained the satisfaction of the cleric's imprisonment.[114] The League period thus prompted intense popular interest in politics and offered significant opportunities for inhabitants to take action based on their convictions. For some, the League also provided the context for fundamental criticisms of the governing elite.

In the third volume of his *De Vinculo Religionis et Imperii Libri tres,* Adam Blacvod (Blackwood), conseiller in the presidial court of Poitiers, recounted his run-in with a craftsman during the time of the League. Attempting to defend a Catholic friend from violence at the hands of a group of League advocates, Blacvod found himself reviled in turn. A soap maker in the band told Blacvod that if he was suffered to remain in Poitiers, this was only because he was generally thought a good Catholic, although at heart he was nothing but a partisan of the Béarnais, just like other members of the presidial court. Several months later, the same man accosted Blacvod in the street and accused him of having taken money to turn the town over to the Huguenots. When the conseiller replied that this was a false rumor manufactured by the soap maker himself, the artisan defended his character as a good Catholic and free Poitevin. Further insults were exchanged, after which Blacvod predicted that his accuser would end his life on the scaffold. This event indeed came to pass, but the spectators, instead of applauding the circumstance, declared the soap maker a saint and a martyr. The Holy Spirit, went the common report, had landed on his shoulder in the shape of a dove, to bring him consolation in his extremity.[115]

The League in Poitiers therefore led to the same kinds of social hostilities and radical differences of opinion that in Paris were eventually preserved in the *Dialogue d'entre le maheustre et le manant.*[116] Craftsmen who normally

[113] ACP Reg. 48, 465–67.

[114] ACP Reg. 52, 170 (13 Mar. 1592).

[115] Adam Blacvod, *De Vinculo Religionis et Imperii Libri tres, adversus eos qui perdellionem fuco pietatis adumbrant* (Poitiers, 1612), cited in [Jean-François] Dreux-Duradier, *Histoire littéraire du Poitou: précédée d'une introduction et continuée jusqu'en 1849 par une société d'hommes de lettres* (1842–49; reprint, Geneva, 1969), 218–20.

[116] This famous pamphlet, a product of the Parisian radical League in its first version, presented a discussion between a high-status moderate and a low-status radical Leaguer. For a modern edition, see François Cromé, ed., *Dialogue d'entre le maheustre et le manant* (Geneva, 1977). See also Baumgartner, *Radical Reactionaries*, 210–17.

did not have a chance to play a conspicuous role on the public political stage now seized the opportunity to make their opinions known and even to threaten social superiors whom they judged to hold antithetical political and religious beliefs. Pride in their own status as members of the urban community also characterized the artisans' challenge. The soap maker's description of himself as a "good Catholic and free Poitivin" no doubt deepened his intended contrast with Blacvod's elite origins and Scottish nationality. This conviction that common people had a worth greater than their reputed superiors was not unique to this incident. In the spring of 1589, Hillerin witnessed a similar confrontation between two conseillers and an armed group of inhabitants. When the judicial officials ordered the group to withdraw, the small crowd "began to insult them, and even menaced them with worse treatment if they did not retire immediately, and that the life of the least of their children was more dear to them than that of princes and kings."[117] This tendency of the League to give voice to expressions of social radicalism was precisely what led Blacvod, in retrospect, to condemn the whole movement. His clash with angry craftsmen only confirmed the central contention of his treatise: royal power was absolute and received its best support from religion. The radical Catholicism of the League had disrupted the lines of authority, leading inferiors to feel entitled to criticize their social betters.[118] Yet if Blacvod had become an absolutist by the reign of Louis XIII, in the early 1590s he was a firm supporter of the League in Poitiers.[119] It is this fact that makes the craftsmen's accusation so revealing: although the conseillers in the presidial court were some of the strongest advocates of the League, the soap maker and his fellows chose to identify this body with support of Navarre. Clearly, Poitiers harbored the makings of a socially and ideologically radical League. That these convictions did not gain the upper hand testifies to the success of elites in maintaining their authority within the urban community even as they held out against Navarre's assertion to be king of France.

Although Poitiers's inhabitants found increased opportunities to influence the political life of their city during the League period, significant limitations on popular agency still existed during this time. Blacvod's encounter with the armed band of artisans illustrates both aspects quite well: for all of the group's pride and audacity in confronting two of the city's magistrates, the soap maker

---

[117] Hillerin, *Chariot chrestien*, 36. It is possible, however, that the incident that Hillerin witnessed was in fact the same one that Blacvod described.

[118] J. W. Allen, *A History of Political Thought in the Sixteenth Century* (London, 1961), 378; J. H. M. Salmon, "Catholic Resistance Theory, Ultramontanism, and the Royalist Response, 1580–1620," in *The Cambridge History of Political Thought, 1450–1700*, ed. J. H. Burns (Cambridge, U.K., 1991), 233–34.

[119] On Blacvod as an absolutist: see Allen, *History of Political Thought;* Salmon, "The Paris Sixteen"; and Church, *Constitutional Thought*, 248–54. On Blacvod as a League advocate: Blacvod remained in Poitiers for the entire five years that the city held out against Henri IV. He was also one of the new bourgeois elected in 1589 to replace the large number who had departed and became an échevin during the League period. ACP Reg. 53, 55–58 (8 Jan. 1593).

did indeed end his career with a rope around his neck. Blacvod's contempt for his opponent is evident in his not bothering to indicate his name, and the soap maker evidently received little sympathy at the hands of François de Brilhac, lieutenant criminel, despite the magistrate's active support of the Holy Union. For all of their active commitment for the League, expressed in verbal confrontations, militia activities, and armed uprisings, Poitiers's inhabitants left it to urban elites to decide whether and when the city would join the Sacred Union. As the dramatic events of spring 1589 yielded only uncertainty during the summer, inhabitants wondered what was being discussed in the secret council at the Cordeliers and attempted to interpret police decisions, in an effort to determine what their governors had decided. As the summer progressed, pressures mounted on the members of governing institutions to determine whether Poitiers had adhered to the League or would remain loyal to the crown. Recounting that the preachers had begun to reject the traditional texts counseling submission to civil authority, Hillerin remarked of Poitiers's magistrates and corps de ville:

> I do not know whether they have the same sentiment, and although up until now they have kept their opinions quiet and hidden, it will nevertheless be necessary for them to reveal them very soon, since they are pushed to do so by those who importune them to extremity.[120]

In the final instance, therefore, it fell to the members of the hôtel de ville and the presidial court, the same individuals who traditionally set municipal policy, to determine whether Poitiers would or would not formally recognize the Holy Union.

Political Ambiguities

The events of May 1589, culminating with the denial of the king's entry, signaled to many the victory of the League in Poitiers. Notable royalists left town, beginning with Biron's expulsion on 30 April and accelerating with the alarms of 17 May. On 25 May, new militia officers were selected to replace those who had departed.[121] The tone of everyday life became more urgent, as secret councils met, fear of attack increased, and preachers began to call for war.[122] In the mayoral election of 30 June, the corps de ville chose a League supporter for mayor, after having provided him with the place of

---

[120] Hillerin, *Chariot chrestien*, 40–42, 45; quotation, 45.

[121] Pierre Rat, lieutenant général, had left as a result of the Biron incident; Brilhac, 24. The absence of Jacques Tillier and Antoine Dupré, échevins, is mentioned on 25 May; ACP Reg. 48, 425–27. Militia replacements: Reg. 48, 427–28. By 29 May 1589 Jean Palustre was the only trésorier present at the meetings of the bureau; ADV C74, 106r et seq.

[122] Hillerin, *Chariot chrestien*, 40–42, 44–45.

bourgeois only two days before.[123] Henri III also recognized the ramifications of events in Poitiers. Sometime in early June, he declared the city guilty of lèse-majesté and transferred the university, bureau, *recette général,* presidial court, éléction, and corps de ville to Parthenay.[124] Poitiers's inhabitants, the edict recited, "set about to surpass the other cities in the kingdom in perfidies . . . by acts so monstrous that their simple memory will leave such a stain on their posterity that it can never be effaced." Specifically, after obtaining a royal pardon for refusing to admit their king, they continued their outrageous indignities against their governor, Malicorne.[125] The hôtel de ville was soon complaining of the actions of the king's troops in the surrounding area and trying to prevent transfer of the royal courts and financial institutions out of the city.[126]

Yet until Poitiers had actually declared for the Catholic League, uncertainties within the town and room for negotiations with the monarch could persist. The town council registers refer only cryptically to the confrontations of early May and mention not at all the deaths of 11 May and the denial of the king's entry.[127] Such silences may be due to the fact that throughout the weeks of unrest both royalists and Leaguers continued to attend the meetings in the hôtel de ville. But this refusal to recognize a rupture with Henri III also allowed the possibility for reconciliation. Indeed, after each succeeding incident, the municipal government dispatched deputies to the king to excuse the disorders that had occurred and to testify to the town's continuing obedience.[128] Henri III was even willing to receive them after 17 May, and Hillerin specifically reasoned that if Poitiers chose to send deputies at all, this fact indicated that the League had not gained universal support in the town.[129] As late as 17 July, there were negotiations with Malicorne, in which his reentry into Poitiers was discussed.[130]

Within Poitiers, inhabitants could not help but be aware of the political struggle taking place but did not automatically interpret the disorders as a victory for the Catholic League. Shortly after the confrontations of 2–3 May, for example, Hillerin commented that he could still write "frankly and in the liberty that we still have here," despite the rumors and factions that made

---

[123] ACP Reg. 48, 473–83 (28 and 30 June 1589).

[124] BNF MS Fr 18976, 115r–116v. This copy of the edict lacks the date and place of issuance. I speculate that it dates from early June, because Poitiers's deputies were trying to prevent transfer of the financial and judicial bodies by the middle of that month.

[125] BNF MS Fr 18976, 115r–v; quotation, 115r.

[126] ACP Reg. 48, 443–48 (7 June 1589); 458–62 (14 June); 463–65 (19 June); 471 (26 June); 489–92 (6 July); ADV C74, 108r.

[127] The secretary recorded royal letters dated 5 May 1589 in which Henri III commended the town for quelling the recent disorders in Poitiers. ACP Reg. 48, 415–20 (6 May 1589).

[128] ACP Reg. 48, 415–20 (6 May 1589); 422–23 (10 May); 423–25 (15 May); 443–48 (7 June); 458–62 (14 June); BNF MS Fr 20157, 161r–v; Hillerin, *Chariot chrestien,* 40; *Response d'vn catholiqve,* 14–15, 17.

[129] Hillerin, *Chariot chrestien,* 40–41.

[130] ACP Reg. 49, 2–3 (17 July 1589); *Response d'vn catholiqve,* 17–18.

everything uncertain but had not progressed so far as to interfere with his studies.[131] After 17 May, he was still in doubt concerning the present situation and the ultimate outcome of events. On the one hand, the license taken by the preachers seemed to indicate that the town had declared for the League, but the message of obedience that deputies had recently delivered to the king seemed to militate against this interpretation, "which many, and some of the most elevated, do not believe."[132] That the royal courts, bureau, and university continued to operate was further sign that Poitiers had not yet succumbed to war. Hillerin would therefore continue to express himself as "a true Christian, a good Frenchman, and a good Catholic," until he saw something other than liberty in Poitiers, because nothing else had yet been declared.[133]

The royalist memorialist also remarked on Poitiers's persisting refusal to make any definitive declaration of its allegiances. This citizen, living in self-imposed exile since early May, claimed to see through all of his former associates' assurances of loyalty, which he thought were only calculated to mislead the king into believing that all of the disorders had been unplanned manifestations of the people's disobedience. Actually, he asserted, everyone in Poitiers was "united in the same spirit of ingratitude and infidelity," although different considerations led them to arrive at their unified stance.[134] If the city's leaders sought to maintain Poitiers in a position of neutrality, in which they appeared to recognize the king but all along favored the affairs of the duc de Mayenne, their efforts were calculated to advance their own interests. The League leaders, our royalist explained, sought to keep the city's affairs in the same undecided state in order simultaneously to retain a new-found influence over the people that enabled them to dictate their every move and to keep the door open to side with the victor in the standoff between the king and the League. "Whatever predilection they held for the good of the League," the memorialist asserted, "they were not such enemies to their particular [gain] that they did not wish to retain the ability one day to join the faction that would be victorious." Even as Poitiers adopted the marks and standards of the League in late July on the prompting of Mayenne and the exhortations of Porthaise, some of the most notable inhabitants would have preferred to maintain the city's neutrality.[135]

Assigning the worst motivations to League advocates, therefore, the royalist narrator identified the continuing ambiguities of Poitiers's allegiances as a calculated policy of the leaders, at the same time that he acknowledged that differences of opinion existed among the city's notables. For a man who had made his decision early on, the choice between the king and the League

---

[131] Hillerin, *Chariot chrestien*, 33.
[132] Hillerin, *Chariot chrestien*, 41.
[133] Hillerin, *Chariot chrestien*, 41–42; quotation, 42.
[134] BNF MS Fr 20157, 161v.
[135] BNF MS Fr 20157, 162r.

seemed perfectly clear. Yet what the long and complex history of Poitiers's declaration for the League shows is that the decision to break with the king was anything but simple. There were great obstacles, both institutional and mental, against overtly renouncing royal authority. The hôtel de ville, in conjunction with the other governing bodies, greatly preferred a practical resistance and messages of recalcitrance encoded within the terms of political exchange to cutting all ties with the crown. Even strong League supporters, who would hold out after Henri IV's conversion and Paris's reduction, hesitated to transfer full allegiance to Mayenne and the League. The victory of the Holy Union in Poitiers involved a complicated series of events, in which factional positioning, popular uprisings, and the seizure of military advantage translated into unquestionable acts of defiance only when elites finally united in declaring them so. And although Poitiers was clearly moving toward full adhesion to the League in late July 1589, when it finally decided to allow the vicomte de la Guierche, Mayenne's choice for governor, to enter the city with a small suite,[136] it still took a full two weeks after the death of the Henri III for the corps de ville and the presidial court to agree to swear the Holy Union. While a king of even questionable Catholic comportments still sat on the throne, the advantages of the provincial capital's traditional relationship with the crown enticed some League adherents to keep open the channels for negotiation. With the self-proclaimed advent of a heretic, however, the choice for militant Catholicism became clear.

The long series of events that led up to the swearing of the Oath of Union had involved, on some level, all of Poitiers's inhabitants in the battle between militant Catholicism and royal obedience. But even the disorder associated with the struggle had not succeeded in entirely overturning the traditional relationships that had dictated the broad lines of civic decision making. When Pierre Humeau described obedience as the height of Christian liberty and enlightened governance as a prime duty of the urban elite, therefore, he referred to an idealized model of government that nevertheless had some basis in fact. Yet although the active participation of members of Poitiers's governing institutions meant that the opportunities for the expression of the most socially radical League sentiments were limited and that these bodies would attempt to preserve the balance of authority, certain changes were inevitable during the League period. The development of alternative institutions, the situation of military threat, the tendency to religious activism, and the precautions taken by all the inhabitants to survive a period of great violence and uncertainty—all these factors had an impact on politics within Poitiers and on the city's relationship to the center of royal authority. In places like Paris, the League may have revived a municipal style slowly falling victim to the growing dominance of royal officials and their culture, but in

[136] ACP Reg. 49, 4–6 (24–25 July 1589). La Guierche did not enter Poitiers until sometime in August, probably on the 14th. Reg. 49, 14–16 (7 and 14 Aug. 1589).

Poitiers both kinds of approaches had coexisted for most of the century. The effects of the League period were therefore quite different in the two cities. Ironically, as Poitiers gained in autonomy and military importance, traditional elites found that new political challenges tended to destabilize their previous authority. By 1591, moreover, the excitement of Poitiers's new-found independence was wearing thin, so that the city's ambitions turned to the protection and prestige of a good League prince.

9   *Autonomy or Security?*

The Urban League and the French Crown

In a letter to his friend Scévole de Sainte-Marthe written shortly before the Edict of Nemours, Étienne Pasquier speculated on the role that the towns might play in the developing conflict between the League and the crown. In his opinion, France's cities would attempt to profit from the situation by obtaining greater military independence for themselves and might therefore allow the princes to dictate terms to the king. The outcome, remarked Pasquier, was uncertain "especially seeing the towns now, by a new police, take things into their own hands, without wanting to accept a garrison from the king or other seigneur."[1] His assessment of urban desires for greater autonomy was echoed a decade later by another convinced royalist, Pierre Victor Palma-Cayet. In explaining the veritable explosion of League support after the assassinations at Blois, Palma-Cayet described many of the towns as acting "under the good hopes that they had imagined to themselves of living in the future in the Swiss manner [i.e. as federated republics] and to be exempt from paying the taille and seigneurial dues. . . ."[2]

The thesis that hopes for greater independence guided urban allegiances is therefore as old as the Catholic League itself. It was even a natural one for men such as Pasquier and Palma-Cayet. The former a committed royalist despite his devout Catholicism and associations with the house of Lorraine and the latter a former Protestant attached to the household of Catherine de Bourbon, neither was disposed to credit the religious concerns or disinterested motivations of adherents of the League. Modern historians, while renouncing the politiques' cynicism concerning adherents' religious beliefs, have generally affirmed their view that desires for greater urban autonomy

[1] Pasquier, *Oeuvres*, 2:288.
[2] Palma-Cayet, *Chronologie novenaire*, 102.

lay at the heart of the League movement. Bernard Chevalier has described the revolt as the parting finale of an older political system in which France's bonnes villes acted as independent agents from the crown, and Denis Richet has identified the League with "a reaction for autonomy" on a provincial level supported by the princes and urban bourgeois.[3] Yves Durand modifies this view by arguing that although the four "urban republics" he analyzes fulfilled their ambitions by achieving a significant measure of independence in joining the Sacred Union, their stopping short of complete sovereignty made them most akin to the imperial cities of the Holy Roman Empire.[4]

The ways in which League cities are said to have distanced themselves from the monarchy depend heavily on historians' estimations of the internal dynamics of the movement. For Drouot, the merchants and lawyers who dominated Dijon's mairie were not seeking independence from the crown but acting on their desire to govern the community without competition from other corporate bodies.[5] For Descimon, similar ambitions led to a more fundamental challenge to the monarchy, as Parisians rejected the political styles of royal officials to revive the more inclusive culture of traditional civic government.[6] Constant, in his synthetic interpretation of the League, places even more emphasis on the relationship between political innovations within the city and radical challenges to the structure of the monarchy. In his estimation, the Seize in Paris envisioned fundamental constitutional changes during the Estates of 1588 that other deputies were less resolute to support. Outside Paris, Constant acknowledges, a city's adhesion to the League could be the product of military force rather than of local enthusiasm, but he also points to the extent to which governing elites seized on their situations to promote their community's independence and even provincial ascendancy over nearby locales.[7] Indeed, where traditional elites retained control during the League era, it has been tempting to interpret their adhesion as a form of self-interest. Thus, Troyes's decision to join arose from a determination of the city's best interests, and even royalist Châlons-sur-Marne acted similarly in taking advantage of the assassinations at Blois to reject its Leaguer governor, allowing it to experience the same kind of increased autonomy thereafter as League cities enjoyed.[8]

Poitiers's experiences during the League period do not support this almost universal consensus that League centers were rejecting the institutions and cultural assumptions of the monarchy or acting on desires for greater autonomy in swearing the Sacred Union.[9] The provincial capital, as we have

[3] Chevalier, *Bonnes villes*, 93–112; Denis Richet, *La France moderne: l'esprit des institutions* (Paris, 1973), 114.

[4] Durand, "Républiques urbaines," 243–44.

[5] Drouot, *Mayenne et la Bourgogne,* 1:154.

[6] See chapter 8 n. 8.

[7] Constant, *Ligue*, 165–74, 186–201, 259–312.

[8] Roberts, *City in Conflict,* 194; Konnert, *Civic Agendas,* 146–9, 166.

[9] For exceptions to this interpretation, see Harding, "Revolution and Reform," 414, 416; Stocker, "Governance of Orléans," 14.

seen, depended heavily on its royal courts and university for its prosperity and consequence and generally sought to preserve and even to increase its advantages through a careful management of its relationship with the crown. Yet Poitiers's example is important not because it provides one exception to a virtually universal rule, but because it reminds us that there is a fundamental difference between goals and outcomes. Cities such as Poitiers declared for the League because they were convinced that a Protestant king would pose the ultimate threat to their salvation, community, and way of life. If their decisions led to fundamental changes in political relationships within the urban sphere and between cities and outside authorities, as they frequently did, this occurrence was an implicit result of their actions rather than the chief motivation for them.[10] Historians, eager to place the League within the narrative of the developing French nation,[11] have mistakenly focused on urban independence as the goal of League leaders rather than seeing it as a consequence of a new political situation. Especially after the death of Henri III, League cities suddenly found themselves on new ground, where they had to handle finances, military initiatives, and political disorder in ways that they had not previously had to face. Not surprisingly, their attempts to survey this unaccustomed terrain usually drew on the political structures and ambitions that had helped to shape their community's identity until that point. This range of possible models in part explains the great variation in responses to the League.

In Poitiers, as elsewhere, the League brought important political changes. New institutions altered the balance of governing bodies, providing opportunities for different groups to claim authority over urban policy. Increased responsibilities for financial and military operations in the region allowed a significantly wider range of political activities that the city could handle without supervision. Many of these changes were very welcome, too, at least for a time. Yet they were not the results of any fundamental innovation in understandings of Poitiers's place within the kingdom. Poitiers's League leaders continued to acknowledge their city's relationship with a central authority, of which Mayenne's leadership and Paris's example constituted the essential elements. Although they firmly refused to recognize Henri IV as king of France, even after his conversion, there is no evidence that they rejected the values of the monarchy or even questioned the importance of the royal administration. In fact, faced with the challenges of the League period, the city came to desire what it had never wanted before: a prince who, as an active governor, would not only fight heresy and enhance the prestige of the

[10] Although the focus of this book prompts analysis of the League as a political phenomenon, this approach is not meant to exclude the crucial religious factors determining general outlook and inciting choices of allegiance. On the subject of religious interpretations of the religious wars, see Mack P. Holt, "Putting Religion Back into the Wars of Religion," *French Historical Studies* 18, no. 2 (1993): 524–51.

[11] See Miriam Yardeni, *La conscience nationale en France pendant les guerres de religion (1559–1598)* (Paris and Louvain, 1971).

city but also inevitably take control of much urban decision making. By 1591, Poitiers's leaders were looking to give up the military command of the province that they had been most eager to claim in 1589. Far from seeking to establish Poitiers as an "urban republic," League leaders looked to the distant and not-so-distant past to formulate their ambitions and envisioned their city as a vital provincial power base with strong emotional ties to a very Christian king.

The Internal Balance of Authority

With the signing of the Oath of Union, Poitiers became an important stronghold of the Catholic League and, for a brief period, actually possessed the military and political importance that its citizens had been ascribing to it since the Hundred Years' War. Poitiers became both a center for the alternative League financial administration and a vantage point from which to launch military campaigns throughout Poitou, with occasional digressions into Angoumois and Brittany. The state of war greatly altered the tenor of life within the city. Captains, soldiers, and their horses filled the streets, and the hotels divided their business between these military men and the captives who overflowed from the prisons as they waited for their ransoms to be paid. As some houses fell into ruin, others became subject to dispute from competing tenants. Provisioning the city required attention but did not turn out to be as difficult as might be expected. For all of the destruction in the countryside, captured goods streamed into Poitiers, merchants obtained passports to transport foodstuffs, and the surrounding parishes were kept in order by the new financial administration. While some institutions, such as the university, all but ceased to function,[12] others, such as the presidial court, remained active. Security within the city was assured by the militia, and the numerous disputes that arose concerning guard duty were generally resolved within this hierarchy.

All of these changes had an impact on the way that Poitiers was governed. Existing institutions by no means fell into abeyance: the hôtel de ville and presidial court continued to meet, to hand down decisions, to enforce orders, and to replenish their personnel. At the same time, Poitiers's greater military and financial role required the development of urban institutions that came to alter the balance of authority within the city. A very short time after it swore the Oath of Union, a Conseil de l'Union (Union Council) was instituted in Poitiers, and the militia took on discrete judicial functions to aid its role of assuring security within the walls. Neither of these institutions was entirely new. Even the Union Council, though inspired by the Parisian orga-

---

[12] The number of students obtaining degrees dropped radically after July 1589 from an average of ninety-seven in 1580–83 to an average of twenty in 1590–93. ACP Casier 78, Reg. 1.

nization, was based on a previously existing council that met in Poitiers's Cordeliers convent. Neither institution, moreover, provided the medium for common inhabitants seriously to challenge the command of elites over the League movement. Although the Union Council in theory represented the three estates of the city, in practice the body was composed so as to limit attendance to notables. This is not to say, however, that League politics in Poitiers followed the status quo. The existence of a variety of institutions with overlapping functions but no predetermined set of privileges or customary relationships encouraged arguments about the nature of political authority. Individuals who had rested their ambitions on obtaining a place in municipal government or other corporate bodies now found that their membership did not necessarily allow them to keep their thumb on the pulse of decision making under the Union. Instead, other groups, such as the clergy and noble captains, now came to enjoy a much greater influence over civic policies than they ever had before. If urban independence is to be gauged by freedom from such influences, then Poitiers became increasingly less independent as the period progressed.

Poitiers's hôtel de ville survived the transition to the League without significant changes to its functions or the character of its membership. It continued to meet as before. Indeed, the numbers of town council meetings were high throughout the League period, and the rates of attendance for both échevins and bourgeois were consistently above average.[13] Retaining its prior functions, the municipal government assured the police of the city, passed ordinances concerning the guard, and maintained institutions subsidiary to it such as the communauté des pauvres. Extending its powers to the new situation, the municipal government helped to determine the city's stance toward exterior authorities, particularly through its correspondence with the League princes and the city of Paris. Because so many of Poitiers's influential League advocates were members of the corps de ville, the municipal government stood a good chance to retain its influence in the urban sphere. This continuity was of course much more easily assured in Poitiers, where municipal offices were held for life, than in other League cities, where new elections could oust previous members, but the city's declaration for the League did require changes in membership nonetheless. At the time that Poitiers officially recognized the Catholic League, thirty-two members of the hôtel de ville had left their municipal functions,[14] and by 1590, nine new échevins and twenty-nine new bourgeois had been elected to fill the vacancies that had accrued.[15] These choices reflected League concerns, especially

[13] Registers survive only for parts of 1589 and 1590, but the council convened eight and sixteen times, respectively, during these two years.

[14] This number included thirteen échevins and nineteen bourgeois. I count as absent those individuals who were not present at the mayoral election of 1589, did not swear the Oath of Union on 18 August, and were not listed as members of the municipality in 1590.

[15] The elections were conducted sometime between September 1589 and July 1590, but the

for the city's security, but did not significantly alter the composition of the body. Of the échevins, three at least were officers in the militia, and one had been attempting to gain access to the council for several years. Their professions reflected a range typical for members of the council, and their previous length of service as bourgeois was variable (indicating that they did not owe their original offices to the League). Of the bourgeois, eight had the same last name as current members of the Cent, and three others were from families traditionally supplying members to the municipality. Four, at least, were officers in the militia, and only two were listed without the title of maître. Granted, the overall social makeup of this group of new bourgeois was slightly below recent practice; interspersed with the lawyers and financial officers were notaries, hotel owners and receveurs. Still, the comment made by a resentful royal commissioner in 1601 that there was a "great number of people of low condition who made their way [into municipal government] during the troubles" was far from accurate.[16]

The expanded pressures of League government nevertheless required the newly replenished corps de ville to acknowledge new decision-making bodies, whose actions belied municipal pretensions to determine civic policy. The Union Council, loosely modeled on the equivalent body in Paris and considered the administrative arm of the League in Poitiers, was the most important,[17] and, thanks to the unusual survival of one of its registers of decisions, we can assess its functions in detail.[18] In theory, at least, it received directives from the duc de Mayenne and claimed jurisdiction over Poitou and parts of surrounding regions. Through its *conseil des finances* (financial council), it rivaled the royal fiscal system and collected the necessary funds to continue the war effort. As a council of war, it was responsible for determining military strategy, for extending or maintaining League control wherever possible, and for assuring the safety of Poitiers. Catholic nobles now arrived in great numbers in the provincial capital, ready to lead forces against the Protestant and politique forces of Henri de Navarre. Some, such as the

---

disappearance of most of the town council register for the 1589 municipal year makes it impossible to determine exactly when.

[16] BNF MS Fr 15899, 869r.

[17] The Union Council of Paris was officially constituted on 17 February 1589. See *Registres des délibérations du bureau de la ville de Paris*, 9:295–96. Henri Drouot was the first to call attention to the importance of these provincial League councils and to provide an overview of their functions in "Les conseils provinciaux de la Sainte-Union (1589–1595): notes et questions," *Annales du Midi* 65 (July 1953): 415–33. Jean-Pierre Andrault examines the actions of the Union Council of Poitiers, with particular attention to its military functions, in "Une capitale de province sous les armes au temps de la Ligue: la guerre de course menée par Poitiers entre 1589 et 1593," in *Les malheurs de la guerre*, vol. 1, *De la guerre à l'ancienne à la guerre réglée*, ed. André Corvisier and Jean Jacquart (Paris, 1996), 39–63.

[18] The register of the decisions of the Union Council from 16 July 1591–4 November 1592 is included among the registers of deliberations of the hôtel de ville as ACP Reg. 52. Drouot signaled the rarity of the survival of these deliberations and found only a portion of one other register from Le Mans. Drouot, "Conseils provinciaux," 418 n. 4.

young gentilhomme Pierre Yongue, sieur de la Brossardière, even died there of wounds they had suffered in the service of the Holy League.[19] The Union Council coordinated the Catholic forces' activities and determined which châteaux or houses in the region should be defended or captured. As a corollary to planning military exploits, the council also arranged for limited observances of peace, as in the case of an accord between Boisseguin, the vicomte de la Guierche, and the sieur de Verac dictating the terms for a cession of hostilities in the bourg of Couhé.[20]

The Union Council also ruled on the taking of prisoners and set ransoms for their release, according to criteria agreed on by Henri de Navarre and the duc de Mayenne.[21] Every military captain or soldier who had captured either persons or goods in Poitou was required to report his activity to the Union Council, to receive judgment on whether his booty was of fair or unfair capture (*bonne prise* or *mauvaise prise*). If the Union Council decided that a prisoner had been fairly taken, it then set the ransom and declared the terms of imprisonment. This aspect of the council's responsibilities imposed on it a high volume of business and sometimes involved it in lengthy adjudications. At virtually every meeting it had to rule on a capture, and all complaints from prisoners desiring their freedom, from soldiers impatient for their ransom money, or from hotel owners seeking payment for the prisoners' board were directed to it.

Such a broad range of competencies made the Union Council a powerful institution and encouraged the inhabitants and corporations of Poitiers to resort to its authority for favorable rulings on special requests. When the chapter of Ste. Radegonde found that Henri de Navarre had seized its seigneury of Vouillé and awarded it to a royalist supporter, it complained of the loss in the Union Council and received satisfaction.[22] Anne Denis also approached the council on 15 May 1592 to request that a Captain Curzay depart from a house she owned. Curzay was ordered to leave the dwelling and, one month later, was himself asking that the council take his services to the League into consideration when it set his uncle's ransom.[23]

This introduction into Poitiers of a powerful new institution created tensions with existing bodies. While the hôtel de ville relied on the authority of

[19] ADV 1H¹⁸49 (Cordeliers): testament of Pierre Yongue, dated 24 Apr. 1590. "Item Je veux Quil Soict faict vng Tableau honorable Auquel sera descripte La Cause pour Laquelle Je seray decedde Qui est pour Le Service de la Saincte Union." Another copy of the testament can be found in ADV 1H¹⁸76, chap. 1, art. XV (Jacobins).
[20] MMP Dom Fonteneau, 16:371–72.
[21] Exactly when these articles were passed is unclear, but they were mentioned in the Union Council on 22 July 1591. ACP Reg. 52, 7–10. On 16 December 1589, Charles X (Charles de Bourbon) had issued letters patent defining when royalist property was subject to seizure, and they were published in the presidial court of Poitiers on 6 February 1590. See *Declaration du roy tres-chrestien Charles X. de ce nom, pour la conseruation des maisons appartenans aux Gentilz-hommes & autres Catholicques qui assistent le Roy de Nauarre* ... (Poitiers, 1590).
[22] ADV G1596, 38v–39r; ACP Reg. 52, 246–47 (21 July 1592).
[23] ACP Reg. 52, 199–200 (15 May 1592); 222–25 (25 June 1592).

the Union Council to handle affairs with expedition and especially made use of its superior monetary resources, it also resented the inevitable diminishment in its own authority. In addition to adjudicating a wide range of issues and requests, the Union Council also trespassed on areas within the municipality's traditional purview, such as the fortifications and matters of police.[24] Members of the corps de ville therefore attempted to limit their loss of authority, either by gaining access to the Union Council itself or by regulating the relationship between the two bodies. In October 1590, in response to the complaints of several échevins that the Union Council was refusing to admit them, the Monday council decided to discuss the matter with the governor, "in order to preserve and maintain the authority of the échevins of this body, since they hold this city and its guard by oath."[25] (They seem not to have reflected that their oath was to the king.) Two days later, they were still complaining that the Union Council had been overturning municipal decisions, "which should not be suffered to occur."[26] It was perhaps in an attempt to monitor the League council more closely that the municipality requested its secretary to submit lists of prisoners currently being held in town.[27] Members of the city government thus approached the Union Council with a mixture of approval and frustration: the former for its active pursuit of the League's military goals, the latter for the inevitable alterations in the balance of authority that such wide-ranging functions produced.

Jealousies and competition among councils with overlapping functions were so common to the political culture of French cities that it would be surprising to find the Leaguers of the hôtel de ville and Union Council in perfect agreement over their mutual rights and roles in city government. But the Union Council was not like other urban institutions: it was not a corporate entity with specific privileges, but an elective body that combined its unprecedented jurisdiction over war and finances with its claim to represent the three estates of the city through its membership. Here, in the redefinition of the sources of political authority and the willingness to craft new institutions to meet the necessities of the occasion, some would argue, lay the essence of the radical political tendencies of the League. But how innovative were these impulses? In cities such as Toulouse and Orléans the League councils reproduced traditional practices in their composition and patterns of consultation. In Toulouse, the *bureau d'estat* took exactly the same form as the council of eighteen that usually advised the capitouls on important issues.[28] In Poitiers, both Henri Drouot and Robert Harding have speculated, the Union Council grew out of a preexisting governor's council, of the kind that became common in the last three decades of the sixteenth century.[29] A close look at

---

[24] For examples, see ACP Reg. 52, 4–5 (20 July 1591); 32–33 (1 Oct. 1591).
[25] ACP Reg. 50, 50–52; quotation, 52.
[26] ACP Reg. 53, 5–10 (20 July 1592); quotation, 7.
[27] ACP Reg. 53, 16 (5 Aug. 1592).
[28] Greengrass, "Sainte Union," 481; Stocker, "Orléans and the Catholic League," 16–17.
[29] Drouot, "Conseils provinciaux," 425; Harding, *Anatomy of a Power Elite*, 89, 92.

these councils confirms this hypothesis of filiation and shows that although League assumptions concerning political participation had changed, they were nevertheless a result of a long process of evolution. There were also wide divergences between theory and practice. Despite ideas that the Union Council should represent the three estates of the city, if anything, it afforded less opportunity for popular input than the exclusive corps de ville.

In times of war, Poitiers's municipal government had consistently enhanced its deliberative opportunities by meeting in special, extraordinary sessions outside the hôtel de ville. Until the fifth religious war (1574–76), these assemblies met most frequently in the judicial palais, where the mayor, échevins, and a few bourgeois generally still predominated among the assembled company. When Poitiers gained a city governor in the person of Jean Jay, sieur de Boisseguin, he shared the council's leadership with the mayor. In 1574, the council began to meet regularly in the Cordeliers convent, whence it made important decisions concerning the police and security of the town. To identify this assembly as a governor's *conseil de guerre,* however, would be misleading: the deliberations were recorded integrally in the town council register; the mayor still held responsibility as the captain of the city; and although a cleric or militia captain appeared from time to time, these meetings almost exclusively involved the same members of the municipal government who met in the hôtel de ville.[30] In fact, these councils of war may have met in the Cordeliers convent to avoid having the city's noble governor appear too often in the hôtel de ville itself. This essentially municipal council, however, had undergone a change by 1586. Still a council of war under the purview of the governor and the mayor, it now regularly included a good number of the city's eighteen militia officers (six captains, lieutenants, and ensigns, respectively). Yet since several of the captains were échevins and the militia existed under the ultimate authority of the mayor, the Cordeliers council had not yet departed from the model of municipal authority.

The oppositions associated with the League movement in Poitiers changed the character of the Cordeliers council. Because perceptions of military threat now depended on opinions concerning the succession of Henri de Navarre and attitudes toward the Catholic princes and their Holy Union, this extraordinary council became the prime political forum in which many crucial decisions were made. A League pamphlet accuses the politiques of turning out in force at the Cordeliers council each morning, in order to threaten the good Catholics and to chase them away from the meeting.[31] After the League faction had succeeded in barring Henri III access to the city, opinion in Poitiers was divided concerning whether the Cordeliers council was a council of war or a secret council—meaning an organ of the League.[32]

---

[30] An exception occurred in July–September 1576, when Boisseguin was absent and Joseph Doyneau, sieur de Sainte-Soline, presided over the council. At this time, the attendance of clerics and militia captains was much higher and more frequent.

[31] *Response d'vn catholique,* 5–6.

[32] Hillerin, *Chariot chrestien,* 41.

It is evident that by 1588, individuals attended council sessions in large numbers. High rates of attendance made control of the forum extremely difficult, and desires to assure mastery therefore led to attempts to limit the group. During the first incidence of regulation, the Cordeliers council was still conceived as a municipal body. On 15 December 1588, the Mois limited it to the mayor, four échevins, four bourgeois, the six militia captains, and Boisseguin, governor of Poitiers.[33] By 29 December, however, attendance had expanded to include numerous seigneurs and notables, and there were complaints of "disorders" occurring in the council. The company itself therefore limited the group to meet in the future, including Leaguers and royalists, and composed of the governor, mayor, chief judicial officials, a trésorier, an échevin, and the militia captains.[34] These attempts at regulation were clearly ineffective, since by 10 March 1589, the Mois was again complaining of "the confusion of people who overrun the council that is ordinarily held at the Cordeliers convent."[35] A new reorganization after the events of May 1589 therefore sought to provide for greater input in its deliberations. Recognizing that the inhabitants desired some form of access to this influential political body, the council decreed that each militia company could depute one individual to represent the interests of his fellows at its meetings.[36] From this time, as well, representatives of the clergy became regular members.

Despite being an outgrowth of the municipal governing process, the Cordeliers council gradually abrogated to itself some of the authority and a good part of the attention previously wielded by and bestowed on the hôtel de ville. It had become the critical forum where the city's political loyalties were established and thus drew large numbers of people, eager to witness the confrontations that would determine their future. Although members of the municipality made up a sizable proportion of its personnel, some of their colleagues were barred from attendance. Instead, by the summer of 1589, the Cordeliers council had come to include individuals from all sectors of the urban community. The inclusion of deputies from the militia companies and clergy indicates that understandings of proper political inclusion were changing; to be legitimate, governing bodies should incorporate all components of the community of the faithful.[37] Yet the novelty of this composition should not be overemphasized. Deputies from the clergy had been invited, after all, to attend deliberative assemblies on many occasions. Clerics also belonged

[33] ACP Reg. 48, 195–203.
[34] ACP Reg. 48, 215–20.
[35] ACP Reg. 48, 341–47; quotation, 344.
[36] ACP Reg. 48, 436–37 (2 June 1589).
[37] Drouot originally posed the question of whether League councils were simply extensions of governor's councils or something qualitatively different because of their ideas of representation. Poitiers's example indicates that they could in fact be both. See Drouot, "Conseils provinciaux," 426–28.

to the dominicale and bureau, supplementary councils that the hôtel de ville had created to handle poor relief and the plague epidemic of 1586, respectively. With the only popular interventions taking place within the hierarchical cadre of the militia, moreover, inhabitants' opportunities for expressing a unique point of view were minimal. With their captains and lieutenants present at the Cordeliers, what complaints could the companies expect to lodge and what influence could they really wield? It was not that models for popular political involvement in important issues affecting the city were entirely lacking. Average parishioners, as we have seen, gathered after Mass to elect tax deputies and took turns fulfilling the duties of poor relief. Yet the League in Poitiers did not draw on parochial institutions, and the impact of common people on urban policies remained small.

What was true for the Cordeliers council remained true for the Union Council, which ultimately replaced it.[38] Much of the Union Council's activity and membership must remain uncertain before 1591, but the register that begins with the council's "reformation" in July 1591 makes its deliberations and composition clear for the next year and a half. Although its membership was supposed to be elective and to include members of the three estates, the Union Council did not in fact depart from the kind of corporate representation that had made up supplementary deliberative bodies in the past. Its twenty-five members were to be drawn from the four leaders of the League (two governors, the mayor, and the bishop), along with representatives of the clergy, judicial officials, third estate, nobility, financial officers, and militia captains. Yet although the clergy and nobility did gain representation on the council, each of the members of the "third estate" also belonged to the corps de ville.[39] By 1592, the idea of including any members of the third estate as such had been dropped, and elections proceeded among the clergy, nobility, judicial officials, and municipal government, with each body selecting its own deputies.[40] In fact, compared with the assemblies that the hôtel de ville had called together to treat urgent matters in the past, League government limited the possibilities for notables without corporate memberships to participate. In the assembly called to discuss the threat of the gabelle uprising in 1548, for example, several notable merchants had been able to express their opinions. The Union Council afforded their descendants no similar opportunity.

Despite continuities of elite membership, the League did alter the control that traditional civic notables could exercise over the city. Continual warfare, in which Poitiers played not only a defensive but also an offensive role,

[38] On 28 August 1589, the Monday council asked Boisseguin, one of the leaders of the Cordeliers council, to consult with the Union Council concerning the "confusion" at the Cordeliers. Since no more is heard of the Cordeliers council thereafter, the Union Council must have concluded that it be discontinued. See ACP Reg. 49, 22.

[39] ACP Reg. 52, 1–3.

[40] ACP Reg. 52, 155–57 (19 Feb. 1592); Reg. 51, 174–75 (4 May 1592).

increased the importance of military experience and leadership. Although Poitiers had asked the advice of the local nobility in the past to help assure its defense, the influence of nobles in governing the city increased immeasurably under the League. The change did not so much rest in the fact that Boisseguin and the vicomte de la Guierche, governors for the League in Poitiers, presided on the Union Council, since the mayor also constituted one of its leaders and co-signed all of its ordinances until 1592.[41] Rather, the second estate now constituted one of the groups with a right to representation in the deliberative body. The complement of nobles had been officially fixed at four members, two of whom were members of the corps de ville, but in practice a significant number of noble captains attended meetings whenever they were in town. From February to June 1592, there were consistently more nobles from the surrounding region than members of the municipal government attending the meetings of the Union Council, and from December 1591 to September 1592 nobles outnumbered municipal officials on average (see table 9.1). Such a presence of noble captains within the city would of course have been viewed with great suspicion at any other time. Yet the military situation partially suspended civic privileges and united the efforts of the urban and noble Leagues.

The Catholic League, then, brought numerous changes to relationships within Poitiers. The creation of new councils and the exigencies of the war effort altered the institutional balance of government and created new settings for judicial decisions. As these deliberative bodies established their competing claims to authority over the city, so too did individuals seek to assure their influence through overlapping memberships. The League opened channels for some to play a much larger role in urban government than they ever had. Clerics, as officers of the militia and members of the Union Council, found their role much enhanced from occasional advisors to regular participants in formulating civic policy. Noble captains, too, parlayed their practical knowledge of military tactics into a definite voice in the Union Council's rulings. It is tempting to see these changes as arising from a new definition of political authority founded in the three estates. Yet the more amorphous third estate continued to be defined, and its political activities delineated, by the corporate groups that traditionally maintained privileged positions within the urban sphere. Poitiers's general position within the Catholic League reflected the same interplay between innovation and conservatism. In adhering to it, Poitiers's leaders implicitly questioned some of

[41] The mayor enjoyed a seat of precedence within the council, since his name almost always heads the second column of participants of the sessions recorded in Reg. 52. Co-signature of ordinances: a notary contract dated 21 April 1590 mentions an ordinance dating from 27 November 1589 signed by the governor, the mayor, and the secretary. In October 1592 the current mayor complained that former holders of that office were improperly continuing to sign the Union Council's orders. See ADV E⁴24.20, contract between Guillaume Pain and Richard Rougier; ACP Reg. 53, 36 (22 Oct. 1592).

Table 9.1.
Attendance of the Union Council, July 1591–November 1592

Month	Number of meetings	Average total attendance	Corps de ville	Nobles	Clergy
July 1591	10	13.0	7.6	2.5	2.9
Aug. 1591	20	14.8	8.1	3.9	2.8
Sept. 1591	15	18.7	7.2	4.6	6.9
Oct. 1591	16	12.6	6.6	3.5	2.6
Nov. 1591	11	13.6	6.5	4.6	2.5
Dec. 1591	15	12.7	5.5	5.9	1.3
Jan. 1592	17	12.1	4.7	5.2	2.2
Feb. 1592	9	10.7	3.8	4.4	2.4
Mar. 1592	9	11.8	4.9	5.2	1.7
Apr. 1592	11	10.6	3.3	5.4	1.9
May 1592	15	13.2	4.6	6.5	2.1
June 1592	11	13.8	3.7	6.9	3.2
July 1592	21	13.3	4.3	5.7	3.3
Aug. 1592	19	11.0	4.2	4.4	2.4
Sept. 1592	12	11.3	4.1	4.3	2.9
Oct. 1592	8	7.0	3.0	2.5	1.5
Nov. 1592	1	7.0	3.0	2.0	2.0

Source: ACP Register 52.
Note: Attendance of the Union Council is divided into three categories: members of the municipality (corps de ville), nobles, and clergy. Each individual has been assigned to only one category, with membership in the hôtel de ville taking precedence. Therefore, even a noble échevin is placed in the municipal category. Nobles include not only the noble captains but also Poitiers's governors. All clerics have been placed in the category of clergy, including those who attended the council as captains of the urban militia. The sum of these three categories of attendance does not always equal Average total attendance because of rounding.

the attributes of royal sovereignty, but they persisted in seeing the Sacred Union as a representative of a central authority that continued to integrate France's towns and seigneurs into a political whole.

Greater Urban Autonomy?

For Poitiers, swearing the Oath of Union involved an increase in the powers of local administration. In the state of civil war, simply maintaining the city's safety and supply would have required greater military efforts and attention to police. But in the first years of adherence to the League, Poitiers's inhabitants envisioned much more than a position of defense; they sought to spread the League's influence over the entire region. Ideally, Poitiers was to be instrumental in leading nearby localities to take up the cause of religious fervor. Practically, the city sought to reinforce and to extend its control over the region through military domination and administrative force. As a provincial capital, Poitiers had long been the center of judicial and financial authority in the region. Yet now, with assertions of political authority contested and both the king and the League princes occupied elsewhere, the city's League leaders enjoyed a level of independence in making and implementing policies impossible under royal supervision.

Almost immediately after Poitiers adhered to the Sacred Union, the religious zeal of its inhabitants and leaders generated plans for the victory of a truly militant Catholicism. On 29 August 1589, the Mois, citing the attacks of enemy forces and the desire to uphold the privileges of the mayor and échevins, took the unprecedented step of forming a light horse company under the mayor's authority.[42] No longer would Poitevins sit idly by while their property was attacked, nor would they have to enroll haphazardly in companies under the command of the local nobility. Instead, they could realize their ardor for the Catholic cause in a structure officially condoned and administered by the hôtel de ville. According to Hillerin, spending his last days in Poitiers before fleeing to his father's estate, expectations of military glory in the service of the Holy Union ran high in Poitiers in the autumn of 1589. "The talk here now is of nothing but soldiers and outfittings," he wrote,

> which will be carried out with such order and justice that honorable people, found to be good Catholics, will be conserved, and the evil, Béarnois and Calvinists, will be punished. Such laws will be established as well that our predecessors will be made to see that they did not understand anything, nor wished to understand, of the military art, which maintains justice without doing damage to anyone, of which one could validly complain.

Soldiers were being equipped with such expedition, continued Hillerin, that it was expected that they would be able to secure all of the surrounding towns for the League before the enemy was even aware of their activity. Already, several towns had sent their keys to Poitiers to avoid attack.[43]

The League, then, created expectations for a military dominance that would simultaneously assure punishment to enemies and spread justice and security to good Catholics. The realities of civil war were quite different, however, as early League victories in Poitou gave way to retrenchment by the summer of 1591. Throughout, the authority of the Union Council and its subsidiary council of finances allowed for a much more localized formulation of military objectives and a more independent use of funds. Only the Union Council's validation could convert captured men and goods into military prisoners and booty, and the taxes previously collected by royal officials were now funneled to support Poitiers's war effort, civic expenses, and charities.[44] That receipts from the taille and *taillon* of Poitou were still not

---

[42] ACP Reg. 49, 23–25.

[43] Hillerin, *Chariot chrestien,* 48.

[44] ACP Reg. 52, 41–42 (13 Feb. 1591); Casier 53, 1591–95, deliberations of 5 May and 28 July 1591; Reg. 50, 22–24 (13 Aug. 1590).

adequate to meet expenses is implied by the Union Council's decision to extend its collections into the *généralités* of Tours, Limoges, and Moulins.[45]

Increased responsibilities for military and financial affairs fell mostly to Poitiers's Union Council, but the presidial court also found its privileges materially enhanced during the League period. On 22 December 1589, the Parlement of Paris, citing the difficulties of travel, authorized Poitiers's presidial court to judge in first instance and by appeal all civil cases arising in the courts of its jurisdiction and to judge criminal cases in last resort. The *arrêt* was duly registered in Poitiers on 6 February 1590 at the same time as—and perhaps in compensation for—several other important League decisions, including recognition of Charles de Bourbon as king of France.[46] The decision was of course designed to reinforce the authority of the presidial court in the face of its royal transfer to Niort and the Parlement of Tours's inhibitions against it.[47] But it may also have allowed the court in general and François de Brilhac, lieutenant criminel, in particular to maintain their judicial rights against the variety of adjudicating bodies created in Poitiers under the Union.

Despite these changes in the important areas of defense, finance, and justice, Poitiers continued to recognize the institutional ties of the French monarchy. Although maintaining a special relationship of loyalty to the crown was no longer possible, provincial League leaders continued to look to the "center" for administrative authority and guidance. Months before Poitiers had joined the Catholic Union, a Union Council had been formed in Paris and had named Charles de Lorraine, duc de Mayenne, *lieutenant général de l'État et Couronne de France*. Throughout the League period, Poitiers accepted this model for the transfer and custody of central authority and routinely referred to Mayenne and the Union Council of Paris as the ultimate arbiters of government. Yet complications arose in this stewardship of the French monarchy. Dual ties to the Parisian Union Council and to Mayenne allowed for considerable ambiguity in Poitiers's sympathies and definition of authority within the League. Although leaders continued to refer to the Parisian Union Council throughout the period of their adhesion to the Union, Mayenne had in fact disbanded it in its original form after Charles de Bourbon was named king, despite the protests of the more radical Seize.[48]

---

[45] ACP Reg. 52, 115–18 (9 Dec. 1591).

[46] *Arrest de la cour de Parlement de Paris, pour l'ampliation du pouuoir & iurisdiction des iuges presidiaux de Poictiers* (Poitiers, 1590). For concurrent registrations, see *Arrest de la cour de Parlement, de recognoistre pour roy Charles diziesme de ce nom* (Poitiers, 1590); *Arrest de la cour de Parlement, povr la conuocation & assemblée des trois Estatz de ce Royaume, assignés en la Ville de Melun, au vingtiesme de Mars prochain* (Poitiers, 1590); *Declaration du roy treschrestien Charles X*; and *Lettres patentes addroissantes av seneschal de Poictou, ou son Lieutenant, pour la conuocation & assemblée du Ban & Arrieban* . . . (Poitiers, 1590).

[47] The inhibitions of the royalist parlement are mentioned in the *Arrest* dated 22 December. The presidial court of Poitiers had earlier been obliged to forbid anyone in its jurisdiction from taking cases elsewhere to be heard. See *Ivgement donne en la covr presidiale de Poictiers, pour la conseruation de la Iustice en Poictou* (Poitiers, 1589).

[48] *Registres des délibérations du bureau de la ville de Paris*, 9:556 n. 2. The Seize petitioned

In acknowledging two sources of authority at the heart of the Holy Union, the provincial capital may have been trying to maintain unity among its own factions competing to define and to control the movement.

Whatever decisions were actually made in Poitiers, local governing institutions, from the hôtel de ville and presidial court to the Union Council and financial council, all made reference to a superior authority to justify their actions. The Catholic League claimed to hold the French monarchy in custody until a new king could be freed or elected, and Poitiers's political bodies continued to operate in preexisting administrative channels that no longer emanated from the king but still issued from the guardians of the crown. Although many in the Holy Union considered Charles de Bourbon king of France until his death in May 1590, Poitiers's League leaders displayed little enthusiasm for the cause of Charles X, imprisoned at nearby Fontaine-le-Comte. The presidial court did not register the Parlement of Paris's official recognition of him as sovereign until February 1590, and René de Brilhac, a League supporter, identified him only as the cardinal de Bourbon in recording his death.[49]

Instead, Poitiers's administrative decisions abounded in references to the governing powers of Mayenne and the Union Council of Paris. Mayenne was seen to exercise all powers of appointment to offices that were still perceived as royal. When the Union Council elected a new master of the mint in 1591, it sent to Mayenne for confirmation.[50] In the financial realm, the endorsements of the League prince and the Union Council of Paris were equally sought for the appointment of a new receveur of the financial council, and when Jean Palustre wished to pass his office of trésorier général on to his son-in-law François Fumé, he resigned it into the hands of Mayenne and the chancellor.[51] In the judicial sphere, Mayenne was recognized to possess powers of appointment over offices that ranged in importance from royal sergeant to lieutenant général of the sénéchaussée.[52] Mayenne also named Pierre de la Chappellerie, sieur de Rouilly, and his son to the important posts of sénéchal of Poitou and *maître des eaux et forêts* for their past and future services to the League.[53] Executive authority, too, was seen to emanate from Mayenne and the Union Council of Paris as it previously had from the king and his council. In order to begin collection of the taille in 1591, for example, the Union Council of Poitiers applied to both Mayenne and the Paris

Mayenne to reconstitute the council in February and April 1591. Baumgartner, *Radical Reactionaries*, 174–75.

[49] Brilhac, 22. Baumgartner points out that most of the Leaguer parlements did not officially recognize Charles X until December–January 1590 (*Radical Reactionaries*, 162).

[50] ACP Reg. 51, 50–54 (6 Sept.).

[51] ACP Reg. 52, 114–15 (7 Dec. 1591); ADV E⁴27.27, procuration of Jean Palustre, 3 Sept. 1593.

[52] ACP Reg. 52, 143–44 (15 Jan. 1592). Mayenne appointed Louis de Sainte-Marthe lieutenant général on 26 February 1593, and he was officially sworn in on 12 October. Brilhac, 25.

[53] BNF MS Fr 15643, 17r.

council for a commission.[54] Finally, Poitiers turned to League commanders in matters of military authority. When the Mois created its light horse company in 1589, for example, it did so subject to the approval of Mayenne, the Union Council of Paris, Boisseguin, and the Union Council of Poitiers.[55] Mayenne, moreover, maintained the right to name the governors of Poitiers and Poitou. To the duc de Mercoeur's offer to provide a governor for the province of Poitou, the hôtel de ville responded—evasively—that it could not accept a candidate without the approval of Mayenne and the Union Council of Paris. Similarly, after the death of Boisseguin in 1592, the municipality decided to request of Mayenne that no new governor be named.[56]

In spite of such recognition of a higher authority, the League's command of the monarchical system was predictably weaker than had been Henri III's. Although the leaders of the Holy Union in Poitiers retained the traditional model of interactions with the crown, they did not adhere to it as strictly as before. In creating its light horse company in 1589 the Mois subjected its decision to every authority under the League, but this proviso could not obscure the fact that its act was unprecedented. When the Union Council sought to begin tax collections in 1591, moreover, it duly applied to Mayenne and to the Union Council of Paris for a commission. Yet when the council realized that the royalists had already begun their collections in the area and the requisite permission to do likewise was not forthcoming, it decided to begin the process on its own. This decision is revealing: collecting the taille without a specific commission when a Valois sat on the throne would have been unthinkable. Some people also experienced confusion over proper jurisdiction. Although Jean Palustre made clear provisions to resign his office, Pierre Liege seems to have been less sure of how to dispose of his post as assessor of the value of movable goods. He therefore passed a power of attorney providing that it could be resigned in the hands of the council of state, the Union Council of Paris, the Union Council of Poitiers, the sénéchal of Poitou or his lieutenant général, the mayor and échevins of Poitiers, "or of anyone else as necessary."[57] Elie Barnavi has argued that Paris tended to adopt a model of "federalism" as opposed to "centralism" in its relations with other cities adhering to the League.[58] From the provincial perspective, this approach accords well with the expanded responsibilities of the Union Council and the increased authority of the presidial court. It accounts poorly, though, for the city's expectations about the nature of authority emanating from a center that Poitevins still recognized, even if the trials of religious war often confused or diminished the effectiveness of the tie.

[54] ACP Reg. 52, 115–18 (9 Dec. 1591).
[55] ACP Reg. 49, 23–25.
[56] ACP Reg. 51, 154–55 (14 Mar. 1592); Reg. 53, 31–34, 41–42 (8 Oct. and 9 Nov. 1592).
[57] ADV E⁴26.16, procuration of Pierre Liege, 29 Sept. 1591.
[58] Elie Barnavi, "Centralisme ou fédéralisme? Les relations entre Paris et les villes à l'époque de la Ligue (1585–1594)," *Revue historique* 526 (1978): 335–44.

The Radical League and the Crown

Poitiers's League leaders could preserve many of their habits of deference to a central authority without contradiction, because although some insisted that Henri III had forfeited his right to rule and all vociferously opposed Henri IV's claim to the throne, none went on record to reject the structures and underlying assumptions of the French monarchy. This state of affairs may seem surprising, given the emphasis on the radical political theories of the urban League and the undeniable presence of a radical wing in Poitiers itself. In Paris, League tracts justified the assassination of the "tyrant" Henri de Valois by arguing that he had violated the contract that bound him to the French people by infringing their fundamental right to property and ruling against the laws of the republic. Radical preachers such as Jean Boucher upheld the Estates as a political authority predating the monarchy and responsible to God for the actions of the king.[59] Parisian proposals to the Estates of 1588 and of 1591 (called but not held) reflected radical Leaguers' attempts to redefine the monarchy by subjecting the king to the supervision of the wider political community in the form of regular meetings of the Estates and appointment of royal counselors.[60] The Seize valued Catholic orthodoxy and unity so highly that they willingly encouraged Spanish backing for their enterprise and even countenanced the election of a Spanish ruler to the French throne.[61] In Poitiers, as well, the League gave rise to political assertions that any French king would have considered treasonous. Pierre Humeau, in his address to the presidial court recommending the swearing of the Oath of Union, insisted that one's duties to God must precede obedience to kings and magistrates, and he wrapped in the authority of a Ciceronian tag the idea that kings are elected by the people for their virtues.[62] Jean Porthaise, the radical League preacher frequently compared to Jean Boucher, exerted an important influence in Poitiers both through frequent attendance at the Union Council meetings and his delivery and publication of strong League sermons.[63] From Porthaise, Poitiers's inhabitants could learn that monarchy was the best form of government only if kings adhered to certain laws and conditions;[64] that princes were subject to the law and responsible

---

[59] Baumgartner, *Radical Reactionaries*, 153–54, 204–5.

[60] Constant, *Ligue*, 165–74; Baumgartner, *Radical Reactionaries*, 179–82.

[61] Baumgartner, *Radical Reactionaries*, 175–76. On the competing interests of the "French" and "Spanish" Leagues, see De Lamar Jensen, *Diplomacy and Dogmatism: Bernardo de Mendoza and the French Catholic League* (Cambridge, Mass., 1964); Yardeni, *Conscience nationale*; René de Bouillé, *Histoire des ducs de Guise*, 4 vols. (Paris, 1850).

[62] Humeau, *Devx harangves*, 43–62, 69.

[63] Labitte was the first to draw attention to Porthaise's League sermons in his *La démocratie*, 279–87. Ouvré also discusses his contribution to the League in Poitiers, "Essai sur l'histoire de la Ligue," 218–24.

[64] Jean Porthaise, *Defence a la responce, faicte aux intenditz de B. De-par-Dieu, par les ministres de l'eglise pretenduë reformée* (Poitiers, 1580), a3r–v.

to their subjects;[65] that kings were not constituted through succession only, but through a combination of succession, election, anointment, and coronation;[66] and that in 1593 it fell to the Estates and the Pope to elect a new king.[67] Further, Poitiers's League adherents showed similar impulses to those of the Seize to place Catholic unity above Gallican freedoms and Mayenne's leadership through their independent correspondence with the Spanish ambassador and willingness to allow a garrison of Spanish troops within the city.[68]

In spite of the radical implications of these actions and tracts produced by the Catholic League in Poitiers, the city's most enduring expressions of League ideas did not emphasize reinventing the terms of the relationship between the monarchy and the people. Pierre Humeau may have placed secular obedience distinctly below sacred duties, but he retained a highly traditional vision of kingship, informing his audience that "justice is the end of the law, the law the work of the prince, and the prince the image of God, who rules all and governs forming himself from the mold and guidance of God through the means of virtue."[69] In insisting so firmly on the necessity for obedience to kings, governors, and magistrates, he sought to maintain existing hierarchies and refused any idea that political authority should originate in the people. Indeed, for Humeau, the exercise of virtue that guaranteed authority and majesty was not to be located in the people meeting in the Estates, but in the Parlement of Paris established by the kings of France:

> And with this beautiful virtue and constancy has always reflected and shined the authority and majesty of the sovereign Parlement of our France, established, ordered and situated by our ancient, valorous, and magnanimous kings in their principal city of Paris, as the true, unique, and supreme asylum and sacred place of the oracles of piety, justice, and all other virtues above all peoples and nations of the world.[70]

As if to confirm his reverence for royal justice, the avocat dedicated the text of his speeches to Barnabé Brisson, president of the Parlement of Paris.[71] It

---

[65] First sermon in Jean Porthaise, *Six sermons faictz en l'eglise cathedralle de S. Pierre de Poictiers, aux processions generalles contre la peste. 1584* (Poitiers, 1584), A8r–v.

[66] "Sermon svr l'arrest donné a Tovrs le 5. Aoust 1591" in *Cinq sermons dv R. P. F. I. Porthaise de l'ordre S. François, theologal de l'Eglise de Poictiers, par luy prononcez en icelle. Esquels est traicté tant de la simulée conuersion du Roy de Nauarre, que du droict de l'absolution Ecclesiastique* . . . (Paris, 1594), 83–84.

[67] "Sermon de la conversion, et absolvtion, diuulgee, Ad cautelam, Le 25. de Iulliet 1593. à Sainct Denys en France," in *Cinq sermons*, 24–25.

[68] The hôtel de ville wrote and received eight letters to and from the Spanish ambassador from 9 September 1591 to 2 March 1592. See ACP Reg. 51, 54–57, 69–71, 96–97, 137–42, 146–49. For Spanish troops, see Reg. 52, 131–32 (26 Dec. 1591); Reg. 51, 171–72 (20 Apr. 1592).

[69] Humeau, *Devx harangves*, [20].

[70] Humeau, *Devx harangves*, 69.

[71] Humeau, *Devx harangves*, Aiir–Aiiiv.

is true, of course, that the magistrates of the Parlement of Paris had declared their adherence to the League by refusing to leave when Henri III transferred their body to Tours, but it is significant that of all places to situate the practice of virtue that assured political authority, Humeau chose the same royal institution that Étienne Pasquier would champion in his *Recherches de la France*.[72]

Humeau's reluctance to dispense with the structures and values of the French monarchy, even if he firmly rejected Henri de Navarre's claim to the throne, found considerable support in Poitiers. The League adherent who drafted the *Response d'vn catholiqve* retained such a strong sense of Poitiers's traditional relationship with the kings of France and the city's duty of obedience that he insisted that without the assassinations at Blois, the evil intentions of the heretics and supporters of Navarre would have met with no resistance. He also insisted that, despite the schemes of the *politiques* throughout the spring of 1589, "the inhabitants . . . persisted in their service and obedience to the king up until his death."[73] That a League adherent in 1590 still felt obliged to maintain that his city remained loyal in the face of murders, provocations, and pacts with a heretical heir to the throne is significant. His lingering respect for the monarchy, moreover, is only confirmed in his complaints about Henri IV, who had trampled the dignity of the crown not only through his usurpation of it, but also through his belittling of royal institutions. He had transferred all of Poitiers's political institutions to that pathetic hole-in-the-wall, Parthenay, and had consigned the august Parlement of Paris to the narrow walls of Tours without the consent or authority of any of the parlements of France.[74] Clearly, for this Leaguer, the French crown never died, even if the person of the king was fiercely under dispute. This respect for the royal administration proved so strong that even the Franciscan friar Jean Porthaise cited with approval a ruling and the general catholicity of the royalist Parlement of Bordeaux.[75]

It is unfortunate that of all the speeches and sermons delivered in Poitiers under the League, we have only the testimonies of Humeau, Porthaise, and an anonymous pamphleteer with which to gauge the aspirations and beliefs of the inhabitants. Yet because these texts form our only evidence, they must suffice to indicate if not what Leaguers actually believed, then at least what views were considered important enough to be preserved in print. From their most well-known League preacher, Poitiers's inhabitants heard less about the trespasses of royal government and the nature of political authority than about the dignity of the clergy and the role of the Catholic Church. Porthaise's chief interest did not lie in the relationship between king and peo-

---

[72] Nancy Lyman Roelker, *One King, One Faith: The Parlement of Paris and the Religious Reformations of the Sixteenth Century* (Berkeley, 1996), 86.
[73] *Response d'vn catholiqve*, 8, 18; quotation, 18.
[74] *Response d'vn catholiqve*, 33–34.
[75] "Sermon svr l'arrest," 82.

ple, but between Church and society. From his earliest published writings, he declaimed against any political rule that did not take its inspiration from the teachings of the church and held that true prophets, rather than astrologers or self-interested political advisors, should advise kings.[76] Porthaise compared the nature of secular and religious authority to prove the primacy of the latter. Although he had earlier denounced the kind of political theorizing that had spawned books such as Bodin's *République,* the preacher took the opportunity of his dedication to the Catholic inhabitants of Poitiers to make such a comparison.[77] Secular rule, on the one hand, was based only on human law, so that its particular form was highly mutable and inessential to its exercise. Monarchy, to be sure, was the best form, but any combination of monarchy, aristocracy, and democracy was possible. The church, on the other hand, had always held the monarchical form, and the authority of the pope was therefore paramount.[78] The church, moreover, not only concerned itself with spiritual matters, but also was very much involved in the affairs of the world. As Porthaise succinctly put it, the church is not *of* this world, but *in* it.[79]

Poitiers's théologal continued to emphasize these ideas in his published sermons during the League era. Many of his arguments against Henri IV's claim to the throne center more on his denial of the pope's authority than on a faulty relationship with the French people. Porthaise fulminates, for example, against the Parlement of Tours, which not only rejected the bull excommunicating Henri de Navarre but also had it burned. Having no jurisdiction over papal authority, the parlement had no right to render a judgment and was moreover entirely mistaken to claim that the pope could not absolve the French people from obedience to a heretic. The pontiff could not make a king, explained Porthaise, but he could certainly declare in matters of conscience who was capable of rule and whom it would be pernicious to obey.[80] Faced with Henri IV's conversion in 1593, Porthaise was even more adamant concerning the pope's authority. Navarre's claim to have received absolution and to be a practicing Catholic was entirely specious, since he had not received this absolution from the power that had excommunicated him in the first place. With a legalism that must have appealed to Poitiers's legal personnel, Porthaise explained that the French bishops could not absolve the pretender to the throne *ad cautelam* (provisionally, as guar-

---

[76] Jean Porthaise, *De la vraie et favlce astrologie contre les abuseurs de nostre siecle* (Poitiers, 1578).

[77] *De la vraie et favlce astrologie,* dedication to Louis de Bourbon, duc de Montpensier, c3v: "Car on ne tient plus conte de la conscience, & lon s'amuse aux inuentions auares des hommes, & aux vaines predictions des deuins, qui sont plus obeis que les Theologiens, & pour ce, Dieu laisse regner ces liures de Republique, de l'estat du Prince, & semblables, qui sont tresperni-cieux aux Monarques, qui doibuent ioindre la Religio[n], & l'estat."

[78] *Defence a la responce,* a2r–a5r.

[79] "Sermon svr l'arrest," 80.

[80] "Sermon svr l'arrest," 69–79, 86–88.

antors) and that Henri IV was rather proving his recalcitrance by refusing to await the pope's decision in humility and penitence. There was no reason, therefore, for Poitiers to reconsider its political loyalties, given that the Béarnais was as unfit to rule as ever.[81]

In comparing Porthaise's sermons on the conversion of Henri IV with those of Jean Boucher, Frederic Baumgartner points to their similarity while identifying Porthaise's greater emphasis on the power of the clergy. Part of the difference, he maintains, stemmed from the fact that the League preacher in Poitiers was free from having to satisfy the expectations of the Seize.[82] Whether the differences arose from the predilections of the preachers or the preferences of their audiences, the differing emphases of these two sets of reactions to the conversion of Henri IV point to significant divergences in the concerns of the urban League. In Paris, radical Leaguers expressed their deep resentment toward royal officials by executing the president of the Parlement of Paris. In Poitiers, at no time did League leaders betray any hostility to the idea of royal authority, nor did they diminish their respect for the royal institutions that supported it. Poitiers's Leaguers were determined, however, to root out the Protestants, who threatened the state and their own security, as well as the "false Catholics" who placed other concerns before the purity of their religion. Jacques de Hillerin, in describing the mounting tensions of the spring of 1589, had referred to the "liberty" that still held in Poitiers as long as the town continued to recognize Henri III as king.[83] League adherents were equally concerned with their "liberty," but by this they meant the integrity of Catholic worship, untainted by the threat of a rival worldview. Yet since "liberty" in the sixteenth century did not carry the connotations it would develop in the eighteenth, Poitiers could deny the royal pretensions of Henri de Navarre without questioning the monarchical system per se. In fact, as the disorders of the religious wars wore on, Poitiers became increasingly eager to subsume much of its newfound autonomy to the protection and prestige of a good League prince.

A *bon prince:* The Search for a Governor

Although the noble and urban Leagues may have arisen from different concerns and pursued different goals, most cities maintained their adherence to the Holy Union under the guidance of a governor.[84] Even a proud provin-

[81] "Sermon de la conversion," and "Sermon faict le xxiiiie. d'Octobre, 1593. en l'Eglise de Poitiers, par le Theologal ordinaire: Auquel est traicté de l'absolution Ecclesiastique, qui ne se doit impartir aux des cheuz de la Foy: & moins aux recheuz, soit par renegation, par Apostasie, par Heresie, ou par Sorcelerie, sans grande difficulté, & longue exploration, de leur penitence," in *Cinq sermons,* 2:3–62.

[82] Baumgartner, *Radical Reactionaries,* 207–8.

[83] Hillerin, *Chariot chrestien,* 33, 44–48.

[84] On noble aspirations during the Wars of Religion and League period, see Stuart Carroll,

cial capital such as Toulouse repeatedly pestered Mayenne for a "bon prince" despite the reassuring presence of its parlement.[85] The prestige and military experience of the nobility did much to maintain League cities in their allegiances. Many cities were led to declare for the League in the first indignation at the death of the Guises or in the initial shock of a Protestant's claiming the throne. But most of the cities to persevere in the Union possessed a capable local governor and were located within the sphere of a great League prince, as attendance records of the Estates General of 1593 confirm.[86] Poitiers, in this respect, was in an unusual situation. Located between Protestant La Rochelle and royalist Tours, the city had seen itself as an essential node in the network of League loyalties from the beginning. By the summer of 1591, however, Poitiers was virtually isolated in an overwhelmingly royalist region. The Mayenniste governor of Poitou, the vicomte de la Guierche, failed to inspire confidence because of his poor military record. When the young duc de Guise managed to evade his captors and escape from prison in August 1591, therefore, Poitiers jumped at the chance to obtain its own League prince. The city's leaders showed themselves little interested in preserving the opportunities for autonomous action or administrative independence that they had experienced since their declaration for the League. Instead, they sought the prestige of a great noble, who in protecting the city and carrying on the fight against heresy, would simultaneously remind inhabitants of the best moments of their history and offer the hope of increased advantages in the future. Never, therefore, did Poitiers's urban administrators have less practical independence than when they had finally obtained a noble governor with the clout and convictions they desired.

By the summer of 1591, the heady enthusiasm of the autumn of 1589 and the assurance that the League would, in conquering its enemies, provide for a truly Catholic society had largely subsided. In place of the early capitulations reported by Hillerin and victories such as the successful siege of the town and château of Chauvigny, which Henri IV acknowledged in June 1590, Poitiers found itself isolated and on the defensive.[87] Jean Le Roy recorded the League's heroic but ineffectual defense against the forces of the prince de Conti in Poitou, as Belac, Chauvigny, Saint-Savin, and numerous

---

Noble Power during the French Wars of Religion: The Guise Affinity and the Catholic Cause in Normandy (Cambridge, U.K., 1998); Nicolas Le Roux, "The Catholic Nobility and Political Choice during the League, 1585–1594: The Case of Claude de la Châtre," *French History* 8, no. 1 (1994): 34–50; Laurent Bourquin, *Les nobles, la ville et le roi: l'autorité nobiliaire en Anjou pendant les guerres de Religion* (Paris, 2001), 137–202; Constant, *Ligue*, 178–83, 325–49.

[85] Greengrass, "Sainte Union," 491.

[86] For example: out of all of Guyenne, only Poitou and Périgueux sent deputies, while Champagne and Brie were represented by Troyes, Chaumont, Sens, Meaux, and Mezières. See Auguste Bernard, ed., *Procès-verbaux des États généraux de 1593* (Paris, 1842), 3–13.

[87] [Jules] Berger de Xivrey, ed., *Recueil des lettres missives de Henri IV*, 9 vols. (Paris, 1843–76), 3:201–2.

other strongholds fell to the royalists.[88] In July 1591, Henri IV confidently assured the duc de Montmorency that the prince de Conti would soon have cleaned up (*nettoyé*) the entire province of Poitou, and that after the château of Mirabeau fell, "there will remain in enemy hands only Poitiers, which can also be recovered by love or force."[89] The king tried force. In June, the chapter of St. Hilaire-le-Grand had been obliged to delay its general chapter meeting, because of enemy attack on the Cueille Mirebalaise, a strategically important suburb of Poitiers, and on 12 August, the mayor and échevins were forced to cut short their Monday council meeting in order to help defend the same location from Conti's attack.[90]

La Guierche: A Governor Opposed

Such setbacks intensified oppositions in Poitiers to its League governor, Georges de Villequier, vicomte de la Guierche. The city's League leaders had accepted him only reluctantly from the beginning of their association, and the governor had been forced to handle repeated challenges to his authority. He had attempted to gain entrance to Poitiers as early as May 1589, but it was only after the city adhered to the Union that the hôtel de ville reluctantly agreed to admit him with a small suite.[91] Mayenne had reportedly appointed the gentilhomme governor of Poitou as the price of obtaining the support of his father-in-law, the sieur de Boisseguin, commander of Poitiers's château, for the League, but La Guierche clearly felt obliged to confirm this appointment by obtaining and having published a commission from "Charles X."[92] By December 1590, opposition to La Guierche had solidified, and the duc de Mayenne was forced to write to Poitiers's leaders and the local nobility in an attempt to smooth over the conflict.[93] These tensions erupted into a veritable armed coup against La Guierche in January 1591, when certain inhabitants of Poitiers led by some of the town's prominent League advocates

---

[88] MMP MS 574, 40r.

[89] Berger de Xivrey, ed., *Recueil des lettres*, 3:433–35; quotation, 435.

[90] ADV G534, 115v (26 and 29 June 1591); ACP Reg. 51, 34–36 (12 and 14 Aug. 1591); Berger de Xivrey, ed., *Recueil des lettres*, 3:445. On these events, see also Aubigné, *Histoire universelle*, 8:232–4; De Thou, *Histoire universelle*, 7:807–11; Palma-Cayet, *Chronologie novenaire*, 304.

[91] *Response d'vn catholique*, 13–14; BNF MS Fr 20157, 158v; ACP Reg. 49, 14–16 (7 and 14 Aug. 1589).

[92] On La Guierche's appointment, see Hillerin, *Chariot chrestien*, 41–42. The anonymous royalist account dates Boisseguin's espousal of League interests somewhat earlier and ascribes his change of position to his son-in-law; BNF MS Fr 20157, 154r. The commission, dated 25 December 1589 and registered in the presidial court on 8 February 1590, was subsequently printed by Poitiers's most dedicated and officially authorized League publisher, Aymé Mesnier. See *Le povvoir de monseignevr le viconte de la Gvyerche, capitaine de cent hommes d'armes gouuerneur pour le roy au pays & comté de Poictou* (Poitiers, 1590).

[93] E. Henry and Ch. Loriquet, eds., *Correspondance du duc de Mayenne publiée sur le manuscrit de la bibliothèque de Reims*, 2 vols. (Reims, 1860), 1:184, 213–15, 233–34, 240–49.

determined to wrest control of the château from him and his father-in-law. According to René de Brilhac, the group assembled at the sound of the toc-sin outside the cathedral and set off with Geoffroy de Saint-Belin, bishop of Poitiers. When Boisseguin refused to yield, the group took La Guierche pris-oner and began to fire at the fortress. Three days later a series of negotia-tions finally allowed a reconciliation of the parties, and the château was dismantled on the town side soon afterward.[94]

The siege and partial dismantling of the château removed the threat of force that Poitiers's two League governors had possessed over the city. No one in Poitiers had forgotten the sack of 1562, made possible when the receveur général, ensconced in the château, had trained its guns on the in-habitants instead of the royal forces; indeed, René de Brilhac explicitly mentioned this precedent in his account of events in 1591.[95] Yet the con-frontation did not succeed in radically altering the dynamics of League lead-ership within the city, so that the military defeats of the following summer only accentuated tensions. By the end of August 1591, oppositions to La Guierche had become so intense that rumors of his possible return to Poitiers after a round of campaigning prompted illicit assemblies. The Mois, assem-bled to deliberate on the problem, ruled that La Guierche was not to enter Poitiers, but to proceed directly to the League princes' camp.[96] Negotiations nevertheless continued by letter,[97] but on 17 September, La Guierche put an end to all attempts to prevent his return by slipping through a gate at which he was not expected late in the evening. His actions prompted an urgent as-sembly of the Mois, in which the mayor presented an account of the gover-nor's recent activities that, while seeming to praise them, shed doubt on his motivations. In particular, the mayor pointed out that the governor had raised troops reputedly for the town's defense but now stationed only a few leagues from Poitiers. Concluding that the unusual circumstances of La Guierche's arrival threatened to cause disorders among the people, the Mois ruled that La Guierche leave Poitiers to join the forces of the duc de Mayenne.[98] Correctly interpreting these conclusions as hostile to his son-in-law, Boisseguin determined to leave Poitiers as well, but the hôtel de ville asked him not to go.[99]

[94] The attack took place on 22 January and the reconciliation on 25 January. Brilhac, 22–23; MMP MS 574, 40r; Berger de Xivrey, ed., *Recueil des lettres*, 2:339. The curé of St. Jean Baptiste recorded that the château was not dismantled until 4 March. *Extraits de l'Obituaire de Sainte-Opportune de Poitiers (1366–1631), des registres paroissiaux de cette ville (1539–1790) et du journal de Pierre Charmeteau, maître perruquier (1731–1767)*, AHP 15 (Poitiers, 1885), 344.

[95] Brilhac, 22.

[96] ACP Reg. 51, 44–46 (28 Aug. 1591); 50–54 (6 Sept. 1591); Bouillé, *Histoire des ducs de Guise*, 4:58.

[97] ACP Reg. 51, 50–58 (6, 13, and 16 Sept. 1591).

[98] ACP Reg. 51, 60–63 (18 Sept. 1591).

[99] ACP Reg. 51, 60–63 (18 Sept. 1591); 63–65 (19 Sept. 1591).

From the beginning of his association with Poitiers, therefore, La Guierche experienced difficulties in obtaining the confidence and cooperation of the city's League leaders, and the troubles of the summer of 1591 only intensified dissatisfaction and distrust. To hold the position of governor of Poitou, not just any gentilhomme would do. La Guierche and his family had been long known in the region, but the governor's military abilities and loyalties were subject to question.[100] He had been a chief League captain in the unsuccessful attempt to win Limoges for the League in 1589, and in 1591 his troops had been chased back to Poitiers from Belac, a town that De Thou, admittedly a hostile witness, accused him of trying to seize simply because he had previously been royal governor of La Marche.[101] During the alarms of the summer of 1591, La Guierche had been far from Poitiers, pursuing his own military goals or ostensibly attempting to collect troops for the town's defense. Absence and defeat at such a time constituted serious failings, but hostilities against the governor of Poitou also surpassed what such weaknesses might be expected to produce. A struggle to exert power and to guide League policy in Poitiers was under way, and La Guierche found his chief opponents in the very leaders who had been most adamant that the city join the League in the spring of 1589. Saint-Belin, François de Brilhac, and Jean Palustre led armed inhabitants to seize the château, and the hôtel de ville complained to the League princes of "the divisions that are causing factions to form in the city, that is, between the vicomte de la Guierche and his reverence [the bishop] of Poitiers, due to the causes for dissatisfaction they claim to have against each other."[102] Because La Guierche owed his position to Mayenne, it is possible that hostilities against him also reflected dissatisfactions with the Mayenniste wing of the Catholic League. If this was the case, a permanent breach never occurred. Despite the firm resolve expressed in the Mois, La Guierche did not in fact retreat from Poitiers, and by 27 September, after a week of extreme tension, the governor and the bishop appeared together in the Union Council.[103] Yet La Guierche had continually fallen short of the qualities that Poitiers's leaders desired in a governor. Poitiers therefore turned eagerly to a noble with great promise and star quality: they wanted the leadership of the young duc de Guise.

[100] Michel Le Riche frequently mentions the La Guierche family in his journal and in 1578 commented on a disagreement between the League governor's father and Joseph Le Bascle, sieur des Défends. Le Riche, 300.

[101] BNF MS Fr 20153, 325–26; De Thou, *Histoire universelle*, 7:807–8. Palma-Cayet describes La Guierche's failed siege of Belac as a major defeat (*Chronologie novenaire*, 267–68).

[102] ACP Reg. 51, 43 (26 Aug. 1591).

[103] On 19 September, the mayor reported that several noble captains had approached him to insist that he expel La Guierche from town. Attendance at the Union Council from 16–19 September was also extremely low, most likely because of the conflict. ACP Reg. 51, 65; Reg. 52, 68–69, 72–74.

Guise: A Governor Desired

On 15 August 1591, Charles de Lorraine managed to elude his guard and to escape from his imprisonment at Tours, where he had been held ever since the assassination of his father in 1588. While Paris celebrated the escape, commentators speculated on the effect Guise's presence would have on League leadership. Reporting the news to the comte de Sanzay, Étienne Pasquier recounted that "the naysayers [*mesdisans*] would have us believe that if the king is annoyed, Monsieur de Mayenne will not be less so, since he has now been given a co-rival in greatness, based on the sole memory of his [i.e. Guise's] father."[104] Pasquier then went on to contradict this opinion, and Guise was careful neither to alienate his uncle nor to set himself up as a rival power.[105] Nevertheless, many persisted in seeing in him the ideal combination of radical religious sympathies and natural political leadership. For Poitiers, Guise's escape seemed providential. Surrounded by enemy forces and in the midst of a crisis of command, the city's leaders jumped at the opportunity to obtain the promise of protection of Guise's presumed military abilities and undoubted prestige. If Poitiers had been chafing under the dubious qualifications of a governor of low standing and subordinate ties to Mayenne, the stature of the Guise family and its reputation for militant Catholicism offered the hope that the provincial capital would soon be able to place full confidence in its leadership and to regain its status as a crucial League center. The members of the hôtel de ville thus invested no time in debating whether Guise's presence would reduce the city's newfound autonomy. Rather, they imagined the enhanced prestige that intimate ties to an influential peer of the realm would assure them in a future securely Catholic France.

Poitiers obtained news of Guise's escape early, and immediately set about to convince him to pay a visit to the town.[106] By the end of the month, no fewer than three or four messengers had been sent to Guise, and the hôtel de ville was urgently marshaling its arguments to persuade him to come. The town, its deputies were to argue, was beset by internal contention between the bishop and the governor and was threatened externally to such an extent that it was on the point of succumbing. To preserve Poitiers from this perilous situation and to conserve it for the cause of Catholicism, God had providentially sent the young duc de Guise to carry out the destiny of his family. The deputies were to inform the duke

---

[104] Pasquier, *Oeuvres*, 2:429–30.

[105] Bouillé, *Histoire des ducs de Guise*, 4:36–37, 48–58.

[106] A letter from Guise dated 16 August from Selles is recorded in the town council register, as is an account of his escape written by René Blaye, sieur de la Lande, citizen of Poitiers and seemingly a member of his suite having similarly escaped. See ACP Reg. 51, 40 (26 Aug. 1591).

that the town of Poitiers, at the time of its extreme necessity, when it had arrived at the very threshold of the abyss, had been saved through the will of God
by the help of the departed and dearly remembered duc de Guise, his father.
Further, that God by this same will, as through a hereditary destiny, seems to
have desired to deliver his Grace, the duc de Guise, his son, in order to conserve this very town of Poitiers in its liberty of the Catholic religion.[107]

To resolve the divisions plaguing the city, Poitiers therefore turned to a memory of unity and heroic resistance to heresy that many associated with the
siege of 1569. Just as Henri de Lorraine—quite young at the time and eager
to measure up to *his* father's famous defense of Metz—had played such an
important part in that endeavor, his son was now to defend the city against
external threat and internal strife.[108] The town's eagerness to welcome Guise
within the walls was quite marked. In order to facilitate the prince's arrival,
the deputies were also to assure him that all of his expenses would be duly
met. Before the Mois had even received word that he would come, it ordered
grain to be milled and appointed an individual to keep track of the expenses
that would be incurred by his presence.[109]

In inviting Guise to come to Poitiers, the town had assured him that he
would "chase away all the clouds" hovering over it, and indeed, conflict
within the League in Poitiers had become intense.[110] League leaders had recently taken drastic actions to preserve a semblance of unity within the movement: they had recently executed a dozen people suspected of "perfidy" and
had all once again sworn the oath of Union.[111] The duc de Mayenne had
written to the new mayor, Jean Chevalier, charging him to preserve the city
within the League.[112] The municipal government, for its part, was writing
and receiving letters to and from all sides in an attempt to assure its defense
and to resolve the gubernatorial impasse. While some of these letters were
to the duc de Mayenne, others might have given the lieutenant général cause
for concern. In September 1591, the hôtel de ville was corresponding directly
with the Spanish ambassador, as well as with the duc de Mercoeur, a League
prince who responded from the veritable stronghold he had fashioned for
himself in nearby Brittany.[113] Such divisions, as we have seen, reflected real
opposition to La Guierche. Guise's eminence made him so universally ap-
pealing in Poitiers that his arrival was to dispel all conflict and to reunite the
city in its holy endeavors.

Although the corps de ville dwelt on external threats and internal conflicts

[107] ACP Reg. 51, 42–43.
[108] Henri de Lorraine's role in the siege of 1569 helped to establish his reputation for military success. Carroll, *Noble Power*, 138.
[109] ACP Reg. 51, 44–46 (28 Aug. 1591).
[110] Papiers de Simancas, B69, pièce 168, quoted in Bouillé, *Histoire des ducs de Guise*, 4:50.
[111] Ibid.
[112] Letter dated 2 Aug. 1591, recorded in ACP Reg. 51, 40–41.
[113] ACP Reg. 51, 50–58, 69–71.

in its attempts to persuade the duc de Guise to come to Poitiers, it by no means saw the city as a pathetic victim dependent on disinterested noble aid. Rather, members' desire for such a prominent leader reflected their ambitions for the urban community. Thus, deputies were to inform the duke of the city's dire need, but they were also to instruct him of its importance. The only sure refuge for the Catholics of Poitou, Saintonge, Angoumois, much of Anjou, part of Touraine, and La Marche, the provincial capital was represented as a site worthy of Guise's person and best efforts.[114] Poitiers's leaders, moreover, do not seem to have voiced any concerns about their own level of authority with such an important noble within the walls. La Guierche was perceived as enough of a threat to prompt the demolition of the château from the town side, but Guise's presence would presumably confer enough benefits on the city to justify any loss of command that elites might suffer. It was to be imagined that with the ultimate victory of the League, the duc de Guise would have a crucial role to play and that Poitiers would benefit accordingly. Poitiers's League leaders may even have nurtured a more ambitious hope. They may have reasoned that if Guise were ultimately selected as the king of France, a possibility that Porthaise indirectly supported, he would retain the same amount of affection for Poitiers as Charles VII had done after the Hundred Years' War.[115] Should the city succeed in repeating this medieval pattern of succoring the heir to the throne in his time of need, then it could happily subsume any impulses to gain independence from the monarchy to more effective expectations of obtaining an extra complement of privileges that would mark a secure relationship with the sovereign.

Despite its best efforts, Poitiers never succeeded in obtaining the duc de Guise as its leader. It was not that he was unwilling. The young nobleman seems to have been persuaded by the town's representations and seriously considered taking up residence there. He was deterred only by his advisors, who counseled him not to provoke his uncle's distrust by establishing a base apart.[116] Mayenne, for his part, recognized Poitiers's desire for Guise's presence, and frequently assured the hôtel de ville that he would spare his nephew after the expected arrival of the duke of Parma.[117] The lieutenant général did in fact commission the duke to command all League forces in Anjou, Touraine, Maine, Berry, Orléans, and Guyenne (including Poitou) shortly afterward, but despite Guise's willingness to accede to this arrangement, the commission was never carried out.[118] Instead of the duc de Guise, Poitiers

---

[114] ACP Reg. 51, 38–44.

[115] Porthaise may have been referring to the possibility of Guise being elected king, when he commented that he would not criticize Henri IV's conversion as an act of political expediency, "Car alors on m'accuseroit d'estre Espagnol, ce que ie ne suis, car ie cognois assez de Princes & Gentils-hommes Catholiques & François, pour commander en ce Royaume quand il en sera besoin, sans introduire vn Prince Espagnol, ou Alleman"; "Sermon de la conversion," 14.

[116] Bouillé, *Histoire des ducs de Guise*, 4:51.

[117] See, for example, ACP Reg. 51, 113–19 (16 Dec. 1591).

[118] Bouillé, *Histoire des ducs de Guise*, 4:77–78.

remained under the military protection of the vicomte de la Guierche until he was killed at the hands of royal forces in a skirmish over his own seigneury in February 1592.[119]

Brissac: A Governor Obtained

The defeat of the governor at La Guierche[120] dramatically altered the terms of League politics in Poitiers. Not only had La Guierche been killed as he attempted to cross a river in an overloaded boat, but many of the nobles sympathetic to his cause were also drowned. Poitiers's own François Palustre, échevin and captain of the municipal company, was also lost. The event inevitably brought changes, both in the internal alignment of League factions and in the external relations between the town and the Catholic princes. The governor of Poitou suddenly removed, each League commander sought to recommend his own replacement. Poitiers therefore found itself in a position to negotiate with a full spectrum of League powers, in the quest for a suitable leader. Although the town was therefore able to assert a measure of autonomy in its decision, its objective was not permanently to distance itself from all noble influence. Rather, Poitiers's League leaders were concerned, as they had been earlier, with obtaining a figure of sufficient stature and energetic religious sympathies to make his command palatable and to assure the city's consequence in the greater political community. They finally got their wish in Charles de Cossé, comte de Brissac, a noted military commander and supporter of the radical League. Yet the presence of an important, perhaps imperious, noble also had its drawbacks, and Poitiers's traditional leaders soon found that they paid for their newly gained security in the coin of their active role in government.

The military disaster at La Guierche altered the political balance in Poitiers. The municipal military company, reduced from light horse to soldiers (*gendarmes*) in January, was disbanded.[121] The bishop took advantage of the death of his rival to attempt to assert even greater authority within the town and tried to insist that meetings of the dominicale be held in the episcopal palace.[122] At the same time, complaints surfaced concerning the way that the Union Council had been run, and there were both clandestine and official calls for reform. On 3 March, Mayor Jean Chevalier contended in the Mois that a document had been found at the house of Julien Millet, bourgeois and League activist, requesting on behalf of the "poor people, inhabitants of the town," that almost every aspect of the Union Council be

---

[119] There is an account of the battle in ACP Reg. 51, 134–42 (10 Feb. 1592). Aubigné also describes the engagement (*Histoire universelle,* 8:230–32), as does De Thou (*Histoire universelle,* 8:90–93) and Palma-Cayet (*Histoire novenaire,* 303).

[120] La Guerche-sur-Creuse (Indre-et-Loire).

[121] ACP Reg. 51, 125–28 (4 Jan. 1592); Reg. 53, 17–19 (7 Aug. 1592).

[122] ACP Reg. 51, 152–54 (9 Mar. 1592).

changed. Questions put to Millet himself and then to François Le Page (a printer with League sympathies who was revealed to have provided a clean copy of the manuscript request) soon revealed a secret network of support for the document.[123] The Union Council itself had recently called for new elections, but by the time of the request they had not been carried out.[124] Although we can only speculate concerning the specifics, these calls for reform and alterations in governmental responsibility likely reflected competing pressures to shape a newly emerging political situation. The governor's death having weakened the lines of authority within the town, rival interests sought to take advantage of this lapse and to impose their own conceptions of the proper form of League government. While political factions disputed mastery of Poitiers's Union Council, the town was in close contact with a full array of League powers.[125] In negotiating its acceptance of a new governor, Poitiers was also determining the exact form its political loyalties would take.

The first reaction of the Mois, on hearing a full account of the fatal skirmish at La Guierche on 10 February, was to advise that letters be sent to solicit help. It therefore asked the mayor to write immediately to the duc de Mercoeur, the Spanish ambassador, and the duc de Nemours, to obtain their aid, and to inform Mayenne and Guise of the disaster. Letters were also dispatched to Paris, Boisdauphin, the marquis de Villars, the maréchal de Retz, and the sieur de Richmont on this occasion.[126] Having informed virtually every influential League noble of the town's loss of a governor, the municipal government could then expect to receive offers of a replacement from all directions. Many in Poitiers still hoped to obtain the duc de Guise, even insisting that the city would "maintain and preserve itself while awaiting the good fortune and fitness [*Lheur & commodite*] that it would please God to send [them] a prince for the relief and government of this area" when the duc de Nemours was suggested instead.[127] It also evaded offers from other quarters, including the sieur de Boisdauphin, governor of Maine and Anjou, and the duc de Mercoeur, governor of Brittany.[128] By the time that Poitiers had evaded Mercoeur's ambitions, however, Mayenne had altered his plans for the disposition of League command. In a letter dated 1 March, the comte de Brissac informed the hôtel de ville that he had agreed to replace La Guierche as governor of Poitou, and the following day Mayenne wrote to assure the municipality that both Guise and Brissac would be leaving mo-

---

[123] ACP Reg. 51, 149–52.
[124] ACP Reg. 52, 155–57 (19 Feb. 1592). The hôtel de ville elected its new delegates on 4 May 1592. Reg. 51, 174–75.
[125] Nobles began to dominate the Union Council in a way that they had not earlier, from February to July 1592 (see table 9.1).
[126] ACP Reg. 51, 134–42 (10 Feb. 1592); 146–47 (22 Feb. 1592).
[127] ACP Reg. 51, 130–32; quotation, 130.
[128] ACP Reg. 51, 146–47; 154–55 (14 Mar. 1592).

mentarily for Poitiers.[129] Yet the town's wait would be a long one. Brissac would not finally arrive until the following autumn, and Guise would soon be appointed governor of Champagne and Brie.[130]

Obliged to renounce their ambition of receiving Guise as governor, Poitiers's leaders nevertheless welcomed Mayenne's selection of Brissac. Having early revealed his dedication to the League at Angers and encouraged Parisian Leaguers on the Day of the Barricades, Brissac would later be appointed governor of Paris, to prevent the comte de Belin from coming to agreement with Henri IV.[131] The municipality showed its approval of Brissac's appointment by making everything ready for his arrival. When in early June the mayor informed the Mois that he had received word of the count's imminent appearance, it concluded that a residence and furniture should be provided.[132] Although Brissac did not in fact arrive until 28 September, his entry inspired high hopes among League supporters. Many probably agreed with the curé of the parish of St. Jean-Baptiste, who was moved to write a short poem on the occasion. Brissac, he was sure, would deliver Poitiers from Protestants and false Catholics and restore the town to tranquility.[133]

Whether Brissac was as effective a military leader, as zealous a persecutor of heretics, and as successful a reconciler of political factions as Poitiers's leaders desired, his presence certainly altered the balance of authority in the town. No sooner had the League noble arrived in Poitiers than he began to assign to himself the structures for decision making and military administration. Just as Mayenne had early on converted the Union Council of Paris into an advisory council attached to his person and Nemours would replace Lyon's Union Council with his own men in 1593, Brissac disbanded the Union Council of Poitiers as it had functioned until his arrival.[134] Less than a month after his entry, the mayor declared in the Mois that the governor had begun to judge the captures brought to Poitiers on his own, and that he

---

[129] The letters seem to have been long in arriving, since Mayenne's was recorded on 23 March and Brissac's one day later (assuming that the delay was not due to a dispute within Poitiers about whether to accept them). ACP Reg. 51, 159–60, 167.

[130] Mayenne in fact appointed Guise as governor of Champagne and Brie on the very day following his letter assuring Poitiers of his nephew's proximate arrival. Bouillé indicates that the duc d'Elbeuf served as League governor of Poitiers for a short time in 1592, but no local source reveals his presence. See Bouillé, *Histoire des ducs de Guise*, 4:78 n. 1, 93–94, 98.

[131] Palma-Cayet, *Chronologie novenaire*, 540–41; Constant, *Ligue*, 22.

[132] ACP Reg. 51, 178–82 (8 June 1592). Ironically, it was suggested that the furniture previously supplied to Malicorne should now be used for Brissac.

[133] The curé's poem, reprinted in *Extraits de l'obituaire*, 344, began as follows:

> Entra dans Poictiers unne rouze
> Nommée le conste de Briçacq
> Qui les meschantz mettra à sacq,
> Et nous rendra tous passiphiques . . .

Jean Le Roy also noted the date of Brissac's entry in MMP MS 574, 40v.

[134] Drouot, "Conseils provinciaux," 428.

had instructed his secretary to sign the ordinances instead of the mayor. Indeed, since Brissac's first attendance at the Union Council on 1 October, attendance had declined drastically, and by 10 October, the council was evidently meeting only in the governor's absence.[135] The death of Boisseguin, governor of the château, on 6 October at the ripe age of eighty probably facilitated this important governmental change.[136] Presented with the mayor's complaint, the Mois decided to remonstrate with the count concerning the mayor's participation but further ruled that it would not press the issue if the governor proved adamant.[137] As it turned out, Brissac *was* adamant. When a group of municipal deputies approached him to remonstrate that in accordance with the town's privileges the mayor, who was also captain of the city, had always participated in councils of war, the count responded "that he intended to cut back the said council of war and name whatever secretary he saw fit, and [himself] sign the conclusions that would result."[138] That he saw his command as verging on sovereign authority is indicated in the ordinance by which he accorded the friars of the order of St. François de Paul of Plessis-lès-Tours the currently vacant buildings of the collège de Gellesis. Adapting the royal formula, *car tel est nostre plaisir,* he concluded: "car ainsi l'avons estime Juste et raisonnable."[139] Although the Union Council continued to meet,[140] it certainly no longer claimed to act as the representative of the three estates of Poitiers, did not make any reference to municipal authority for its actions, and was composed of personnel of the governor's selection. Poitiers's elite had in effect ceded all military decision making to the governor.

With Brissac's installation, Poitiers's notables turned over much of the active administration of League concerns. If urban elites had been able to extend the range of their decision-making powers during the first years of the League, the price of a prestigious governor, willing to assure the town's security and to act on its most zealous religious proclivities, was a retrenchment of this autonomy. Whether this situation produced any resentment is uncertain, but it certainly allowed Poitiers to continue firm in its adherence to the League. Indeed, the town's commitment to the Catholic Union remained strong enough to enable it to hold out in the face of a blockade against it in the summer of 1593.[141] Brissac's military command must have

---

[135] ACP Reg. 52, 296–307. After 10 October, the Union Council met in its previous form only three times. Because Brissac insisted that his secretary now sign the ordinances, the register of Union Council sessions kept by its secretary, Jacques Barraud, ends on 4 November.

[136] MMP MS 574, 40v–41r.

[137] ACP Reg. 53, 37–38.

[138] ACP Reg. 53, 38–41 (26 Oct. 1592); quotation, 39.

[139] ADV 1H^{18} 95 (Minimes), ordinance dated 29 Oct. 1592.

[140] Its existence is mentioned on 7 June 1593 in ACP Reg. 53, 81–82.

[141] The blockade was maintained by Malicorne and other royalist nobles beginning in May 1593 and lasted until a truce between Henri IV and Mayenne was concluded on 14 August. See MMP MS 574, 41r; Brilhac, 24–25; Aubigné, *Histoire universelle,* 8:235–41. The hôtel de ville

played an active role, since he was seriously wounded in a sortie.[142] Fortified by the sermons of Jean Porthaise, the city also refused to be swayed by Henri IV's conversion to Catholicism, an act that convinced many towns and nobles to accept him as legitimate king of France. For a time, the city even ignored Paris's recognition of the Bourbon king, although the capital's capitulation in March 1594 was probably an important spur to Poitiers's beginning negotiations with Henri IV.

Thanks in part to the good offices of Scévole de Sainte-Marthe and with the cooperation of its new governor, Charles de Lorraine, duc d'Elbeuf, Poitiers obtained an Edict of Reduction to royal obedience in July 1594.[143] The edict granted amnesty for all actions taken during the League period, confirmed all individuals in their offices, and as was usual for edicts of pacification, consigned all hostilities to forgetfulness. Maurice Roatin, recently elected mayor of Poitiers, reinforced this idea of mutual forgiveness. In the first meeting of the Mois in which both former Leaguers and royalists were present (although a mere two royalists appeared at this early date), Roatin pointed out that determining right and wrong was impossible in civil war and that the parts of moderation and vehemence were equally acceptable where religious differences were concerned. Neither Leaguers nor royalists were therefore to blame. "Because, then, gentlemen," concluded Roatin,

> foreign examples set us, our Christian faith obliges us, the king's ordinance constrains us, to forgetfulness, let us all bury with willing hearts the memory of things past in the joy and happiness of our reconciliation, from which, for my part, I will never withdraw, and from this moment forward, I embrace you and recognize you all without distinction as my relations, friends, and fellow citizens.[144]

The memory of the League period in Poitiers would not be as easy to efface as Roatin intimated, and the process of civic government after 1594 was no more harmonious than previously. Nevertheless, after its recognition of

---

took measures to prepare for it on 22 May, and wrote to Mayenne concerning it on 28 June. ACP Reg. 53, 74–76, 93–95. According to the curé of St. Jean-Baptiste, royal forces attacked Poitiers on 8 July. *Extraits de l'obituaire*, 344.

[142] Berger de Xivrey, ed., *Recueil des lettres*, 3:809.

[143] The text of the edict, as copied into the town council register, gives the date of July 1594, whereas other texts give the date as 16 June (actually the date that Henri IV sent letters after agreement with Poitiers's deputies). The version in Register 54, 40–54, was reportedly copied from a printed copy, since the text is entitled "Edict et declaration du Roy sur la Reduction de la ville de Poictiers en son obeissance/ a Poictiers par Ayme Mesnier Imprimeur ordinayre de Lad ville et de Luniversite mil V^c iiii^xx^xiiii Avecq permission." For a printed version of the edict, see Thibaudeau, *Abrégé de l'histoire du Poitou*, 5:192–208. Aubigné notes the good offices of Sainte-Marthe in securing Poitiers's reduction (*Histoire universelle*, 9:39–40).

[144] ACP Reg. 54, 64–73 (5 Sept. 1594); quotation, 69. Andrault provides both a facsimile version and a transcription of this speech in an appendix of his "Capitale de province."

Henri IV, Poitiers set about to reconstruct the same relationship of loyalty and privilege with the new king as it had enjoyed under his Valois predecessors. Unfortunately for Poitiers, Henri IV had a good memory and was not as willing as he had first declared to retain unaltered the terms of his relations with the provincial city.

10 *After the League*

Change and Continuity under Henri IV

The image of the first Bourbon king of France has undergone considerable reevaluation in recent years. In place of an earlier assumption that everyone eagerly capitulated before Henri le Grand, scholars now recognize that the first ten years of Henri IV's reign involved a "struggle for stability," in which the king had to take active measures to prevent disorder and to ensure his authority.[1] Against the view that the new king deliberately imposed a policy of strict royal control on the cities and thereby launched the absolutist style of rule that would reach its full development under Louis XIV has been countered the interpretation that Henri IV had no systematic urban policy but reacted within the traditional bounds of royal authority to curb the very real threat of disorder in the cities. This he achieved by bolstering his own influence and strengthening his ties to local elites, chiefly through ensuring that trustworthy men were appointed or elected to city governments, themselves often made more manageable through limitations of their size and electorates.[2] For Poitiers, as for other League cities, the king's attitude toward his erstwhile enemies was of critical importance. Would the king truly consign the past to oblivion, as the numerous edicts of reduction insisted that repentant communities must, and would he adopt the relationship of royal magnanimity and urban service that formed the fundamental underpinnings of urban privileges and thus of civic society as it was presently constituted?[3] This is the crucial question that we must now examine: to what extent did

[1] Mark Greengrass, *France in the Age of Henri IV: The Struggle for Stability,* 1st ed. (London, 1984).

[2] Finley-Croswhite, *Henry IV and the Towns;* Descimon, "Échevinage parisien."

[3] Michael Wolfe, *The Conversion of Henri IV: Politics, Power, and Religious Belief in Early Modern France* (Cambridge, Mass., 1993), 184; Thibaudeau, *Abrégé de l'histoire du Poitou,* 5:197–98 (Edict of Reduction, Article VI).

Poitiers's experiences during the League period mark a break in the city's relationship with the crown and thus in the assumptions of urban government?

Poitiers's experiences under Henri IV confirm many of the conclusions of recent scholars concerning the king's relationship with the towns. Although a full range of the city's leaders rushed to assure their newly recognized monarch of the inhabitants' joy and prompt obedience, Poitiers did not immediately settle down in peace and tranquility. The tensions of factionalism associated with the League continued to plague urban life, and resistance to the city's new position of royal obedience kept alive a palpable military threat. Toward this situation of potential disorder, however, Henri IV behaved remarkably mildly. Poitiers was not one of the French cities to see its privileges impugned. Despite the provocation of an attempted fiscal revolt, the provincial capital kept almost all of its substantial privileges intact throughout the reign and owed the slight alterations that took place to the hôtel de ville's own misrepresentations in court. Neither did the city experience any radical new burden in royal fiscal demands, although the king and his counselors complained in more than one instance of Poitiers's poor record in this regard.

Yet if Poitiers's relations with the crown show a king ready at first to overlook internal strife and willing to preserve the privileges that ensured its governing traditions, they also reveal a king who was not quite the "Renaissance monarch" that some have emphasized.[4] Henri IV was not "absolutist"—if by that we mean that he systematically tried to enforce a policy of urban subservience to the royal will. But he did develop a noticeably different style from his predecessors in dealing with the cities and corporate groups that composed his kingdom, and this shift of approach changed the terms of Poitiers's relationship with the crown. The city's leaders soon found that Henri IV was much more willing to threaten his dire displeasure when his will was not obeyed, and these threats carried weight because he had occasionally carried them out elsewhere. The king also used the prestige and awesome authority of the crown readily to intervene personally in the city's affairs. His interventions were not only punitive but preventative as well, and they resulted from a tendency to closer supervision than the city had experienced before.

With these shifts in the king's behavior went changing royal expectations of how his subjects were to represent their relationship to him. Perhaps because he had had to win back his kingdom city by city, Henri IV put much greater stock in evidence of present obedience than in recitals of past loyalty. He insisted that subjects' current actions prove their intentions and was impatient with professions of fidelity based on past relationships. Thanks to the advice that the hôtel de ville received from all sides, Poitiers learned the new vocabulary of obedience relatively quickly. The city's governors stopped

---

[4] Finley-Croswhite, *Henry IV and the Towns*, 147–48.

trying to make the kinds of historical arguments that had been key to their community's identity throughout the sixteenth century and began to represent their objectives in terms of utility. The new relationship, however, was more precarious from the city's point of view, since any present disobedience could dispel the effects of years of fidelity. Thus, although Henri IV sought to preserve the traditional ties between king and city and used a tried-and-true array of methods to achieve this goal, his vigorous and personal style of rule did influence the ways that this relationship was understood. For a city such as Poitiers, whose present importance as an administrative capital and center of learning was intimately tied to its past, the change proved significant.

The Struggle for Stability

Once Poitiers received its Edict of Reduction in July 1594, the city's leaders acted in concert to present an image of united obedience to their lawful king. Negotiations with the city's deputies were apparently concluded on 16 June, when Henri IV wrote to the clergy, presidial court, and city of Poitiers to express his pleasure at their intent to recognize him, and the edict was formally published in the presidial court on 5 August 1594.[5] This event, the king was assured, was an occasion of general rejoicing. The three estates of the city, presided by the duc d'Elbeuf, the bishop, and the lieutenant général, had received the edict "with such great joy," and at a general assembly at the cathedral, the entire town thanked God for having unbound its eyes to recognize its duty.[6] A Te Deum was sung, and later that evening, fireworks were set off in the streets and a cannon fired to mark the people's joy.[7] Repeated letters from the mayor, the presidial court, the bishop, and the duc d'Elbeuf reinforced this image of peaceful unity under royal authority, and all sides praised the actions of the duc d'Elbeuf for helping to bring calm to the city and for disposing the people to recognize their king.[8] These reports not only recounted Poitiers's situation with numbing consistency but also reassured the king of an awareness that any authority his officials exercised devolved uniquely from his own majesty. Such pious assertions, Poitiers's officials knew, accorded well with the king's own views, since the officials' recognition of political dependence closely echoed language they had received in royal letters. Recognizing that the authority and respect due to magistrates

---

[5] ACP Casier 43, Reg. 16, 169–72; Berger de Xivrey, ed., *Recueil des lettres*, 4:169–71; Brilhac, 25.

[6] BNF MS Fr 23194, 245r.

[7] MMP MS 574, 41r; Brilhac, 25.

[8] For these letters to Henri IV, see BNF MS Fr 23194, 5 Aug.: from Elbeuf (249r), from the presidial court (253r), two letters from the mayor (255r, 257r); 6 Aug.: from the bishop, lieutenant général, and mayor (259r); 20 Aug.: from Elbeuf (243r); 23 Aug.: from the officers of the presidial court (241r–v); undated: from the bishop (247r–248r).

could not exist without royal majesty, they acknowledged the king's reminder that "their offices, without [royal authority], could have no firm basis or foundation."[9] Poitiers was also careful to reinforce this picture of obedience by celebrating royal victories against the League. On 14 September, for example, the mayor reported to Henri IV that everyone in Poitiers was so overjoyed to hear of the reduction of Amiens that they immediately repaired to the cathedral, where a Te Deum was chanted in the presence of the duc d'Elbeuf, the bishop, the entire clergy, and many of the inhabitants.[10] In the months after Poitiers recognized Henri IV, therefore, the city's leaders sought to smother any lingering doubts of their loyalty in a barrage of assurances to the contrary.

Despite such declarations, tensions associated with the League and hostilities to Henri IV had far from subsided in Poitiers, and the king was deeply aware of this fact. As in 1589, the sieur de Malicorne, governor of Poitou, undermined the city's attempts to present a united front to the crown. After Poitiers's reduction, he inconveniently accused the duc d'Elbeuf of attempting to keep alive League sentiments and of supporting his own mayoral candidate against the royalist supporter of good reputation who was ultimately elected.[11] In contrast to the chorus of letters describing Poitiers's joyful acceptance of the Edict of Reduction, Malicorne also commented that those who had tried to forestall this submission now acquiesced with heavy hearts, more out of constraint than voluntarily.[12] If Henri IV might have reasoned that Malicorne's irritation arose equally from his jealousy of Elbeuf's new authority as from his concern for the provincial capital's loyalties, the same could not be said for other indications that Poitiers's reduction to royal obedience had not gone as smoothly as represented. Once François Roatin, mayor of Poitiers, saw his own interests shift from supporting this vision of instant unity to emphasizing his own activity in the king's service, he revealed that there had been "difficulties" that he and Louis de Sainte-Marthe, lieutenant général, had worked to overcome, "although the passions of some then posed a certain obstruction."[13]

Indeed, factionalism persisted despite the terms of the edict. When Pierre des Fontaines, canon of Ste. Radegonde, returned to Poitiers, he found that his chapter insisted on seizing his assets and denying him the fruits of his

---

[9] Compare the following: ". . . noz charges les reconnoissans de vostre seule Maiesté, sans l'authorite delaquelle le pouuoir et respect deus aux Magistratz et a la Justice ne peuuent subsister" (BNF MS Fr 23194, 241r) and "Aussy vous pouvés croire que le vostre [contentement] en accroistra de jour en jour par la participation que vous avés au public, que la conservation de nostre auctorité porte avec soy et pour le lustre qu'elle donne à vos charges, qui ne peuvent, hors icelle, avoir ferme subsistance ny fondement . . . ." (Berger de Xivrey, ed., *Receuil des lettres*, 4:171).

[10] BNF MS Fr 23194, 273r–v.

[11] BNF MS Fr 23194, 204r–v.

[12] BNF MS Fr 23194, 251r–v.

[13] BNF MS Fr 23194, 299r, 245r.

prebend because of his years' absence from the city, despite a royal arrêt of 1592 moving the chapter to Saint-Maixent. When he protested, the presidial court of Poitiers presumed to judge the case, in flagrant contravention of the terms of the Edict of Reduction.[14] Many people relinquished the convictions that had fueled the recent troubles only reluctantly. Geoffroy de Saint-Belin, bishop of Poitiers, on the one hand complained to the king that the city was in constant danger from the scheming of the Huguenots and their allies and on the other assured the king of steps he had taken to banish a Jacobin preacher who had sermonized on the biblical limitations of the power of kings in his cathedral.[15] The persistence of these tensions, moreover, posed a serious threat to the stability and loyalties of the city. When the duc d'El-beuf was to be absent from Poitiers for a period in the fall of 1594, the mayor assured the king that the inhabitants would maintain a vigilant guard and punish any Leaguer gentilshommes who attempted to gain entrance.[16] This strategy, however, would have been only minimally effective, since there were still nobles in Poitiers who had not yet sworn obedience to the crown.[17] The possibility that Poitiers could rescind its recognition of Henri IV and return to the League camp was also very real. Until the duc de Mercoeur finally came to terms with the crown in 1598, a powerful League presence persisted on the borders of Poitou. It was for this reason that Henri IV kept the provincial capital so well-informed of the ups and downs of his negotiations and truces with Mercoeur.[18]

Henri IV's strategy for reasserting his authority in Poitiers fit well with his general pattern of showing leniency to his former enemies and relying on individuals who could preserve order in precarious times.[19] In Poitiers, these approaches were inseparable, since the very leaders to whom the king turned to maintain the city in his obedience were precisely those who had presided under the League. All échevins and bourgeois who had been elected to the hôtel de ville during the League were permitted to remain.[20] Louis de Sainte-Marthe had been appointed lieutenant général of the sénéchaussée by the duc de Mayenne in 1593. On 16 June 1594, Henri IV confirmed this appointment, divesting his own appointee.[21] Saint-Belin also found it in his interest to exchange his support for the League for loyalty to the king, expressed in a steady stream of obsequious letters to the sovereign. In return, Henri IV sent him commissions to execute and

[14] ADV G1534, account of Pierre des Fontaines, 1595; Thibaudeau, *Abrégé de l'histoire du Poitou,* 5:196–98 (Articles V–VI).

[15] BNF MS Fr 23194, 247r–248r, 301r.

[16] BNF MS Fr 23194, 306r.

[17] Berger de Xivrey, ed., *Recueil des lettres,* 4:233–34.

[18] ACP Reg. 55bis, 5 (2 July 1595); Berger de Xivrey, ed., *Recueil des lettres,* 4:383–84.

[19] Greengrass, *France in the Age of Henri IV,* 59; Wolfe, *Conversion of Henri IV,* 163–64, 177–80; Finley-Crosswhite, *Henry IV and the Towns.*

[20] Thibaudeau, *Abrégé de l'histoire du Poitou,* 5:198–99 (Article VIII).

[21] BNF MS Fr 18159, 223v–224r, arrêt of the Conseil d'État, 5 July 1594; Brilhac, 25.

added the abbey of Saint-Savin to his large collection of ecclesiastical properties.[22]

The king's largest and most shrewd act of reconciliation, however, was reserved for Charles de Lorraine, duc d'Elbeuf. Thanks to a sizable cash gift from the crown, the nobleman consented to make the transition from Poitiers's last League governor to the king's best agent for preserving peace in the provincial capital.[23] On 21 July 1595, Henri IV confirmed the relationship by granting Elbeuf the position of governor and lieutenant général for the king in Poitiers, and on 2 September, he made his official entry as governor of the city.[24] This choice was significant. It deeply upset the sieur de Malicorne, governor of Poitou, who resented that his years of loyal service to Henri IV and his predecessors should be so poorly rewarded.[25] The choice also appears to have been necessary. The unanimous praise of Elbeuf's actions that Poitiers's inhabitants forwarded to the king indicates their strong preference for the former Leaguer's leadership, as does the decision of the hôtel de ville to mount a careful guard against troops led by the sieur de Lavardin, Malicorne's nephew.[26] When the prince de Condé passed through Poitiers in October 1595, Malicorne and his troops had to wait to escort the prince to Châtellerault from a point conspicuously distant from the town walls.[27]

Not only did Henri IV look to former Leaguers to maintain royal authority in Poitiers, but he also gave them considerable latitude to remain in his good graces. The king was fully aware of the tensions and divisions that continued to fester in the provincial capital. For this reason he enjoined the inhabitants to reconcile themselves with each other, since, he believed, God's benediction was sure to follow such union.[28] The king was also informed of the dubious loyalties of the very men whom he had charged to impose order and to encourage peace in Poitiers. Yet so long as their ambiguous intentions did not materialize into manifest disloyalty, the king declared himself willing to discount rumors and to found his good opinion on their notable actions. In December 1594, therefore, Henri IV calmed Elbeuf's fears about reports reaching the royal camp at Amiens concerning the nobleman's intentions and told him to convey similar reassurances to the city of Poitiers. In March 1595, the king similarly wrote to the mayor, to express his ap-

[22] BNF MS Fr 23194, 275r, 301r.

[23] Poitiers's reduction was very expensive, costing 209,833 écus "A M. d'Elbeuf et autres, pour Poictiers," when Paris and Brisson combined cost only slightly more than double this sum, and Troyes's obedience rated at only 35,000 écus. See the figures provided by Claude Groulart: "Mémoires de Messire Claude Groulart, Premier Président de Normandie, ou Voyages par lui faicts en cour," in *Nouvelle collection des mémoires pour servir à l'histoire de France, depuis le XIIIe siècle jusqu'à la fin du XVIIIe*, ed. Michaud and Poujoulat, 1st ser. (Paris, 1838), 11:569.

[24] ACP Reg. 55bis, 42 (6 Sept. 1595); Brilhac, 26–27.

[25] Berger de Xivrey, ed., *Recueil des lettres*, 4:233–34; ACP Reg. 55bis, 17 (7 Aug. 1595).

[26] ACP Reg. 55bis, 17. Lavardin's troops may have also formed the focus of complaint a few weeks earlier. Reg. 55bis, 7 (17 July 1595).

[27] ACP Reg. 55bis, 62–63 (29 Oct. 1595).

[28] Berger de Xivrey, ed., *Recueil des lettres*, 4:209.

proval that Elbeuf had commissioned him as one of the six militia captains and to assure him that he had never doubted Roatin's fidelity, despite what he had learned from some letters that had been intercepted![29] Clearly, in these first years of reconciliation between the king and the former League city, Henri IV was willing to overlook a considerable amount of ambivalence, so long as urban leaders maintained order and assured the city's practical obedience in the form of military security. This tendency to look to the practical implications of his subjects' actions would continue to guide Henri IV's relations with Poitiers. Yet as the monarch became more secure of his kingdom, he developed a more imposing and interventionist style of rule, which changed the terms of the relationship between king and city.

A New Royal Style

On the evening of 28 July 1606, word reached Poitiers that a troop of five hundred to six hundred mounted men were heading toward the city's Pont-à-Joubert gate. In the general alarm that followed, the canons of St. Hilaire-le-Grand rang the tocsin in their bourg, without consulting the mayor, captain of the city.[30] The council decided to begin a judicial inquiry into the event and to send the resulting information to Maximilien de Béthune, duc de Sully, governor of Poitou since December 1603.[31] Their findings clearly provoked royal anger. Facing imprisonment, the *doyen* and sénéchal of St. Hilaire hurried to court, where they implored the king's mercy and vowed never to fall into a similar offense. Their contrition had the desired effect. The king received them back into his good graces and instructed the corps de ville to welcome them back in the spirit of civic harmony; Sully advised that punishments should be limited to short sentences of banishment for some of the culprits who were least socially prominent.[32] This obscure incident typifies many of the aspects of Henri IV's style of rule. Faced with the possibility of disorder, the crown reacted decisively in directing local elites; it took an active role in overseeing punishment for disturbers of the civic peace and in preventing any future unrest. Royal representatives dished out threats of dire consequences for disobedience as promptly as the king rewarded contrite journeys to court with his magnanimous forgiveness. As a result, the culprits' brush with royal authority acted as powerfully as any limitation of privileges to make them remember their duty in the future. In this way, the crown sought to manage the local scene with an attention at once more systematic and more personal than Poitiers had previously faced.

[29] Berger de Xivrey, ed., *Recueil des lettres*, 4:279, 318.
[30] ACP Reg. 62, 11–12 (29 July 1606).
[31] ACP Reg. 62, 14 (14 Aug. 1606); 19 (16 Sept. 1606); Henri Ouvré, *Essai sur l'histoire de Poitiers depuis la fin de la ligue jusqu'à la prise de La Rochelle (1595–1628)* (Poitiers, 1856), 26.
[32] ACP Casier 8, C42; Reg. 62, 24–30 (10 Oct. 1606).

Poitiers had occasion to experience the full brunt of Henri IV's attention at least twice in the first decade of the seventeenth century. In May 1601, the city was on the verge of a fiscal revolt against the unpopular *pancarte,* or *sol pour livre* tax on merchandise sold in Poitiers, and only the threats of military intervention and loss of important privileges induced the corps de ville and presidial judges to drop their temporizations with the royal commissioner and to lend their weight to his efforts to carry out the king's will.[33] In 1609, Henri IV was informed of irregularities in Poitiers's municipal elections and militia appointments. After deputies were summoned to court to explain, the royal council issued an arrêt ruling on the procedures to be observed in future. Members of the Cent were unhappy about several of the new provisions, but the hôtel de ville heard from all sides that it was lucky to have escaped with such limited alterations to its customs. Well-known to contemporaries, these incidents have also been cited by more modern historians as characteristic of Henri IV's attitude toward the towns, whether as examples of the king's innovatory policies or as evidence of his more traditional approaches to urban problems.[34] In fact, these two incidents show that neither interpretation adequately accounts for the king's relationship with the capital of Poitou. Although the royal hand was considerably lighter in correcting local abuses than theories of his absolutist intentions would predict, the king's readiness to intervene both dramatically and consistently in local affairs helped to change the terms with which the city's elites approached the crown.

Henri IV no doubt learned of Poitiers's resistance to the pancarte through the frustrated and self-justifying series of letters that Pierre d'Amours, the *conseiller du roi* commissioned to publish the tax, sent to Chancellor Bellièvre and Secretary of State Villeroy to report on his lack of progress.[35] Having arrived in Poitiers on the evening of 29 April 1601, d'Amours quickly became aware of popular opposition to his commission.[36] The inhabitants feared that he intended to establish the gabelle, the salt tax from which Poitiers had successfully negotiated exemption for the province in 1548, and with tempers rising, they were soon confronting the commissioner with

---

[33] On the pancarte, see Finley-Croswhite, *Henry IV and the Towns,* 139–42; Greengrass, *France in the Age of Henri IV,* 95.

[34] In 1617, Jean Chenu made reference to the arrêt in his discussion of municipal elections and used it as a source to discuss Poitiers's particular privileges in his *Recveil des antiqvites,* 128, 481–93. In July 1609, Pierre de l'Estoile reported receiving a pamphlet hot from Poitiers concerning the 1609 mayoral election: Pierre de l'Estoile, *Journal de l'Estoile pour le règne de Henri IV, 1601–1609* ([Paris], 1958), 486. For modern accounts, see Ouvré, *Essai sur l'histoire de Poitiers,* 12–19; Finley-Croswhite, *Henry IV and the Towns,* 143–48.

[35] These letters are all recorded in BNF MS Fr 15899. Since Annette Finley-Croswhite has already made full use of these letters to give a detailed narrative of the events in Poitiers (*Henry IV and the Towns,* 143–46), I shall refrain from providing the full account again here but shall limit myself to the essential for the analysis.

[36] ACP Reg. 59, 96 (30 Apr. 1601).

threats and insults.[37] Popular hostilities quickly became dangerous in a way typical of fiscal uprisings.[38] On 15 May, d'Amours received word that two hundred to three hundred people were stationed to ambush him on his way to a meeting at the hôtel de ville, and he was convinced that had the mayor not forborne to send for him as promised, he would have "met his fate" (*Jeusse couru fortune*).[39] The following day, a man of low condition accosted him near the Augustinian convent and announced that he should be thrown in the river. The commissioner withdrew safely from this confrontation thanks to the protection of the mayor, only to find his lodgings besieged by a band of men and women carrying stones and knives later that afternoon. Had it not been for the actions of Scévole de Sainte-Marthe, who went downstairs to calm the crowd, and of the mayor, who arrived shortly afterward to disperse the group, d'Amours was sure his life would have been forfeit.[40]

In addition to popular hostilities, d'Amours complained about the temporizations of the local magistrates, if not their downright collusion with the people. When he represented his commission to the officials of the presidial court, they refused to lend him any support for fear of losing the goodwill of the inhabitants and went so far as to challenge its validity. He could not find a single sergeant to help him complete his publications.[41] An assembly at the palais achieved nothing, and the corps de ville refused to attend on the grounds that any communications should be imparted to it at the hôtel de ville.[42] Yet by 18 May, the commissioner had asked four times without success that a Mois be assembled to hear him.[43] Even the bishop had promptly left town when he heard of d'Amours's arrival.[44] Whether Poitiers's governors feared to lose control of a dangerous situation or tacitly supported the inhabitants' opposition, they certainly evaded the royal official's request to help him carry out the king's will in their city.

Not only did d'Amours blame his difficulties on the complacency and spinelessness of the local magistrates, but he also opined that their failure in obedience sprang implicitly from the composition of Poitiers's governing bodies. Because d'Amours assumed that when magistrates recognized their authority and were willing to use it, the people remained quiescent, he in-

---

[37] Gabelle: BNF MS Fr 15899, 868r (letter dated 14 May 1601). Threats and insults: BNF MS Fr 15899, 298r (letter dated 18 May 1601); 866r (letter dated 14 May 1601).

[38] Beik, *Urban Protest*; Yves-Marie Bercé, *Histoire des Croquants: étude des soulèvements populaires au XVIIe siècle dans le sud-ouest de la France*, 2 vols. (Paris, 1974), pt. 2, chap. 2, esp. 1:294–95, 300–2, 317–20, 324–25; Boris Porchnev, *Les soulèvements populaires en France de 1623 à 1648* (Paris, 1963), 132–260.

[39] BNF MS Fr 15899, 869r (letter dated 14 May 1601).

[40] BNF MS Fr 15899, 298r (letter dated 18 May 1601).

[41] BNF MS Fr 15899, 866r (letter dated 14 May 1601); 298v (letter dated 18 May 1601).

[42] BNF MS Fr 15899, 866r, 868r (letters dated 14 May 1601); ACP Reg. 59, 98–102 (3–7 May 1601).

[43] BNF MS Fr 15899, 298v (letter dated 18 May 1601); 866r (letter dated 14 May 1601); ACP Reg. 59, 102–3 (9 May 1601); 105 (15 May 1601).

[44] BNF MS Fr 15899, 868r (letter dated 14 May 1601).

sisted that the local officials' fears, inattention to their duty, and even contempt for his endeavors led to the indignities that he, and by extension royal authority, had suffered in the city.[45] Without serious redress, therefore, the king's authority would continue to be recognized "only verbally, by pretty words" and not in deed.[46] From the commissioner's point of view, Poitiers's civic institutions were both too popular and too exclusive. He was convinced that men of low condition, who had gained access to the corps de ville during the League era, were now encouraging the people to oppose him, and that factional politics prevented loyal servants of the king, such as the current mayor, from exercising the authority they ought.[47] His proposed solution would contract urban government to a limited group of reliable elites, while permitting offices to circulate among members of the trusted circle:

> One could make a selection of persons to exercise judicial office who will have the courage to maintain the authority of the king and make the people obedient to it. It is [also] necessary to alter the council and corps de ville, reducing it into the form of the *pairie*; otherwise the king will never be obeyed. In so doing, you will please the men of honor in the city, for giving them hope to accede to office, and you will avoid the monopolies and scheming of those who care for nothing but the good will and favor of the people.

If the crown wished to go further and to revoke Poitiers's privileges, d'Amours could see merit in this approach. Nothing would rouse city councillors to their duty more effectively, and the privileges could be restored later as a reward for good behavior.[48] These suggestions were hardly original, since Henri IV had carried out similar measures in cities such as Lyon, Abbeville, and Amiens.[49] Yet since such attitudes toward local elites and dire predictions that "as long as the corps de ville retains its present composition, the king will never be served, obeyed, nor have his necessities met" resonated with existing royal assumptions about urban government, they were sure to provoke a strong reaction in court.[50]

Henri IV's response to Poitiers's resistance admirably illustrates the style of his interactions with urban centers. Furious at the opposition and concerned that it would set a bad example for other cities, the king first desired to intervene personally and immediately; he was determined to gain the upper hand by any means necessary and planned to confront the city in person at the head of his troops.[51] Yet the crown soon came to consider the shock of royal forces alone as an effective first strike. The king agreed to send the

[45] BNF MS Fr 15899, 296r (letter dated 8 June 1601); 306r (letter dated 28 June 1601).
[46] BNF MS Fr 15899, 866v (letter dated 14 May 1601).
[47] BNF MS Fr 15899, 869r (letter dated 16 May 1601); 866r (letter dated 14 May 1601).
[48] BNF MS Fr 15899, 296r (letter dated 8 June 1601).
[49] Barbier, *Recueil des privileges*, 49–53; Finley-Croswhite, *Henry IV and the Towns*, 79–86.
[50] BNF MS Fr 15899, 869r (letter dated 16 May 1601).
[51] Berger de Xivrey, ed., *Recueil des lettres*, 5:417–18.

duc d'Elbeuf, still governor of Poitiers, to confront the city, and the royal council concluded that the threat of garrisoning three companies of cavalry to ensure that justice was maintained would be held in reserve pending Elbeuf's success. Although several councillors recommended depriving Poitiers of its privileges immediately as a fit punishment for a city full of seditious mutineers, the king restrained himself to angry denunciations of Poitiers's disloyal magistrates while awaiting the results that the city's governor could achieve.[52] These provisions produced an immediate response. No sooner had Poitiers received the royal council's ruling than the hôtel de ville and presidial court each dispatched two deputies to Châtellerault, to plead with d'Amours to return to Poitiers and to promise their full cooperation.[53] When the commissioner reentered the city shortly afterward in the company of the duc d'Elbeuf, he was pleased to find the people disposed to humility and submission and the municipal and judicial officials abject in their assurances of obedience and profuse in their offers of assistance.[54]

Yet if the purport of d'Amours's letters now shifted from angry denunciations of urban leaders to sympathetic advocacy of their difficulties in raising large sums in a poor city, these messages of obedience and contrition did not entirely mollify the king. Having issued royal letters stating that the hôtel de ville was not to elect a new mayor until receiving further instructions, Henri IV continued to maintain this prohibition, despite d'Amours's recommendation to the contrary because of the distress this caused the notable citizens.[55] The king also insisted that the corps de ville supplement its written protestations of obedience and repentance with deputies' verbal assurances of submission and regret in court.[56] The prospect of apologizing to the king in person clearly filled Poitiers's best representatives with anxiety, since of all of the prospective deputies selected by the Mois and confirmed by d'Amours and Elbeuf, only one agreed without special persuasion to make the trip.[57] In any event, their fears were for naught. Henri IV assured them that as long as Poitiers's inhabitants showed him their love and fidelity, he would treat

[52] Berger de Xivrey, ed., *Recueil des lettres*, 5:418, 421–23; Groulart, "Memoires," 586. Although Finley-Croswhite maintains that Henri IV revoked Poitiers's privileges (144), Groulart's account of the discussion in the royal council indicates that he did not.

[53] ACP Reg. 59, 108 (8 June 1601); BNF MS Fr 15899, 296r (letter dated 8 June 1601); 296v (letter dated 10 June 1601).

[54] BNF MS Fr 15899, 293r (letter dated 13 June 1601).

[55] ACP Reg. 59, 115 (25 June 1601); 118–19 (29 June 1601); BNF MS Fr 15899, 293r (letter dated 13 June 1601); 306r (letter dated 28 June 1601). The Mois voted to honor the king's orders and asked Scévole de Sainte-Marthe, as senior échevin, to carry out the duties normally performed by the mayor. Reg. 59, 118–19 (29 June 1601); 124–25 (13 July 1601). I have found no evidence that Henri IV appointed him mayor, pace Finley-Croswhite, *Henry IV and the Towns*, 145.

[56] The hôtel de ville first resolved to send deputies on d'Amours's suggestion on 12 June, and on 2 July 1601, it was reported that d'Amours and Elbeuf had received royal letters ordering Poitiers to send its deputies to court. ACP Reg. 59, 110–11, 120.

[57] ACP Reg. 59, 120–23 (3 and 9 July 1601); Reg. 60, 1–2 (mid-July 1601). François Lucas consented to go only if he were offered a place of échevin. See Reg. 63, 195–98 (2 Apr. 1608).

them as a good king and solicitous father. So little did he wish to destroy their privileges, granted and confirmed by his predecessors, that he instructed them to punish anyone spreading rumors that he sought to reinstitute the gabelle or to impose citadels on his people.[58] The king's insistence on these punitive measures may have arisen from the city's continuing attempts to avoid the full effects of the institution of the pancarte. Even after Poitiers's leading officials agreed to aid d'Amours in executing his commission, debate continued over whether the city should offer the king a lump sum in exchange for the tax, give its *ferme* to the highest bidder, or arrange for its collection internally.[59] This residual recalcitrance may explain why, even after welcoming Poitiers's deputies so magnanimously, Henri IV waited until his personal visit to the provincial capital in May 1602 to allow mayoral elections to proceed once more in their traditional form.[60]

Poitiers's experiences during the pancarte incident help to reveal the pattern of Henri IV's interactions with the cities. Because, as Annette Finely-Croswhite has shown, the first Bourbon king depended heavily on urban elites to keep order, he reacted forcefully and with anger against any failures to enforce obedience or to uphold unity. In 1601, Poitiers's civic governors revealed themselves wanting and risked bringing down on themselves not only a range of institutional reprisals, but also the armed intervention of the king in person. Although these threats immediately convinced municipal officials of the danger of their position, they were still obliged to proffer assurances of respectful obedience personally in court to allay royal suspicions and to regain his goodwill. Such interactions between sovereign and city stand in strong contrast to Henri III's relations with the capital of Poitou. Facing a loss of control of elite loyalties in 1588 and 1589, Henri III attempted to regain them through compromise and assurances of continuing favor. Even the royalist narrator of the League takeover in Poitiers implied that Henri III was too gentle in his approach and in his instructions to intermediaries and only tried to make use of his royal presence when it was too late.[61] Still, although Henri IV professed himself far more willing than his predecessor to use force, to deal out punishments, and to exhibit his anger in person, these demonstrations were designed to convince subjects that the consequences for disloyalty were so damaging that he could later count on displaying his generosity of spirit rather than his wrath. This is why, for all of the king's anger and for all of the suggestions that Poitiers's governing in-

[58] ACP Reg. 60, 15–17 (10 Sept. 1601).

[59] For these lengthy negotiations, see ACP Reg. 59, 111–17 (15–27 June 1601); 123–25 (13 July 1601); Reg. 60, 5 (2 Aug. 1601); 7–12 (13–20 Aug. 1601); 70–71 (18 Mar. 1602); BNF MS Fr 15899, 294r–v (letter dated 16 June 1601); 302r (letter dated 23 June); 307r (letter dated 8 July).

[60] Brilhac, 28–30; MMP MS 574, 42r–v. Both René de Brilhac and Jean Le Roy describe the king's entry into Poitiers and his lifting of the interdiction against electing a new mayor, but neither gives any hint of the cause of royal displeasure.

[61] BNF MS Fr 20157, 155v–156r, 159v–161v.

stitutions be reformed, the city ultimately lost none of its privileges and managed to fix the sol pour livre tax at a level that did not satisfy the crown.[62] These patterns of interaction, moreover, held in less urgent situations. In 1609, as in 1601, Henri IV revealed a tendency to intervene personally, to threaten strong consequences for disorder, but once satisfied of the city's loyalty, to institute only minimal change.

In January 1609, Henri IV wrote to the mayor, échevins, and inhabitants of Poitiers concerning possible disruptions of that year's mayoral election. Having been alerted that monopolies and cabals (*brigues*) were already under way—a serious matter since the election would not take place until late June—the king decided to resolve the situation himself. He therefore ordered the corps de ville to send two échevins to court, where the deputies would inform him of municipal electoral privileges and receive his resulting judgment.[63] After hearing the letters read aloud on 14 February, the Mois duly elected two representatives to go to court. One was Marc Jarno, the man who had led the deputation to court in 1601.[64] Although the municipal government had less cause to expect royal anger now than during the resistance to the pancarte, the king's intimation that electoral disputes threatened the repose of the city and the union of the inhabitants must have given warning that Henri IV was disposed to see local frictions as having important implications for the peace of the kingdom.[65] Elite factionalism could now be taken for disloyalty. Further, even though the king's letter promised that his decision would be to the city's advantage, any review of mayoral electoral privileges must have worried municipal officials; they were no doubt aware that Poitiers belonged to a tiny minority of major urban centers that did not have to submit mayoral candidates for the king's ultimate selection. They may also have known, as Robert Descimon has found, that he had been routinely choosing the prévôts des marchands of Paris for most of his reign.[66]

Indeed, the crown's temptation to alter Poitiers's electoral privileges must have been great. Irregularities had surfaced in several mayoral elections of recent years: in both 1600 and 1608, the Mois had found it necessary to cast ballots three times, since in each case extra, illegal ballots were discovered during the first two attempts. In 1608, there were even accusations that the

---

[62] For the king's comments that the sum was derisory, see AN E*3b, 167v (audience of the Conseil des finances, 27 Sept. 1601). The pancarte in Poitiers was fixed at five thousand livres in 1602. A copy of the letters of the Conseil d'État, dated 14 Aug. 1608, providing a final regulation for the city's accounts of its collection, is recorded in ACP Reg. 64, 128–29 (16 Feb. 1609).

[63] ACP Reg. 64, 123 (14 Feb. 1609). A printed copy of the letter may also be found in Berger de Xivrey, ed., *Recueil des lettres*, 7:671–72. Although the letter is dated 23 January in the register, Berger de Xivrey dates it to 13 January.

[64] ACP Reg. 64, 122–23.

[65] Berger de Xivrey, ed., *Recueil des lettres*, 7:671. Sully reiterated these concerns and emphasized the king's displeasure with the actions of the corps de ville in a letter dated 5 February 1609 that he wrote to accompany the king's. ACP Reg. 64, 123–25.

[66] Descimon, "Échevinage parisien," 130–31.

outgoing mayor had sequestered some of the ballots, thus allowing his preferred candidate to win.[67] Selections of new bourgeois and échevins had been
equally dubious. Since Poitiers's Edict of Reduction had provided that both
the politiques who had left the city during the League period and the Leaguers who had been elected to fill their places would retain their positions in
the corps de ville, it also stipulated that no new elections could take place on
the death of current members until the Cent had been reduced to its original
size.[68] Faced with this unwanted moratorium on elections, the hôtel de ville
fulfilled the letter, but certainly not the spirit, of the law. Bourgeois now resigned their offices to their sons, brothers, nephews, sons-in-law, and brothers-in-law in unprecedented numbers. Michel Ferrand, after obtaining his
place of bourgeois on the resignation of his father, even arranged that because of his business in Paris, the office be conferred on his brother, François,
instead.[69] On occasion, the hôtel de ville even violated the edict's provisions
outright. In November 1600, for example, the council decided that although
the Cent still contained more than one hundred members, three new bourgeois should be elected with the stipulation that each successful candidate
contribute two hundred écus to the municipal government's debts.[70] Even
elections of militia captains were subject to dispute. When the council
dunned Mayor Jean Martin to replace the recently deceased Jean Estourneau
as captain, a sergeant in the company opposed the election. The disagreement finally went to the royal council for adjudication, and as the municipal government attempted to resolve the opposition to the pancarte in July
1601, the duc d'Elbeuf finally appointed his own candidate to lead the company.[71] Such electoral tensions indicate that frictions were still pronounced
among Poitiers's elites with aspirations to municipal office and suggest that
Henri IV's concern for the city's stability was not misplaced. Reform would
not be remiss.

Despite such ample evidence of disorder, Poitiers emerged from the king's
inspection with almost all of its privileges intact. Thanks to the good offices
of Sully, governor of Poitou, who vouched for the city's fidelity and devotion
to its sovereign, Henri IV simply adjusted municipal procedures but left its
liberties alone. In a letter to the municipal officials and inhabitants, the king
explained:

> [A]nd even though the disorder that has occurred [in the election of your
> mayor] until now and the importance of this affair have given us much reason

---

[67] ACP Reg. 58, 88–91 (30 June 1600); Reg. 63, 247–52 (27 June 1608).

[68] Thibaudeau, *Abrégé de l'histoire du Poitou*, 5:198–99 (Article VIII).

[69] ACP Reg. 63, 123–31 (26–28 Nov. 1607).

[70] ACP Reg. 59, 49–50 (6 Nov. 1600). The three new bourgeois in fact agreed to contribute
only 150 écus each. Reg. 59, 51–52 (10 Nov. 1600).

[71] ACP Reg. 58, 29 (20 Sept. 1599); 31 (23 Sept. 1599); 45 (29 Nov. 1599); 69–70 (28 Feb.
1600); Reg. 59, 120 (2 July 1601).

to make greater changes, nevertheless, placing a more narrow observation of your duty after the consideration of your entreaties, we have simply aimed to remedy the confusion in your procedures and not to detract from your customs, although there are some that are quite extraordinary.[72]

Sully protested against any special merit in saving the city's privileges but confirmed its good luck in retaining them where others had seen them retrenched.[73]

The arrêt of the Conseil d'État was not quite as sparing of the prerogatives of the hôtel de ville as the king and the governor implied, but it did largely focus on preventing further electoral abuses. All elections were henceforth to proceed by ballot rather than by voice vote, as had frequently been municipal practice, and procedures for printing and casting ballots were elaborated. Soliciting votes through visits to prospective supporters was categorically forbidden, as was election of any new bourgeois until their number had been reduced to the requisite seventy-five. Henceforth, a bourgeois could resign his office only to a son, and only provided that the young man had reached twenty-five years of age. Apparently to ensure that the municipality's choice of mayor met with the king's approval, future mayors were enjoined to swear their oaths to the governor of the city or the province. Further, militia offices were simultaneously opened to rotation but limited to municipal elites; the four lay captains were now to be elected yearly, and eligible candidates were limited to échevins.[74] Revealingly, these provisions were not designed to invest municipal office with the permanence and proprietary rights of royal ones after the *paulette*. On the contrary, the crown seems to have been attempting to restore, as far as was possible in Poitiers, a freer circulation of offices among a trusted group of notables—a principle that Descimon identifies with an older, civic conception of government.[75]

As limited as these changes to Poitiers's municipal customs were, several met with discontent and were quickly modified. When the hôtel de ville received the arrêt on 18 April, the Mois made a great show of reading it, recording it, and executing it in every detail, yet attempts to repeal specific measures were quickly under way.[76] The article most potentially damaging to urban

[72] Letter of Henri IV dated 9 Apr. 1609, recorded in ACP Reg. 64, 151–52, and Berger de Xivrey, ed., *Recueil des lettres*, 7:694. I quote from the printed version.

[73] ACP Reg. 64, 152–53 (18 Apr. 1609). Sully's letter is dated 12 April 1609.

[74] For the text of the 9 April arrêt of the Conseil d'État, see ACP Reg. 64, 146–51; ACP Casier 4, B21 (a pamphlet copy dating from 1751); and BNF MS Clair. 361, 113r–114r. For discussion of how the provisions of the arrêt related to Poitiers's particular electoral practices, see my "Benefit of the Ballot?" Finley-Croswhite's contention that Henri IV "reduced the size of the town council in Poitiers from ninety-three to seventy-five" (*Henry IV and the Towns*, 148) is slightly misleading, since the king was only insisting that the group of bourgeois be returned through attrition to its normative number.

[75] Descimon, "Échevinage parisien," 120–21, 145.

[76] ACP Reg. 64, 142–56.

liberties, requiring the mayor to swear his oath of fealty to the governor of the city or the province, was simply ignored once the council felt that it had observed due diligence. After the mayoral election of 1609, the mayor-elect wrote to the duc de Roannais, now the city's governor, to ask him to attend the swearing-in. Yet the day before the ceremony, when it was apparent that neither governor would be present in the city, the council decided that the mayor would swear his oath in the accustomed manner to the lieutenant général instead.[77] On hearing the article providing that the lay militia captains were now to be elected annually, moreover, the captains and sergeant-major immediately protested the measure.[78] The council ruled that all documents relating to militia elections be turned over to the interested parties, and armed with these papers, the captains succeeded in obtaining an arrêt of the Conseil d'État overturning the previous stipulations.[79] The militia captains were once more permitted to hold their offices for life or until their demission, and both échevins and bourgeois were now eligible to hold them. To obtain this result, the existing captains had argued that the arrêt of 9 April unfairly introduced a distinction between lay captains, whose positions would be annual, and ecclesiastical ones, whose offices had not been altered. Further, they maintained that militia offices had never been subject to elections by the corps de ville, and to prove this point, they had all produced their commissions signed by governors from Boisseguin through Roannais. This contention was patently untrue. Militia offices had been subject to election, sometimes in the Mois and sometimes by the officers themselves.[80] Ironically, while this reasoning seems to have convinced the royal council, it also introduced the single most important limitation of Poitiers's privileges to result from the 1609 reforms. The corrective arrêt contented the militia captains, but it also ruled that in future, Sully, as governor of the province, would not only issue the captains' commissions, but would also select the new captains himself. Poitiers, therefore, had only itself to thank for the single provision that truly detracted from the city's established liberties.

If Poitiers escaped relatively unscathed from the crown's scrutiny, noble patrons admonished urban elites to take this experience as an important lesson. Sully, in informing the hôtel de ville of how fortunate it had been compared with other city governments, enjoined municipal officials to take the king's leniency to heart and to "redouble [their] devotions to his service," since, as he had earlier remarked, the king's "authority must always be the principal foundation of your prerogatives."[81] The sieur de la Clyelle, who

[77] ACP Reg. 64, 219–23 (5–13 July 1609).

[78] ACP Reg. 64, 144–46.

[79] ACP Reg. 64, 157–59 (27 Apr.–4 May 1609); 170–71 (27 May 1609). Copies of the arrêt, dated 16 May 1609 from Paris, may be found in Reg. 64, 175–79 (29 May 1609), and BNF MS Clair. 361, 133r–134v.

[80] For examples, see ACP Reg. 46, 386–89 (8 July 1587); Reg. 47, 305–6 (20 Jan. 1588); Reg. 51, 11–13 (17 July 1591); 152–54 (9 Mar. 1592).

[81] ACP Reg. 64, 152, 124.

had also intervened on the city's behalf at court, seconded Sully's admonitions. After acknowledging Poitiers's thanks, he remarked:

> And I will only tell you that you must henceforth make yourselves such watchful observers of the intentions of his Majesty . . . that no further subject for his displeasure nor complaint may arise from your actions, which must conform to his will. For otherwise, you must fear the entire abolition of your privileges, as the result of his indignation.[82]

Poitiers's leaders, therefore, were being instructed from many sides to learn from their mistake and to pay greater attention to satisfying the king, whose concerns for order now made even electoral campaigning a subject for royal obedience. That Henri IV required exceptional assurances of urban loyalties, though, was a lesson that Poitiers had already been at least partially successful in mastering.

Terms of Obedience

Under the reign of Henri IV the climate of royal relations with the cities underwent a noticeable shift. The crown made attempts to subject municipal governments to greater supervision and insisted that royal favors depend on justifiable grounds. As a result, Poitiers found that its royal grants were no longer renewed as automatically as before. When a royal gift of one hundred livres per year came up for renewal in 1608, Sully, as finance minister, refused to allow the verification of the letters of continuation until he had checked how the funds had been used in the past. Almost an entire year later, having examined the municipal account, the minister finally declared himself satisfied and raised his previous restriction on spending the money.[83] Urban elites, as we have seen, were expected to prove their loyalties through prompt attention to the king's will. Poitiers's hôtel de ville acceded to the requirement by taking even minute opportunities to record how punctiliously it had carried out royal orders. When Henri IV recommended to the corps de ville that it welcome and lodge a Spanish nobleman, the council not only recorded the text of the letters, but called a special meeting of the Mois to deliberate on the most honorable means of receiving the visitor.[84] Poitiers was equally eager to show compliance with a royal command banishing all gypsies from Poitou. The council concluded that the orders should be published aloud in the city, and the municipal secretary recorded both the royal order and Sully's introductory letter in the town council register.[85] It was rel-

[82] ACP Reg. 64, 153–54 (letter dated 12 Apr. 1609).
[83] ACP Reg. 63, 163 (18 Feb. 1608); Reg. 64, 105 (10 Jan. 1609).
[84] ACP Reg. 63, 243–46 (16–18 June 1608).
[85] ACP Reg. 63, 176–77 (10 Mar. 1608).

atively easy, of course, to make a show of obedience when the matter had virtually no effect on local interests.

Henri IV, however, was not satisfied with mere protestations of loyalty. Where his predecessors had credited recitations of historical relations of obedience and favor between corporate groups and the crown, the new Bourbon king insisted that these bodies' current actions prove their loyalty and justify his favor. His reprimand to the city of Bourges for its attempts to substitute assurances of fidelity for hard cash in 1600 was characteristic. "If the state of our affairs and the difficulties that weigh upon us could be cured by nice words and the thanks that you give for the results that you expect from them, in which resides your tranquility and the conservation of all of your means and domestic faculties in the future," he retorted,

> you would be perfectly right. But since [our affairs] require another remedy, we ask that you provide it, and cause us to be more pleased and satisfied than we are with your letters and offers, in hard silver and absolutely not in cloth or other merchandise. Believe that by the help that you give us on this occasion, we will judge the good will and affection you have to serve us.[86]

Not only were current professions of loyalty ineffectual in mitigating royal demands, but the king also professed great impatience with his subjects' attempts to cite historical acts of great fidelity in negotiating with him. When the Parlement of Bordeaux tried to use the fact that it had remained loyal to Henri IV throughout the troubles of the League period to allay his anger at its refusal to register the Edict of Nantes in 1599, its arguments were forcefully repulsed. Pointing out that the court had remained royalist only because the maréchal de Matignon had forced it to do so, the king warned the judges that although he had always recognized their infection, he now had the means to remedy the situation and to force those who were opposing his commands to repent.[87] Henri IV thus demolished the parlement's appeal to history by contrasting his former comparative weakness with his current menacing strength. This is not to say, however, that the king was ready to put the past entirely behind him. In his anger at Poitiers for resisting the publication of the pancarte, he compared the city's actions to Bordeaux's revolt against the gabelle in 1548 and Rouen's attack against Protestants in 1571. Further, remembering Poitiers's shocking refusal to admit Henri III in 1589, he justified his plans to exact a severe retribution for the city's current resistance as a God-given opportunity to punish its past faults along with its present disobedience.[88]

Poitiers, when negotiating with the crown, did not repeat the mistakes of Bourges or Bordeaux. Rather than emphasizing the city's historical relation

---

[86] Berger de Xivrey, ed., *Recueil des lettres*, 5:307–8 (letter dated 22 Sept. 1600).
[87] Berger de Xivrey, ed., *Recueil des lettres*, 5:180–81 (Response du Roy, 3 Nov. 1599).
[88] Berger de Xivrey, ed., *Recueil des lettres*, 5:418, 422.

of fidelity and service with the kings of France, which recent events rendered difficult anyway, municipal officials learned a new language of obedience that elaborated the city's current utility and abilities to serve the crown. Worried that the king's intent to raise the duchy of Thouars to a peerage in 1595 would upset the jurisdiction of Poitiers's sénéchaussée, the hôtel de ville drafted a brief arguing that, as the capital of the province, the city was the surest means to preserve the king's authority and to assure the peace and repose of the region. If the authors could not help marshaling history to make their point, they referred only to the long period during which the region had been subject to the same royal law and custom and neglected to recite the special authority and privileges of Poitiers's sénéchaussée and the signal acts of loyalty that lay behind them.[89] This change of approach was equally apparent when the city's deputies made their representations before the conseil des finances in an attempt to dispel the unpleasant consequences of the pancarte incident in September 1601. Assuring the council that the hôtel de ville had not elected a new mayor since the king's prohibition, the deputies expressed concern that the current interdiction threatened to damage the city's privileges. Here, they certainly pointed out that the privileges in question had been granted by preceding monarchs more than three hundred years before in recognition for the humble services of their forefathers. This historical relationship, however, was not expected to be convincing in and of itself. Rather than evoking Poitiers's signal acts of loyalty and reciting a litany of privileges granted by grateful kings, the deputies focused on the privileges' utility. Previous monarchs, they explained, had recognized that Poitiers was so lacking in wealth and the means to achieve it that they had granted these privileges as a means of support. "Without them," they concluded, the city "would have been immediately abandoned and would not have possessed any means to subsist nor to render itself useful to the state and service of His Majesty."[90] The king, therefore, should not maintain Poitiers's privileges because, or only because, they represented centuries of good relations between city and sovereign, but rather because they allowed Poitiers to be useful to the crown.

Such changes may seem subtle, but they represent a noticeable evolution in the understanding of the relationship between the cities and the king. The arguments of Poitiers's deputies constituted a step toward a view of privileges that, as Gail Bossenga has explained, based them on current utility and therefore subjected them to the changeable pleasure of the monarch.[91] Their representations downplayed, on the other hand, the character of privileges as constituting a historical pact between cities and the crown, in which notable

[89] ACP Reg. 55bis, 75–76 (23 Nov. 1595). Despite Poitiers's opposition, the Parlement of Paris ruled that the duchy of Thouars would be raised to a peerage and the duc de la Trémoille would be received to swear the oath of a duke and peer of France. ACP Casier 8, C41 (decisions of the Parlement of Paris, 1 and 4 Dec. 1599).

[90] AN E*3b (audience of the Conseil des finances, 27 Sept. 1601).

[91] Gail Bossenga, *The Politics of Privilege: Old Regime and Revolution in Lille* (Cambridge, U.K., 1991), 44–45.

actions in the past should override any royal desires to change them without significant cause. When Étienne Pasquier appeared before the Parlement of Paris in February 1576 to defend the city of Angoulême from charges of treason, for example, he took just this position in his oral argument. Angoulême had angered the crown by closing its gates against the duc de Montpensier and refusing to be granted to the duc d'Anjou at the end of the fifth religious war. Pasquier, however, reminded the Parlement that the city's privileges specified that it could not be alienated to a lesser power without its consent. He pointed out that these privileges had been granted "not through a free gift, if I should so express it, but at the cost of our blood and our lives," alluding to Angoulême's refusal to bow to the Black Prince after the treaty of Brétigny (1360). Privileges, when the result of special historical circumstances, therefore possessed a moral weight that could not be sloughed off for royal convenience, just as the royal domain should not be alienated to meet fiscal difficulties.[92] In the sixteenth century, history provided one of the key languages through which cities and other corporate bodies interacted with the crown, in order to retain current advantages and to negotiate new ones. After the Wars of Religion, and especially after the Catholic League period, however, the bright memory of the loyalties of the Hundred Years' War were somewhat tarnished, and cities duly shifted the terms of their main arguments to prove their mettle to the king. As Poitiers's experiences under Henri IV show, this newer language could work well in retaining privileges and maintaining the authority of elites within the urban community. At the same time, though, by reducing the moral weight of historical tradition, this approach inevitably rendered urban privileges less stable and reduced the effectiveness of each community's claims for special consideration.

Conclusions: Poitiers and the French Crown

Henri IV's assassination does not seem to have filled Poitiers with intense regret. In his eulogy delivered in the cathedral St. Pierre on 21 June 1610, the abbot of Noaillé paid virtually no attention to the unique circumstances of the reign and declined to discuss at any length the particular virtues of the departed king. Instead, the cleric stuck to generalities and even praised Henri IV for his ardent religious faith and submission to the Pope![93] It is hard to imagine that such a speech would have satisfied anyone who was genuinely mourning the king's passing.[94] Such lack of enthusiasm stands in stark con-

---

[92] Pasquier, *Oeuvres*, 2:139–54; quotation, 150.

[93] *Oraison fvnebre de tres-chrestien, tres clement, et tres-debonnaire prince, Henry IIII. roy de France & de Nauarre. Prononcée le iour de son seruice en l'Eglise Cathedrale de Poictiers, le 21. Iuin 1610. . . . Iouxte la copie imprimee à Poictiers par Anthoine Mesnier* (Paris, 1610).

[94] René de Brilhac noted that on receiving news of the king's death, the clergy, judicial officials, and corps de ville of Poitiers immediately swore obedience to Louis XIII but nowhere recorded any expression of regret for Henri IV. Brilhac, 33.

trast with the shock that greeted the sudden death of Charles VIII in 1498, when someone recorded in the current book of statutes of the hôtel de ville that the people were "deeply angered and grieved" at the death of a king who had campaigned actively in Guyenne and granted Poitiers important privileges.[95] Henri IV thus had good reason to doubt the goodwill of the capital of Poitou, for despite local assurances of obedience and comparisons between the first Bourbon king and the Emperor Constantine, the religious tensions of the League period likely continued to fester among urban elites, who did what they could to render the Edict of Nantes inoperative in their city.[96] Poitiers's relationship with the crown was therefore far from consistent; it rather adapted to each side's evolving expectations for the other.

Despite the variations in royal approaches to the cities in the sixteenth century and the changing circumstances rendering communities more or less responsive to individual kings, the relationship between the French crown and urban elites was vital for the interests of both. Although the French kings from François I to Henri IV never developed a consistent policy toward the cities of their realm, they all acknowledged the role that urban centers played in maintaining order, meting out justice, lending financial support, and preserving military security. The means by which the monarchs sought to assure these objectives certainly varied. François I, who tended to work with urban governing bodies as corporate groups, assigned a range of municipal accountants and controllers to assure that urban elites were funneling resources into military and police measures, and not enriching themselves by siphoning off royal funds.[97] Henri IV took a different approach to urban supervision by establishing special relationships with individual elites, whom he could then call on to govern the local community in a way sanctioned by the crown. Both therefore worked within political hierarchies already established in the urban sphere to assure that cities fulfilled their desired roles within the wider political order. Henri II and Charles IX, by contrast, experimented with policies that could have had significant effects on local decision making. By decreeing that men of the law and royal officials should not sit on city councils, Henri II emphasized the fiscal responsibilities of urban governments over their judicial functions and sought to alter the patterns of political authority and prestige within the cities. Charles IX, by giving merchants, ordinary bourgeois, and lesser urban notables authority over judicial matters and police decisions, also intended to readjust the balance of civic responsibilities for keeping order without redefining its essential characteristics.[98]

[95] ACP Casier 42, Reg. 11, A [front endpaper]. Charles VIII's death was recorded opposite the accounts of his royal entry into Poitiers in 1483, at which he acceded to requests to augment Poitiers's privileges, and his martial exploits in Guyenne and Brittany (1r–v).

[96] *Oraison fvnebre*, 12; ACP Reg. 58, 21–26 (26–29 Aug. 1599).

[97] Edict dated Mar. 1515 from Paris, Isambert, 12:26–29; edict dated 30 June 1517 from Montreuil, Isambert, 12:119–37. Cities frequently reacted by repurchasing these royal offices.

[98] Edict dated Nov. 1563 from Paris, creating the jurisdiction of the *juges consuls* in Paris;

Yet despite differences, the French kings always recognized the importance of existing urban institutions. This is why François I and Henri IV, who each demanded much of urban elites but sought to achieve their goals in different ways, expressed remarkably similar frustrations with what they saw as the failure of civic bodies to perform their functions adequately. Where Henri IV denounced corrupt electoral practices in the city of Troyes for creating disorder and resulting in "the little care of those who have been admitted for the last few years to the positions of mayor and other public [offices] of this city, neglecting the good of the people in the administration of communal affairs of the said city, [and] regarding nothing beyond their private interests,"[99] François I equally blamed such practices for the graft of urban officials eager to sidetrack royal funds for their own purposes. "We are duly alerted and well informed," ran the preamble to the edict of March 1515 creating controllers to oversee city governments' use of royal grants,

> that the mayors, échevins, and other officials of the said towns, cities, and fortresses are selected by means of cabals and intrigues, [and] not for the zeal that they should have for us or for the common good, but for their individual profit and great gains [*acqets*] that they know to exist from the said city offices.[100]

If both François I and Henri IV were especially critical of city governments and the self-interested elites who composed them, this displeasure arose from their very reliance on such groups to respond to royal objectives and to assure peace, order, and productivity within their local communities.

For municipal elites, their city's relationship with the crown was equally important, since royal authority guaranteed their own status within urban society. City councillors did not forget that royal privileges underwrote municipal authority. Explicit theories of urban government were rare in the sixteenth century, but each attempt to define its nature viewed civic political bodies as mediating a relationship between the crown and the urban community. In Poitiers, members of the corps de ville went particularly far in associating their rights to govern with monarchical rule, since they defined their authority over the urban population as seigneurial.[101] That Poitiers, a city with strong ultra-Catholic sentiment, waited until the death of Henri III definitively to espouse the Catholic League testifies to the overwhelming benefits that elites enjoyed in such justifications for the political order. Despite religious upheaval, distrust of the king, and intense factional disputes, many

---

Ordinance of Moulins, dated Feb. 1566, article 72, providing that each parish or quartier elect one or two bourgeois to rule on police matters up to 60 sous; edict dated Jan. 1572 from Amboise, creating police assemblies in every city with a royal court, Isambert, 14 (1):153–58, 208–9, 241–45. See also Stocker, "Urban Police," 2–6.

[99] Berger de Xivrey, ed., *Recueil des lettres*, 8:767.

[100] Isambert, 12:27.

[101] See chapter 1.

members of the hôtel de ville joined other royal officials and notables in attempting to retain intact the structures of authority within Poitiers and between the city and the crown. This is not to say, of course, that the variations in royal approaches to city governance had no effect in Poitiers. On the contrary, François I's enthusiasm for improving projects encouraged a group of échevins and bourgeois to take on the burden of rendering the Clain River navigable and implicitly to augment the hôtel de ville's rights of police within Poitiers. Conversely, Henri II's edict of October 1547 threatened seriously to disrupt the patterns of political authority within municipal government. Ultimately, the degree to which municipal elites and the French kings concurred in their approach to urban government and the extent to which they shared assumptions about how to mediate their own relations helped to determine how successful local notables could be in imposing and carrying out their own views of civic order.

Yet as important as Poitiers's relationship with the French crown was to both sides and as much as municipal elites wished to view themselves as able to command the urban population, civic political culture in the sixteenth century was far more inclusive than either crown or corps de ville would have liked to admit. Because of Poitiers's practices of lifelong office and co-optive electoral procedures, access to the hôtel de ville was very limited. Yet the nature of civic government admitted possibilities for inclusion, if not of personnel, then at least of the principle that a range of interests had to be considered. Practically, the process of making and implementing decisions that were to affect the entire community dictated that if opposition to the corps de ville's assessment of the "common good" was too pronounced, the municipal government would be forced to reconsider its position. If lesser notables found themselves shut out of holding coveted places as échevins and bourgeois, moreover, their participation in numerous bodies from the militia to the poor-relief regime was essential in maintaining a shared definition of civic order. That their cooperation was far more common than their resistance is due to the fact that all levels of urban society were familiar with, and placed value in, a shared definition of Poitiers's civic identity. Because understandings of Poitiers's unique character incorporated the city's historical tradition of loyalty to the French crown with a strong religious, then specifically Catholic, identity, a broad spectrum of inhabitants could gain access to a language specifically describing the value of their city, the capital of Poitou. Historical narratives and religious values, therefore, helped to form the basis of a shared urban political culture—one based not in rational discourse, but in a set of guiding assumptions about the specificity and importance of the city. This shared language certainly did not prevent strong social hostilities or political disagreements from breaking out, but it did provide a pole of local pride toward which even royal officials could express their allegiance and a model to which poor Poitevins could appeal when they felt their values and interests under attack.

How, then, did Henri IV's predilection for assurances of current obedience over expressions of past loyalties influence the terms of this civic identity? The king worked within the guidelines of Poitiers's past interactions with the monarchy by preserving virtually all of the city's privileges and upholding Catholicism in the urban context. The crown also did much to reinforce the authority of local elites by relying on them to govern the city and to maintain order in ways acceptable to itself. Yet by de-emphasizing the weight of historical relations between Poitiers and the French kings, Henri IV helped to sever a political language that had been an important element of mutual comprehension and negotiation between provincial city and crown from the terms of a local understanding of the meaning of the civic community. If the Catholic League did not represent a last attempt of French cities to regain a failing independence from the monarchy, then, the uprising and its aftermath did have an effect on the political culture of cities like Poitiers. As Henri IV's officials began to take a more active interest in assuring that urban elites performed their functions properly, Poitiers's historical tradition retained its local importance, but it lost some of its ability to define the value, significance, and therefore rights of the provincial capital in the wider arena of the French kingdom.

Conclusions: Cities and Sixteenth-Century Political Culture

Based on the example of Poitiers, this book has made a number of arguments about urban political culture. It has argued that municipal government, despite its exclusive membership and pretensions to authority, nevertheless allowed for a measure of consent and consensus within the urban political sphere. It has shown that this measure of consent in a hierarchical system was possible because inhabitants shared a common political vocabulary based on the historical identity of their city. It has revealed that the stylized rules of decision making and limitations on acceptable political language within city government normally acted to reinforce the points of view of dominant members, at the same time that they provided a space for negotiation when disagreement threatened to disrupt public order. It has revealed that the relationship between the city and the king was crucial to each, and that advantages accrued to both civic elites and the monarch in conceiving of and representing it in terms of cooperation rather than antagonism. It has argued, finally, that the potential benefits of this mutual support were so great that despite growing tensions over religious and financial policies, Poitiers held to its official stance of loyalty to the French crown until the death of Henri III and never questioned the structures of the monarchy even as the city denied Henri IV's right to be king. Yet to what extent can these findings be generalized? Poitiers was one French city among many. Its active courts and university, combined with its comparatively weak commercial life, allowed royal officials and legal personnel to gain an earlier and greater ascendancy than in many French cities, and its particular history since the reign of Charles VII encouraged elites to turn to royal favors rather than to seek their own fortunes independently through foreign trade. After all, Poitiers's near neighbor, La Rochelle, had early been singled out for its loyalty to the French crown only to become a target of royal hostility and isolation during the religious wars for its adoption of the Protestant faith.[102] Cities such as Bordeaux and Toulouse put much greater emphasis on an ancient tradition of municipal government extending back to the Roman world, and the customs of cities such as Nantes and Dijon allowed for greater political enfranchisement among householders below the level of the elites.[103] If in Poitiers the League period did not lead to radical alterations in the nature of political authority or the social order, in Paris the Seize and their supporters constituted a much greater threat to both.[104] How, then, is Poitiers's example important, and what does it teach us about early modern political culture more generally?

Poitiers's example shows that the phenomenon of growing state control and the inexorable rise of ideas and practices associated with it did not exclusively dominate early modern political life. Even in a city where royal officials had early gained the upper hand, particular values and customs of urban governance and a strong local identity thrived. It is understandable that the importance of cities and civic culture to the wider structures of the kingdom has been underestimated. Theorists of the French monarchy radically downplayed the importance of cities. Jean Bodin's republic was made up of households, not cities, and he viewed towns and communes as simply one kind of corporate group, with special rights of bourgeoisie to be sure, but inessential to the constitution of the commonwealth.[105] Exponents of a tempered, rather than an "absolute," monarchy did not locate the opposite poles of authority in cities, but in judicial institutions, religious values, or a more amorphous third estate.[106] Indeed, cities did not participate as such in national political institutions such as the Estates General, but rather drafted the complaints and helped to elect the deputies of the province in which they were situated. Very few people in the sixteenth century theorized about the role of cities or how they functioned as political communities. Claude de

---

[102] Jean Froissart, *Les chroniques de Sire Jean Froissart*, ed. J. A. C. Buchon, 3 vols. (Paris, 1840), 1:452; Robbins, *City on the Ocean Sea*.

[103] Lurbe, *Chronique bovrdeloise*; La Faille, *Annales*; Saupin, "Élections municipales à Nantes sous l'ancien régime, 1565–1789," *Annales de Bretagne et des pays de l'Ouest* 90, no. 3 (1983): 429–50; Holt, "Popular Political Culture."

[104] Descimon, *Qui étaient les Seize?*; Constant, *Ligue*.

[105] Bodin, *République*, 1:39–49, 111–39.

[106] Seyssel, *Monarchy of France*; François Hotman, *Francogallia*, ed. and trans. Ralph E. Giesey and J. H. M. Salmon (Cambridge, U.K., 1972); Julian H. Franklin, ed. and trans., *Constitutionalism and Resistance in the Sixteenth Century: Three Treatises by Hotman, Beza, and Mornay* (New York, 1969).

Rubys and Jean Chenu, who described the municipal customs of Lyon and placed the practices of Bourges within the context of a variety of other French cities, respectively, were unusual, and Charles Loyseau, who had something to say about urban officials and dignities, was highly critical of civic pretensions.[107] As cities and their customs did not strike contemporaries as phenomena needing explanation, so have modern historians tended to underestimate their importance, except as localities in which broader trends were carried out.

Yet the development of royal institutions did not lead inexorably to the decline of urban ones, because in the sixteenth century these two spheres of authority were still mutually reinforcing. Despite Bernard Chevalier's well-known thesis of the *trahison des bourgeois,* royal officials did not withdraw uniformly from civic life in the sixteenth century, but remained active in several public spheres simultaneously. The tendency to focus on Paris and other cities with sovereign courts to the relative exclusion of smaller provincial centers has obscured this fact, as have the visibility and prestige of parlementary families compared with the relative obscurity of middle and lesser officials.[108] Indeed, Chevalier's chief example to prove his point is Michel de Montaigne, hardly a man to stand as representative for an entire social group.[109] Within these urban enclaves, city councillors, whether jurists or commercial elites, ascribed to a set of practices and political values that contradicted those of royal office holding and ran counter to the hierarchies of civil society as these hierarchies were evolving in the sixteenth century. This is not to deny that local elites were looking for personal benefits in participating in urban government, that they routinely attempted to exclude others from similar advantages, and that they championed a particular and exclusive view of municipal authority based in a desire to uphold their own privileges and to assert power. At the same time, though, they could be the foremost advocates of local, civic traditions. The particular values of urban political life grew from the practices and identities that they helped to shape for their communities.

When we turn our attention from the inroads of royal institutions to the values of urban government in a city such as Poitiers, the ways in which French cities shared many of the characteristics of urban centers throughout late medieval and early modern Europe become more apparent. The seemingly firm dichotomy between cities existing under strong royal authority, such as in France and England, and those with a much larger complement of independence, such as on the Italian peninsula and in the Holy Roman Empire, must be mitigated when we privilege the processes and values of urban

---

[107] Rubys, *Privileges;* Chenu, *Recveil des antiqvites;* Loyseau, *Oevvres,* 817–27; *A Treatise of Orders and Plain Dignities,* ed. and trans. Howell A. Lloyd (Cambridge, U.K., 1994).

[108] For an attempt to reverse this trend, see Michel Cassan, ed., *Les officiers "moyens" à l'époque moderne: pouvoir, culture, identité* (Limoges, [1998]).

[109] Chevalier, *Bonnes villes,* 147.

government over the ability to conduct foreign affairs. We have seen that in Poitiers independence from the French crown never formed a specific goal, even when the city resolutely held out against Henri IV. "Turning Swiss" was not a temptation for Poitiers's governing elites, who knew that their authority was linked with that of the crown.[110] Yet even in a city dominated by men who made their livings from the royal courts and administration, ideas existed favoring the "equality" of the city's governors in decision making, the value of regular circulation of offices, the need for consultation with the different interests in the city defined by corporate status or profession, and above all, a political process that recognized that government could function only with the tacit support of the populace. Such ideas echoed the more developed political ideologies of the Renaissance republics of the Italian peninsula and the elaborately balanced constituencies of the German imperial cities, where the challenge to reconcile assumptions of inclusiveness with the realities of political exclusion was particularly pronounced.[111] Cities, therefore, were neither the guardians of democratic values nor the progenitors of community feeling, but they did offer particular solutions to the question of the nature of political authority and its relation to the social order.

To understand properly the nature of French early modern public life, therefore, we cannot neglect the political environments of cities such as Poitiers. They were of real concern to the French monarchs and factored into royal conceptions of right order for their kingdom, even if royal policies varied in assessing how best to achieve this goal. The crown alternated between privileging cities' commercial importance with an eye to their fiscal contributions and emphasizing their judicial role of enforcing order on the local level. The kings of France also evolved different strategies for assuring that their will was obeyed in the cities: François I's confidence in dealing with corporate groups eventually ceded to Henri IV's marked preference for communicating with a selected group of trustworthy individuals, and the personal styles of the monarchs influenced how urban elites could represent their cities' relationship to the crown. Yet despite these changes during the sixteenth century and beyond, cities remained an essential element in the political community, and the crown continued to see the importance of man-

[110] The reference is to Thomas A. Brady, *Turning Swiss: Cities and Empire, 1450–1550* (Cambridge, U.K., 1985).

[111] The literature on Italian and German cities in the Renaissance and Reformation is voluminous, but see John M. Najemy, *Corporatism and Consensus in Florentine Electoral Politics, 1280–1400* (Chapel Hill, 1982); Nicolai Rubinstein, *The Government of Florence under the Medici (1434 to 1494)* (Oxford, 1966); Hankins, ed., *Renaissance Civic Humanism*; Thomas A. Brady Jr., "In Search of the Godly City: The Domestication of Religion in the German Urban Reformation," in *Communities, Politics and Reformation in Early Modern Europe* (Leiden, 1998), 169–88; Robert W. Scribner, "Civic Unity and the Reformation in Erfurt," *Past and Present* 66 (1975): 29–60; Lorna Jane Abray, *The People's Reformation: Magistrates, Clergy, and Commons in Strasbourg, 1500–1598* (Ithaca, 1985); Rhiman A. Rotz, "'Social Struggles' or the Price of Power? German Urban Uprisings in the Late Middle Ages," *Archiv für Reformationsgeschichte* 76 (1985): 64–95.

aging its relationship with them. This is why François I encouraged improvement projects, Henri III issued privileges indulging in litanies of cities' past signal services to the monarchy, and Henri IV thought it worth his while to look into debatable urban electoral practices.

Yet as much as cities mattered to the crown, they were more essential for the citizens themselves. They provided a meaningful setting in which inhabitants could engage in public life—whether their activities included collecting donations and linens for the poor, voting on parish business, or attending weekly meetings at the hôtel de ville—and in which families could compete for advancement and prestige. Municipal government was attractive to so many because it combined both of these advantages. It allowed individuals to advance the concerns of the families and interest groups to which they belonged at the same time that it provided them with a sense that they were acting for the wider public benefit. The elaborate decision-making procedures and particular customs of the hôtel de ville frequently assured that those who already possessed authority within the urban sphere could keep it, but they were also important to members because they reinforced the sense that the civic polity possessed its own traditions and history that assured its special identity. The nature of this identity certainly underwent revision, and the characteristics and obligations of the "public good" that municipal officials sought to promote were subject to disagreement. The debates over the navigation project, the enforcement of Henri II's edict of October 1547, the course that Poitiers should navigate during the religious wars and the Catholic League period, and the city's interactions with Henri IV all illustrate this clearly. Yet despite these profound disagreements, commitment to civic life endured. This is why Jean Le Roy's 1609 compendium of mayoral arms displays a pride in civic culture and cultivated memory of political events that Jean Bouchet, Renaissance historian of his city, dramatist of royal entries, and bourgeois of Poitiers, would have understood and approved.

Bibliography

Archival and Manuscript Sources

Archives communales and Mediathèque municipale de Poitiers

Registers of Deliberation

Reg. 4 (19 Jan. 1450–18 Jan. 1466); 8 (Dec. 1501–Apr. 1502); 9 (26 July 1506–13 Dec. 1507); 10 (5 Aug. 1510–25 July 1511); 11 (28 July 1511–23 June 1513); 12 (1 July 1513–22 July 1513); 13 (7 Nov. 1513–10 July 1514); 14 (14 July 1514–13 July 1515); 15 (14 July 1515–24 July 1517); 16 (26 July 1517–24 July 1518); 17 (Aug. 1519–7 July 1522); 18 (14 July 1522–11 July 1524); 19 (31 July 1531–18 July 1533); 20 (14 July 1536–7 July 1539); 21 (15 July 1538–7 July 1539); 22 (14 July 1539–12 July 1540); 23 (14 July 1540–2 Aug. 1541); 24 (3 Aug. 1541–11 July 1542); 25 (31 July 1542–25 July 1544); 26 (28 July 1544–20 July 1545); 27 (24 July 1545–19 July 1546); 28 (23 July 1546–15 July 1547); 29 (22 July 1547–30 July 1548); 30 (7 Aug. 1548–26 July 1549); 31 (19 July 1549–14 July 1551); 32 (26 July 1551–24 Feb. 1556); 33 (25 Feb. 1556–11 June 1556); 34 (24 July 1556–19 July 1557); 35 (23 July 1557–22 July 1558); 36 (26 July 1558–10 July 1559); 37 (14 July 1559–28 June 1560); 38 (14 July 1561–16 June 1562); 39 (14 July 1571–21 Apr. 1572); 40 (14 July 1571–7 June 1572); 41 (28 July 1572–25 June 1574); 42 (May 1574–11 July 1580); 43 (25 July 1580–14 July 1581); 44 (31 July 1582–14 July 1583); 44bis (15 July 1583–14 July 1584); 46 (18 July 1586–14 July 1587); 47 (17 July 1587–14 July 1588); 48 (15 July 1588–14 July 1589); 49 (17 July 1589–4 Sept. 1589); 50 (16 July 1590–29 Oct. 1590); 51 (15 July 1591–14 July 1592); 52 (16 July 1591–4 Nov. 1592); 53 (20 July 1592–14 July 1593); 54 (1 July 1594–14 July 1595); 55bis (17 July 1595–14 July 1596); 56 (17 July 1597–14 July 1598); 57 (17 July 1598–14 July 1599); 58 (16 July 1599–10 July 1600); 59 (17 July 1600–14 July 1601); 60 (c. 30 July 1601–1 Apr. 1602); 61 (18 July 1603–14 July 1605); 62 (17 July 1606–14 July 1607); 63 (16 July 1607–14 July 1608); 64 (10 July 1608–14 July 1609)

Casier 1, A2: Établissements de Rouen, 1204

Casier 1, A19: Letters patent, 1372, re: nobility

Casier 2, A26–28: Letters patent, 1463, 1467, 1472, re: *arrière ban*

Casier 2, A31: Letters patent, 1488, re: *drapperie*
Casier 3, A43: Letters patent, 1576, re: judicial privileges
Casier 4, B2, B7: Election dispute of 1458
Casier 4, B13–15: Letters patent, 1548–49, re: merchant dispute
Casier 4, B17: Inventory of municipal documents submitted by Maixent Poitevin
Casier 4, B19: Deliberations on precedence, 1582
Casier 4, B21: *Arrêt* of Conseil d'État, 1609
Casier 7, C40: Estates General, 1588
Casier 8, C41: Decisions of Parlement of Paris, 1599
Casier 8, C42: Letter of Henri IV, 1606
Casier 9, D14: Jurisdiction dispute with *lieutenant criminel*, 15th century
Casier 9, D27: *Aumôneries* of Poitiers, 1506
Casier 9, D34: *Procès-verbal* in dispute with lieutenant criminel, 1527
Casier 9, D35–Casier 10, D39: Navigation project, 1537–40
Casier 10, D40–42: Tax collections for navigation project, 1540–42
Casier 10, D43: Letters patent, 1542, re: navigation project
Casier 10, D44: Procès-verbal of meeting with clergy, 1542
Casier 10, D46: Aumôneries of Poitiers, 1559
Casier 10, D47: Request of hatters
Casier 10, D48, 51: Bourg of St. Hilaire, 1565, 1567
Casier 10, D53: Documentation re: *police* ordinances of 1567
Casier 10, D55: Request of carpenters, 1567?
Casier 11, D58: Sentence of Grands Jours of 1579 re: aumôneries
Casier 13, E52: Artillery, 1586–90
Casier 13, E53: Arrêt of Chambre des Comptes, 1594
Casier 17, F112: Contract, 1544, re: municipal domain
Casier 17, F130: Municipal loan, 1582–83
Casier 20, G49–G53: Letters re: *dixième,* 1539–75
Casier 22, H43: Letters patent, 1584, re: taxation
Casier 23, H37: Royal ordinance, 1587, re: office of *jaugeur*
Casier 23, I17–21: Letters patent, 1538–44, re: taxation
Casier 23, I23–24: Documentation concerning taxation, 1546–1560s
Casier 33, J1329–31: Sentences, 1538–39, re: clock tower
Casier 36, K11: Account of navigation expenses, 1542
Casier 36, K14: Municipal account, 1545–47
Casier 37, K21: Account of Mayor Maixent Poitevin, 1566–69
Casier 37, K24: Account of entry of Henri III, 1577
Casier 37, K25–26: Mayoral accounts, 1581–84
Casier 37, K28–31: Municipal accounts, 1586–89
Casier 37, K32: Account of tax collections for artillery, 1589
Casier 40, Reg. 1: Tax roll, 1552
Casier 40, Reg. 2: Tax roll, 1568
Casier 40, Reg. 3: Account of war magazine, 1594
Casier 42, Reg. 11: Statutes and memoranda, 15th and 16th centuries
Casier 42, Reg. 12: Copies of municipal documents, 17th century
Casier 42, Reg. 13: Inventory of 1506
Casier 43, Reg. 15: Copies of confirmations of municipal privileges, 17th century
Casier 43, Reg. 16: Copies of municipal documents, 17th century
Casier 43, Reg. 18, No. 1: Narratives of mayoralties of Lauzon and Lucas. No. 2: Mayoral list

Casier 44, 1506–7, 1523–63, 1560–86, 1583: Mayoral jurisdiction
Casier 45, 1601–15: Mayoral jurisdiction
Casier 49, 1544–45: Rolls of Communauté des pauvres
Casier 49, 1565, 1584: Rolls of the poor
Casier 49, 1589: Account of Communauté des pauvres
Casier 53, 1544, 1555–56, 1570–73, 1587–90, 1591–95: Deliberations of *dominicale*
Casier 54, 1556–57, 1568, 1592–94: Accounts of Aumônerie Notre-Dame
Casier 54, 1558–59, 1562, 1564, 1565–66, 1572–74, 1581: Accounts of Communauté des pauvres
Casier 56, 1636, 1638: Armorials of university rector.
Casier 59, K79: Account of dixième, 1531
Casier 70, No. 1605: Ordinance concerning *fabriqueurs*, 1562
Casier 72, No. 1674: Documents concerning Humeau family
Casier 78, Reg. 1: University register, 1575–95
Reg. Paroissial 142: Baptisms, St. Jean-Baptiste, 1543–49
Reg. Paroissial 238: Baptisms, Ste. Opportune, 1539–84
MS 48 (309): Book of Hours belonging to Barthommé Aubert
MS 51 (Manuscrit Saint-Hilaire): Livre de la police, 15th and 16th centuries
MS 272 (196): Inventory of royal police ordinances recorded in Châtellet, 16th century
MS 381 (401), 388 (117): Lists of mayors
MS 574: *Recueil des maires,* 1609
Dom Fonteneau, 3:23–29: Letters patent, 1587, re: Jean Porthaise.
Dom Fonteneau, 9:475, 479–80: château de la Guierche; certificate of fidelity, 1595
Dom Fonteneau, 16:371–72: Accord between Boisseguin, Guierche, and Verac, 1590
Dom Fonteneau, 20:377–78: Letters patent, 1591, re: Niort
Dom Fonteneau, 23:173–83: Édit du Roy sur l'élection d'un juge et trois consuls des marchands en la ville de Poitiers, 1566
Dom Fonteneau, 23:185–86: Reglement pour le rang des Maire et Eschevins de Poitiers dans les assemblées de la Noblesse de Poitou, 1588
Dom Fonteneau, 25:629: Commission issued by Guierche, 1591
Dom Fonteneau, 76:187: Description of Clain River

Archives départementales de la Vienne

Carton 30: Autographs
B^Supp277: Criminal jurisdiction of presidial court of Poitiers, 16th–18th centuries
C74–76: Registers of Généralité, 1588–89, 1594, 1596
C203: Commissions and ordinances, 1596–1656
C280: Receipts presented to *trésoriers*, 1578–1765
C306: Documents concerning palais, 1570–1702
C308: *Greffe* of presidial court, 1587–1789
C347: Declarations of butchers, 1581–1709
C545: Declarations of *domaines* of Vouvant and Mayrevent, 1548
E⁴24.19–20: Notarial contracts of Jean Bourbeau, 1588–93
E⁴26.13–17: Notarial contracts of Jacques Herbaudeau, 1588–92
E⁴27.3: Notarial contracts of M. A. Chaigneau, 1548
E⁴27.5–6: Notarial contracts of Jean Chauveau, 1542–43
E⁴27.27: Notarial contracts of François Guyonneau, 1592–94
E⁶58: City of Poitiers
E⁸3–5: Confraternity of Notre-Dame celebrated in St. Didier

E^{8}8–9: Inventories of titles of confraternity of Notre-Dame, celebrated in St. Didier, 1559, 1714

E^{8}10: Confraternity of Ste. Catherine, celebrated in St. Germain

E^{8}11: Accounts of confraternity of Ste. Catherine, celebrated in St. Germain, 1587

F8: Grands Jours of Poitiers, 1531–1635

G182: Statutes of chapter of St. Pierre

G503, 505: Chapter of St. Hilaire, church documentation, 1506–19, 1547–81

G521: Accounts of vestry of St. Hilaire, 1519–1645

G522: Ecclesiastical jurisdiction of St. Hilaire, 1413–1776

G533–34: Deliberations of chapter of St. Hilaire, 1582–87, 1590–91

G571: Extracts of acts of chapter of St. Hilaire, 1376–1784

G588: Inventory of titles of St. Hilaire, 1573

G590: Chapter of St. Hilaire, 1378–1719

G639: Chapter of St. Hilaire, judicial and police rights, 1204–1541

G640–42: Jurisdiction of St. Hilaire, 1449–1564

G645: Police ordinances, *sénéchal* of St. Hilaire

G646–47: Bourg of St. Hilaire, minutes of *greffe,* 1482–1685

G681: *Cure* of Notre-Dame-de-la-Chandelière, 1411–1773

G686: Cure of Ste. Triaise, 1535–1771

G687: Confraternity of Notre-Dame-de-Mars, celebrated in Ste. Triaise, 1371–1538

G899: *Châtellenie* of Masseuil

G1097: Acts of rogations jurisdiction of Notre-Dame-la-Grande, 1257–1733

G1100: Aumônerie of Notre-Dame

G1108: *Rentes* of chapter of Notre-Dame-la-Grande in St. Cybard parish

G1118, 1226: Notre-Dame-la-Grande, mills of La Jonchière in Dissay

G1286–1289: Accounts of vestry of Notre-Dame-la-Grande, 1534–52, 1580–83, 1585–86, 1599–1600

G1293: Extracts of rentes, memoirs, and receipts of chapter of Notre-Dame-la-Grande

G1301: Deliberations of chapter of Notre-Dame-la-Grande, 1573–75

G1346–47: Chapter of Ste. Radegonde, church documentation, 16th and 17th centuries

G1353/Carton 25, No. 2: Statutes of chapter of Ste. Radegonde

G1364: Chapter of Ste. Radegonde, parish documents

G1534: Account of chapter of Ste. Radegonde, 1589–95

G1589, 1591–92, 1594–96: Deliberations of chapter of Ste. Radegonde, 1562–65, 1573–76, 1583–87, 1591–94

G1687: Rentes of chaplains of Ste. Radegonde, 1491–1746

G1693–94: Deliberations of chaplains of Ste. Radegonde, 1573–75, 1578–1642

G1770: Chapter of St. Pierre-le-Puellier, Fief-le-Comte and Charruau mill

G^{9}84–85: Cure of St. Cybard, 1414–1599

G^{9}90–91: Cure of St. Didier, 1266–1640

G^{9}95: Cure of St. Étienne, 1342–1600

G^{9}98: Cure of St. Germain, 16th century

G^{9}102: Cure of St. Michel

G^{9}104: Cures of Montierneuf, 1485–1787; Notre-Dame-l'Ancienne, 1517–1784

G^{9}105: Cure of Notre-Dame-la-Grande, 1281–1774

G^{9}106: Cure of Notre-Dame-la-Petite, 1295–1600

G^{9}109: Cure of Ste. Opportune, 1360–1600

G^{9}112: Cure of St. Paul, 1501–1700

G^{9}114: Cure of St. Porchaire, 1441–1600

G^{9}119: Vestry of St. Porchaire, 1630–80

G^{9}120: Cure of Ste. Radegonde

$G^{10}7$: Chapelle de l'Échevinage en l'Hôtel Dieu de Poitiers, 1587–1764
$1H^17$: St. Cyprien
$1H^{13}9$: St. Hilaire-de-la-Celle
$1H^{18}49$: Cordeliers of Poitiers
$1H^{18}76$: Jacobins of Poitiers
$1H^{18}95$: Minims of Poitiers, 1505–1611
$2H^13$: Ste. Croix, abbey, 1526–1630
$2H^113$, 15, 22–23: Ste. Croix, mills and fisheries
$2H^229$: La Trinité, fief of Tison and Tison mill
J25–28: Presidial court of Poitiers
J116: List of mayors, jubilee of 1554
J118: Ceremonial of episcopal entries
J629: Account of *receveur* of *sénéchaussée*, 1557
J1021: Vestry of St. Cybard, 1559; confraternity of Ste. Catherine, 1512–88
SAHP 20: Papers and titles of Brilhac family, 1565–1722 (Fonds de Bernay)
SAHP 36: Family papers: Pelisson
SAHP 49: Register of debts and affairs of Jean and François de Brilhac, 1586
SAHP 51: *Papier journal* of Jean de Brilhac, 1535–38
SAHP 84, 86: Assorted papers
SAHP 88: *Coutumes* of Poitou, 1505–1698
SAHP 97: Legal notes, Brilhac family
SAHP 102: Papier journal of Jean de Brilhac, 1539–65
SAHP 203: Family papers: Brochard, Ferrand, Dupuy
SAHP 314: Genealogy: Pidoux family
SAHP 316: Genealogy: Rogier/Rougier family
SAO 144: Collection Bonsergent, Nos. 110, 113, 116, 117
SAO 150: Family papers: Sanzay
SAO 245: Ceremonial of episcopal entry
SAO 259: Notable events in history of Poitiers
SAO 260 (Manuscrit d'Auzance): copies of municipal documents

Archives nationales, Paris

E^*3b: Audiences of Conseil des finances, Sept.–Dec. 1601
$X^{1A}9205$: Registre des ordonnances civiles des Grands Jours à Poitiers, 1579
$X^{1A}9208$: Registre du Grands Jours à Poitiers, Sept.–Dec. 1579

Bibliothèque nationale de France

MS Clair. 361: Mayoral elections in Poitiers, 1609
MSS Fr 3310, 3405, 3614, 15559, 15569, 15572, 15574, 15643, 15876, 15899, 18976, 20153, 20157, 23194: Letters, 1570s–1601
MS Fr 18153: Register of Conseil Privé, 1547–54
MS Fr 18159: Register of Conseil d'État, 1594

Printed Primary Sources

Affiches du Poitou
Ample discovrs et veritable, des choses plus notables arriuées au siege memorable de la renommée ville de Paris. . . . Poitiers: Aymé Mesnier, 1590.

Arrest de la cour de Parlement de Paris, pour l'ampliation du pouuoir & iurisdiction des iuges presidiaux de Poictiers. Poitiers: Aymé Mesnier, 1590.

Arrest de la cour de Parlement, de recognoistre pour roy Charles diziesme de ce nom. Poitiers: Aymé Mesnier, 1590.

Arrest de la cour de Parlement, povr la conuocation & assemblée des trois Estatz de ce Royaume, assignés en la Ville de Melun, au vingtiesme de Mars prochain. Poitiers: Aymé Mesnier, 1590.

Arrest de la covrt des Grandz Iours seant en la ville de Poictiers donné le dixneufiesme iour de Decembre, 1579. Sur le faict de la visitation des Benefices. Poitiers: Aymé Mesnier, 1579.

Arrest de la covrt des Grandz Iours seant en la ville de Poictiers donné le dixneufiesme iour de Decembre, 1579. Sur le faict du renvoy des Contumax. Poitiers: Aymé Mesnier, 1579.

Arrest de la covrt des Grandz Iovrs seant en la ville de Poictiers, donné le dix-neufiesme iour de Septembre. 1579. Poitiers: Aymé Mesnier, 1579.

Arrest de la covrt des Grandz Iovrs seant en la ville de Poictiers, donné le septiesme iour de Decembre. 1579. Poitiers: Aymé Mesnier, n.d.

Arrest de la covrt des Grandz Iovrs seant en la ville de Poictiers. Donné le vingt-deuxiesme iour de Septembre. 1579. Poitiers: Aymé Mesnier, 1579.

Arrest de la covrt des Grandz Iovrs seant en la ville de Poictiers. Donné le vingt-sixiesme iour de Septembre. 1579. Poitiers: Aymé Mesnier, 1579.

Arrestz de la covrt des Grandz Iovrs seant en la ville de Poictiers do[n]nez le septiesme iour de Nove[m]bre. 1579. Sur le faict des Benefices Cures, Hospitaulx, Aulmosneries, Maladeries estant du ressort desdict Grandz Iours. Poitiers: Aymé Mesnier, n.d.

Arrestz de la covrt des Grandz Iovrs seant en la ville de Poictiers, donnez les sept & quatorziesme iours de Nouembre. 1579. Contre les defaillans & contumax condamnez à mort. Poitiers: Aymé Mesnier, n.d.

Les arrestz de la covrt des Grandz Iovrs seant en la ville de Poictiers. Ensemble les lettres patentes du Roy pour la continuation d'iceulx. Poitiers: Aymé Mesnier, 1579.

Au tresillustre duc de Guyse, pair de France, sur la deffence de Poictiers, vers imitez du Latin de I.V. N.p., 1569.

Aubigné, Agrippa d'. *Histoire universelle.* Ed. Alphone de Ruble. 10 vols. Paris: Librairie Renouard, 1895.

Audouin, E., ed. *Recueil de documents concernant la commune et la ville de Poitiers.* 2 vols. AHP 44, 46. Poitiers: Imprimerie de N. Renault, 1923; Imprimerie de Poitou, 1928.

Avtre arrest donné en la covrt des Grandz Iovrs seant en la ville de Poictiers. Contre les deffaillans & Contumax condemnez à mort. Poitiers: Aymé Mesnier, 1579.

Barbier, Alfred. "Chroniques de Poitiers aux XVe et XVIe siècles, deuxième partie: première guerre civile à Poitiers (1562)." *MSAO,* 2d ser., 14 (1891): 1–222.

Barbier, Guillaume. *Recveil des privileges, avthoritez, povvoirs, franchises, & exemptions des preuost des marchands, escheuins, & habitans de la ville de Lyon.* Lyon: Gvillavme Barbier, 1649.

Barbot, Amos. *Histoire de La Rochelle.* 3 vols. Ed. Denys d'Aussy. Publication de la Société des Archives Historiques de la Saintonge et de l'Aunis. Paris and Saintes: Pichard & Mortreuil, 1886–90.

Beauchet-Filleau, H[enri], ed. *Le siége de Poitiers par Liberge suivi de la bataille de Moncontour et du siége de Saint-Jean-d'Angély.* Poitiers: Létang, 1846.

Berger de Xivrey, [Jules], ed. *Recueil des lettres missives de Henri IV.* 9 vols. Paris: Imprimerie Royale, 1843–76.

Bernard, Auguste, ed. *Procès-verbaux des États généraux de 1593.* Paris: Imprimerie Royale, 1842.

Bèze, Théodore de. *Histoire ecclésiastique des églises réformées au royaume de France*. 3 vols. Paris: Libraire Fischbacher, 1883–89.

Bodin, Jean. *Les six livres de la République*. 6 vols. Paris: Fayard, 1986.

Bouchet, Guillame. *Les serées de Guillaume Bouchet, sieur de Brocourt*. Paris: Alphonse Lemerre, 1873.

Bouchet, Jean. *Les Annales d'Aquitaine. Faicts et gestes en sommaire des roys de France et d'Angleterre, pays de Naples & de Milan. . . .* Poitiers: Abraham Movnin, 1644.

——. *Lhistoire et cronicque de Clotaire Premier de ce nom. vii. roy des fra[n]cois. et monarque des gaulles. Et de sa tresillustre espouse: madame saincte. Radego[n]de extraicte au vray de plusieurs croniq[ue]s antiq[ue]s & modernes*. [Poitiers: Enguilbert de Marnef, 1518.]

Bourgueville, Charles de. *Les recherches et antiquitez de la province de Neustrie, à présent duché de Normandie, comme des villes remarquables d'icelle, mais plus specialement de la ville et université de Caen*. Caen: T. Chalopin, 1833.

Catalogue des actes de François Ier. 10 vols. Paris: Imprimerie Nationale, 1887–1908.

Catalogue des actes de Henri II: collection des ordonnances des rois de France. 5 vols. Paris: Imprimerie Nationale, 1979, and CNRS, 1986–98.

Célier, Léonce, ed. *Recueil de documents concernant le Poitou contenus dans les registres de la Chancellerie de France, XIV (1486–1502)*. AHP 56. Poitiers: Imprimerie P. Oudin, 1958.

Chenu, Jean. *Recveil des antiqvites et privileges de la ville de Bovrges, et de plvsievrs autres villes capitales du royaume*. Paris: Robert Foüet, 1621.

Contareno, Gasper [Gasparo Contarini]. *The Commonwealth and Gouernment of Venice*. 1599. Reprint, Amsterdam and New York: Da Capo Press and Theatrum Orbis Terrarum, 1969.

Copie des lettres escrites par le dvc d'Epernon av roy de Nauarre, touchant les affaires de ce temps, enuoyees par vn bourgeois de Poictiers, à vn sien amy estant en ceste ville de Paris. N.p., 1588.

Copie d'une lettre missive, escrite par un advocat de Paris, à un conseiller esta[n]t aux grans Iours à Poictiers, surprise pres ladicte ville de Poictiers. N.p., 1568.

Covstvmes dv compte, et pais de Poictov, anciens ressorts & enclaues d'iceluy, mises & redigees par escript. . . . Paris and Poitiers: Iehan Dallier and les Marnefs, & Bouchet, freres, 1560.

Covelle, Alfred L., ed. *Le livre des Bourgeois de l'ancienne République de Genève*. Geneva: J. Jullien, 1897.

Coyecque, Ern[est], ed. "L'assistance publique à Paris au milieu du XVIe siècle." *Bulletin de la Société de l'Histoire de Paris et de l'Ile de France*, 15 (1888): 105–18.

Cromé, François, ed. *Dialogue d'entre le maheustre et le manant*. Geneva: Droz, 1977.

Darnal, Jean. *Supplement des chroniques de la noble ville & cité de Bourdeaus*. Bordeaux: Iac. Millanges and Cl. Mongirovd, 1620.

De par le roy et monseigneur le conte du Lude cheuallier de l'ordre dudict seigneur, gouerneur & lieutenant general pour sa maiesté en Poictou. Il est ordonné que toutes personnes obeiront au contenu en ceste presente sur peine d'estre penduz & estranglez, & porteront croix blanche en la forme y contenue. Poitiers: Bertrand Noscereau, 1567.

De par le roy, et Monsieur le comte du Lude. Il est enioinct à tous ceulx qui ont vsé & vsent du baptesme tel qui se faict en la Religion pretendue Reformée, obeyr au contenu en ces presentes. Poitiers: Bertrand Noscereau, 1565.

Declaration du roi par laqvelle il deffend de ne faire presche, assemblées, ny administrations de sacrementz de la nouuelle Religion, pretendue Reformée, en sa court ne suitte, ny es maisons de sa maiesté. Poitiers: Françoys Boyzateau, 1563.

Declaration du roy tres-chrestien Charles X. de ce nom, pour la conseruation des maisons appartenants aux Gentilz-hommes & autres Catholicques qui assistent le Roy de Nauarre. . . . Poitiers: Aymé Mesnier, 1590.

Desaivre, Léo., ed. *Lettres missives de Jehan de Chourses, seigneur de Malicorne gouverneur du Poitou de 1585 à 1603: lettres missives à lui adressées et autres documents relatifs à l'histoire du Poitou pendant cette periode.* AHP 27:249–509. Poitiers, 1896.

La description dv plant dv theatre faict à Orléans, pour l'assemblée des troiz estats, auec vn brief discours de la seance des tenans & representans lesdictz estatz. Paris: Vincent Sertenas, Gilles Corrozet, & Guillaume Niuerd, 1560.

Discovrs des choses les plvs remarcables auenues par chacu[n] iour dura[n]t le siege de Lusignen, en Ian. 1574. N.p., 1575.

Discovrs dv svcces des affaires passez au siege de Poictiers, despuis le dixneufiesme iour de Iuillet, 1569. iusques au vingtvniesme de Septembre audict an: Enuoyé à Mo[n]seigneur de Mandelot Gouuerneur de Lyon. Paris: Au mont S. Hilaire à l'enseigne du Pelican, 1569.

Discovrs miracvlevx advenv en l'an M.D.LXXXVI. pres la ville de Potiers, en la personne d'vn nommé Bernardeau, aduocat au siege presidial de Poictiers. Paris: Anthoine Guyueriot, 1586.

Edict concernant la preseance des officiers des sieges presidiaux par dessus les Maire & Escheuins en toutes assemblées publiques & honnoraires. Auec l'Arrest de nos Seigneurs de la Cour de Parlement du 5. iour de Juin, 1559. Poitiers: I. Thoreav & la vefue d'A. Mesnier, 1637.

Edict du roy Charles nevfieme de ce nom, faict par le conseil & aduis de tous les parlemens de ce royaume, pour la tranquilité & repos vniuersel de ses subiets, touchant le faict de la Religion. Poitiers: Ian de Marnef, n.d.

Edict dv roy svr la pacification des troubles de ce royaume. Selon la copie imprimée à Poictiers. N.p.: François le Page, 1577.

Edict dv roy svr la revocation des edicts de la Ligue, faits és années mil cinq cens quatre vingts cinq, & quatre vingts huict. Tours: Iamet Mettayer, 1591.

Edict dv roy, svr le faict de la religion. Publié en la court de Parlement à Paris, le dernier iour de Iuillet, M.D. LXI. Poitiers: Nicolas Pelletier, n.d.

Edict & declaration dv roy svr la reduction de la ville de Poictiers en son obeissance. Poitiers: Iean Blachet, 1594.

Edict et ordonnance du roy pour le bien & reiglement de la Iustice, & police de son Royaume. Poitiers: Bertrand Noscereau, 1565.

[Ex]traict [de l'or]donnance [de par] le roy Charles IX. sur le reiglement de la Iustice. Publié en la court ordinaire de la seneschaucée de Poictou, tenu à Poictiers, sceant monseigneur le conte du Lude cheualier de l'ordre, & lieutenant dudit seigneur ondit pays de Poictou le XII. iour de nouembre 1563. Poitiers: Bertrand Noscereau, 1563.

Extraits de l'obituaire de Sainte-Opportune de Poitiers (1366–1631), des registres paroissiaux de cette ville (1539–1790) et du journal de Pierre Charmeteau, maître perruquier (1731–1767). AHP 15:333–426. Poitiers: Imprimerie Oudin, 1885.

Franklin, Julian H., ed. and trans. *Constitutionalism and Resistance in the Sixteenth Century: Three Treatises by Hotman, Beza, and Mornay.* New York: Pegasus, 1969.

Froissart, Jean. *Les chroniques de Sire Jean Froissart.* Ed. J. A. C. Buchon. 3 vols. Paris: Auguste Desrez, 1840.

Geisendorf, Paul-F., ed. *Livre des habitants de Genève.* 2 vols. Geneva: Droz, 1957–63.

La grande trahison descouverte en la ville de Poictiers, sur les entreprises de Richelieu, & Malicorne. Paris: Denis Binet, 1589.

Groulart, Claude. "Mémoires de Messire Claude Groulart, Premier Président de Normandie, ou Voyages par lui faicts en cour." In *Nouvelle collection des mémoires pour servir à l'histoire de France, depuis le XIIIe siècle jusqu'à la fin du XVIIIe*. Ed. Michaud and Poujoulat. 1st ser., 11:549–98. Paris: Éditeur du Commentaire Analytique du Code Civil, 1838.

Guicciardini, Francesco. *Dialogue on the Government of Florence*. Trans. and ed. Alison Brown. Cambridge: Cambridge University Press, 1994.

Henry, E. and Ch. Loriquet, eds. *Correspondance du duc de Mayenne publiée sur le manuscrit de la bibliothèque de Reims*. 2 vols. Reims: P. Dubois, 1860.

Heures de Nostre Dame, à l'vsage de Poictiers. Poitiers: Françoys le Page, 1576.

Hillerin, Jacques de. *Le Chariot chrestien a quatres roues, menant a salut, dans le souvenir de la mort, du iugement, de l'enfer, & du paradis. . . .* Paris, n.d.

Hotman, François. *Francogallia*. Ed. and trans. Ralph E. Giesey and J. H. M. Salmon. Cambridge: Cambridge University Press, 1972.

Humeau, Pierre. *Les devx harangves ov remonstrances faictes en la cour ordinaire de la seneschavcee de Poictou & siege presidial à Poictiers, Sur la publication du reglement general faict pour remedier aux desordres aduenus à l'occasion des troubles presens*. Poitiers: François le Page, 1590.

Des inhumanitez et cruaultez de l'armee du roy de Navarre au Poictou. . . . N.p., 1588.

Isambert, [François André] et al., eds. *Recueil général des anciennes lois françaises depuis l'an 420 jusqu'à la révolution de 1789*. 29 vols. Paris: Belin-Le-Prieur, 1822–33.

Ivgement donne en la covr presidiale de Poictiers, pour la conseruation de la iustice en Poictou. Poitiers: Aymé Mesnier, 1589.

Laborde, Léon de. *Les comptes des bâtiments du roi*. 2 vols. Paris: J. Baur, 1877–80.

La Faille, G[ermain] de. *Annales de la ville de Toulouse depuis la reunion de la comté de Toulouse à la couronne*. 2 vols. Toulouse: Guillaume-Louïs Colomyez and Jerôme Posuël, 1687–1701.

La Fontenelle de Vaudoré, [Armand-Désiré] de, ed. *Chroniques fontenaisiennes, contenant 1. La chronique d'une commune rurale de la Vendée (Le Langon, près Fontenay-le-Compte); 2. La chronique des guerres civiles en Poitou, Aunis, Xaintonge et Angoumois, de 1574 à 1576; 3. Et la chronique de la guerre des trois Henri, en Bas-Poitou; où se trouvent des détails curieux sur les desséchements des Marais et sur les guerres de Religion*. Fontenay-le-Comte: Gaudin, 1841.

———. *Journal de Guillaume et de Michel Le Riche, avocats du roi à Saint-Maixent (de 1534 à 1586)*. 1846. Reprint, Geneva: Slatkine Reprints, 1971.

La Haye, Jean de. *Les memoires et recherche de France, et de la Gaule Aqvitaniqve*. Poitiers: Abraham Movnin, 1643.

Lalourcé, Charlemagne, ed. *Recueil de pièces originales et authentiques, concernant la tenue des États-Généraux d'Orléans en 1560, sous Charles IX, de Blois en 1576, 1588 sous Henri III, de Paris en 1614, sous Louis XIII*. 9 vols. Paris: Barrois, l'aîné, 1789.

Ledain, Bélisaire, ed. *Journal historique de Denis Généroux, notaire à Parthenay 1567–1576*. Niort: L. Clouzot, 1865.

———. *Journaux de Jean de Brilhac conseiller en la sénéchaussée de Poitou de 1545 à 1564 et de René de Brilhac conseiller au présidial de Poitiers de 1573 à 1622*. AHP 15:1–48. Poitiers: Imprimerie Oudin, 1885.

———. *Lettres adressées à Jean et Guy de Daillon, comtes du Lude, gouverneurs de Poitou de 1543 à 1557 et de 1557 à 1585*. AHP 13–14. Poitiers: Imprimerie Oudin, 1882–83.

———. *Lettres des rois de France, princes et grands personnages à la commune de Poitiers*. Parts 1 and 2. AHP 1: 143–201; 4: 275–340. Poitiers: Imprimerie Oudin, 1872, 1875.

L'Estoile, Pierre de. *Memoires-Journaux 1574–1611. . . .* 14 vols. Paris: Tallandier, 1982.

Lettre des dessains et entreprises de Henry de Bovrbon, et de d'Espernon, enuoyee aux Roch-

elois, où sont contenues toutes leurs intentions, pour ruiner l'Eglise & les catholiques, trouvée n'agueres en la possession d'vn heretique à Poitiers. Et comme elle a esté communiquée à M. le duc de Mayenne. Paris: Iouxte la copie imprimée à Poitiers, 1589.

Lettres dv roy, addroissantes a monseigneur de Boisseguin, gouuerneur pour sa Majesté en sa ville de Poictiers, sur l'esmotion aduenuë à Paris. Poitiers: Pierre de-Marnef, 1588.

Lettres dv roy, contenant les moyens de la detestable conivration et conspiration, entreprinse contre sa maiesté, tendant a la subuersion du royaume. Poitiers: Nicolas Pelletier, 1560.

Lettres dv roy et de la royne, des troubles commencez, & de ce qu'on à voulu executer contre luy estant en sa ville de Meaux, au mois de septembre mil cinq cens soixante sept. Addroissantes à Monsieur le conte du Lude. . . . Poitiers: Bertrand Noscereau, 1567.

Lettres du roy, povr maintenir ses sviets en tranquillité & repos, & les faire viure, & se contenir doucement & paisiblement suiuant ses edits & ordonnances. . . . Poitiers: Nicolas Logerois, 1567.

Lettres dv roy tres-chrestien Charles IX. de ce nom, par laquelle il veut & ordonne que court & iurisdiction qu'on appelle vulgairement les Grans Iours, soit tenue & exercee en sa ville de Poitiers. . . . Poitiers: André Bodin, 1567.

Lettres patentes addroissantes av seneschal de Poictou, ou son Lieutenant, pour la conuocation & assemblée du Ban & Arrieban, au iour assigné en la presente. Poitiers: Aymé Mesnier, 1590.

Lettres patentes du roy, Charles IX. par lesquelles il defend à toutes personnes d'entrer en debat, esmouuoir seditions, & de se reprocher aucunes choses les vns aux autres pour le faict de la religion, sur peine de la hart, & sans aucun espoir de grace ou remissio[n]. Poitiers: Nicolas Pelletier, 1561.

Lettres patentes dv roy Henry III. de ce nom, roy de France & de Polongne, sur l'entretenement de son edict de pacification. Donné à S. Germain en Laye, le xv. iour d'aruil, mil cinq cens quatre vingts. Poitiers: Aymé Mesnier, 1580.

Les lettres patentes du roy nostre sire, contenans pardon, remission & abolition geneneralle, à tous ses subiects, de quelque qualité & condition qu'ilz soient, pour le passé, des crimes & cas concernans le fait de la foy & religion. Poitiers: Nicolas Pelletier, 1560.

Lettres patentes dv roy tres-chrestien Charles IX. contenants ampliation de pouuoir à messieurs tenants les grands iours en sa ville de Poictiers, ceste presente année mil cinq cens soixante sept. Poitiers: Bertrand Noscereau, 1567.

Loyseau, Charles. *Oevvres . . . , diuisees en deux tomes. . . .* Geneva: Estienne Gamonet, 1636.

——. *A Treatise of Orders and Plain Dignities.* Ed. and trans. Howell A. Lloyd. Cambridge: Cambridge University Press, 1994.

Lurbe, Gabriel de. *Chroniqve bovrdeloise composee cy devant en latin.* Bordeaux: Simon Millanges, 1619.

Martel, Marie-Thérèse de, ed. *Catalogue des actes de François II.* 2 vols. Paris: Éditions du CNRS, 1991.

Mennechet, Éd., ed. *Histoire de l'estat de France, tant de la république que de la religion, sous le regne de François II: par Régnier, sieur de la Planche.* Paris: Techener, 1836.

Le moyen par leqvel aisement tous troubles & differens tant toucha[n]t la croix, de laquelle y à si dangereuse altercation en la ville de Paris, que autres concernants la religion seront assopis & ostez a Messieurs les habitans de Paris. . . . Poitiers: Bertrand Noscereau, & Aymé Mesnier, 1572.

Neron, Pierre, and Estienne Girard. *Les edicts et ordonnances des Tres-Chrestiens Roys, François I. Henry II. François II. Charles IX. Henry III. Henry IV. Lovys XIII. et Lovys XIV. Sur le faict de la Iustice & abreuiation des Procez.* Paris: Lovis Billaine, 1666.

Nicollière-Teijeiro, S. de la, ed. "Comptes de la fabrique de Saint-Martin de Cangtenay, 1481–1506." *Revue de Bretagne, de Vendée et d'Anjou* 37 (1875): 174–85.

Oraison fvnebre de tres-chrestien, tres clement, et tres-debonnaire Prince, Henry IIII. Roy de France & de Nauarre. Prononcée le iour de son Seruice en l'Eglise Cathedrale de Poictiers, le 21. Iuin 1610. . . . Iouxte la copie imprimee à Poictiers par Anthoine Mesnier. Paris: Nicolas Rovsset, 1610.

Ordonnance du roy svr le faict de la police de la ville de Poictiers, & des aultres villes du plat païs de Poictou, establie par les co[m]missaires deputez par sa maiesté. . . . Publiee à Poictiers le xxiii. xxiiii. & xxv. iours du moys de Ianuier, Mil cinq cens lxxviii. Poitiers: les Bouchetz, 1578.

Ordonnance povr la garde de Poictiers, faicte par monseigneur de Vieilleuille, conte du Restal, mareschal de France & lieutenant general pour sa maiesté en ses païs d'Aniou, Poictou, Angoumoys, Xanctonge, & la Rochelle. Poitiers: Bertrand Noscereau, 1568.

Ordonnances des rois de France de la troisième race, recueillies par ordre chronologique. 21 vols. Paris: Imprimerie Royale (Impériale, Nationale), 1723–1899.

Ordonnances des rois de France: règne de François Ier. 9 vols. Paris: Imprimerie Nationale, 1902–92.

Ordonnances faictes par la court des grans iours seant à Poictiers en l'an mil cinq cens quaranteung, sur le faict de la polyce de ladicte uille, forsbourgs, banlieue, & Seneschaulcée de Poictou. Poitiers: [Marnef], 1542.

Palma-Cayet, Pierre Victor. *Chronologie novenaire, contenant l'histoire de la guerre sous le règne du tres-chrestien roy de France et de Navarre Henry IV, et les choses les plus memorables, advenues par tout le monde, depuis le commencement de son règne. . . .* In *Nouvelle collection des mémoires pour servir à l'histoire de France, depuis le XIIIe siècle jusqu'à la fin du XVIIIe.* Ed. Michaud and Poujoulat. 1st ser., 12. Paris and Lyon: Guyot Frères, 1850.

Pasquier, Étienne. *Les oeuvres d'Estienne Pasquier. . . .* 2 vols. Amsterdam: Compagnie des libraires associez, 1723.

Le passage heureux de l'armee du Roy au Poictou, à la barbe de ses ennemis, qui n'y ont sçeu donner aucun empeschement. Paris: Pierre Mercier, 1588.

Porthaise, Jean. *Cinq sermons dv R. P. F. I. Porthaise de l'ordre S. François, theologal de l'Eglise de Poictiers, par luy prononcez en icelle. Esquels est traicté tant de la simulée conuersion du Roy de Nauarre, que du droict de l'absolution Ecclesiastique. . . .* Paris: Guillaume Bichon, 1594.

———. *De la vraie et favlce astrologie contre les abuseurs de nostre siecle.* Poitiers: François le Paige, 1578.

———. *Defence a la responce, faicte aux intenditz de B. De-par-Dieu, par les ministres de l'eglise pretendüe reformée.* Poitiers: Francoys le Page, 1580.

———. *Six sermons faictz en l'eglise cathedralle de S. Pierre de Poictiers, aux processions generalles contre la peste. 1584.* Poitiers: Iean Main, 1584.

Le povvoir de monseignevr le viconte de la Gvyerche, capitaine de cent hommes d'armes gouuerneur pour le roy au pays & comté de Poictou. Poitiers: Aymé Mesnier, 1590.

Privileges de la ville de Bovrges et confirmation d'iceux. Avec la liste chronologiqve des prvd'hommes maire et eschevins, qvi ont govverné la ville depvis l'an 1429. ivsqves a la presente année 1661. Bourges: Iean Chavdiere, 1661.

Les propos qve le roy a tenvz a Chartres aux deputez de sa cour de Parlement de Paris. Poitiers: Pierre de Marnef, 1588.

Rat, Pierre. *Petri Rat Pictauiensis decurionis, in patrias Pictonum leges, quas vulgus consuetudines dicit, glossemata.* Poitiers: Ex officia Marnefiorum fratrum, 1548.

Recueil d'arrêts de la cour des grands jours de Poitiers, 1579.

Rédet, [Louis-François-Xavier], ed. *Documents pour l'histoire de Saint-Hilaire de Poitiers.* 2 vols. *MSAO,* 1st ser., 14 and 19. Poitiers: Société des Antiquaires de l'Ouest, 1847, 1852.

——. "Extraits des Comptes de la Ville de Poitiers, aux XIVe et XVe siècles." Parts 1 and 2. *MSAO,* 1st ser., 6 (1839): 385–427; 7 (1840): 381–446.

Registres des déliberations du bureau de la ville de Paris. 19 vols. Paris: Imprimerie Nationale, 1883–1958.

Reglement et ordonnance politqve, faicte svr les mestiers de boulangiers, & meusniers, tant en ceste ville & faux-bourgs de Poictiers, qu'autres forains, faicte par messieurs les maire escheuins, & bourgeois de ladicte ville. Poitiers: Vefve Iehan Blanchet, 1606.

Reglement et ordonnances pollitiqves, faictes par les maire pairs, conseillers, escheuins, & bourgeois de la ville de Poictiers, . . . pour le repos public & reglement du fait de la police en ladicte ville. Poitiers: Vefve Iehan Blanchet, [1606].

Remonstrance faicte a monsieur d'Espernon, entrant en l'eglise cathedrale de Rouën, le troisiésme de May, 1588. . . . Poitiers: Pierre de-Marnef, 1588.

Remonstrances du clergé et du tiers-état de Poitou, 1560–1588. AHP 20:325–83. Poitiers, 1889.

Response d'vn catholiqve citoien de Poictiers à la lettre d'vn sien ami cy deuant son concitoien & catholique, mais a present partisan des heretiques & mescreans. N.p., 1590.

La routte et deffaitte du camp de monsieur de Malicorne, devant la ville de Poitiers, par les habitans de ladite ville. N.p., 1590.

Ruben, Émile, ed. *Registres consulaires de la ville de Limoges.* 6 vols. Limoges: Imprimerie de Chapoulaud Frères, 1867–97.

Rubys, Claude de. *Les privileges, franchises et immunitez octroyees par les roys treschrestiens, aux consuls, eschevins, manans, & habitans de la ville de Lyon, & à leur posterité.* Lyon: Antoine Gryphius, 1574.

Saint-Belin, Geoffroy de. *Commandement.* Poitiers: Aymé Mesnier, 1590.

Sainte-Marthe, Scévole de. *Opera Latina et Gallica.* 2 vols. Geneva: Slatkine Reprints, 1971.

Sansay, René, comte de. *Remonstrances tres-hvmbles faites a Henry III. tres-chrestien & inuincible roy des François, des Gaulles & de Polongne . . . aux estats generaux de la monarchie françoise, en l'an 1588. Sur la reformation de tous les ordres, extirpation des heresies, & poursuite contre les heretiques rebelles.* Paris: Iean Richer & Clavde de Montr'oeil, 1588.

Seyssel, Claude de. *The Monarchy of France.* Ed. Donald R. Kelley, trans. J. H. Hexter. New Haven: Yale University Press, 1981.

Sincerus, Joducus. [Zinzerling, Justus.] *Voyage dans la vieille France, avec une excursion en Angleterre, en Belgique, en Hollande, en Suisse et en Savoie.* Trans. Thalès Bernard. Paris and Lyon: Dentu, 1859.

Sommaire discovrs des cavses de tovs les trovbles de ce royaulme, procedentes des impostures & coniurations des heretiques & des rebelles. . . . Poitiers: Emé Mesnier & Anthoine Delacourt, 1573.

Stances svr la victoire obtenve par le roy, contre les ennemis de son estat. N.p., 1590.

Theveneau, Nicolas. *Annotations, ov paraphrase avx loix mvnicipalles, et covstvmes dv comte, et pays de Poictov.* Poitiers: Nicolas Pelletier, 1561.

——. *Coustumes du pays & comté de Poictov. Commentees & paraphrasees, auec sommaire sur chascun article d'icelles. . . . Auec l'edict du roy sur l'eslection d'vn iuge, & trois consulz des marchans en la ville de Poictiers.* Poitiers: Bouchetz, freres, 1586.

Thou, Jacques-Auguste de. *Histoire universelle de Jacques-Auguste de Thou, avec la suite par Nicolas Rigault.* 11 vols. La Haye: Henri Scheurleer, 1740.

Triumphes dhonneur faitz par le commandement du roy a lempereur en la ville de Poic-

tiers ou il passa venant Despaigne en france pour aller en flandres le neufuiesme iour de dece[m]bre lan mil ci[n]q ce[n]s xxxix. Paris: Jehan du pre, 1539.

Vaissière, Georges-Pierre-Charles de, ed. *Journal de Jean Barrillon, secrétaire du Chancellier Duprat.* 2 vols. Paris: Renouard, 1897–99.

Vinet, Elie. *L'antiqvité de Bovrdeavs, et de Bovrg.* Ed. Henry Ribadieu. Bordeaux: Paul Chaumas, 1860.

Le vray discovrs de la deffacite des reistres, par monsievr le duc de Guise, le lundy dixiesme iour d'Octobre M.D.LXXV. Poitiers: Pierre Boizateau, n.d.

Secondary Works on Poitiers and Poitou

Andrault, Jean-Pierre. "Une capitale de province sous les armes au temps de la Ligue: la guerre de course menée par Poitiers entre 1589 et 1593." In *Les malheurs de la guerre.* Vol. 1, *De la guerre à l'ancienne à la guerre réglée,* 39–63. Ed. André Corvisier and Jean Jacquart. Paris: Éditions du CTHS, 1996.

Auber, [Charles-Auguste]. *Étude sur les historiens du Poitou depuis ses origines connues jusqu'au milieu du XIXe siècle.* Niort: L. Clouzot, 1870.

——. "Jacques de Hillerin, Poitevin et conseiller au parlement de Paris: biographie des XVIe et XVIIe siècles." *BSAO,* 1st ser., 6 (1850–1852): 53–102.

Babinet, Charles. "Les échevins de Poitiers de 1372 à 1675 ou le livre d'or de la bourgeoisie poitevine." *MSAO,* 2d ser., 19 (1896): 1–50.

Babinet, Léon. "Le siège de Poitiers en 1569." *MSAO,* 2d ser., 11 (1888): 463–613.

Barbier, Alfred. "Chroniques de Poitiers aux XVe et XVIe siècles." *MSAO,* 2d ser., 13 (1890): 431–517.

——. "Trois ordonnances inédites de François Ier relatives aux privilèges de la ville de Poitiers." *BSAO,* 2d ser., 7 (1896): 303–9.

Beauchet-Filleau, H[enri] and Ch[arles] de Chergé. *Dictionnaire historique et généalogique des familles du Poitou.* 4 vols. 2d ed. Poitiers: Oudin, 1891–1912.

Besson-Léaud, Théophile. *Conférence Boncenne: la coutume du Poitou; son passé, ses vestiges dans le droit français.* Niort: Imprimerie Th. Mercier, 1900.

Boissonnade, Prosper. *Essai sur l'organisation du travail en Poitou depuis le XIe siècle jusqu'à la Révolution.* 2 vols. *MSAO,* 2d ser., 21–22. Poitiers, 1898–99.

——. *Histoire de Poitou.* Paris: Ancienne Librairie Furne Boivin & Cie, 1926.

Bonvalet, Adrien. "Jean d'Amoncourt, Évêque de Poitiers (1551–1558)." *BSAO,* 2d ser., 2 (1881): 347–53.

Camus, Marie-Thérèse. *Sculpture romane du Poitou: les grands chantiers du XIe siècle.* Paris: Picard, 1992.

Chergé, Charles de. "Notice bibiographique sur Jean de la Haye, lieutenant général de Poitou." *MSAO,* 1st ser., 8 (1842): 173–220.

Colette-Pattyn, Marie-Noëlle. "Le processional de Saint-Hilaire-le Grand à Poitiers (XVIe siècle), deuxième partie: édition des rubriques, commentaire, résumé d'itinéraires." *BSAO,* 4th ser., 15 (1979): 93–142, 165–222.

De La Croix, Camille. "Inscriptions du XVIe et du XVIIe siècles." *BSAO,* 2d ser., 3 (1884): 371–72.

Desayre, [Léo]. "Charles-Quint en Poitou en 1539." *BSAO,* 2d ser., 6 (1894): 410–20.

Desgraves, Louis. *Répertoire bibliographique des livres imprimés en France au seizième siècle, 115: Poitiers.* Baden-Baden: Librairie Heitz GMBH, 1970.

Dez, Gaston. *Histoire de Poitiers. MSAO,* 4th ser., 10. Poitiers: Société des Antiquaires de l'Ouest, 1969.

Dez, Pierre. *Histoire des protestants et des églises réformées du Poitou.* La Rochelle: Imprimerie de l'Ouest, 1936.

Dreux-Duradier, [Jean-François]. *Histoire littéraire du Poitou: précédée d'une introduction et continuée jusqu'en 1849 par une société d'hommes de lettres.* 1842–49. Reprint, Geneva: Slatkine Reprints, 1969.

Eygun, F. "Les Trois Pilliers de Poitiers." *BSAO,* 3d ser., 12 (1941): 744–60.

Favreau, Robert. "Aspects de l'Université de Poitiers au XVe siècle." *BSAO,* 4th ser., 5 (1959): 31–71.

——. "Le palais de Poitiers au moyen âge." *BSAO,* 4th ser., 11 (1971): 35–65.

——. *La ville de Poitiers à la fin du moyen âge: une capitale régionale.* 2 vols. Poitiers: Société des Antiquaires de l'Ouest, 1978.

Favreau, Robert, ed. *Histoire de Poitiers.* Toulouse: Privat, 1985.

Faye, Léon. "Le Parlement et les Grands Jours de Poitiers." *MSAO,* 1st ser., 21 (1854): 13–40.

Fracard, M.-L. "Les ventes de biens d'église par ordonnances légales au XVIe siècle." *BSAO,* 4th ser., 10 (1969): 219–30.

Gaillard, Nicias. "De quelques descriptions de Poitiers et du Poitou qu'on rencontre dans des ouvrages de géographie et des voyages publiés aux XVIe et XVIIe siècles." *MSAO,* 1st ser., 2 (1836): 120–74.

Gaulon, Françoise. "Manuscrits et annales municipales de Poitiers au moyen âge." *BSAO,* 5th ser., 11 (1997): 19–40.

Genesteix. "Le logis de la famille de Sainte Marthe à Poitiers." *BSAO,* 2d ser., 5 (1890): 376–87.

Gennes, Ch. de. "Les avocats du roi à Poitiers." *MSAO,* 1st ser., 27 (1863): 5–26.

——. "Étude historique sur la coutume du Poitou commentée par les jurisconsultes poitevins, et spécialement par le présidial de Poitiers." *MSAO,* 1st ser., 33 (1868): 277–395.

——. "Notice sur la famille de Brilhac." *BSAO,* 1st ser., 10 (1863): 314–17.

——. "Notice sur le livre des actions publiques faites sur divers sujets au siège présidial de Poitiers, par M. Antoine Citoys, docteur ès lois, avocat audit siège." *BSAO,* 1st ser., 10 (1862): 173–90.

——. "Notice sur le présidial de Poitiers." *MSAO,* 1st ser., 26 (1860–61): 359–528.

Ginot, Emile. "Notes sur la Confrérie des Pèlerins de Saint-Jacques de Poitiers et sa Chapelle." *BSAO,* 3d ser., 9 (1932): 494–509.

——. "À travers les siècles; à travers les rues: introduction à la topographie historique de la ville de Poitiers." *BSAO,* 3d ser., 5 (1921): 515–45.

——. "Vieilles histoires d'hôtelleries à Poitiers." *BSAO,* 3d ser., 7 (1927): 551–84.

Jahan, Sébastien. "Approches qualitatives de la pauvreté en haut Poitou au XVIIIe siècle." *BSAO,* 5th ser., 5 (1991): 97–136.

——. *Profession, parenté, identité sociale: les notaires de Poitiers aux temps modernes, 1515–1815.* Toulouse: Presses Universitaires du Mirail, 1999.

——. "Réproduction professionelle et mobilité sociale: les Chesneau, notaires royaux à Poitiers (1519–1617)." *BSAO,* 5th ser., 6 (1992): 185–209.

Jarousseau, Gérard. "L'élection du maire de Poitiers, Pierre Régnier, en 1516: observation sur les institutions communales de cette ville." *BSAO,* 4th ser., 14 (1978): 567–86.

——. "Essai de topographie historique: le marché neuf de Poitiers créé à la fin du XIe siècle." *BSAO,* 5th ser., 4 (1990): 99–118.

——. "Un rôle d'imposition de Poitiers en 1552: étude des structures sociales et économiques de la ville." *Actes du 87e Congrès des Sociétés Savantes, Poitiers 1962, Bulletin philologique* (1962): 481–92.

La Bouralière, Auguste de. *Bibliographie poitevine ou dictionnaire des auteurs poitevins et des ouvrages publiés sur le Poitou jusqu'à la fin du XVIIIe siècle.* 1907. Reprint, Geneva: Slatkine Reprints, 1972.

——. "Les bornes de l'ancien bourg Saint-Hilaire." *BSAO*, 2d ser., 4 (1886): 88–96.

——. "L'imprimerie & la librairie à Poitiers pendant le XVIe siècle." *MSAO*, 2d ser., 23 (1899): 1–392.

——. "Un pamphlétaire au XVIe siècle: François Le Breton." *MSAO*, 2d ser., 6 (1883): 19–35.

La Marsonnière, Jules-Levieil de. "La navigation du Clain." *BSAO*, 2d ser., 7 (1896): 237–58.

——. "Le salon de Mesdames Desroches aux Grands Jours." *MSAO*, 1st ser., 8 (1842): 37–58.

La Ménardière, [Joseph-Camille-Arnault] de. "Introduction à l'histoire des établissements de charité à Poitiers." *MSAO*, 1st ser., 37 (1873): 3–40.

Lecointre-Dupont. "Mémoire sur le miracle des clefs et sur la procession du lundi de pâques." *MSAO*, 1st ser., 12 (1845): 209–56.

——. "Notice sur le monument nommé La Pierre Qui Pue." *MSAO*, 1st ser., 9 (1843): 65–76.

Ledain, Bélisaire. "Les livres de raison et journaux historiques du Poitou." *Revue poitevine et saintongeaise: histoire, archéologie, beaux-arts & littérature* 4, no. 47 (1888): 21–334.

——. "Les maires de Poitiers." *MSAO*, 2d ser., 20 (1897): 215–770.

——. "Notice sur l'ancien couvent des Augustins de Poitiers." *BSAO*, 2d ser., 7 (1895): 179–98.

Legrand. "La corporation des boulangers de Poitiers en 1609." *MSAO*, 2d ser., 7 (1884): 339–42.

Le livre à Poitiers 1479–1979: catalogue de l'exposition organisée par la bibliothèque municipale à l'occasion du 500e anniversaire de l'imprimerie à Poitiers. Poitiers: Musée Sainte-Croix, 1979.

Longuemar, [Alphonse Le Touzé] de. *Essai historique sur l'église royale et collégiale de Saint-Hilaire-le-Grand de Poitiers. MSAO*, 1st ser., 23. Poitiers: A. Dupré, 1857.

Marcadé, Jacques. "Fabriques et fabriciens dans le diocèse de Poitiers, au XVIIIe siècle." *BSAO*, 4th ser., 13 (1975): 189–99.

——. "Les Protestants dans le Centre-Ouest de 1534 à 1660." *BSAO*, 5th ser., 1 (1987): 99–115.

Ouvré, Henri. "Essai sur l'histoire de la Ligue à Poitiers." *MSAO*, 1st ser., 21 (1854): 85–243.

——. *Essai sur l'histoire de Poitiers depuis la fin de la ligue jusqu'à la prise de La Rochelle (1595–1628). MSAO*, 1st ser., 22. Poitiers: A. Dupré, 1856.

Pellegrin, Nicole. *Les bachelleries: organisations et fêtes de la jeunesse dans le Centre-Ouest XVe–XVIIIe siècles. MSAO*, 4th ser., 16. Poitiers: Société des Antiquaires de l'Ouest, 1982.

Péret, Jacques. "Habitat et famille dans une petite paroisse de Poitiers, La Résurrection, à la fin du XVIIIe siècle." *BSAO*, 4th ser., 16 (1981): 237–49.

Rambaud, Pierre. "Contribution à l'étude des confréries religieuses dans les maîtrises et corporations de Poitiers." *BSAO*, 3d ser., 1 (1909): 673–712.

——. "Contribution à l'étude des maîtres fondeurs en Poitou." *BSAO*, 3d ser., 3 (1914): 230–44.

——. "Étienne Thevet maître chirurgien à Poitiers (1586–1618)." *BSAO*, 3d ser., 1 (1908): 382–95.

——. "La juridiction consulaire de Poitiers (1566–1791)." Parts 1 and 2. *BSAO*, 3d ser., 6 (1924): 643–72; 7 (1925): 210–31.

——. "Un médecin chanoine de l'église de Poitiers au XVIe siècle: Guillaume Sacher, docteur en médecine." *BSAO*, 3d ser., 5 (1920): 381–407.

——. "La police des rues de Poitiers du XVe au XVIIIe siècle." *BSAO*, 3d ser., 4 (1918): 482–99.

——. "Les statuts de la faculté de médecine de Poitiers (1533–1616)." *BSAO*, 3d ser., 3 (1913): 33–63.

Rédet, [Louis-François-Xavier]. *Inventaire des archives de la ville de Poitiers. MSAO*, 2d ser., 5 (1882). Poitiers: Tolmer, 1883.

——. "Mémoire sur les halles et les foires de Poitiers." *MSAO*, 1st ser., 12 (1845): 61–97.

Richard, Alfred. *Histoire des comtes de Poitou, 778–1204.* 2 vols. Paris: Alphonse Picard & Fils, 1903.

——. "Le Manuscrit Nᵒ51 de la Bibliothèque de Poitiers. A-t-il eu un caractère officiel?" *BSAO*, 2d ser., 3 (1883–85): 297–306.

——. "Notes biographiques sur les Bouchet, imprimeurs et procureurs à Poitiers au XVIe siècle." *BSAO*, 3d ser., 2 (1912): 544–84.

Richard, Hélène. "Les Livres d'Heures imprimés poitevins conservés à la bibliothèque municipale de Poitiers." *BSAO*, 4th ser., 16 (1982): 343–58.

Rivaud, David. "La crise militaire de 1512–1513 et ses conséquences politiques sur le corps de ville de Poitiers." *BSAO*, 5th ser., 8 (1994): 31–49.

Rondeau, Philippe. "L'ancien hôtel de ville de Poitiers." *MSAO*, 1st ser., 34 (1869): 129–60.

Tarrade, Jean. "La population de Poitiers au XVIIIe siècle: essai d'analyse socio-professionnelle d'après les contrats de mariage." *BSAO*, 4th ser., 12 (1974): 331–52.

——. "La réforme municipale de 1787 en Poitou." *BSAO*, 4th ser., 19 (1986): 429–46.

Thibaudeau, [Antoine-René-Hyacinthe]. *Abrégé de l'histoire du Poitou, contenant ce qui s'est passé de plus remarquable dans cette province, depuis le règne de Clovis jusqu'au commencement de ce siècle.* 6 vols. Paris: Demonville, 1782–88.

Thouvenin, Georges. "La fondation de Poitiers selon les humanistes de la Renaissance: à propos d'une ode de Scévole de Sainte-Marthe." *BSAO*, 3d ser., 7 (1927): 734–63.

Villard, François. "Jean de la Trémoille, administrateur du diocèse de Poitiers (1505–1507)." *BSAO*, 4th ser., 10 (1969): 205–18.

——. "Le conflit entre l'évêque Pierre d'Amboise et le chapitre cathédral pour la juridiction ecclésiastique." *BSAO*, 4th ser., 9 (1968): 341–60.

Yver, Jean. "Les caractères originaux du groupe de coutumes de l'Ouest de la France." *Revue historique de droit français et étranger* ser. 4, no. 30 (1952): 18–79.

General Secondary Works

Abray, Lorna Jane. *The People's Reformation: Magistrates, Clergy, and Commons in Strasbourg, 1500–1598.* Ithaca: Cornell University Press, 1985.

Adams, Christine. *A Taste for Comfort and Status: A Bourgeois Family in Eighteenth-Century France.* University Park: Pennsylvania State University Press, 2000.

Allen, J. W. *A History of Political Thought in the Sixteenth Century.* 2d ed. London: Methuen, 1961.

Antoine, M[ichel]. "La monarchie absolue." In *The French Revolution and the Creation of Modern Political Culture.* Vol. 1, *The Political Culture of the Old Regime*, 3–24. Ed. Keith Michael Baker. Oxford: Pergamon Press, 1987.

Armstrong, Megan. "The Franciscans and the Catholic League: A Question of Civic Ties and Spirituality." *Proceedings of the Western Society for French History* 24 (1997): 130–38.

Arnade, Peter. *Realms of Ritual: Burgundian Ceremony and Civic Life in Late Medieval Ghent.* Ithaca: Cornell University Press, 1996.

Babeau, Albert. *La ville sous l'ancien régime.* 2 vols. Paris: Didier et Cie, 1884.

Babelon, Jean-Pierre. *Paris au XVIe siècle.* Paris: Hachette, 1986.

Barel, Yves. *La ville médiévale: système social, système urbain.* Grenoble: Presses Universitaires de Grenoble, 1977.

Barnavi, Elie. "Centralisme ou fédéralisme? Les relations entre Paris et les villes à l'époque de la Ligue (1585–1594)." *Revue historique* 526 (1978): 335–44.

——. *Le parti de dieu: étude sociale et politique des chefs de la Ligue parisienne, 1585–1594.* Brussels and Louvain: Nauwelaerts, 1980.

Barnavi, Elie, and Robert Descimon. *La Sainte Ligue le juge et la potence: l'assassinat de Président Brisson (15 novembre 1591).* Paris: Hachette, 1985.

Baumgartner, Frederic J. *Henry II, King of France 1547–1559.* Durham: Duke University Press, 1988.

——. *Radical Reactionaries: The Political Thought of the French Catholic League.* Geneva: Droz, 1975.

Beik, William. *Absolutism and Society in Seventeenth-Century France: State Power and Provincial Aristocracy in Languedoc.* Cambridge: Cambridge University Press, 1985.

——. "The Culture of Protest in Seventeenth-Century French Towns." *Social History* 15, no. 1 (1990): 1–23.

——. "Magistrates and Popular Uprisings in France before the Fronde: The Case of Toulouse." *Journal of Modern History* 46 (1974): 585–608.

——. *Urban Protest in Seventeenth-Century France: The Culture of Retribution.* Cambridge: Cambridge University Press, 1997.

Benedict, Philip. *Rouen during the Wars of Religion.* Cambridge: Cambridge University Press, 1981.

Benedict, Philip, ed. *Cities and Social Change in Early Modern France.* London: Unwin Hyman, 1989.

Bercé, Yves-Marie. *Histoire des Croquants: étude des soulèvements populaires au XVIIe siècle dans le sud-ouest de la France.* 2 vols. Paris: Librairie Droz, 1974.

Bernstein, Hilary J. "The Benefit of the Ballot? Elections and Influence in Sixteenth-Century Poitiers." *French Historical Studies* 24, no. 4 (2001): 621–52.

Billot, Claudine. "Chartres et la navigation sur l'Eure à la fin du moyen âge." *Annales de Bretagne et des pays de l'Ouest* 85, no. 2 (1978): 245–59.

Black, Antony. *Guilds and Civil Society in European Political Thought from the Twelfth Century to the Present.* Ithaca: Cornell University Press, 1984.

Bloch, Jean-Richard. *L'anoblissement en France au temps de François Ier: essai d'une définition de la condition juridique et sociale de la noblesse au début du XVIe siècle.* Paris: Librairie Félix Alcan, 1934.

Bornecque, Robert. *La France de Vauban.* Paris: Éditions Arthaud, 1984.

Bosseboeuf, L. A. "La fabrique des soieries de Tours." *Mémoires de la société archéologique de Touraine* 41 (1900): 193–528.

Bossenga, Gail. *The Politics of Privilege: Old Regime and Revolution in Lille.* Cambridge: Cambridge University Press, 1991.

Bouillé, René de. *Histoire des ducs de Guise.* 4 vols. Paris: Amyot, 1850.

Boulton, Jeremy. *Neighbourhood and Society: A London Suburb in the Seventeenth Century.* Cambridge: Cambridge University Press, 1987.

Bourquin, Laurent. *Les nobles, la ville et le roi: l'autorité nobiliaire en Anjou pendant les guerres de Religion*. Paris: Belin, 2001.

Boutier, Jean, Alain Dewerpe, and Daniel Nordman. *Un tour de France royal: le voyage de Charles IX (1564–1566)*. Paris: Aubier Montaigne, 1984.

Bouwsma, William J. "Lawyers in Early Modern Culture." *American Historical Review* 78, no. 2 (1973): 303–27.

Brady, Thomas A. Jr. "In Search of the Godly City: The Domestication of Religion in the German Urban Reformation." In *Communities, Politics and Reformation in Early Modern Europe*, 169–88. Leiden: Brill, 1998.

——. *Ruling Class, Regime, and Reformation at Strasbourg, 1520–1555*. Leiden: Brill, 1978.

——. *Turning Swiss: Cities and Empire, 1450–1550*. Cambridge: Cambridge University Press, 1985.

Britnell, Jennifer. *Jean Bouchet*. Edinburgh: Edinburgh University Press for the University of Durham, 1986.

Bryant, Lawrence M. *The King and the City in the Parisian Royal Entry Ceremony: Politics, Ritual, and Art in the Renaissance*. Geneva: Droz, 1986.

Burns, J. H. *The Cambridge History of Political Thought 1450–1700*. Cambridge: Cambridge University Press, 1991.

Carré, Henri. *Le Parlement de Bretagne après la Ligue (1589–1610)*. Paris: Maison Quantin, 1888.

Carroll, Stuart. "The Guise Affinity and Popular Protest during the Wars of Religion." *French History* 9, no. 2 (1995): 125–52.

——. *Noble Power during the French Wars of Religion: The Guise Affinity and the Catholic Cause in Normandy*. Cambridge: Cambridge University Press, 1998.

Cassan, Michel. "Laïcs, Ligue et réforme catholique à Limoges." *Histoire, économie et société* 10, no. 2 (1991): 159–75.

——. "Marchands, bourgeois et officiers en Haut-Limousin au XVIe siècle." *Bulletin de la société archéologique et historique du Limousin* 113 (1986): 16–23.

——. "Mobilité sociale et conflits religieux: l'exemple limousin (1550–1630)." In *La dynamique sociale dans l'Europe du Nord-Ouest (XVIe–XVIIe siècles): colloque, 1987*. Association des historiens modernistes de l'Université 12, 71–92. Paris: PUPS, 1987.

——. *Le temps des guerres de religion: le cas du Limousin (vers 1530–vers 1630)*. [Paris]: Publisud, 1996.

Cassan, Michel, ed. *Les officiers "moyens" à l'époque moderne: pouvoir, culture, identité*. Limoges: Presses Universitaires de Limoges, [1998].

Cerutti, Simona. *La ville et les métiers: naissance d'un langage corporatif (Turin, 17e–18e siècle)*. Paris: Éditions de l'ÉHÉSS, 1990.

Chartier, Roger and Henri-Jean Martin, eds. *Histoire de l'édition française*. 4 vols. Paris: Promodis, 1983–86.

Chatel, Jean-Yves. *Les projets de transnavigation de Loire en Seine par les rivières d'Eure et du Loir et leur abandon: 150 ans d'utopie (1685–1840)*. Chartres: Société archéologique d'Eure-et-Loir, 1995.

Chevalier, Bernard. *Les bonnes villes de France du XIVe au XVIe siècle*. Paris: Aubier Montaigne, 1982.

——. "L'état et les bonnes villes en France au temps de leur accord parfait (1450–1550)." In *La ville, la bourgeoisie et la genèse de l'état moderne (XIIe–XVIIIe siècles)*, 71–85. Ed. Neithard Bulst and J.-Ph. Genet. Paris: Éditions du CNRS, 1988.

——. "The Policy of Louis XI towards the *Bonnes Villes*: The Case of Tours." In *The Re-*

covery of France in the Fifteenth Century, 265–93. Ed. P. S. Lewis. London: Macmillan, 1971.

——. "Pouvoir royal et pouvoir urbain à Tours pendant la guerre de Cent ans." Parts 1 and 2. *Annales de Bretagne et des pays de l'Ouest (Anjou, Maine, Tourraine)* 81, no. 2 (1974): 365–92; 83, no. 4 (1974): 681–707.

——. *Tours, ville royale (1356–1520): origine et développement d'une capitale à la fin du moyen âge.* Louvain and Paris: Vander/Nauwelaerts, [1975].

Church, William. *Constitutional Thought in Sixteenth-Century France: A Study in the Evolution of Ideas.* Cambridge: Harvard University Press, 1941.

Cloulas, Ivan. *Henri II.* Paris: Fayard, 1985.

Collins, James. *Fiscal Limits of Absolutism: Direct Taxation in Early Seventeenth-Century France.* Berkeley: University of California Press, 1988.

Congar, Yves M.-J. "Quod Omnes Tangit, Ab Omnibus Tractari et Approbari Debet." *Revue historique de droit français et étranger.* 4th ser., 35 (1958): 210–59.

Constant, Jean-Marie. *La Ligue.* [Paris]: Fayard, 1996.

Coornaert, Émile. *Les corporations en France avant 1789.* 2d ed. Paris: Les Éditions Ouvrières, 1968.

——. "La politique économique de la France au début du règne de François Ier." *Annales de l'Université de Paris* 8, no. 5 (1933): 414–27.

Corcia, Joseph di. "*Bourg, Bourgeois, Bourgeois de Paris* from the Eleventh to the Eighteenth Century." *Journal of Modern History* 50, no. 2 (1978): 207–33.

Corvisier, André, ed. *Histoire du Havre et de l'estuaire de la Seine.* Toulouse: Privat, 1987.

Craig, J. S. "Co-operation and Initiatives: Elizabethan Churchwardens and the Parish Accounts of Mildenhall." *Social History* 18, no. 3 (1993): 357–80.

Crouzet, Denis. *Les guerriers de dieu: la violence au temps des troubles de la religion vers 1525–vers 1610.* 2 vols. [Paris]: Champ Vallon, 1990.

——. "Recherches sur les processions blanches, 1583–1584." *Histoire, économie et société* 1 (1982): 511–63.

Crue, François de. *Le parti des politiques au lendemain de la Saint-Barthélemy: La Molle et Conconat.* Paris: Plon, 1892.

Darquennes, Achille. "Représentation et bien commun." In *IXe congrès international des sciences historiques, Paris 1950,* 35–51. Louvain: Bibliothèque de l'Université, Bureaux du Recueil, 1952.

Davis, Barbara Beckerman. "Poverty and Poor Relief in Sixteenth-Century Toulouse." *Historical Reflections* 17 (1991): 267–96.

Davis, Natalie Zemon. "The Sacred and the Body Social in Sixteenth-Century Lyon." *Past and Present* 90 (1981): 40–70.

——. *Society and Culture in Early Modern France.* Stanford: Stanford University Press, 1975.

Descimon, Robert. "Les assemblées de l'Hôtel de Ville de Paris (mi-XVIe–mi-XVIIe siècles." *L'administration locale en Île-de-France: mémoires de la Fédération des Sociétés historiques et archéologiques de Paris et de l'Île de France* 38, no. 1 (1987): 39–54.

——. "Le corps de ville et le système cérémoniel parisien au début de l'âge moderne." In *Statuts individuels, statuts corporatifs et statuts judiciaires dans les villes européennes (moyen âge et temps modernes): actes du colloque tenu à Gand les 12–14 octobre 1995,* 73–128. Ed. Marc Boone and Maarten Prak. Leuven-Apeldoorn: Garant, 1996.

——. "Le corps de ville et les élections échevinales à Paris aux XVIe et XVIIe siècles: codification coutumière et pratiques sociales." *Histoire, économie et société* 13 (1994): 507–30.

——. "L'échevinage parisien sous Henri IV (1594–1609): autonomie urbaine, conflits politiques et exclusives sociales." In *La ville, la bourgeoisie et la genèse de l'état moderne (XIIe–XVIIIe siècle): actes du colloque de Bielefeld (29 novembre–1er décembre 1985)*, 113–50. Ed. Neithard Bulst and J.-Ph. Genet. Paris: Éditions du CNRS, 1988.

——. "La Ligue à Paris (1585–1594): une révision." *Annales: E.S.C.* 37 (1982): 72–111.

——. "Milice bourgeoise et identité citadine à Paris au temps de la Ligue." *Annales: E.S.C.* 48, no. 4 (1993): 885–906.

——. "Prise de parti, appartenance sociale et relations familiales dans la Ligue parisienne (1585–1594)." In *Les réformes: enracinement socio-culturel: XXVe colloque international d'études humanistes, Tours, 1er–13 juillet 1982*, 123–36. Ed. Bernard Chevalier and Robert Sauzet. Paris: Éditions de la Maisnie, 1985.

——. *Qui étaient les Seize? étude sociale de deux cent vingt-cinq cadres laïcs de la Ligue radicale parisienne (1585–1594)*. Mémoires de la Fédération des sociétés historiques et archéologiques de Paris et de l'Île-de-France 34. Paris: Klincksieck, 1983.

——. "Les scrutateurs des élections échevinales à Paris (mi-XVIe/mi-XVIIe siècle): des médiateurs de fidélité." In *Paris et ses compagnes sous l'ancien régime: mélanges offerts à Jean Jacquart*, 195–209. Ed. Michel Balard, Jean-Claude Hervé, and Nicole Lemaître. Paris: Université de Panthéon-Sorbonne, 1994.

——. "La vénalité des offices politiques de la ville de Paris (1500–1681)." *Le bulletin de la S.H.M.C.* (1994), nos. 3–4: 16–27.

Descimon, Robert, and Jean Nagle. "Les quartiers de Paris du moyen âge au XVIIIe siècle: évolution d'un espace plurifonctionnel." *Annales: E.S.C.* 34, no. 5 (1979): 956–83.

Dewald, Jonathan. *The Formation of a Provincial Nobility: The Magistrates of the Parlement of Rouen 1499–1610*. Princeton: Princeton University Press, 1980.

Diefendorf, Barbara B. *Beneath the Cross: Catholics and Huguenots in Sixteenth-Century Paris*. Oxford: Oxford University Press, 1991.

——. *Paris City Councillors in the Sixteenth Century: The Politics of Patrimony*. Princeton: Princeton University Press, 1983.

Diefendorf, Barbara B., and Carla Hesse, eds. *Culture and Identity in Early Modern Europe (1500–1800): Essays in Honor of Natalie Zemon Davis*. Ann Arbor: University of Michigan Press, 1993.

Dolan, Claire. *Entre tours et clochers: les gens d'église à Aix-en-Provence au XVIe siècle*. Sherbrooke, Canada, and Aix-en-Provence, France: Centre d'Études de la Renaissance de l'Université de Sherbrooke and Edisud, 1981.

——. "L'identité urbaine et les histoires locales publiées du XVIe au XVIIIe siècle en France." *Canadian Journal of History* 27 (1992): 277–98.

——. "Des images en action: cité, pouvoir municipal et crises pendant les guerres de religion à Aix-en-Provence." In *Les productions symboliques du pouvoir XVIe–XXe siècle*, 65–86. Ed. Laurier Turgeon. Québec: Septentrion, 1990.

——. *Le notaire, la famille et la ville (Aix-en-Provence à la fin du XVIe siècle)*. Toulouse: Presses Universitaires du Mirail, 1998.

Dolan, Claire, ed. *Évenement, identité et histoire*. Québec: Septentrion, 1991.

Doucet, Roger. *Les institutions de la France au XVIe siècle*. 2 vols. Paris: Picard, 1948.

Drouot, Henri. "Les conseils provinciaux de la Sainte-Union (1589–1595): notes et questions." *Annales du Midi* 65, no. 23 (1953): 415–33.

——. *Mayenne et la Bourgogne: étude sur la Ligue (1587–1596)*. 2 vols. Dijon: Bernigaud & Privat, 1937.

Dubois, Claude-Gilbert. *Celtes et Gaulois au XVIe siècle: le développement littéraire d'un mythe nationaliste*. Paris: J. Vrin, 1972.

Duby, Georges, ed. *Histoire de la France urbaine*. 5 vols. Paris: Seuil, 1980–85.

DuPlessis, Robert S. *Lille and the Dutch Revolt: Urban Stability in an Era of Revolution 1500–1582*. Cambridge: Cambridge University Press, 1991.

Durand, Yves. "Les républiques urbaines en France à la fin du XVIe siècle." *Société d'Histoire et d'Archéologie de l'Arrondissement de Saint-Malo, Annales 1990*, 205–44.

Dutens, Joseph-Michel. *Histoire de la navigation intérieure de la France, avec une exposition des canaux à entreprendre pour en compléter le système*. 2 vols. Paris: A. Sautelet, 1829.

Farr, James R. *Hands of Honor: Artisans and Their World in Dijon, 1550–1650*. Ithaca: Cornell University Press, 1988.

Febvre, Lucien. *Life in Renaissance France*. Trans. Marian Rothstein. Cambridge: Harvard University Press, 1977.

Fédou, René. *Les hommes de loi lyonnais à la fin du moyen âge: étude sur les origines de la classe de robe*. Annales de l'Université de Lyon 3d ser., 37. Paris: Société d'Édition "Les Belles Lettres," 1964.

Filhol, René. *Le premier président Christofle de Thou et la réformation des coutumes*. Paris: Recueil Sirey, 1937.

Finley-Croswhite, S. Annette. "Absolutism and Municipal Autonomy: Henry IV and the 1602 Pancarte Revolt in Limoges." In *Society and Institutions in Early Modern France*, 80–97. Ed. Mack P. Holt. Athens: University of Georgia Press, 1991.

———. "Engendering the Wars of Religion: Female Agency during the Catholic League in Dijon." *French Historical Studies* 20, no. 2 (1997): 127–54.

———. *Henry IV and the Towns: The Pursuit of Legitimacy in French Urban Society, 1589–1610*. Cambridge: Cambridge University Press, 1999.

Fumaroli, Marc. *L'âge de l'éloquence: rhétorique et 'res literaria' de la Renaissance au seuil de l'époque classique*. Hautes Études Médiévales et Modernes 43. Geneva: Librairie Droz, 1980.

Gal, Stéphane. *Grenoble au temps de la Ligue: étude politique, sociale et religieuse d'une cité en crise (vers 1562–vers 1598)*. Grenoble: Presses Universitaires de Grenoble, 2000.

Gallais, Vincent. "Entre apprentissage et ambition: la culture politique d'un procureur du roi au présidial de Nantes, Jean Blanchard de Lessongère (1602–1612)." In *Les officiers "moyens" à l'époque moderne: pouvoir, culture, identité*, 367–86. Ed. Michel Cassan. Limoges: Pulim, [1998].

Galpern, A. N. *The Religions of the People in Sixteenth-Century Champagne*. Cambridge: Harvard University Press, 1976.

Garrioch, David. *Neighbourhood and Community in Paris, 1740–1790*. Cambridge: Cambridge University Press, 1986.

Gascon, Richard. *Grand commerce et vie urbaine au XVIe siècle: Lyon et ses marchands (environs de 1520–environs de 1580)*. 2 vols. Paris: SEVPEN, 1971.

Giry, A. *Les établissements de Rouen: études sur l'histoire des institutions municipales de Rouen, Falaise, Pont-Audemar, Verneuil, La Rochelle, Saintes, Oléron, Bayonne, Tours, Niort, Cognac, S-Jean-d'Angély, Angoulême, Poitiers, etc*. 2 vols. Paris: F. Vieweg, 1883.

Glidden, Hope H. *The Storyteller as Humanist: The Serées of Guillaume Bouchet*. Lexington, Ky.: French Forum Publishers, 1981.

Greengrass, Mark. "The Anatomy of a Religious Riot in Toulouse in May 1562." *Journal of Ecclesiastical History* 34, no. 3 (1983): 367–91.

———. *France in the Age of Henri IV: The Struggle for Stability*. 1st ed. London: Longman, 1984.

———. "The Sainte Union in the Provinces: The Case of Toulouse." *The Sixteenth Century Journal* 14 (1983): 469–98.

Guignet, Philippe. *Le pouvoir dans la ville au XVIIIe siècle: pratiques politiques, notabilité et étique sociale de part et d'autre de la frontière franco-belge.* Paris: ÉHÉSS, 1990.

Guilmoto, Gustave. *Étude sur les droits de navigation de la Seine de Paris à la Roche-Guyon du XIe au XVIIIe siècle.* Paris: Alphonse Picard, 1889.

Habermas, Jürgen. *The Structural Transformation of the Public Sphere: An Inquiry into a Category of Bourgeois Society.* Trans. Thomas Burger and Frederick Lawrence. Cambridge: MIT Press, 1989.

Hamon, Auguste. *Un grand rhétoriqueur poitevin: Jean Bouchet 1476–1557?* Paris: H. Oudin, 1901.

Hanawalt, Barbara A., and Kathryn L. Reyerson, eds. *City and Spectacle in Medieval Europe.* Minneapolis: University of Minnesota Press, 1994.

Hankins, James, ed. *Renaissance Civic Humanism: Reappraisals and Reflections.* Cambridge: Cambridge University Press, 2000.

Hanley, Sarah. "Engendering the State: Family Formation and State Building." *French Historical Studies* 16, no. 1 (1989): 4–27.

Hanlon, Gregory. *L'univers des gens de bien: culture et comportements des élites urbaines en Agenais-Condomois au XVIIe siècle.* Bordeaux: Presses Universitaires de Bordeaux, 1989.

Harding, Robert. *Anatomy of a Power Elite: The Provincial Governors of Early Modern France.* New Haven: Yale University Press, 1978.

———. "Revolution and Reform in the Holy League: Angers, Rennes, Nantes." *Journal of Modern History* 53 (1981): 397–416.

Hardwick, Julie. *The Practice of Patriarchy: Gender and the Politics of Household Authority in Early Modern France.* University Park: Pennsylvania State University Press, 1998.

Heller, Henry. *The Conquest of Poverty: The Calvinist Revolt in Sixteenth Century France.* Leiden: Brill, 1986.

Hindle, Steve. "Hierarchy and Community in the Elizabethan Parish: The Swallowfield Articles of 1596." *The Historical Journal* 42, no. 3 (1999): 835–51.

Hoffman, Philip T. *Church and Community in the Diocese of Lyon, 1500–1789.* New Haven: Yale University Press, 1984.

Holmès, Catherine E. *L'éloquence judiciaire de 1620 à 1660: reflet des problèmes sociaux, religieux et politiques de l'époque.* Paris: Nizet, 1967.

Holt, Mack P. *The Duke of Anjou and the Politique Struggle during the Wars of Religion.* Cambridge: Cambridge University Press, 1986.

———. "Order and Community in Sixteenth-Century Burgundy." *Proceedings of the Annual Meeting of the Western Society for French History* 16 (1989): 60–71.

———. "Popular Political Culture and Mayoral Elections in Sixteenth-Century Dijon." In *Society and Institutions in Early Modern France,* 98–116. Athens: University of Georgia Press, 1991.

———. "Putting Religion Back into the Wars of Religion." *French Historical Studies* 18, no. 2 (1993): 524–51.

———. "Wine, Community, and Reformation in Sixteenth-Century Burgundy." *Past and Present* 138 (1993): 58–93.

Holt, Mack P., ed. *Society and Institutions in Early Modern France.* Athens: University of Georgia Press, 1991.

Hunt, Lynn, ed. *The New Cultural History.* Berkeley: University of California Press, 1989.

Huppert, George. *Les Bourgeois Gentilshommes: An Essay on the Definition of Elites in Renaissance France.* Chicago: University of Chicago Press, 1977.

———. *The Idea of Perfect History: Historical Erudition and Historical Philosophy in Renaissance France.* Urbana: University of Illinois Press, 1970.

Irvine, Frederick M. "From Renaissance City to Ancien Régime Capital: Montpellier, c. 1500–c. 1600." In *Cities and Social Change in Early Modern France*, 105–33. Ed. Philip Benedict. London: Unwin Hyman, 1989.

Jacquart, Jean. *François I.* Paris: Fayard, 1981.

James, Mervyn. "Ritual, Drama and Social Body in the Late Medieval English Town." *Past and Present* 98 (1983): 3–29.

Jensen, De Lamar. *Diplomacy and Dogmatism. Bernardo de Mendoza and the French Catholic League.* Cambridge: Harvard University Press, 1964.

Jouanna, Arlette. *L'idée de race en France au XVIe siècle et au début du XVIIe.* 2 vols. Montpellier: Université Paul Valéry, 1981.

——. "La première domination des réformés à Montpellier (1561–1563)." In *Les réformes: enracinement socio-culturel: XXVe colloque international d'études humanistes, Tours, 1er–13 juillet 1982*, 151–60. Ed. Bernard Chevalier and Robert Sauzet. Paris: Éditions de la Maisnie, 1985.

Juvigny, Rigoley de, ed. *Les bibliothéques françoises de La Croix du Maine et de Du Verdier sieur de Vauprivas.* Vol. 2, *La Croix du Maine.* Paris: Saillant & Nyon; Michel Lambert, 1772.

Kaiser, Wolfgang. *Marseille au temps des troubles, 1559–1596: morphologie sociale et luttes de factions.* Trans. Florence Chaix. Paris: Éditions de l'ÉHÉSS, 1992.

Kantorowicz, Ernst H. *The King's Two Bodies: A Study in Medieval Political Theology.* Princeton: Princeton University Press, 1957.

Kelley, Donald R. *Foundations of Modern Historical Scholarship: Language, Law, and History in the French Renaissance.* New York: Columbia University Press, 1970.

Kent, D. V., and F. W. Kent. *Neighbours and Neighbourhood in Renaissance Florence: The District of the Red Lion in the Fifteenth Century.* Locust Valley, N.Y.: J. J. Augustin, 1982.

Keohane, Nannerl O. *Philosophy and the State in France: The Renaissance to the Enlightenment.* Princeton: Princeton University Press, 1980.

Kettering, Sharon. *Judicial Politics and Urban Revolt in Seventeenth-Century France: The Parlement of Aix, 1629–1659.* Princeton: Princeton University Press, 1978.

Knecht, R. J. *Renaissance Warrior and Patron: The Reign of Francis I.* Cambridge: Cambridge University Press, 1994.

Konnert, Mark W. *Civic Agendas and Religious Passion: Châlons-sur-Marne during the French Wars of Religion, 1560–1594.* Sixteenth Century Essays and Studies 35. Kirksville, Mo.: Sixteenth Century Journal Publishers, 1997.

Labitte, Charles. *La démocratie chez les prédicateurs de la Ligue.* Paris: Durand, 1865.

Lagarde, Georges de. "Les théories représentatives du XIVe–XVe siècle et l'Église." In *Xe congrès international des sciences historiques, Rome, 1955: études présentées à la Commission Internationale pour l'Histoire des Assemblées d'États*, 63–75. Louvain and Paris: Publications Universitaires de Louvain, Éditions Béatrice-Nauwelaerts, 1958.

La Lande, [Joseph Jérôme Le Français] de. *Des canaux de navigation, et spécialement du canal de Languedoc.* Paris: Chez la Veuve Desaint, 1778.

Latreille, André, ed. *Histoire de Lyon et du Lyonnais.* Toulouse: Privat, 1975.

Laverret, Michel. "L'iconographie de Sainte Radegonde dans les manuscrits." *BSAO*, 5th ser., 2 (1988): 85–112.

Lebigre, Arlette. *La révolution des curés: Paris 1588–1594.* Paris: Albin Michel, 1980.

Le Roux, Nicolas. "The Catholic Nobility and Political Choice during the League, 1585–1594: The Case of Claude de la Châtre." *French History* 8, no. 1 (1994): 34–50.

Levi, Giovanni. *Le pouvoir au village: histoire d'un exorciste dans le Piémont du XVIIe siècle.* Trans. Monique Aymard. Paris: Éditions Gallimard, 1989.

Lillich, Meredith Parsons. *The Armor of Light: Stained Glass in Western France, 1250–1325*. Berkeley: University of California Press, 1994.

Luchaire, Achille. *Les communes françaises à l'époque des capétiens directs*. Paris: Hachette, 1890.

Lusignan, Serge. *Préface au Speculum Maius de Vincent de Beauvais: réfraction et diffraction*. Montreal and Paris: Bellarmin and Vrin, 1979.

Macfarlane, Alan. "History, Anthropology and the Study of Communities." *Social History* 1–2 (1977): 631–52.

Maclean, Ian. *Interpretation and Meaning in the Renaissance: The Case of Law*. Cambridge: Cambridge University Press, 1992.

Maillard, Jacques. *Le pouvoir municipal à Angers de 1657 à 1789*. 2 vols. Angers: Presses de l'Université d'Angers, 1984.

Mailles, Thierry. "Les relations politiques entre le Parlement de Toulouse et les Capitouls, de 1540 environ à 1572." In *Les parlements de province: pouvoirs, justice et société du XVe au XVIIIe siècle*, 509–21. Ed. Jacques Poumarède and Jack Thomas. Toulouse: Framespa, 1996.

Major, J. Russell. "The French Renaissance Monarch as Seen through the Estates-General." *Renaissance Quarterly* 9 (1962): 113–25.

——. *From Renaissance Monarchy to Absolute Monarchy: French Kings, Nobles, and Estates*. Baltimore: Johns Hopkins University Press, 1994.

——. *Representative Government in Early Modern France*. New Haven: Yale University Press, 1980.

Mantellier, Philippe, and Denis Jeanson. *Histoire de la Communauté des Marchands fréquentant la rivière de Loire et fleuves descendant en icelle*. 2 vols. 1864. Reprint, Tours, 1987.

Marongiu, Antonio. "*Q.o.t.*, principe fondamental de la Démocratie et du Consentement, au XIVe siècle." *Album Helen Maud Cam: Studies presented to the International Commission for the History of Representative and Parliamentary Institutions, XXIV*, 101–15. Louvain and Paris: Publications Universitaires de Louvain; Éditions Béatrice-Nauwelaerts, 1961.

Martin, Xavier. "L'escamotage d'une réforme municipale: Angers, 1589." *Annales de Bretagne et des pays de l'Ouest (Anjou, Maine, Touraine)* 91 (1984): 107–34.

——. "Les faux-semblants d'une réforme municipale: Angers, 1584." Parts 1 and 2. *Annales de Bretagne et des pays de l'Ouest (Anjou, Maine, Touraine)* 89 (1982): 291–312, 425–50.

Maugis, Édouard. *Recherches sur les transformations du régime politique et social de la ville d'Amiens des origines de la commune à la fin du XVIe siècle*. Paris: Alphonse Picard et fils, 1906.

Michaud-Quantin, Pierre. *Universitas: expressions du mouvement communautaire dans le moyen-âge latin*. Paris: J. Vrin, 1970.

Miron de l'Espinay, A[lbert]. *François Miron et l'administration municipale de Paris sous Henri IV de 1604 à 1606*. Paris: Plon, 1885.

Moeller, Bernd. *Imperial Cities and the Reformation: Three Essays*. Ed. and trans. H. C. Erik Midelfort and Mark U. Edwards Jr. Durham, N.C.: Labyrinth Press, 1982.

Mollat, Michel, and Philip Wolff. *Ongles Bleus, Jacques et Ciompi: les révolutionaires populaires en Europe aux XIVe et XVe siècles*. [Paris]: Calmann-Lévy, 1970.

Moulakis, Althanasios. "Civic Humanism, Realist Constitutionalism, and Francesco Guicciardini's *Discorso di Logrogno*." In *Renaissance Civic Humanism: Reappraisals and Reflections*, 200–222. Ed. James Hankins. Cambridge: Cambridge University Press, 2000.

Mousnier, Roland. "L'opposition politique bourgeoise à la fin du XVIe et au début du XVIIe siècle: l'oeuvre de Louis Turquet de Mayerne." *La plume, la faucille et le marteau: institutions et société en France du moyen âge à la révolution,* 57–76. Paris: Presses Universitaires de France, 1970.

——. *La vénalité des offices sous Henri IV et Louis XIII.* 2d ed. Paris: Presses Universitaires de France, 1971.

Muir, Edward. *Civic Ritual in Renaissance Venice.* Princeton: Princeton University Press, 1981.

Najemy, John M. *Corporatism and Consensus in Florentine Electoral Politics, 1280–1400.* Chapel Hill: University of North Carolina Press, 1982.

Norberg, Kathryn. *Rich and Poor in Grenoble, 1600–1814.* Berkeley: University of California Press, 1985.

Nouillac, J. *Villeroy: secrétaire d'état et ministre de Charles IX, Henri III, et Henri IV (1543–1610).* Paris: Champion, 1909.

Nussdorfer, Laurie. *Civic Politics in the Rome of Urban VIII.* Princeton: Princeton University Press, 1992.

Olivier-Martin, François. *Histoire du droit français des origines à la révolution.* Paris: Domat Montchrestien, 1948.

——. *L'organisation corporative de la France d'ancien régime.* Paris: Sirey, 1938.

Ouvré, Henri. *Notice sur Jean Bouchet: poète et historien poitevin du XVIe siècle.* Poitiers: A. Dupré, 1858.

Parker, David. *La Rochelle and the French Monarchy: Conflict and Order in Seventeenth-Century France.* London: Royal Historical Society, 1980.

Pernot, Michel. *Les guerres de religion en France 1559–1598.* Paris: SEDES, 1987.

Petit-Dutaillis, Charles. *Les communes françaises: caractères et évolution des origines au XVIIIe siècle.* Paris: Albin Michel, 1947.

Pirenne, Henri. *Medieval Cities: Their Origins and the Revival of Trade.* Trans. Frank D. Halsey. Princeton: Princeton University Press, 1952.

Pocock, J. G. A. *The Machiavellian Moment: Florentine Political Thought and the Atlantic Republican Tradition.* Princeton: Princeton University Press, 1975.

Porchnev, Boris. *Les soulèvements populaires en France de 1623 à 1648.* Paris: SEVPEN, 1963.

Powicke, Maurice. *The Loss of Normandy 1189–1204: Studies in the History of the Angevin Empire.* 2d ed. Manchester: Manchester University Press, 1960.

Pythian-Adams, Charles. "Ceremony and the Citizen: The Communal Year at Coventry 1450–1550." In *Crisis and Order in English Towns 1500–1700: Essays in Urban History,* 57–85. Ed. Peter Clark and Paul Slack. London: Routledge & Kegan Paul, 1972.

Ramet, Henri. *Le Capitole et le Parlement de Toulouse.* Toulouse: Imprimerie Régionale, 1926.

Rappaport, Steve. *Worlds within Worlds: Structures of Life in Sixteenth-Century London.* Cambridge: Cambridge University Press, 1989.

Reynolds, Susan. *An Introduction to the History of English Medieval Towns.* Oxford: Clarendon Press, 1977.

Richet, Denis. *La France moderne: l'esprit des institutions.* Paris: Flammarion, 1973.

Robbins, Kevin C. *City on the Ocean Sea: La Rochelle, 1530–1650; Urban Society, Religion, and Politics on the French Atlantic Frontier.* Leiden: Brill, 1997.

——. "The Social Mechanisms of Urban Rebellion: A Case Study of Leadership in the 1614 Revolt at La Rochelle." *French Historical Studies* 19, no. 2 (1995): 559–90.

Roberts, Penny. *A City in Conflict: Troyes during the French Wars of Religion.* Manchester: Manchester University Press, 1996.

———. "Religious Conflict and the Urban Setting: Troyes during the French Wars of Religion." *French History* 6, no. 3 (1992): 259–78.

Roelker, Nancy Lyman. *One King, One Faith: The Parlement of Paris and the Religious Reformations of the Sixteenth Century.* Berkeley: University of California Press, 1996.

Rörig, Fritz. *The Medieval Town.* Berkeley: University of California Press, 1967.

Rotz, Rhiman A. "'Social Struggles' or the Price of Power? German Urban Uprisings in the Late Middle Ages." *Archiv für Reformationsgeschichte* 76 (1985): 64–95.

Rubinstein, Nicolai. *The Government of Florence under the Medici (1434 to 1494).* Oxford: Clarendon Press, 1966.

Salmon, J. H. M. "Catholic Resistance Theory, Ultramontanism, and the Royalist Response, 1580–1620." In *The Cambridge History of Political Thought, 1450–1700,* 219–53. Ed. J. H. Burns. Cambridge: Cambridge University Press, 1991.

———. "The Paris Sixteen, 1584–1594: The Social Analysis of a Revolutionary Movement." *Journal of Modern History* 44 (1972): 540–76.

Sanfaçon, André. "Traditions mariales et pouvoir ecclésiastique à Chartres sous l'Ancien Régime." In *Les productions symboliques du pouvoir XVIe–XXe siècle,* 45–64. Ed. Laurier Turgeon. Québec: Septentrion, 1990.

Saupin, Guy. "Les élections municipales à Nantes sous l'ancien régime, 1565–1789." *Annales de Bretagne et des pays de l'Ouest (Anjou, Maine, Touraine)* 90, no. 3 (1983): 429–50.

———. "Les habitants et l'élaboration de la politique municipale à Nantes sous l'ancien régime." *Annales de Bretagne et des pays de l'Ouest (Anjou, Maine, Touraine)* 91, no. 4 (1984): 319–50.

———. *Nantes au XVIIe siècle: vie politique et société urbaine.* Rennes: Presses Universitaires de Rennes, 1996.

Sawyer, Jeffrey K. *Printed Poison: Pamphlet Propaganda, Faction Politics, and the Public Sphere in Early Seventeenth-Century France.* Berkeley: University of California Press, 1989.

Schneider, Robert A. "Crown and Capitoulat: Municipal Government in Toulouse, 1500–1789." In *Cities and Social Change in Early Modern France,* 195–220. Ed. Philip Benedict. London: Unwin Hyman, 1989.

———. *Public Life in Toulouse, 1463–1789: From Municipal Republic to Cosmopolitan City.* Ithaca: Cornell University Press, 1989.

Scribner, Robert W. "Civic Unity and the Reformation in Erfurt." *Past and Present* 66 (1975): 29–60.

Sée, Henri. *Louis XI et les villes.* 1891. Reprint, Geneva: Slatkine-Megariotis Reprints, 1974.

Shalk, Elery. *From Valor to Pedigree: Ideas of Nobility in France in the Sixteenth and Seventeenth Centuries.* Princeton: Princeton University Press, 1986.

Skinner, Quentin. *The Foundations of Modern Political Thought.* 2 vols. Cambridge: Cambridge University Press, 1978.

Sluhovsky, Moshe. *Patroness of Paris: Rituals of Devotion in Early Modern France.* New York: Brill, 1998.

Squatriti, Paolo. *Water and Society in Early Medieval Italy, A.D. 400–1000.* Cambridge: Cambridge University Press, 1998.

Stocker, Christopher W. "The Confraternity of the Holy Name of Jesus: Conflict and Renewal in the Sainte Union in 1590." In *Confraternities and Catholic Reform in Italy, France, and Spain,* 155–89. Sixteenth Century Essays and Studies 44. Ed. John Patrick Donnelly and Michael W. Maher. Kirksville, Mo.: Thomas Jefferson University Press, 1999.

——. "Orléans and the Catholic League." *Proceedings of the Annual Meeting of the Western Society for French History* 16 (1989): 12–21.

Swartz, Marc J., ed. *Local-Level Politics: Social and Cultural Perspectives.* Chicago: Aldine Publishing, 1968.

Terpstra, Nicholas. "Apprenticeship in Social Welfare: From Confraternal Charity to Municipal Poor Relief in Early Modern Italy." *Sixteenth Century Journal* 25, no. 1 (1994): 101–20.

——. *Lay Confraternities and Civic Religion in Renaissance Bologna.* Cambridge: Cambridge University Press, 1995.

Thierry, Augustin. *Essai sur l'histoire de la formation et des progrès du Tiers État suivi de fragments du Recueil des monuments inédits de cette histoire.* 2d edition. Paris: Furne, Jouvet et Cie, [1853].

——. *Recueil des monuments inédits de l'histoire du Tiers État.* 4 vols. Paris: Firmin Didot Frères, 1850–70.

Tierney, Brian. *Religion, Law, and the Growth of Constitutional Thought 1150–1650.* Cambridge: Cambridge University Press, 1982.

Tully, James, ed. *Meaning and Context: Quentin Skinner and His Critics.* Princeton: Princeton University Press, 1988.

Turgeon, Laurier, ed. *Les productions symboliques du pouvoir XVIe–XXe siècle.* Québec: Septentrion, 1990.

Venard, Marc. "Les confréries dans l'espace urbain: l'exemple de Rouen." *Annales de Bretagne et des pays de l'Ouest* 90, no. 2 (1983): 321–32.

Vermeesch, Albert. *Essai sur les origines et la signification de la commune dans le nord de la France (XIe et XIIe siècles).* Heule: UGA, 1966.

Warren, W. L. *King John.* London: Eyre & Spottiswoode, 1961.

Wolfe, Martin. *The Fiscal System of Renaissance France.* New Haven: Yale University Press, 1972.

Wolfe, Michael. *The Conversion of Henri IV: Politics, Power, and Religious Belief in Early Modern France.* Cambridge: Harvard University Press, 1993.

Yardeni, Myriam. *La conscience nationale en France pendant les guerres de religion (1559–1598).* Paris and Louvain: Béatrice Nauwelaerts; Éditions Nauwelaerts, 1971.

——. "Histoires de villes, histoires de provinces et naissance d'une identité française au XVIe siècle." *Journal des savants* (Jan.–June 1993): 111–34.

Zubov, V. P. *Leonardo da Vinci.* Trans. David H. Kraus. Cambridge: Harvard University Press, 1968.

Dissertations and Unpublished Secondary Work

Andrault, Jean-Pierre. "Une capitale de province à l'âge baroque: le corps de ville de Poitiers, 1594–1652." Ph.D. diss., Université de Poitiers, 1988.

Bernstein, Hilary. "Politics and Civic Culture in Sixteenth-Century Poitiers," Ph.D. diss., Princeton University, 1996.

Breen, Michael P. "Legal Cultue, Municipal Politics and Royal Absolutism in Seventeenth-Century France: The *Avocats* of Dijon (1595–1715)." Ph.D. diss., Brown University, 2000.

Read, Kirk D. "French Renaissance Women Writers in Search of Community: Literacy Constructions of Female Companionship in City, Family, and Convent. Louise Labé, Lionnoize, Madeleine and Catherine des Roches, Mère et Fille, Anne de Marquets, Soeur de Poissy." Ph.D. diss., Princeton University, 1991.

Stocker, Christopher W. "The Governance of Orléans under the Catholic League." Paper presented at Sixteenth Century Studies conference. St. Louis, Dec. 1993.

——. "Henry IV and the Échevinage of Orléans." Paper presented at French Historical Studies annual meeting. El Paso, Mar. 1992.

——. "Urban Police and Confessional Politics in Sixteenth Century Orléans." Paper presented at the Western Society for French History annual meeting. Santa Barbara, Nov. 1990.

Index

La Guierche, Georges de Villequier, vicomte
   de, 200, 203, 213, 221, 226, 237–40,
   242–45
la Haye, Jean de, 12, 72–73, 87, 158–63,
   179–80, 183–84
La Marche, 240, 243
La Rochelle, 7, 12, 23, 34–36, 132–33, 139,
   148, 159–60, 237, 274
La Trinité (abbey), 113
Lauzon, Jasmes de, 70–71, 94, 115, 117–19,
   124, 133, 139
Le Bascle, Joseph, 158, 196
Le Havre, 110
Le Mans, 195
Le Riche, Michel, 42, 193
Le Roy, Jean, 23, 168, 237, 277
lieutenant général, 28, 72–74, 90
Ligugé, 113
Limoges, 23, 69, 144, 240
Loire River, 6, 107, 110–11, 120
Louis XI (king of France), 16, 31, 34, 108,
   168
Louis XII (king of France), 131
Louis XIV (king of France), 106–7, 250
Loyseau, Charles, 44, 71, 133, 275
Lude, Guy de Daillon, comte du, 31, 158
Lyon, 3, 37, 47, 92, 131, 167, 246
   municipal government of, 34–35, 44, 51,
   70–71, 259, 275

Maine, 243
maior et sanior pars, 98, 101
Malcontents, 12, 87, 159–62, 179–80
Malicorne, Jean de Chourses, sieur de, 193–
   94, 196–201, 203, 211, 253, 255
Marché Vieux, 103, 156, 201
Marnef, Enguilbert de, 10, 135, 143, 145, 148
Marnef, Jean de, 135–36, 138–39, 143
Marnef family, 10, 56, 58
Marseille, 23, 70, 88, 132, 207
   and Catholic League, 189–90, 204
Martin, Jean, 200, 263
Mayenne, Charles de Lorraine, duc de, 158
   as Catholic League agitator, 187, 193,
      195, 212
   as Catholic League leader, 202, 213, 220–
      21, 229–31, 233, 238–40, 242, 245–
      46, 254
   relations of with Charles, duc de Guise,
      241, 243, 245
mayors, 38, 49, 85, 90
   in extraordinary councils, 223–25, 247
   in *hôtel de ville*, 7, 22, 28–30, 32, 76–77,
      92, 96, 137, 139, 148, 265
   See also under elections
Medici, Catherine de', 3, 160
merchants, 7, 15, 48, 133–36, 218
   in *corps de ville*, 3, 66–70, 72, 76, 91,
      133, 136–37, 139, 150

and urban politics, 43, 58, 139–40, 143–
   45, 148–49
Mercoeur, Philipp-Emmanuel de Lorraine,
   duc de, 231, 242, 245, 254
militia, 36, 43, 163, 257, 263–65
   and Catholic League, 207–8, 218, 224
mills, 87, 109, 113, 119, 122
Miracle of the Keys, 14, 155, 158, 161,
   164–66, 173–80
Mois et Cent, 22, 30, 32, 45–46, 74, 77–79,
   90, 96, 99, 258
Montaigne, Michel de, 275
Montierneuf, 51, 75
   parish of, 58, 119
Montpensier, Louis de Bourbon, duc de,
   161, 269
Moulins, 132
municipal government, decision-making
   process in, 12–13, 45, 72, 88, 95–102,
   277
   consultation, 15, 25–26, 45, 48, 141,
      272–73
   disagreement, 87–88, 95–99, 105–6,
      117–18, 123, 137
   distribution of responsibility, 89, 98–99
   family alliances, 94–95, 277
   lawsuits, 97, 123–24
   majority, 13, 83, 95–96, 100–102
   negotiation, 83, 88, 90, 95, 98, 150, 273
   opining, 77–78, 93–95
   political language, 13–14, 50, 82–91, 94–
      95, 104, 153, 171–73, 178, 192, 211,
      251–52, 268, 273
   seniority, 72, 77–79, 92–93, 95
   *See also maior et sanior pars; Quod
      omnes tangit*
municipal government, theories concerning
   authority, 23–24, 27–28, 62, 105–6, 114,
      116, 187
   consultation, 44–45, 273
   customs and traditions, 64, 72, 76–79, 81
   equality, 67, 77, 79–80, 276
   estates, 15, 45–46, 219, 226
   mixed government, 21–23, 44
   representation, 24, 44–46, 219, 225
   seigneurial authority, 12, 24, 28–31, 44
   service, 12, 37, 39–42
   unanimity, 13, 38, 83, 95, 98, 100–102
   See also communes; public good

Nantes, 23, 31, 34, 189, 274
navigation project, 15, 104–5, 107–8, 110–
   13, 116, 125, 272
   funding of, 104, 108, 111, 113, 116,
      118–19, 125, 130
Niort, 7, 29, 196–97, 229
Notre-Dame-la-Chandelière, 55
Notre-Dame-la-Grande
   chapter of, 52, 54, 97, 113, 175